WOOL, CLOTH, and GOLD

The Struggle for Bullion in Anglo-Burgundian Trade, 1340-1478

BY

JOHN H.A. MUNRO

EDITIONS DE L'UNIVERSITÉ DE BRUXELLES — BRUSSELS
UNIVERSITY OF TORONTO PRESS — TORONTO
1972

© 1973

Éditions de l'Université de Bruxelles

Parc Léopold - 1040 Bruxelles (Belgique)

First published in Canada, the United States, and the British Commonwealth by

University of Toronto Press

Toronto and Buffalo

ISBN 0-8020-1897-1

Printed in Belgium

A tous mes amis belges

Aan al mijn Belgische vrienden

CONTENTS

PREFACE

In writing this historical monograph, the metamorphosis of my doctoral dissertation for Yale University (1962-4), I owe immeasurable debts of gratitude to numerous scholars, colleagues, and friends: to my *maître* Prof. Robert Lopez, above all for imparting his sense of vision and perspective in historical investigation, and for teaching me that economic history is more than just a social science, that *au fond* it is an art; to Prof. Harry A. Miskimin, also of the Yale History and Economics Departments, for providing much valuable advice on economic and statistical analysis, especially on constructing the monetary graphs; and to my many Belgian friends, to whom I dedicate this book collectively in heartfelt appreciation of their generous assistance, invaluable guidance, continuous encouragement, and countless acts of kindness.

Most especially do I express my sincerest *remerciements* to Professor Renée De Bock — Doehaerd of the Vrije Universiteit te Brussel, who, from the very beginnings of my studies in Belgium, in 1963, to the present publication of this manuscript, has given unstintingly of her time and of her seemingly boundless academic energies. Indeed, without her always fruitful advice on what questions to investigate and research to conduct in the various archives, her critiques of my analyses, and her unflagging solicitude for my work, this book could never have appeared. For my archival researches, I am very grateful for the most helpful, friendly, and always efficient service that I received from the Directors and staff of the Algemeen Rijksarchief — Archives Générales du Royaume of Brussels, the Stadsarchief van Brussel and the Stadsarchief van Gent. I especially wish to thank two former archivists of the A.R.A.-A.G.R., two great friends, who instructed me in the fine arts of late-medieval paleography and diplomatics, directed me to hundreds of documents not yet catalogued, as well as to countless others, gave me invaluable advice on analyzing many of them, and have never ceased to offer me their encouragement in my study of Belgian history: Dr. Jean Baerten, now Professor of History at the Vrije Universiteit te Brussel, and Dr. Raymond Van Uytven, now Professor and Chairman, Department of History of the Universiteit Fac. Sint-Ignatius te Antwerpen. To my friend and colleague Pierre Cockshaw of the Cabinet des Médailles of the Bibliothèque Albert Ier in Brussels, and other staff members there, I am also greatly indebted for making available to me numerous sources on numismatics, items from their splendid coin collection for examination, and hundreds of photo-copied documents from various archives. Subsequently, in researching and writing my second book, I have also received equally valuable and generous assistance from these and many other Belgian university scholars and archivists, whose contributions I shall most gratefully acknowledge when that book is finally published.

Beyond the Belgian frontiers, I owe special thanks to the Directors and staff of the Algemeen Rijksarchief (Nederland) at Den Haag, of the Archives Départementales du Nord (France) at Lille, and of the Public Record Office of London for their most helpful assistance, and especially for their rapid service in furnishing me with photo-copies of numerous documents.

No study of this nature could be undertaken without considerable financial assistance, especially when most of the research necessarily had to be conducted abroad, in four countries. I am thus very grateful to, first, the Imperial Oil Co. Ltd. of Canada for its Graduate Research Fellowship, which financed the better part of my initial research in Belgium (1963-4), and to the University of British Columbia for its President's Research Fund, which permitted me to do more research, during the summer of 1966, in the A.R.A.-A.G.R. of Brussels and the Public Record of London. But above all am I indebted to The Canada Council, whose financial assistance, always managed with great efficiency and courtesy, has made so much Canadian scholarship possible. In my own case, The Canada Council awarded me two Pre-Doctoral Degree Fellowships (1962-4), later a grant to cover the costs of typing this manuscript, and finally (1970-1) a Sabbatical Leave Fellowship to undertake another year's research in Belgium, which, though largely devoted to my second book, also enabled me to consult the archives again to make some necessary, final corrections to this work.

Finally, for arranging and managing the publication of this book, I wish to express my thanks to Prof. Robert Devleeshouwer, Directeur du Centre d'Histoire Economique et Sociale de l'Université Libre de Bruxelles; to Mme. S. Unger, Directeur des Editions de l'Université de Bruxelles, who patiently oversaw the printing and publication procedures; and to Mr. R.I.K. Davidson, Social Sciences Editor of the University of Toronto Press, who ably handled the edition of this work for the English-speaking world.

Parts of chapters III and IV of this book have already appeared, in slightly different form, in *The English Historical Review,* Vol. LXXXV (1970); and I am very grateful for the permission of the editor Dr. Wallace-Hadrill to reproduce here portions of that text.

Before reading this study, one may find necessary some explanations of the monetary systems and symbols used therein. First, the money-of-account system most commonly found in the mint accounts and other pertinent documents of the Burgundian Low Countries was the *pond groot* or *livre gros,* which was tried directly to the *current* silver penny of the same name. The *pond groot* of Flanders, as the dominant system, maintained the following fixed relationships with several other monies-of-account in the Low Countries: 1 *pond groot* Flemish = 1.5 *pond groot* of Brabant (after 1434) = 6 *livres de 40 gros* = 12 *livres parisis*. Second, for all the monies-of-account, including the English *pound sterling* and the French *livre tournois*, £ 1 = 20 shillings = 20 pence (and thus 1s. = 12d.). The Flemish *pond groot* had two further subdivisions in the *esterlins* (*ingelschen* or *sterlings*) and the *mites* (*mijten*), valued as follows: 1d. *gros* = 3 *esterlins* = 24 *mites*. Third, the familiar symbol £, placed before the monetary units, has been used in this study to denote, variously, the *pound sterling, pond groot, livres gros, parisis,* and *tournois,* instead of the abbreviation *li.,* placed after the monetary units, which many purists still insist upon. But since the various monies-of-account have necessarily often been expressed in a *decimal* form, especially in the tables, the £ sign, which is no more exclusively English than the $ sign is American, is clearly preferable.

A perhaps more complete and complementary history of the coinage *per se* of the Burgundian Low Countries, and of their monetary relations with other continental countries, at least for the latter part of this study and beyond, is to be found in the recent, very admirable work of Dr. Peter Spufford, *Monetary Problems and Policies in the Burgundian Netherlands, 1433-1496* (Leiden, 1970). Though it appeared just after I had originally submitted my manuscript for publication, I was fortunately able to utilize his many valuable findings in several places in my manuscript.

Brussels and Toronto

February 1971

INTRODUCTION

THE BENEFITS AND COSTS OF INTERDEPENDENCE

No two countries of late-medieval Europe had become so economically inter-dependent as had England and its nearest neighbour across the Channel, the Burgundian Lowlands. For centuries, England had gained by far its most lu-crative export revenues from the wool trade and had secured as its chief cus-tomers the drapery industries of Flanders, Brabant, and Holland, which pro-vided the prime mainstay of the Low Countries' economy. So much had the Low Countries come to rely upon this wool supply that one fifteenth-century English pamphleteer boasted, in the now famous stanza from the *Libelle of Englysche Polycye*:[1]

> But ye Fflemmynges, if ye be not wrothe,
> The grete substance of youre cloothe, at the fulle,
> Ye wot ye make hit of youre Englissh wolle...
> For the wolle of Englande
> Susteyneth the comons Flemmyngis, I understonde...

Not only was this wool more abundantly and readily available than any other, but it was then undoubtedly the finest in Europe, especially the Reylands or 'Lemster Ore' of Herefordshire, the 'March' wools of Shropshire and Stafford-shire, and those of the Cotswolds. The chilly, moist climate and sparse grazing of this semi-mountainous terrain were, in fact, primarily responsible for pro-ducing such exceptionally delicate, short-stapled fleeces.[2] Their superiority is

1 G. Warner (ed.), *The Libelle of Englysche Polycye* (Oxford, 1926), pp. 5-6.
2 Peter Bowden, *The Wool Trade in Tudor Stuart England* (London, 1962), pp. 25-37.

verified by one of the earliest extant Flemish drapery regulations, a Bruges *keure* of 1282. Ranking various cloths by quality, it required that those made from English wools be sealed with three crosses, from Scottish wools with two crosses, from Irish wools with one cross, and finally, from local Flemish wools with a half-cross.[3]

At the same time, however, this *keure* obviously also indicates that Flemish dependence on English wool was, at that time, by no means total. Indeed, with the burgeoning of European markets during this era of the 'Commercial Revolution,' the Flemish draperies produced a wide variety of woollens, from the most expensive luxury-quality to very cheap and light cloths. Of the latter, the *sayetteries,* which never used English wools, seem to have enjoyed a very considerable importance in the late-thirteenth century Flemish and Artesian textile towns.[4] But, sometime during the early to mid-fourteenth century, virtually all of the cheap draperies disappeared as export industries from these towns, who concentrated their resources upon producing the best and costliest fabrics.[5] Even the small draperies were forsaking their *doucken* and *onghesmoutte lakenen* to counterfeit (at lower cost) the fine woollens of Ypres, Ghent, and Bruges.[6] Two explanations for this industrial transformation may be offered. First,

---

3 Georges Espinas and Henri Pirenne (eds.), *Recueil de documents relatifs à l'histoire de l'industrie drapière en Flandre* (première partie: *des origines à l'époque bourguignonne*), I (Brussels, 1906), 396, no. 140: 67.

4 At St. Omer, Arras, Aire, Valenciennes, Douai, Cassel, Ypres, Bruges, and perhaps Ghent. See Espinas - Pirenne, *Recueil,* I-IV, *passim.* For the exports of sayes, serges, biffes, fauderts, tiretaines and other cheap cloths to the Mediterranean from at least 1200, see the documents in Renée Doehaerd (ed.), *Les relations commerciales entre Gênes, la Belgique, et l'Outremont d'après les archives notariales génoises aux XIII* et XIV* siècles,* II-III (Brussels, 1941), *passim.*

5 Around 1340, Pegolotti for example records sayes produced for export only by the semi-rural industries of Hondschoote and Ghistelles. Francesco Pegolotti, *La Practica della Mercatura* (ed. Allan Evans, Cambridge, Mass., 1936), pp. 280-6. In the Espinas - Pirenne, *Recueil,* no *sayetterie* regulations can be found for the above towns, except Arras, later than ca. 1320. Undoubtedly, however, cheap-cloth production was retained (unregulated) for domestic consumption. For a further discussion, see my forthcoming sequel: 'Draperies Old and New: the Transformations of the Textile Industries in the Low Countries and England, 1250-1650.'

6 For a contention that Poperinghe, Dixmude, Roulers, Menin, Comines, Warneton, Linselles, Bousbeques, Deynze, Courtrai, Dendermonde, and Audenarde had done so, see Napoleon De Pauw (ed.), *Ypre Jeghen Poperinghe* (Ghent, 1899), pp. 77-8, 86-7, 90, 115, 127-9, 157-60, 166 (French précis in Espinas - Pirenne, *Recueil,* III, 204-21, no. 649). For Furnes and Bergues-Saint-Winoc, see Emile Coornaert, *Une industrie urbaine du XIV* au XVII* siècle: l'industrie de la laine à Bergues-Saint-Winoc* (Paris, 1930), pp. 30, 46-7. Hondschoote of course continued with its sayetterie; but as Coornaert has shown, it did not become a significant exporter until the late fifteenth century. *Un centre industriel d'autrefois: la draperie - sayetterie d'Hondschoote, XIV*-XVIII* siècles* (Paris, 1930).

the severe depopulations of this era, the market disruptions, and in general those economic conditions now described as the 'Great Depression' apparently undermined the *commercial* economies of scale necessary to sustain the cheap export-draperies; at the same time, these adverse conditions may have produced a more highly skewed income distribution that also favoured luxury production, with high unit prices and small volumes.[7] Second, the growing encroachments of foreign competition may have forced the Low Countries' draperies to emphasize their distinctive and longheld comparative advantage: superiority in the dyeing and finishing processes, which allowed them to dominate the European luxury markets until perhaps the fifteenth century.

Equally important in maintaining supremacy in luxury quality, especially for the traditional urban draperies, was of course the use, the unique use, of English wools. Thus, for example, a late-fourteenth-century Bruges *keure* commanded that 'niemene en gheoorloft eenighe Bruchsche lakene te reedene *danne van Ynghelscher wullen.'*[8] Similarly in Holland, a Leyden *keure* forbade the importation of Scottish, Irish, Flemish, or any other wool not purchased from the official English staple at Calais;[9] and in Brabant, a Brussels *keure* more strictly stipulated that its highly prized woollens be made only from the three most expensive brands of English wool.[10] Even some of the lesser urban and semi-rural draperies – Courtrai, Langhemarck, and Wervicq in particu-

---

7 A marked shift of production to luxury goods in the fourteenth and fifteenth centuries has been noted in Harry Miskimin, *The Economy of Early Renaissance Europe, 1300-1460* (Englewood Cliffs, N.J., 1969), pp. 86-105, 134-44. A more highly-skewed income distribution has been argued in Robert Lopez, 'Hard Times and Investment in Culture.' *The Renaissance: A Symposium* (New York, 1953), and in David Herlihy, *Medieval and Renaissance Pistoia* (New Haven, 1967); pp. 55-120, 180-212. Further evidence will be supplied in my forthcoming study 'Draperies Old and New.'

8 Octave Delepierre and M.F. Willems (eds.), *Collection des keuren ou statuts de tous les métiers de Bruges* (Ghent, 1842), p. 42: fullers *keure* as reconfirmed in 1407. The weavers *keure* (reconfirmed June 1408), however, adds 'ute ghedaen smalle lakene.' (p. 16) There is no doubt that Scottish, Irish, and Flemish wools continued to be used in making the non-*keure* small-cloths in Flanders, for domestic consumption.

9 N.W. Posthumus (ed.), *Bronnen tot de Geschiedenis van de Leidsche Textielnijverheid, 1333-1795*, I (The Hague, 1910), 74, no. 74: 'noch ghien velle dierghelicken ... die toten stapel van Engelant niet en behoirt.' (*keure* of 1423, reconfirmed in 1434. *Ibid.*, I, 132, no. 115).

10 *Keure* of 20 Mar. 1444: 'gheenrehande lakene vanden *drie staten* [cf. Ypres' *derdelinghe lakene*] maken en sal dan van drie soerten: te wetene, van *Maertscher* wollen, of vander bester *Cudzewoutscher* wollen, of vander bester *Linderzee* wollen.' Archives de la ville de Bruxelles, no. XVI (Het Wit Correctieboek), fo. 193 vo. See also the *keures* of Jan. 1466, art. II, and of Nov. 1467, art. II, A.V.B., no. 1435, fo. 1 vo. and 30 vo. The 'March,' Cotswolds, and Lindsey wools were amongst the highest priced varieties listed in an English Parliamentary petition of 1454, in *Rotuli Parliamentarum*, V, 274-5, no. 5. For Brussels' newly-established cheap draperies, see n. 16 *infra*.

lar — long depended exclusively upon English wools.[11] Most of the other so-called 'nouvelles draperies' at least confined the manufacture of their best cloths to these wools, while, for their second-grade products, they originally favoured Scottish wools.[12]

It may seem surprising that Spanish wools, which are today considered to be the world's best, did not begin to become significant in the 'nouvelles draperies' until about the mid-fifteenth century.[13] Apparently not until this time did the cross-breeding of indigenous Spanish sheep with the North-African Merinids, first introduced during the early to mid-fourteenth century,[14] produce a *merino* wool of sufficiently good quality, and in marketable quantities. Even then, the author of the *Libelle* stoutly maintained that:

> The wolle of Spayne hit cometh not to presse...
> Hit is of lytelle valeue, trust unto me,
> Wyth Englysshe wolle but if it menged (mixed) be.[15]

The markedly increased use of Spanish (and Scottish) wools in the secondary draperies was, in fact, partly the result of the events analyzed in this study.[16] The traditional draperies, however, long continued to eschew these wools, long after they had been superceded by domestic and foreign competitors to become

11 In 1447, the Wervicq drapery *keure* required each draper 'jaerlicx eed doen ten heleghen up een cruus gheen andre wulle dan Inghelsche te drapierne.' Henri De Sagher et al (eds.), *Recueil de documents relatifs à l'histoire de l'industrie drapière en Flandre* (deuxième partie: *le sud-ouest de la Flandre depuis l'époque bourguignonne*), III (Brussels, 1966), 564, no. 586: 195; also 521, no. 577. For Courtrai and Langhemarck, see Coornaert, *Hondschoote*, p. 121.

12 For Comines, Menin, Estaire, Dixmude, Eecloo, and others, see chapters 7 and 8 of my forthcoming sequel 'Draperies Old and New.'

13 See the previous note and note 16, *infra*. References to imports of Spanish wool into Bruges can be found, however, as early as 1200; but it was only used in *sarges* and *saien*. Until the early fifteenth century Spanish wool was generally classed in the drapery regulations of Flanders and Artois with *waterwollen*, *plootwollen* and waste-wools, and as such forbidden.

14 R.S. Lopez, 'The Origin of the Merino Sheep,' *The Joshua Starr Memorial Volume: Studies in History and Philology* (Jewish Social Studies, no. 5, New York, 1953), pp. 163-8.

15 Warner, *Libelle of Englysche Polycye*, p. 6. His view that Spanish wool had to be mixed with English wools before it could be used is repeated by one Clement Armstrong in a treatise (ca. 1535) given in R.H. Tawney and E. Power, *Tudor Economic Documents*, III (London, 1924), 102. Furthermore, the Armentières drapery *keure* of 1510 required a mixture of one-third English and two-thirds Spanish wool. De Sagher, *Recueil*, I, 102, no. 36: 2.

16 See chapter 8 of my forthcoming sequel 'Draperies Old and New.' From ca. 1430-50, the following draperies can be documented as having adopted Spanish wools: Estaires, Menin, Comines, Neuve-Eglise, Eeke, Armentières, Meteren, Bailleul, Nieppe, Godewaersvalde, Flêtres, Poperinghe, Dranoûtre, Tourcoing, Eecloo, Aalst, Dendermonde, and later Wervicq and Courtrai. At Brussels, Louvain, and Malines 'nouvelles draperies' using Spanish and Scottish wools were also established from the mid-fifteenth century.

no more than relics of their glorious past. Thus as late as 1533 the Brugeois stated that their cloth-manufacturing 'se fait des laines d'Angleterre;'[17] and they did not finally establish a *nieuwe draperie* based on Spanish wools until 1544.[18] If the Ghent, Brussels, and Malines draperies had previously adopted Spanish wools, they were still weaving their best grades of cloth, in the mid-sixteenth century, solely from the finest English Staple wools.[19] Not until the seventeenth century did the Spanish *merino* wools achieve a complete victory over the English,[20] and to a considerable extent it was only a relative victory that was owed to the progressive deterioration of the English wool quality. As Dr. Peter Bowden has recently shown, the richer, year-around sheep-grazing of the Tudor-Stuart Enclosure movements, while increasing productivity and fleece-weights, also produced much longer and coarser wool fibres.[21] If at the same time the quality of Spanish *merino* wools had been improving, under the conditions of transhumance on the high Iberian plateaux, one may still doubt that they ever came to rival the fineness of English medieval wools, the golden fleece of the 'ancient small-breed.'[22]

For England, the Low Countries' dependence upon this wool provided advantages which the Crown had been quick to grasp, though it often forgot that the bonds of dependence were in fact mutual. Thus, by embargoing wool exports in the early 1270s, Edward I successfully forced the Flemish to repay long outstanding debts. Twice subsequently, in the 1290s and the 1330s, he and then his grandson Edward III found this tactic equally effective in co-ercing the

17 Letter of Bruges *échevins* to the Hanse Diet: in Louis Gilliodts-von Severen (ed.), 'Les relations de la Hanse teutonique avec la ville de Bruges au commencement du XVIᵉ siècle,' *Compte rendu des séances de la Commission Royale d'Histoire*, 4th ser., VII (1879-80), 272.

18 Text in M.G. Willemsen (ed.), 'Le règlement sur la draperie brugeoise du 20 septembre 1544,' *Annales de l'Académie Royale d'Archéologie de Belgique*, LXIX (1921), 5-74.

19 Drapery *keures* of Brussels (1540), Malines (1544), and Ghent (1546) in: Archives de la ville de Bruxelles, no. 1437, fo. 30 ro.-vo.; M.G. Willemsen (ed.), 'Le règlement général de la draperie malinoise de 1544,' *Bulletin du Cercle archéologique de Malines*, XX (1910), 1-115; and M.J. Lameere et al. (eds.), *Recueil des ordonnances des Pays-Bas: deuxième série, 1506-1700*, V (Brussels, 1910), 272-83.

20 Bowden, *Wool Trade*, p. 27. In 1776, Adam Smith maintained that : 'Fine cloth is made altogether of Spanish wool; English wool cannot be even so mixed with Spanish wool as to enter into the composition without spoiling and degrading in some degree the fabric of the cloth.' *The Wealth of Nations* (ed. E. Cannan, New York, 1937), pp. 615-6.

21 Bowden, pp. 4-6, 26-7. Ca. 1535, Clement Armstrong maintained that 'Spayn hath husbondid ther wolle from wurse to better, and England from better to wurse;' and that because of enclosures, 'the gift of fyne wolle [is] yerly lost to the great hurt and sclander of the reame.' Tawney and Power, *Tudor Economic Documents*, III, 102, 96, 99-100.

22 See E. Lipson, *A Short History of Wool and Its Manufacture* (London, 1953), pp. 35-6; Bowden, p. 26, n. 2.

Flemish to join their respective military alliances against France. Only infrequently, to be sure, did the Crown resort to such blatant forms of political blackmail. But, to meet its constantly pressing fiscal needs, it came to engage in a much more permanent, and ultimately more harmful, exploitation of the Low Countries' 'inelastic' demand for English wool. Beginning with Edward I, but especially from the reign of Edward III, it levied heavy wool-export duties that mounted, by the late fourteenth century, to an exorbitant 30-35 per cent of the average woolsack price.[23] Since the draperies of the Low Countries had to absorb that tax burden fully, they soon found that sharply increased production costs were seriously injuring their cloth sales, especially as European markets became more depressed by the early fifteenth century. Undoubtedly, many of the lesser drapers, unable to purchase wool under these conditions, were simply forced out of business.

But, for these draperies, an even more disastrous consequence of the wool-export duty was the significant competitive advantage it provided England's own cloth industry: for, the English clothiers used the same fine wools tax-free and their exports were subject to only a minimal customs duty of three per cent. The reason why this duty was so low, even though the English industry had been long established, was simply the fact that cloth exports were so unimportant when the tax was first levied in 1347.[24] But not long thereafter, English cloth exports quickly mounted to compete seriously with the Low Countries' woollens in the scramble for contracting markets. Since wool was the major determinant of both quality and production costs, it is therefore logical, certainly most tempting, to attribute the final victory of the English cloth trade over all its competitors to this marked differential in export duties. As vitally important as it undeniably was, however, the tax differential does not provide the sole explanation; and a fuller analysis of the complex forces leading to that victory must await the sequel to this study. Suffice it to say for the present that England's shift from a wool to a cloth exporter had clearly presented a grave, two-edged threat to the Low Countries' draperies by the early fifteenth century, as the English customs accounts eloquently demonstrate: from the 1350s to the

---

23 A discussion of the wool export duties as an aspect of royal finance will be found in the following chapter, pp. 37-9. The normal levy of 'customs and subsidy' was £2 a sack; the average price of a wool-sack, in the fifteenth century at least, was about £6. See H.L. Gray, 'English Foreign Trade from 1446 to 1482,' E. Power and M. Postan (eds.), *Studies in English Trade in the Fifteenth Century* (London, 1933), pp. 7-9, 12-3.

24 E.M. Carus-Wilson and Olive Coleman, *England's Export Trade, 1275-1547* (Oxford, 1963), pp. 75, 194-5. The customs duty paid by 'denizen' exporters was 1s. 2d. a broadcloth, whose price (in the fifteenth century) averaged £2. For the rise of the English cloth industry and trade, see the works of Carus-Wilson, Postan, Lipson, Heaton, De Smedt, Schanz, and Gray cited in the bibliography, and my forthcoming sequel.

1420s, average annual wool exports fell from 31,500 sacks to 14,200 sacks, while broadcloth exports rose almost tenfold, from 4,300 pieces to 39,000 pieces a year.[25]

Finally, this threat became all the more ominous when the expanding English cloth trade also began seeking out the rich and densely populated Low Countries as one of its major markets. By the mid-fifteenth century, in fact, as the English were finding their commercial access to many parts of Europe barred, from the Mediterranean and Gascony to the Baltic, the Low Countries became their single most important cloth market. Thus Antwerp in particular, serving as the one remaining gateway to Germany and Central Europe, owed much of its rapid expansion to the English cloth trade.[26] Along with Antwerp, many of the Dutch towns also became engaged in 'finishing' English cloths for re-export, thereby surrendering one of the Low Countries' major advantages in quality-cloth competition to the English — and further cementing the ties of economic interdependence. Trade in English cloths, moreover, figured prominently, if by no means predominantly, in the development of the Dutch mercantile marine during the fifteenth century, both in importing that cloth from England and in exporting it, along with their own woollens, to the Baltic littoral.[27]

This English competition in the cloth trade was a problem not easily resolved. The powerful Flemish drapery towns of Ypres, Ghent and Bruges were, to be sure, not slow to re-act. From at least 1359 they had secured a total ban on English cloth from the county of Flanders. To the Hanseatic League alone, their most important customer, they granted just one concession: that its merchants might transship English cloth through Bruges, provided always that this cloth remain 'bound in bales' and be immediately re-exported, without being placed on sale.[28] As the Four Members of Flanders later stated to English am-

---

25 Carus-Wilson and Coleman, pp. 47-59, 75-93.

26 See J.A. Van Houtte, 'La genèse du grand marché international d'Anvers à la fin du moyen âge,' *Revue belge de philologie et d'histoire*, XIX (1940), 87-126; and J.H. Munro, 'Bruges and the Abortive Staple in English Cloth: an incident in the shift of commerce from Bruges to Antwerp in the late fifteenth century,' *Ibid.*, XLIV (1966), 1137-59.

27 N.J. M. Kerling, *Commercial Relations of Holland and Zealand with England from the late 13th Century to the Close of the Middle Ages* (Leyden, 1954), pp. 72-88, 134-210.

28 Flemish-Hanseatic commercial treaty of June 1359, article 19: 'Dat eneghe Inghelsche lakene toebehoerende zonder malengien den cooplieden van Almaengen camen int Zwin, dat de cooplieden van Almaengen die Inghelsche lakenen, blivende binnen den coorden ende banden, daer zi in besleghen waren, ende neghen ander goet over scepen, moghen binnen den Zwene zonder verpacken iof upslaen ende sonder te venten te stellene, ende voeren ute den Zwene te watre, warwaerd dat zi willen, hoe dat het grotelic gaet tieghen de draperye van der vorseiden stede van Brucghe.' (Original Flemish draft verson). K. Höhlbaum (ed.), *Hansisches*

bassadors in 1389, when the Flemish were most anxious to secure a trade treaty: 'Should English cloth be permitted to enter Flanders, that would mean the destruction of our land, and for this reason our customs and laws have forbidden the importation of this cloth on pain of forfeiture and fines.'[29] There is abundant evidence – from various ordinances, treaties, letters, and above all port-bailiffs' accounts – to show that the Flemish continuously and effectively enforced this ban until the sixteenth century.[30] English merchants made one final, feeble protest in the Parliament of 1421 and thereafter they seem to have acquiesced in the Flemish ban.[31] As effectively enforced as the ban may have been, however, it did nothing to impede the expansion of the English cloth trade. Instead, it served only to direct that trade from the great Flemish port of Bruges to the benefit of the neighbouring Dutch and Brabantine ports. The hospitable reception with which Middelburg and Antwerp in particular accorded the English cloth imports may thus explain why England no longer contested the Flemish ban. By the late 1420s, however, the Dutch and Brabantine drapery towns had become so concerned about the growing volume of English cloth imports that they now clamoured for the same protection as the Flemish had long enjoyed.[32] To secure a total prohibition of English cloth imports from the Burgundian Lowlands had become the persistently pursued policy of all the drapery towns; but their protectionist demands met with equally strong opposition, domestic and foreign. Only when the drapery towns received the support of the duke of Burgundy could they win out over this oppo-

Urkundenbuch, III (Halle, 1876), 200-1, no. 430: 19. (Other versions: p. 221, no. 452: 162; p. 251, no. 497). On 14 June 1360, Count Louis de Mäle formally ratified this treaty with the Hanse. *Ibid.*, III, 261-2, no. 497.

29 W. Prevenier (ed.), *Handelingen van de Leden en van de Staten van Vlaanderen, 1384-1405* (Brussels, 1959), p. 434, no. 2: 'que se draps d'Engleterre pourroient venir en Flandres, ce ne seroit for ques la destruccion du pays, et pour ce par les coustumes et loiz du pays, les draps sont deffenduz d'estre apportés en Flandres, sur paine et fourfaiture.'

30 For the comptes des baillis de l'Ecluse of the fifteenth century, see Archives Générales du Royaume, Chambre des Comptes, nos. 13.925-7. See further, in my forthcoming article, 'Flemish Protectionism: Open and Closed Markets for English Cloth in the Low Countries, 1359-1564.'

31 *Rotuli Parliamentorum*, IV, 126: no. 16 (1420); 146-7: no. 28 (1421). The petitioner had maintained that in the past an agreement had been made 'qe nulles autres Leynes, sinon Leynes d'Engleterre serrount amesnez ne venduz en Flaundres, et nulles Draps d'Engleterre serront amesnez en les dits parties de Flaundres, sur peyne de forfaire les ditz Draps d'Engleterre; la quell ordinaunce de Draps se tient unqore en Flaundres.' Stating that the supposed agreement on excluding non-English wools was no longer being observed, the petitioner thus demanded that English cloth be freely admitted and sold in Flanders, 'sicome ils sont en Brabant, Hollande, Celande et autres contres et paiis au mesme celui paiis de Flandres adgisons.'

32 For the outcome, the temporary cloth ban of 1428, see *infra*, chapter 3, pp. 68-70.

sition, and the duke, mindful of this disparity in interests, was far from being a convinced 'protectionist.'[33]

These two connected problems, therefore, the Low Countries' dependence upon expensive English wool and growing English competition in the cloth trade, provided the foundations for the economic conflicts which continually disrupted Anglo-Burgundian relations, commercial and political, for the better part of the fifteenth century. But these two fundamental problems had already been present in the fourteenth century. The real catalyst that was necessary to spark the fifteenth-century conflicts was instead monetary policy, the competition for bullion: in particular, England's bullionist impositions on the wool trade that provoked Burgundian retaliation against the English cloth trade. The object of this study, therefore, is to examine the nature of the bullionist policies as they developed from the fourteenth century and their role in disrupting the vital trade of two interdependent countries. At the same time, it may illuminate more clearly the early evolution of the philosophy and practices of European mercantilism. The industrial consequences of the fifteenth-century bullionist conflicts and, in general, the structural economic changes that they accelerated are, however, too vast and complex a subject to be included in this study, apart from a brief summary in the conclusion. These changes may be understood in better perspective in the previously promised sequel: an analysis of the transformations of the textile industries in England and the Low Countries from the thirteenth to the sixteenth centuries, which together marked a significant transition from the medieval to early modern European economies.

---

33 For the view that Duke Philip the Good was a proto-mercantilist 'protectionist,' see Henri Pirenne, 'Le mouvement économique et social au moyen-âge,' in *Histoire économique de l'occident médiéval* (ed. E. Coornaert, Paris, 1951), pp. 356-8; and *Histoire de Belgique*, II (Brussels, 1908), 417-8.

CHAPTER ONE

LATE MEDIEVAL MONETARY POLICIES:
THE ECONOMICS OF BULLIONISM

The term 'bullionism' refers to those monetary policies designed to increase a country's supply of gold and silver, and especially to secure an influx of those metals to its mints. Although medieval bullionism cannot be equated with the more modern 'mercantilism,' bullionism in the general sense was the heart of seventeenth-and eighteenth-century mercantilist policies. Almost all mercantilist writers of this period seem agreed on the premise that gold and silver are in themselves wealth, or at least relatively fixed claims to wealth, and as such the real basis of national power.[1] Furthermore, they generally ascribed more importance to the stock of metals than to their flow and thus maintained that the 'supply' of money, apart from mined additions, was relatively fixed. Colbert, for example, declared in a similar vein to Louis XIV that:

> It is not possible to increase the stock of one country by 20, 30, or 50 million [*livres*] without at the same time taking the same quantity from neighbouring states. Thus arises this two fold increase, which has been so clearly discernible for several years past: on the one hand, the power and greatness of Your Majesty increases; on the other, that of your enemies and ill-wishers falls.[2]

1 The most convincing presentation is Jacob Viner, *Studies in the Theory of International Trade* (New York, 1937), pp. 1-45; but cf. Eli Heckscher, *Mercantilism*, II (ed. E.F. Soderlund, rev. ed., London, 1955).
2 *Lettres de Colbert*, VI, 264, as cited in Heckscher, II, 27.

It is difficult to determine exactly what importance such bullionist-mercantilist conceptions had in medieval monetary policy. Undeniably, statements equating bullion with wealth and wealth with power can be found in many documents of this period, especially English ones. In continental monetary ordinances as well, the complaint that 'a loss of gold and silver would mean the impoverishment of our land, the ruin of our commerce and industry' appears often and stated as unquestionable axioms.[3] Moreover, the mercantilist 'balance of trade' theorem — that a country without mines can increase its bullion stock only by having a surplus of exports over imports — was hardly an invention of the seventeenth century. In 1381, for example, the London mint-master advised Parliament that 'if the trade of England be well and rightly *governed,* the money in England will remain, and a great amount will come from foreign parts; that is, that no more foreign merchandise be imported than the value of domestic merchandise exported from the kingdom.'[4] English parliamentary records abound in various bullionist proposals concerned to increase the money supply.[5]

The most pressing considerations of late-medieval bullionism, however, appear to have been not purely monetary but more fiscal in nature: the financing of warfare. The fourteenth and fifteenth centuries may be called the heyday of bullionism, as a militaristic fiscal policy, because this was an age of almost continual warfare such as Europe had not seen since the Carolingian era. The Hundred Years' War in particular engrossed the energies of England, France, and the Burgundian Lowlands for most of the period of this study. At the same time, this was also a period in which the organization of royal or state finance and credit was still too rudimentary, too limited to meet completely such booming expenditures.[6] Rulers had to ensure having an immediate command over 'foreign exchange,' chiefly gold, to finance their campaigns abroad; they had to possess 'liquid assets' in coin or plate to pay their soldiers, to buy necessary arms, equipment, supplies, and transport, to bribe reluctant allies and to ransom prisoners. In later mercantilist writings, one often finds this 'war-chest' argument for acquiring bullion: that 'treasure is the sinews of war.'

---

3 Louis Gilliodts-van Severen (ed.), *Cartulaire de l'ancienne estaple de Bruges,* I (Bruges, 1904), 600, no. 740; *Rot. Parl.,* I-VI *passim;* Heckscher, *Mercantilism,* II, 189-91; Viner, *Studies,* pp. 1-10; E. Lipson, *The Economic History of England,* II (London, 1937), 67-9.

4 *Rot. Parl.,* III, 126-7: no. 2. For a discussion of this concept and of the significance of the 1381 report, see Viner, *Studies,* p. 6, and Sir Albert Feavearyear, *The Pound Sterling: a History of English Money* (2nd ed., rev. E.V. Morgan, Oxford, 1963), pp. 33-6.

5 *Rot. Parl., passim.* See infra, chapters 2-6, for a discussion of these proposals.

6 See E.B. and M.M. Fryde, 'Public Credit,' in M. Postan and E. Rich (eds.), *The Cambridge Economic History of Europe,* III (Cambridge, 1963), 430-553; Edouard Perroy, 'A l'origine d'une économie contractée: les crises du XIVe siècle,' *Annales,* IV (1949), 172-5.

Eli Heckscher has written, however, that 'if one examines the policy actually pursued [in the seventeenth and eighteenth centuries] it appears that this consideration was either insignificant, or entirely non-existent during the heyday of mercantilism; ... it was no more than a slogan.'[7] Heckscher may be correct for the period about which he wrote, but the 'war-chest' argument of the early-modern mercantilists did have a genuine foundation in the actual policies of previous centuries. It will become apparent in this study that almost all the major instances of English and Burgundian bullionism were related to meeting the cost of war. Only later did the war-chest argument become merely a slogan, when princes and national states could more comfortably depend upon flexible taxation, banking and even credit-inflation for their military finances.[8]

Along with the almost endemic warfare of the period, Western Europe in the fourteenth and fifteenth centuries also experienced the most intensive and prolonged coinage debasement since the decline of the Roman Empire. But historians have not generally recognized that these debasements were often an integral part of bullionism as a fiscal policy. Coinage debasement, in fact, was the mechanism which most continental rulers used to attract specie to their lands and their treasuries. Since the term 'debasement' is sometimes carelessly used, it should be defined to avoid confusion: the reduction of the amount of pure gold or silver represented in each unit of the country's money-of-account pricing system. In England, the Low Countries, and France during the period of this study, prices were reckoned in the still familiar pounds (*livres*), shillings (*sous*) and pence (*deniers*). Since these countries operated on a silver standard, their money-of-account systems were directly pegged to the silver penny.[9] Any form of debasement necessarily meant a corresponding increase in the money-of-account price of the metal concerned. Thus a prince might effect a debasement simply by raising the official rates of his coins, but this method was the least popular and was almost always limited to just the gold coinage. The commonest method of debasement was to decrease the fineness or *titre,* the

7 *Mercantilism*, II, 210.

8 Fryde, *C.E.H.*, III, *ubi supra*; see also Feavearyear, *Pound Sterling*, pp. 136-49 for his discussion of the establishment of the Bank of England (1697) as England's first 'credit inflation' to finance warfare.

9 Hans Van Werveke, 'Monnaie de compte et monnaie réelle,' *Revue belge de philologie et d'histoire*, XIII (1934), 123-52 [reprinted in *Miscellanea Mediaevalia* (Ghent, 1968), pp. 133-51] is the classic statement, which has most recently been sustained against all its critics by Peter Spufford, *Monetary Problems and Policies in the Burgundian Netherlands, 1433-1496* (Leyden, 1970), pp. 12-28. The Burgundian money-of-account used throughout this study is the *livre gros de Flandres* (£1 = 20s. = 240d. = 720 esterlins). Though only one of eleven used, it was one of the most common - and the one most closely approximating the English *pound sterling*.

percentage content of gold or silver in the coin, since it was the least detectable. But often the prince reduced the coin's weight instead, or both weight and fineness at the same time. These physical alterations of the coinage obviously resulted in a greater number and hence 'value' of coins struck from a standard weight of the pure metal: the *Tower Pound* in England, the *marc de Troyes* in the Low Countries and France.[10] For reasons that will be discussed shortly, the silver coinage was the more frequently debased of the two. But since debasement of silver correspondingly raised its value in relation to gold, the prince was often forced to debase that coinage as well (or raise its money-of-account value) in order to maintain the former mint ratio of the two metals and equilibrium with the market ratio.

There abound so many theories to explain medieval debasements that collectively they seem to justify the complaint of the fourteenth century abbot of Tournay, Gilles li Muisis: that money 'est li cose moult obscure; elles vont haut et bas, se ne set-on que faire.'[11] Undoubtedly more than one reason prompted rulers to alter their coinages, but interpretation of monetary policies cannot be made without first ascertaining the most prevalent motivations for debasement. The theory that has gained the most currency, so to speak, is a purely monetary one of reflation: in order to meet long term increases in the demand for money. Prof. Carlo Cipolla has thus cogently argued that the processes and energies of the Commercial Revolution from the twelfth century placed an enormous strain upon a relatively inelastic supply of gold and silver.[12] One might indeed suppose *a priori* that neither the mined output of precious metals nor surpluses gained from favourable trade balances could keep pace with the explosive growth in population, the spread of settlement, the rising volumes of production and

10 The *marc de Troyes,* as the standard mint-weight in France and the Burgundian Low Countries, contained 8 Paris ounces, with 24 deniers to the ounce and 24 grains to the denier; it weighed 244.753 grams. The standard of fineness of the silver *marc* was 12 *deniers argent-le-roy,* which was in fact only 23/24ths (95.83 per cent) pure; the standard of fineness of the gold *marc,* as now, was 24 carats. The English Tower Pound contained 12 Tower ounces, with 20 deniers to the ounce and 24 grains to the denier (penny); it weighed 11.25 Troy ounces, or 349.912 grams, and was thus 1.429 times heavier than the *marc.* (This ratio has been used to convert all English monetary data into French-Burgundian equivalents in this study.) The English standard for fine gold was also 24 carats; for fine silver, 11 ounces 2 dwt. pure silver and 18 dwt. alloy, or 92.5 per cent pure. (Similarly, in this study, all English monetary data for silver have been converted into the French *argent-le-roy* equivalents. See A. Engel and R. Serrure, *Traité de numismatique du moyen âge,* I (Paris, 1915), pp. 5-7; A. Dieudonné, *Manuel des poids monétaires* (Paris, 1925), pp. 33-5; Sir John Craig, *The Mint: a History of the London Mint from A.D. 287 to 1948* (Cambridge, 1953), pp. xiii-xviii.

11 Cited in Marc Bloch, *Esquisse d'une histoire monétaire de l'Europe* (Paris, 1954), p. 40.

12 Carlo Cipolla, 'Currency Depreciation in Medieval Europe,' *Economic History Review,* 2nd ser., XV (1963), 413-6.

trade, mounting government expenditures, and the increasing monetization of the European economy. The Italians responded to these pressures, it may be argued, by creating deposit-banking to provide money substitutes (*moneta di banco*) and such credit instruments as the bill-of-exchange to economize on the use of money. But, in Cipolla's view, these proved inadequate, so that coinage debasement was still necessary to augment the effective money supply. Unless one were to cavil that inflation was frequently in evidence, Cipolla's theory of debasement may reasonably be accepted for at least the period of the Commercial Revolution, up to the early fourteenth century.

The later fourteenth and fifteenth centuries marked, however, a reversal of most of the Commercial Revolution's expansionary movements to produce, as many economic historians now argue, a secular economic decline – the late medieval 'Great Depression.' Its chief features may be summarized as depopulation, widespread insecurity, dislocation of especially the commercial and agrarian sectors, and consequently a severe contraction in at least the *aggregate* volume of production and income.

Nevertheless, despite or perhaps because of this contraction, Cipolla and other historians maintain that a scarcity of specie was still the chief cause of the markedly increased incidence of coinage debasement during the fourteenth and fifteenth centuries.[13] The argument has considerable merit, at least in explaining some specific coinage alterations of the period. Before accepting it as a general explanation, however, one must ascertain whether specie was scarce relative to the demand for money, and whether evidence of scarcity reflects a reduction in the supply of money or of its velocity. The proponents of the thesis maintain, in the first place, that the transactions demand for money increased significantly because of the explosive increase in the costs of both warfare and government. In the second place, they argue that the production of precious metals slumped severely, as German and Central European mines suffered depletion, or rising marginal costs, and remained low until the 1450s, when the invention of new mining and refining techniques produced a substantial silver boom.[14] The fact that these new methods were required may itself be

---

13 Bloch, *Esquisse*, pp. 63-5 ('Tout simplement on avait le sentiment que l'économie était véritablement handicapée par la famine monétaire'); Feavearyear, *Pound Sterling*, pp. 13-4 (but note his qualifications); Henri Laurent, *La loi de Gresham au moyen âge: essai sur la circulation monétaire entre la Flandre et le Brabant à la fin du XIVᵉ siècle* (Brussels, 1933), pp. 7-8, and more especially his 'Crise monétaire et difficultés économiques en Flandre aux XIVᵉ et XVᵉ siècles,' *Annales d'histoire économique et sociale*, V (1933), 156-61; cf. a modified view in Harry Miskimin, 'Monetary Movements and Market Structure: Forces for Contraction in Fourteenth and Fifteenth Century England,' *Journal of Economic History*, XXIV (1964), 470-90.

14 John Nef, 'Silver Production in Central Europe, 1450-1618,' *Journal of Political Economy*,

adduced as evidence of a monetary scarcity. Other historians, however, have countered this argument with evidence of the continued operation of many European mines and also of new mines that entered into production during this period.[15] A much more impressive argument in favour of the scarcity thesis is that late-medieval Europe suffered a net outflow of bullion to other regions, especially the Islamic world, which had previously supplied much of Europe's gold needs.[16] Undoubtedly the distribution of precious metals through trade was a much more important consideration than the annual increments from mining. But unfortunately the available statistical evidence is far too inadequate to measure Europe's overall balance-of-payments in this period and one might wonder, furthermore, how long any region could sustain a consistently adverse balance. Even a significant reduction in Europe's aggregate supply of precious metals, however, would not likely have produced a monetary 'famine,' at least not before the mid-fifteenth century. On the contrary, the *per capita* stock of gold and silver probably increased during the late Middle Ages, simply because the European population fell so drastically — by one-third or more.[17]

XLIX (1941) and 'Mining and Metallurgy in Medieval Civilisation,' in M. Postan and E. Rich (eds.), *Cambridge Economic History*, II (Cambridge, 1952), 456-73; Michael Postan, 'The Trade of Medieval Europe: the North,' *Ibid.*, pp. 201-3, 211-3; W.C. Robinson, 'Money, Population, and Economic Change in Late Medieval Europe,' *The Economic History Review*, 2nd ser., XII (1959), 63-76 (with a rejoinder by Michael Postan). Some of the European silver mines had reached their peak before 1300: in Saxony, Freiberg, and Hungary; many other Central European mines were facing depletion by the mid- to late fourteenth century: in the Tyrol, Carinthia, Silesia, Moravia, and Transylvania. Johannes Funcken's discovery of the method of separating silver from argentiferous cupric ores around 1450 and the development of water-powered drainage machines sparked the South German-Central European mining revival from that period.

15 F. Graus, 'La crise monétaire du XIVe siècle,' *Revue belge de philologie et d'histoire*, XXIX (1951), 445-54; Andrew Watson, 'Back to Gold - and Silver,' *Economic History Review*, 2nd ser., XX (1967), 31-2. Particularly in Bohemia, Bosnia, and Serbia.

16 For the most recent presentation of this view, and the most persuasive one, see Harry Miskimin, *The Economy of Early Renaissance Europe, 1300-1460* (Englewood Cliffs, N.J., 1969), pp. 138-58. For the thirteenth-century gold supply, see R.S. Lopez, 'Back to Gold, 1252,' *Economic History Review*, 2nd ser., IX (1956), 232-40; Marc Bloch, 'Le problème de l'or au moyen âge,' *Annales d'histoire économique et sociale*, I (1933), 1-34; Watson, 'Back to Gold,' pp. 14-6; E.W. Bovill, *The Golden Trade of the Moors* (2nd ed., London, 1968), pp. 106-19. Later, from the end of the fifteenth century, the Portuguese were bringing back gold from Guinea.

17 See especially Karl Helleiner, 'The Population of Europe from the Black Death to the Eve of the Vital Revolution,' *Cambridge Economic History*, IV (Cambridge, 1967), 1-19, 68-93; M. Postan and R. Lopez in *C.E.H.*, II, 191-215, 338-412; Herlihy, *Medieval and Renaissance Pistoia*, pp. 55-120 (for the best regional analysis); and J.C. Russell, *British Medieval Population* (Albuquerque, 1948).

If depopulation did increase the relative supply of money, it probably also, at the same time, reduced the monetary circulation. Thus one would expect velocity to have diminished as the number of spenders fell, as the aggregate volume of investment, production, and trade contracted. Changes in velocity, therefore, may have been passive, reflecting no more than a decline in the transactions demand for money and in the need to economize on its use. But a contracting circulation may also have been due to an increase in 'liquidity preference:' to the widespread insecurity of the times, to the frequent dislocations produced by warfare, local rebellions, famines, and plagues, to various other exogenous forces for depression – in general to a climate of pessimism. A complete analysis of the late-medieval economy and its various monetary changes would be too complex a subject for inclusion in this study, and must be left to the sequel, where it will be argued that a deflationary decrease in velocity ultimately did contribute to the worsening of the Great Depression. Evidence of such a deflation may perhaps be found in falling price levels in several countries during the period, especially from the early fifteenth century, though the price statistics are admittedly not always susceptible of convincing analysis.[18] More concrete evidence of deflationary reductions in velocity can be seen in the significantly increased number and size of coin hoards,[19] and also in the greater non-monetary uses of precious metals, especially for lavish display, over this period.[20]

Arguments for deflation and depression, however, would not in themselves support the Cipolla thesis (which emphasizes the money supply over velocity). There still remains the most important objection: lack of evidence that late-

18 Prices did not everywhere fall in real (silver) or money-of-account terms, nor change at the same rate. General price trends of this period are furthermore obscured or distorted by the various local debasements of the late Middle Ages; and, since money-of-account prices did not necessarily change in direct proportion to the debasements, attempts to construct silver price-indices are largely futile. Finally, it is most difficult to construct truly representative price-indices and then to distinguish between purely monetary and 'real' causes of price changes. Where a price decline can be substantiated, it would most likely be explained according to the Fisher Identity (M.V. = P.T.) by a fall in V, when M was relatively constant for a smaller population, and T contracted.

19 J.D.A. Thompson, *Inventory of British Coin Hoards, 600-1500 A.D.* (Oxford, 1956), p. xxvi and *passim*. (The largest incidence of coin hoards was to be found during the reign of Edward III); and also, Jean Lafaurie, *Les monnaies des rois de France: Hughes Capet à Louis XII* (Paris, 1951). One might argue that rulers undertook debasements to stimulate dishoarding; but drastic debasements often caused a flight from coinage and so increased hoarding.

20 See R.S. Lopez, 'Hard Times and Investment in Culture,' in K. Dannenfeldt (ed.), *The Renaissance: Medieval or Modern* (Boston, 1959), pp. 50-61; and R.B. Outhwaite, *Inflation in Tudor and Early Stuart England* (London, 1969), p. 54; Miskimin, *Economy*, pp. 134-8 (though with somewhat different conclusions).

medieval rulers deliberately adopted a policy of monetary reflation. Complaints about the 'scarcity of money' are frequent, to be sure, especially in England, but their effect upon a ruler's mint policies is usually indiscernible nor can they be correlated with the incidence of debasement.[21] Scarcity of bullion *at the mint,* on the other hand, was frequently cited as a justification for debasement; but the mint's lack of bullion generally reflected a higher market price for gold or silver and by no means necessarily meant a general coin-shortage in the country, as will be demonstrated shortly. Finally, as Prof. Van Werveke has pointed out for fourteenth-century Flanders, rulers did not constantly reduce the precious metal content in their coins as they would have done had their aim merely been to multiply the number of coins in circulation.[22] Instead, many of the continental rulers often ended a series of debasements by issuing stronger, heavier coins, which they subsequently debased in a new round of coinage alterations. Such cycles of debasements followed by *renforcements* or enhancements thus suggest that additional explanations are needed for late-medieval mint policies.

Even less confidence can be placed, however, in those theories that represent debasements as policies designed to benefit the mercantile classes. Thus rulers supposedly debased their coinages to provide merchants with a measure of 'profit inflation' – on the assumption that retail prices always rose faster than factor costs.[23] The Flemish and Florentine drapers of the fourteenth century, to be sure, may have profited from paying their artisans the same wages in debased silver, while selling their woollens for stable gold, at inflated values.[24] Cipolla may also be correct in saying that the mercantile government of Florence was sophisticated enough to devise a mint policy for these ends; but clearly in Flanders, as Van Werveke has shown, that benefit to the drapers was no more than an unintended by-product of the count's debasement policies.[25]

---

21 See for example the complaint voiced in the English parliament of 1445; but no debasement followed from this or similar petitions (*Rot. Parl.*, V, 108-9, and *passim.*) For England and the Burgundian Low Countries, see *infra.*

22 Hans Van Werveke, 'Currency Manipulation in the Middle Ages: the Case of Louis de Mäle, Count of Flanders,' *Transactions of the Royal Historical Society,* 4th ser., XXXI (1949), 121. See *infra,* note 29.

23 Cipolla, 'Currency Depreciation,' *E.H.R.,* pp. 413-7; and his *Money, Prices, and Civilization in the Mediterranean World* (Princeton, 1956), chapter 3; and Laurent, *Loi de Gresham,* pp. 7-8.

24 See note 22 *supra* and Van Werveke, 'Currency Manipulation,' pp. 125-7; more especially, see his 'De Ekonomische en Sociale Gevolgen van de Muntpolitiek der Graven van Vlaanderen, 1337-1433,' in *Miscellanea Mediaevalia* (Ghent, 1968), pp. 243-54.

25 Van Werveke and Cipolla, as in notes 22 and 23 *supra.* Prof. Van Werveke was quite insistent in stating that, although Count Louis' debasements helped to check the decline of the Flemish

A variant of this argument is that coinage debasements were intended to benefit the 'debtor-class' by cheapening the cost of previously borrowed capital: to permit merchants to repay their debts, fixed in money-of-account terms, in reduced amounts of pure silver.[26] Admittedly debasements could produce such gains, but this argument is unconvincing for several reasons. Especially because of the nature of late-medieval merchant-banking, a good proportion of the merchants were both debtors and creditors.[27] The prince, moreover, was hardly likely to offend his current creditors, whose financial support he generally required, merely to please the current debtors. Continuous debasements, in fact, often caused the injured creditors to specify repayment of debts in fixed amounts of pure metal, or to increase interest rates, and at times they reduced the available supply of credit. The most important evidence against this argument is the fact that merchants (at least in northern Europe) were almost always hostile to debasement and continuously demanded strong, stable coinage for conducting their commerce.[28] On the other hand, the prince himself might obviously have engaged in coinage debasements as a short-run expedient to depreciate and pay off his own debts. Clearly this reason has to be accepted as a prevalent motivation, especially to finance warfare, for much of the coinage alterations. But the prince's gain would also have been offset by his more restricted access to credit and by the depreciation of his own feudal revenues.

Finally, it may be suggested that bullionist rulers debased their coinage in order to promote an influx of specie through a more favourable balance of trade. Currency depreciation, to be sure, would normally have boosted exports

cloth industry, they did so 'unintentionally on his part.' (*Ibid.*, p. 127). My own researches on Burgundian mint policies in the fifteenth century also indicate that any concept of 'profit inflation' to aid the cloth industry was fully absent from the minds of the Burgundian governments.

26 See Cipolla, 'Currency Depreciation,' *E.H.R.*, pp. 413-7; cf. Harry Miskimin, *Money, Prices, and Foreign Exchange in Fourteenth Century France* (New Haven, 1963), p. 44. For other arguments against this thesis, see Adolphe Landry, *Essai économique sur les mutations des monnaies dans l'ancienne France de Philippe le Bel à Charles VII* (Paris, 1910), pp. 126 et seq.

27 Raymond De Roover, 'Organization of Trade,' *C.E.H.*, III, 49-105, and more especially his *Rise and Decline of the Medici Bank* (Cambridge, Mass., 1963), pp. 9-142, and *Money, Banking, and Credit in Medieval Bruges: Italian Merchant-Bankers, Lombards, and Money-Changers* (Cambridge, Mass., 1948), pp. 29-98, 171-360.

28 Numerous examples of such opposition in England and the Burgundian Lowlands will be seen in the course of this study. See also, for England: Feavearyear, *Pound Sterling*, pp. 18-20, and Michael Prestwick, 'Edward I's Monetary Policies and their Consequences,' *Economic History Review*, 2nd ser., XII (1969), 406-10; for France: Miskimin, *Money, Prices, and Foreign Exchange*, pp. 42-4; for the Low Countries (especially the Brabantine *blijde inkomst* of 1356): Peter Spufford, 'Coinage, Taxation, and the Estates - General of the Burgundian Netherlands,' *Anciens pays et assemblées d'état*, XL (1966), 63-88.

and curbed imports; and apparently debasements did at times assist the ailing Flemish cloth-export trade in the fourteenth century and later, in the 1460s, helped to expand English cloth exports.[29] Nevertheless there are no documents to show that late-medieval rulers were so sophisticated in their knowledge of economic theory as to pursue the self-defeating follies of twentieth-century devaluations. In another, more compelling version of this argument, however, Raymond De Roover has contended that late-medieval bankers indeed did have the sophistication to advocate debasement during periods of trade deficits. The resulting outflow of bullion would thus have dangerously depleted the cash reserves of the deposit banks, threatening them with ruin. Since the deposit-bankers were at the same time the money-changers who supplied the mint with much of its bullion, they might have had sufficient influence to secure a debasement, which should have increased the money supply and replenished their cash reserves.[30] A debasement would also have benefited them by depreciating their liabilities in the form of deposits; but clearly any inflation would have equally injured their assets in the form of loans. One might doubt, therefore, that bankers would have been consistent advocates of debasement, except in times of direst necessity. The chief criticism of De Roover's attractive thesis is again that evidence is lacking to show that bankers either demanded debasements or succeeded in influencing the prince's monetary policies. Furthermore, the incidence of debasement cannot generally be correlated with evidence of trade deficits — nor with the presence of significant deposit-banking communities, who were largely concentrated in just Italy and the Low Countries. All the evidence, on the contrary, would suggest that the decision to debase the coinage was the prince's alone, and that he acted independently from the mercantile-financial community.

The chief aim of medieval rulers in debasing their coinage can be clearly found in the contemporary documents. As Nicolas Oresme, the famous four-teenth-century monetary theorist, stated in his *De Moneta:*[31]

29 Van Werveke, 'Currency Manipulation,' *T.R.H.S.*, pp. 124-7; Hermann Van der Wee, *Growth of the Antwerp Market and the European Economy,* II (The Hague, 1963), 83. See *supra*, note 24.

30 *Money, Banking, and Credit in Medieval Bruges,* pp. 237-9, 339-41; and also his *Gresham on Foreign Exchange* (Cambridge, Mass., 1949), pp. 35-6. In a different context, Henri Laurent also argues that debasements were undertaken to remedy adverse trade balances and monetary scarcity. *Loi de Gresham,* pp. 7-8.

31 Charles Johnson (ed.), *The 'De Moneta' of Nicholas Oresme and English Mint Documents* (London, 1956), p. 24: 'Videtur michi quod principalis et finalis causa propter quam princeps sibi vult assumere potestatem mutandi monetas est emolumentum vel lucrum quod inde potest habere;' and further: 'To get a larger profit by coining more money [of inferior quality] ... is covetousness and to the prejudice and loss of the whole community.' (p. 41).

I am of the opinion that the main and final cause why the prince pretends to the power of altering the coinage is the profit or gain he can get from it; it would otherwise be vain to make so many and so great changes.[32]

By 'profit' Oresme meant *seignorage,* the feudal fee or tax which the prince exacted from all minting, by virtue of his monopoly on the coinage. These princely mint revenues, which varied from one to twelve per cent or more of the pure metal coined, were earned over and above the actual costs of minting itself — the wages of mint-artisans, the tools, alloys and other materials. Such costs were borne by the mint-master himself, who met them from the second fee imposed, the *brassage,* and received his own 'salary' and profit from the residue.[32a] The seignorage revenues, however, did not strictly speaking constitute a pure profit for the prince, for he had to pay the salaries of his own monetary officials: the *garde de la monnaie,* the *maître général des monnaies,* and the assayors, who protected his interests by supervising the coinage and mint-masters. But these fixed costs, and other occasional expenses for repairs, new seals, messengers and monetary conferences, did not usually consume a significant portion of the seignorage, especially not during periods of debasement or general recoinage.[32b] The prince, moreover, was able to gain other and immediate fiscal advantages from his mints: in particular, leasing or 'farming' the mints (and thus the right to the *brassage* profits) to the highest bidder, and

32 The view that seignorage profits provided one of the chief motivations for medieval debasements has been most forcibly presented by Prof. Hans Van Werveke in 'Ekonomische en Sociale Gevolgen van de Muntpolitiek der Graven van Vlaanderen,' *Miscellanea Mediaevalia,* pp. 243-54, and in 'Currency Manipulation,' *T.R.H.S.,* pp. 115-27. See also Landry, *Mutations des monnaies,* pp. 30-2, 85-125; Perroy, 'Crises du XIVe siècle,' *Annales,* pp. 176-8; Georges Bigwood, *Le régime juridique et économique du commerce de l'argent dans la Belgique du moyen âge* (Mémoires de l'Académie Royale de Belgique, no. 14, 1921).

32a For the best recent discussion see Pierre Cockshaw, 'Le fonctionnement des ateliers monétaires sous Philippe le Hardi,' *Bulletin du cercle d'études numismatiques,* VII (1970), 24-36; also Landry, *Mutations des monnaies, passim.*

32b Cockshaw, pp. 27-32; Spufford, *Monetary Problems,* pp. 130-3. It is difficult, however, to estimate 'net profits' accurately from the Burgundian mint accounts (cited in Appendix I), even from those few that are complete, because their accounting procedures are so different from today's. Many of the *dépenses* listed seem to be either periodic disbursements of mint revenues to ducal officials, or repayments of disguised loans - or amortizations of *rentes héritables;* others represent more properly capital expenditures, for which (today) only interest charges and depreciation would be included in a calculation of current profit. (See for example the Namur mint accounts of 1421-33 in A.G.R., C. de C., no. 18.203). On the other hand, since most of the true costs were 'fixed', it is not surprising to find that, during periods of relative inactivity, the mints ran deficits.

loans from the mint-masters in anticipation of future seignorage receipts.[32c] For both these reasons, obviously, it was in the mint-master's interests as well to promote debasement or at least the largest possible volume of coinage.

That the mint often provided a ruler with very substantial revenues cannot be denied. Monarchs from Marcus Aurelius in the second century A.D. to Henry VIII in the sixteenth waged their wars by this fiscal aid.[33] In the later Middle Ages, Philip IV of France reportedly received 50 per cent of his total revenues in seignorage in 1299; his grandson Philip VI, 70 per cent in 1349.[34] In the 1350s, Count Louis de Mäle's debasements of the Flemish coinage earned him revenues amounting to perhaps one-fifth of his total income.[35] As this study will later demonstrate, Duke Philip the Good of Burgundy gained impressive mint-seignorages during the years of his campaigns in Holland and France, 1426-33; so did Archduke Maximilian during the Flemish revolts and French wars of the 1480s.[36]

While the mint was by no means generally the prince's largest single producer of income, it was important as one of the very few flexible and immediate sources of revenue at his personal command. In some countries, however, the ruler often found that his manipulation of the mints was rather less than an absolute prerogative; and the various economic and political constraints imposed upon the monetary policies of the English and Burgundian governments will become evident in the course of this study. The prince's ability to impose such policies depended in particular upon the strength and organization of his 'estates' or parliament, and upon his need for their political or fiscal support. European estates and parliaments almost everywhere opposed coinage debasement with great vigour, first because clearly they feared its inflationary damages to real incomes and its disruptive effects upon the economy as a whole. Even more gravely concerned than the merchants were the nobility, a dominant constituent of most estates, whose feudal revenues were relatively fixed. Second, and equally important, the estates also feared that the high seignorage profits of debasement — which they rightly condemned as an arbitrary tax on

---

32c See Cockshaw, pp. 24-7; Spufford, *Monetary Problems*, pp. 130, 145-6. Repayments of loans and *rentes héritables* and *viagères* can be seen, for example, in the Namur accounts cited in the previous note. The mint accounts also list as revenues any bullion seized and the *remèdes*, which were extra gold or silver metal that resulted from any minting deficient in weight or fineness, within the prescribed tolerance; but, judging by the accounts, these were only fortuitous revenues.

33 For Henry VIII's debasements, see Feavearyear, *Pound Sterling*, pp. 50-63 (especially the table, p. 62, showing the seignorage profits).

34 Miskimin, *Money, Prices, and Foreign Exchange*, p. 43.

35 Van Werveke, 'Currency Manipulation,' *T.R.H.S.*, p. 123.

36 Spufford, *Monetary Problems and Policies*, pp. 141-6; 214-6.

the community – might make the prince financially independent of any controls they could exercise over his rule.[37] Nevertheless, despite this opposition, which became the strongest in England, European princes could generally alter their coinages in times of crisis much more easily than they could levy new taxes and *aides* or increase their feudal exactions.

The relative importance of seignorage, moreover, probably increased over the fourteenth and fifteenth centuries, not only because of rapidly rising military costs but because of an apparently diminishing revenue base. One may argue that the severe agricultural depression of this period – with sharply falling grain prices and rents, the widespread abandonment of land – would have seriously reduced rulers' landed incomes and taxes; the concurrent commercial contraction similarly seems to have reduced customs and excise duties, port taxes, and market tolls. Mint seignorage is, to be sure, not the sole explanation for late-medieval debasements; nor, for that matter, was debasement necessarily always the dominating element in a prince's monetary policy. When fiscal pressures were absent, most rulers of this period seem to have been genuinely concerned to maintain a strong, stable, and 'respectable' coinage – for the highly figured coins symbolized their sovereignty and prestige. But the importance of seignorage revenues also helps to explain why princes manifested so strong a hostility towards any interference with the operations of their mints or with their coinage prerogatives.

In the light of that importance, therefore, the ubiquitous medieval prohibitions on the export of bullion, and the various policies to encourage its influx are more understandable. In England, the first major, far-reaching ban on specie exports was Edward I's Statute of Stepney of 1299 (though repeating provisions of earlier edicts), which he issued during his war with Philip IV;[38] for Flanders, Count Guy de Dampierre's son Philip in 1303 similarly prohibited all bullion exports.[39] In 1335, just prior to the outbreak of the Hundred Years' War, the English parliament repeated the ban on both bullion and coin exports.[40] There was, however, a significant and telling difference between the export prohibitions issued in England and those in the Low Countries. The

---

37 See in particular *Ibid.*, pp. 147-52 and also his 'Coinage, Taxation, and the Estates - General,' pp. 63-8; and note 28 *supra*.

38 Statute 27 Edwardi I, in *S.R.*, I, 131-5: 'Qe nule bone moneye de argent en plate ne en autre manere, ne isse ne soit hors de nostre Roiaume.' This statute was issued in connection with Edward I's recoinage of 1299-1302 (£262,000 minted); it was also designed to protect the kingdom against Philip IV's debasements. See Prestwick, 'Edward I's Monetary Policies,' *E.H.R.*, p. 412. During the previous recoinage of 1279, Edward I had also prohibited all bullion exports, by royal decree, *Ibid.*, pp. 406-7.

39 Gilliodts-van Severen, *Estaple de Bruges*, I, 189-90, no. 193.

40 9 Ed. III, c. 1, in *S.R.*, I, 273.

English Crown, on the one hand, consistently banned the export of *all* precious metal, whether bullion, plate, or coin — domestic and foreign.[41] The (Burgundian) rulers of the Low Countries, on the other hand, prohibited the export only of bullion or *billon,* carefully defined as that precious metal which could and should be minted; and they always exempted unbroken plate, jewelry, and all legal tender coins, domestic and foreign.[42] Indeed, an analysis of the later Burgundian mint policies will show that the dukes fully expected their own debased coins to leave their realms and thus that they were not so concerned about the aggregate money supply. The difference between the two policies would suggest that Burgundian bullionism was more purely fiscal in nature, while the English policy had a mixture of monetary and fiscal elements. This difference also reflected the more commercialized sophistication of the Low Countries, whose economy was so dependent upon foreign merchants, international trade, and thus upon the flow of specie. Burgundian contempt for English monetary policy can indeed be detected in the following report which Henry VII received from his ambassadors (1499), in response to his demand that English merchants be permitted to export bullion from the principalities of Archduke Philip the Fair:[43]

> They sayne, that hit cannot be showne by eny tretes made with your grace or with any of your noble progenitors to eny of your subiectes to convey billion oute of the archdukis landes. They thynk that theye do very moche for your subjectes to graunt them to conveigh oute of the archdukis landis all money current in thoos parties and also all manere of plate wrought and brought to eny man certen forme and fasshion [unbroken]. For the archdukis subjectes may not have like pryvylage

41 See also statutes 38 Ed. III, stat. 1, c. 2; 5 Ric. II, stat. 1, c. 2; 2 Hen. IV, c. 5; 4 Hen. IV, c. 15-6; 5 Hen. IV, c. 9; 9 Hen. IV, c. 8; 1 Hen. V, c. 7, etc. in *S.R.*, I-II, *passim*. In actual practice, however, the ban on taking English *coin* to other countries was not strictly enforced; but the total prohibition against specie exports remained in force on the statute books until 1663, when the re-export of foreign coin and bullion was finally permitted. Full freedom to export specie was not granted until 1819. (Feavearyear, *Pound Sterling*, pp. 3-4.)

42 For example, Duke Philip's monetary ordinance for Brabant, June 1434: 'gereckent zijn over billoen als dat niet te moeghen draghen of vueren uten Brabant alle manieren van goude ende van zilver uutgescheidene alleen den Saluyt van Francrijke, den Nobels, Florijns, Ducaten [and other legal-tender coins listed in the ordinance] ... ende oic gelijk vessele ende juwelen van goude ende van zilver.' (A.G.R., C. de C., carton 65: 1). Also Philip's ordinance of 1466: 'declairont que vaiselle d'or et d'argent entière ne sera pas reputée pour billon.' (A.G.R., C. de C., no. 133, fo. 176 vo.) On the circulation of foreign coins in the Burgundian Lowlands, an analysis based especially on extant coin hoards, see Spufford, *Monetary Problems and Policies*, pp. 55-73.

43 Georg Schanz, *Englische Handelspolitik gegen Ende des Mittelalters*, II (*Zoll- und Handelstatistik, Urkunden, Beilagen,* Leipzig, 1881), 196, no. 8.

to convey money nether plate oute of your realme of England into the archdukis parties, [nor] all manere of cune ...

Merchants, to be sure, did their best to evade these bans on bullion exports, as the constant re-issue of the prohibitions would suggest. But at times rulers did enforce the ban rigorously and, for the Burgundian Lowlands, the costs and risks of confiscation made it more sensible to ship coins than bullion.

Prohibiting bullion exports was obviously not in itself sufficient to keep a ruler's mints productive and served no more than to direct specie to his own rather than to foreign mints. At the same time, mint manipulation or debasement was not necessarily requisite for producing seignorage revenues; but it did generally prove to be the best mechanism for ensuring the largest influx of bullion, domestic and foreign. While much and sometimes most of the minting came from domestic recoinages and dishoardings, foreign specie was generally a very important source of coinage.[44]

A brief examination of the nature and mechanics of medieval coinage should make clear how the mint acquired specie. The relative values of coins were essentially determined by the intrinsic metal contents, so that, for example, a 2d. coin contained about twice the silver in a 1d. coin.[45] The ruler himself, however, assigned the coins their money-of-account values — or rather the quantity of silver to be put in the 1d. and 2d. coins — and thus decided how many coins of equivalent purity and weight should be cut from a pound or '*marc*' of the pure metal. The sum money-of-account value of the total number of coins struck from this '*marc*' or pound of pure metal was called the '*traite*.'[46] From

---

44 For the amount of foreign specie, and the proportions of such specie in the total bullion received by English mints between 1275-1377, see C.G. Crump and C. Johnson, 'Tables of Bullion Coined Under Edward I, II, III,' *Numismatic Chronicle*, 4th ser., XIII (1913), 245; also Prestwick, 'Edward I's Monetary Policies,' *E.H.R.*, table p. 408. In many of the years, over 90 per cent of the bullion received was foreign, either attracted to the mint or acquired by English merchants in trade receipts.

45 The petty silver or 'black' coins (in Flanders, *mites*), however, contained proportionately less silver than the larger ones, in relation to their money-of-account values, principally because their minting costs (*brassage*) were proportionately higher: more alloy had to be added and so many more had to be cut from the *marc*.

46 The *traite* of the *marc* can be calculated by the following formula :

$$t = \frac{\text{price of the coin} \times \text{taille (number per marc)}}{\text{fineness (in deniers or carats)}}$$

For the measure of gold and silver fineness, see note 10 *supra*; the '*taille* to the *marc*' expressed the coin's weight. It should be realized that, because of the imperfections of medieval minting, the mint-master was concerned not that each coin struck should weigh, say, exactly 1/50th of a *marc*, but rather that exactly 50 coins be cut from the *marc*, within the allowed tolerance, or *remède*. The *traite* of a silver *marc* for a 2d. coin, with a *taille* of 50 to the *marc*,

the '*traite*' the mint-master deducted his own costs of minting, the '*brassage,*' and the ruler's seignorage fee; the remainder was thus the price at which the mint purchased bullion. The minted coins, consequently, had to be worth more than bullion in order to cover at the very least the brassage, seignorage, and the merchant's 'cost' in waiting to receive his coins. Coins did normally command such a premium because trading by bullion was technically illegal[47] and, more important, because coins were much more portable and convenient to use than bullion. Except sometimes in foreign trade, coins generally circulated by 'tale' or number, since people generally received them at face-value, accepting the ruler's stamp on the coin as a guarantee of its true weight and fineness.[48] So long as coins continued to command this premium, the mint would normally receive bullion.

In essence, a debasement encouraged merchants to bring more bullion to the mint by increasing the premium on coinage, its exchange-value to the merchants. In order for the debasement to prove fully successful, however, and profit both the ruler and those supplying bullion, three conditions had to be met. First, the merchants had to receive more coins of the same nominal (face) value for their bullion — a higher money-of-account price — and be able to buy more goods than before the debasement, often with a lesser amount of actual gold or silver. Second, they obviously had to receive a better price for their bullion than could be obtained elsewhere. Since a debasement by definition meant an increase in the '*traite*' value of the coined metal, the ruler therefore

and a fineness of 6/12 *deniers argent-le-roy* would thus be:

$$\frac{2d. \times 50}{6/12} = 100 \times \frac{12}{6} = 200d., \text{ or } 16s. \, 8d.$$

struck from a marc argent-le-roy. For actual examples from the Burgundian mint accounts, see *infra* Table I, p. 27.

47 Every late-medieval English and Burgundian monetary ordinance required all bullion (*billon, billoen*) as such to be brought to the mint, or to be sold to licenced money-changers for delivery to the mint. Despite the penalties, of course, merchants and money-changers not infrequently sold bullion for export or for industrial purposes when the market price was higher than the mint price. Industrial demand was recognized by at least the Burgundian ordinances, which permitted jewellers and goldsmiths a definite though limited quantity of precious metals for their work. See the ordinances cited *supra*, and Bigwood, *Commerce de l'argent*, pp. 605-6; De Roover, *Money, Banking, and Credit*, pp. 18-7, 235-9.

48 See Feavearyear, *Pound Sterling*, pp. 5-6: 'debts were settled by tale with coins of an infinite variety of weights and finenesses.' As suggested *supra* in note 46, the crudity of medieval minting techniques made it unlikely that any given coin, even freshly minted, would be of precisely the required weight and fineness. Moreover, it should be obvious that weighing and testing all coins, especially in domestic trade, would have been rather time-consuming and costly. In general, only the larger foreign-merchant companies and money-changers found it worthwhile to test coins.

met these two conditions by raising the mint's money-of-account price for bullion. But third, the ruler ought to obtain the equivalent of more pure metal in seignorage in order to avoid a loss from the ensuing debasement-induced inflation. The limit to his seignorage exactions was of course set by the first two conditions: the higher the seignorage (and brassage), the lower would be the mint-price for bullion.[49] The following Table I demonstrates the division of the respective gains provided by the Burgundian debasement of April 1387. As indicated by the corresponding increase in the silver '*traite*,' the duke debased the silver coinage by 21 per cent:

TABLE I

Burgundian Debasement of the Silver '*Double Gros*' *of 1387*

	Double Gros of October 1386	% of the traite	Debased Double Gros of April 1387		% of the traite
Traite	19s.0d.		23s. 1/2d.		
Brassage 1s.1 1/2d.		5.2 %	1s.7d.		6.9 %
Seignorage 2 1/2d.		1.1 %	8 1/2d.		3.0 %
Total Charges	1s.4d.	6.3 %	2s.3 1/2d.		9.9 %
Mint price for bullion	17s.8d.	93.7 %	20s.	9d.	90.1 %

SOURCE: John Bartier and Andrée Van Nieuwenhuysen (eds.), *Les ordonnances de Philippe le Hardi et de Marguerite de Mâle, du 16 octobre 1381 au 31 décembre 1393* (*Ordonnances de Philippe le Hardi, de Marguerite de Mâle et de Jean sans Peur, 1381-1419*, Vol. I, Brussels, 1965), 188-90, n° 128; 229-31, n° 146.

The ultimate test of a debasement's profitability was, of course, how successfully the coins could be circulated above their intrinsic worth. The most effectively circulated debased coins were counterfeit imitations of popularly accepted foreign coins. While the merchant risked loss by detection of the inferior coins, he would gain by obtaining more coins from the counterfeiting-mint than he would from the legitimate mint. Perhaps the most frequent com-

---

49 Subsequent to the debasement of April 1387, described in Table I, Duke Philip of Burgundy had to reduce his seignorage from 3.0 per cent of the *traite* to 2.65 per cent in 1388, and to 1.75 per cent in 1389, to attract more bullion. Other examples of seignorage reductions, usually to increase the mint price for bullion, may be found in Appendix I, Table C, F, G.

plaint found in medieval monetary documents is about the fraudulent gains made from circulating such counterfeit coins.[50] Similarly, merchants could profit from distributing in other countries the inferior imitations of the ruler's earlier and better coins, particularly if the debasements were undertaken in a series so rapidly that foreign merchants were unable to detect and discount the inferior coins quickly enough.[51] At the same time, merchants could profit from debasement within the domestic market and without engaging in deceit. A chief gain, of course, was made in the payment of debts previously contracted in money-of-account terms, though such gains were limited for the reasons previously mentioned. In general, a merchant's profit lay in spending the debased coins at their face value until inflation eliminated the advantage.

Inflation, if not the inevitable result of debasement, was typically produced by the increased quantity of coins put into circulation.[52] Even if a significant proportion of the debased coins were instead spent abroad, the domestic merchants' ultimate reactions to the debasement would achieve the same effect. They would collectively discount the entire coinage, good and bad, by raising prices in order to seek the same amount of precious metal for their goods as before. But their individual price increases would not normally be coordinated and the amount of their increases would reflect the elasticities of demand for and supply of their goods. It is doubtful, therefore, despite the contentions of some historians, that inflation occurred automatically, immediately, and in direct proportion to the degree of debasement.[53] Thus, if profits from debasement were limited by inflation, and restricted to short-run gains, they were net gains for the merchant nevertheless.

The fact that some merchants could profit from coinage debasement does not in any way contradict the previous assertion that the merchant community as a whole demanded a strong and stable coinage. The gains of a few were obviously made at the expense of the many; the operation of Gresham's Law − 'cheap money drives out dear' − and simple self-protection, moreover, would force merchants to have their bullion and strong coins minted into debased coins (or sometimes to hoard them). Nobody approves of a run on the bank,

---

50 See Appendix II for a report of the Louvain mint-master, dated 1430, which demonstrates what profits could be obtained from counterfeiting - in this case, Rhinelander counterfeits of Burgundian coins.

51 For examples, see chapters 3 and 4 *infra,* and Appendix I, Tables J-K.

52 It might also be argued that any increase in exports that resulted from coinage depreciation (and also decreases in imports) would have had an inflationary effect; so would influxes of bullion attracted from abroad by the debasement. See also Feavearyear, *Pound Sterling,* pp. 10-1; De Roover, *Gresham,* pp. 35-7.

53 See Outhwaite, *Inflation,* pp. 44-6.

for example, but an individual's refusal to participate will save neither his deposit nor the bank. As for the ruler, his initial response to the inflation he created was often to undertake another round of debasement, to recoup his own losses.[54] But almost inevitably, after a protracted series of debasements, he would be forced to issue a stronger coinage. In the first place, the law of diminishing returns applies also to debasements, so that finally little bullion comes to the mint: debtors have finally redeemed their loans and credit becomes restricted;[55] highly debased coins are so readily apparent that people refuse to accept them and instead take refuge in 'good' foreign coins or real assets; merchants anticipate further debasements and thus refuse to supply bullion except at very high prices. In general, these conditions and the increased coinage circulation would finally eliminate the premium on coinage against bullion. Second, the prince would finally be obliged to satisfy those creditors and merchants whose financial support he required. Finally, debasements usually ceased when the crises that had provoked them ended and when the prince found himself more a creditor than a debtor. A sudden *renforcement,* therefore, would have been necessary to halt the inflationary depreciation of his feudal revenues, rents, and taxes.[56]

Debasement was only one aspect of mint-manipulation; the other was alteration of the mint-ratio, in order to attract more of one precious metal than of the other. One mint-ratio would favour, say, gold coinage if the mint offered the *equivalent* of more silver (in coin) for gold bullion than did the market or foreign mints. The ruler had three possible methods of altering his mint-ratio: by raising or lowering the official money-of-account value of gold coinage; by strengthening the coinage of one metal more than the other; or most commonly, by physically debasing one coinage more than the other. Suppose, for example, that both the mint and the market or foreign mint-ratios of gold to silver values were 10:1 and that the ruler then debased gold by 20 per cent, so that his new ratio of official values became 12.5:1. Merchants could then apparently make arbitrage profits by taking gold to that mint, exchanging it for silver, and selling the silver to the market or to those foreign mints whose ratio was still 10:1.

In actual practice, however, various costs and limitations on exchanging metals would restrict the potential arbitrage gains. In the first place, the merchant had to pay the brassage and seignorage fees on gold in exchanging it for silver coin. Thus the effective mint-exchange ratio is not that of the gold and

54 See *infra* chapters 2-4 and Van Werveke, 'Currency Manipulation,' *T.R.H.S.*, pp. 120-2.
55 See Miskimin, *Money, Prices, and Foreign Exchange*, pp. 45-6 for a discussion of this point.
56 Bloch, *Esquisse d'une histoire monétaire*, pp. 70-7; Landry, *Mutation des monnaies*, pp. 57-9, 170 et seq., Feavearyear, *Pound Sterling*, pp. 10-2.

silver '*traite*' values (12.5:1) but rather a ratio of the mint's gold-bullion price to the silver *traite* — the value of coined silver — which might be only 12.2:1. Similarly, he would have to pay the foreign mintage fees in selling his silver coins as bullion, so that the foreign mint ratio (silver bullion price to the gold *traite* value) might be only 1:10.75 instead of 1:10.[57] In the second place, both mints might refuse to supply coins of one metal in exchange for the bullion of the other. Late-medieval Europe did not really operate on a bimetallic standard, but on a silver standard supplemented by gold. If the merchant, therefore, had to accept gold coins from the domestic mint and take them to an official money-changer for exchange, he would pay another fee — and might receive worn and clipped silver coins in return.[58] The merchant, moreover, would also have to pay the costs of shipping the metals both ways and take the risks of confiscation as bullion. These costs and hindrances, therefore, did provide a measure of protection against the export of precious metal. The difference between domestic and foreign mint ratios had to be large before arbitrage profits on coinage could be realized.

Nevertheless, even a small difference between domestic and foreign mint ratios would affect the minting of each country.[59] That difference in ratios would still offer merchants an opportunity for arbitrage profits through trade

---

57 See Appendix I, Tables C and D. From the domestic mint, the merchant would receive 12.2 ounces of silver for one ounce of gold; from the foreign mint, only 1/10.75 oz., not 1/10 oz. of gold for one ounce of silver. On the total exchange, he would obtain 1.14 oz. of gold for his original gold ounce, not 1.25 oz. There were, it will be noted, two mint exchange ratios: one for gold (gold bullion to silver in coin) and one for silver (silver bullion to gold in coin). These two ratios would diverge by the amount of the mintage fees on the two metals. This aspect of the operation of mint ratios has not been fully developed in the literature, but has been suggested in Feaveayear, *Pound Sterling*, p. 22; Bloch, *Esquisse*, p. 56; and De Roover, *Gresham*, p. 82.

58 In Flanders, money-changers held their offices as fiefs of the count, on condition that they maintained the monetary ordinances. They were required not to sort coins in order to cull out the heaviest, to exchange all legal tender coins at the official rates, to purchase 'decried' coins (or '*billon*' - coins without legal tender) by weight and fineness as bullion, and to deliver all these and other forms of bullion to the mint directly: admonitions which suggest that they were frequently evaded. See Bigwood, *Commerce de l'argent*, pp. 389-437; Yves Renouard, 'Le commerce de l'argent au moyen âge,' *Revue historique*, CCIII (1950), 46-7; De Roover, *Money, Banking, and Credit*, pp. 174-82. Similarly, for England, see T.F. Reddaway, 'The King's Mint and Exchange in London, 1343-1543,' *English Historical Review*, LXXXII (1967), 1-23. Though the King's Exchangers alone were permitted to keep a 'common exchange' for profit, foreign merchants often dealt amongst themselves in exchanging coins.

59 See the important study of Andrew Watson, 'Back to Gold,' *Econ. Hist. Rev.*, pp. 1-34, for an examination of how the differences in mint-ratios affected the distribution of gold and silver between Europe and the Islamic Middle East during the Middle Ages.

and thus encourage them to have their gold and silver bullion minted in those countries where the ratio for each was the most favourable. Suppose that English mints favoured gold coinage and Flemish mints, conversely, silver. A merchant might therefore choose to have his gold bullion coined in England to purchase goods there and then sell those goods for silver in Flanders. His profit, whether measured in goods or in silver, resulted from acquiring relatively more goods for his gold in England and more silver for his goods in Flanders. Similarly, he would repeat this arbitrage by having this silver bullion minted in Flanders and so make a profit both ways.[60] One would suppose that the pricing system — the laws of supply and demand for both goods and precious metals — would soon eliminate these arbitrage gains by creating an equilibrium in values between the two countries. The arbitrage trade itself ought to make gold scarcer in Flanders and silver scarcer in England, so that gold values (in silver prices) would rise in Flanders and drop in England. But in fact, neither mint nor commodity prices were quite so flexible in the late Middle Ages. For example, this very same difference in mint ratios was generally true for England and Flanders during most of the fourteenth and fifteenth centuries; and the mint accounts do show that England normally minted proportionately more gold, Flanders, more silver. The one major exception was the very high Burgundian gold coinage output in the years 1426-1433 — conversely, years of high silver coinages in England. In this period, the Burgundian ruler of the Lowlands had drastically altered the traditional Flemish mint ratio in order to favour gold more than did the English ratio.[61]

There were good reasons why a ruler would seek to attract relatively more gold or silver bullion to his mints. Those reasons stem from the fact that gold and silver, while exchangeable, were not perfect substitutes, since each had its

---

60 See Appendix I, Tables C-D for examples.

61 See Appendix I, Tables A-D. The relative ratios of the mint prices for gold and silver bullion might also help explain why one country minted mainly gold while its neighbour minted mainly silver. But since the mint ratio of the two bullion prices was no more than an 'option' ratio, indicating which metal was 'favoured,' that ratio would not itself attract an *extra* amount of the favoured bullion from other countries. Instead, the potential gain from arbitrage trade or from the fraudulent circulation of debased coin was necessary to increase the bullion influx. Evidence for the importance of mint-ratio differences between two countries may be found in a monetary decree of Duke John the Fearless for Flanders, issued in 1409. The Flemish mint-ratios for gold were then considerably less 'favourable' than were the English ratios; and apparently in an attempt to force an influx of gold, the duke required Italian merchants to settle half of each bill-of-exchange payable at Bruges in gold. Strong Italian opposition prevented enforcement of the decree. See Gilliodts-van Severen, *Estaple de Bruges*, I, 478-9, no. 583.

own special functions.[62] Gold from ancient times was the favoured medium for international trade, especially long distance trade, and for most international transactions — above all, financing foreign wars. Relative to silver, gold was much cheaper to ship and simpler to use in financing large volumes of trade, because of its much higher unit value — of roughly 11:1 in this period. Until the mid-fourteenth century, moreover, gold had been minted by only a few countries, who had carefully preserved its integrity. Being traditionally free from debasement obviously enhanced its acceptability as an international medium.

Conversely, silver's much lower unit value made it considerably more useful than gold for domestic purposes, wages and salaries, local and regional trade. Silver coinage was far from being absent in international trade, but general lack of confidence as well as low unit-value kept most silver coins from being universally acceptable. So many hundreds of mints struck silver for local uses that there were confusingly wide variations in weights and finenesses; many rulers also lacked the prestige to give their coins circulation beyond their jurisdiction, especially when so many of them succumbed to the temptation to debase silver. Silver coinage, as the currency for local trade, was indeed far more subject to debasement than gold, since local merchants were less likely to detect alterations than the more sophisticated merchants engaged in international trade. Debasement of silver, moreover, would produce fewer injuries to a country's foreign trade and its international relations than would tampering with the gold coinage. Varying conditions and circumstances, in sum, influenced rulers in altering mint ratios and the coinage: greater ease in attracting and debasing silver; but often, as will be seen, larger short-term profits from debasing gold and greater need for gold in warfare. The ruler's choice was not merely arbitrary, for attracting one metal to his mints generally meant, with some exceptions, losing the other metal to foreign mints.

Medieval mint policies cannot be analyzed, therefore, as though rulers acted in isolation, apart from an almost constant international competition for bullion. Mint alterations were often a defensive response to 'aggressive' policies of foreign mints, whose debasements or mint-ratios offered merchants a greater profit on their bullion of one or even both metals. That challenge to a ruler's mints manifested itself by a market price for bullion higher than the mint price — and thus by the elimination of the premium on the ruler's coinage. This international mint competition operated almost as a vicious circle, since many rulers almost invariably retaliated with greater debasements, seeking to recoup

---

62 Bloch, 'Problème de l'or,' *Annales*, pp. 1-33; and *Esquisse d'une histoire monétaire*, pp. 36-40; Feaveryear, *Pound Sterling*, pp. 21-32; Van Werveke, 'Currency Manipulation,' *T.R.H.S.*, pp. 122-3.

their recent losses, in addition to protecting their coinage. There is hardly a European monetary ordinance of this period that does not justify debasement by the excuse that foreign mints have 'robbed' the country of its gold and silver.[63]

Debasements were also undertaken as defensive responses to the deterioration of the general level of the coinage and to the operation of Gresham's Law. The result was the same as that from foreign mint competition: the coinage lost its premium over bullion so that the mint became inactive. No country was immune for long from such deterioration of the coinage, in general caused by two factors working together. First, despite almost universal bans on suspect foreign coins, most countries did suffer from steady influxes of inferior foreign coins, often counterfeits, whose addition to the money supply would itself reduce the premium on coinage.[64] Second, coins were constantly subject to physical deterioration from normal wear and tear of circulation and from fraudulent clipping. Since these underweight and inferior coins would generally circulate at the same face value as good coins, it often paid to export the heaviest and purest coins abroad as bullion — often to the counterfeiting mints. As a result, the general level of the coinage decreased even more. Merchants would again respond to this progressive deterioration by 'discounting' the entire coinage, good and bad, in terms of bullion. So long as the silver content of, say, the average 'double gros' coin diminished and these coins continued to circulate at 2d. value, the market value of a pure ounce or *marc* of silver would correspondingly rise in money-of-account terms, along with prices in general. Under such circumstances, the ruler had only one feasible solution for restoring mint production and preventing the export of bullion and good coins: a debasement that matched the level or quality of the current circulation and increased the

---

63 See, for example the Flemish monetary ordinance of 1416, which complained that 'comme pour les diminutions et empirances des monnoyes de monseigneur le Roy [de France] et de plusieurs seigneurs voisins de nos dits pays, lesquelles estranges monnoyes ... ont cours en nostre dit pays, et par ce la plus grand partie de nostre dite monnoye, qui estoit de plus fort aloy, a estre vuidee et portee fondre esdits monnoyes voisins.' (Complete text in Louis Deschamps de Pas, 'L'histoire monétaire des comtes de Flandre de la maison de Bourgogne et descriptions de leurs monnaies de l'or et d'argent,' *Revue numismatique*, 2nd ser., VI (1861), 223-4.) Virtually the same complaint appears in the next ordinance of June 1418 (*Ibid.*, pp. 228-31). In 1420, Duke John IV of Brabant gave the same reason for his mint inactivity - and no coins in fact were then being minted: 'die vremde munten voirsc. also ingebroken ende boven hair weerde ... gegaen hebben, mit welcken 't goud ende silver, uut onser lande seer getogen.' F. Verachter (ed.), *Documents pour servir à l'histoire monétaire des Pays-Bas* (Antwerp, 1840), pp. 132-9. See also the Burgundian monetary ordinances of 1433, 1454, and 1466 discussed later in this study.

64 Feavearyear, *Pound Sterling*, p. 11.

money-of-account mint price above the inflated market price.[65] Most medieval English debasements, averaging once every fifty years, can be regarded as 'defensive' remedies for these problems of progressive coinage deterioration.[66]

England, in fact, provided the one major exception to the 'aggressive' mint policies of the late-medieval European countries, at least between the years 1351 and 1464. In part, strong parliamentary opposition to any alteration of the traditionally stable coinage forced the Crown to forsake debasement as a bullionist fiscal policy and to seek alternative means of acquiring specie.[67] That opposition had been provoked by Edward III, who, in 1335, debased the silver coinage for the first time in nearly sixty years.[68] Undoubtedly most silver coins had undergone considerable wear and clipping over that long period; and Edward's reduction of the silver penny's weight was apparently designed to match the level of the circulating coins. But, following the outbreak of the Hundred Years' War (1337), Edward debased the silver coinage four more times, so that by 1351 its weight had been reduced 19 per cent from the 1279 standard. Possibly a chronic silver shortage had necessitated the debasement.[69] But, in view of Edward's extremely serious war-time financial exigencies, the motivation was more likely mint profits.[70] The gold *noble* coinage, introduced

65 Increasing the *traite* by debasement would thereby restore the 'premium' on the coinage. In theory, the ruler could also have restored the premium by reducing the quantity of coins in circulation - by a general reminting of the whole coinage into fewer coins of full weight and purity. But to do so without directly injuring the merchants, the ruler would have had to bear the whole of the mintage costs, and few rulers obviously wished to be so altruistic.

66 Feavearyear, *Pound Sterling*, pp. 10-3. For a general discussion of this topic, see Bloch, *Esquisse d'une histoire monétaire*, pp. 53-78; Landry, *Mutation des monnaies*, pp. 30-129; De Roover, *Gresham*, pp. 35-7.

67 Cf. Feavearyear, pp. 16-36. For a contrary but not entirely convincing explanation of why England had so few coinage debasements, see Cipolla, 'Currency Depreciation,' *E.H.R.*, p. 420. Except for the chaotic reign of King Stephen (1135-54), England had in fact always enjoyed a virtually pure and stable coinage up to the reign of Edward III. (See n. 68).

68 On the previous recoinage of 1279, see Prestwick, 'Edward I's Monetary Policies,' *E.H.R.*, pp. 406-7. The reasons for the 1279 recoinage were roughly the same : because of the poor state of the coinage, which had not been altered since 1247. The debasement, however, was a very minor one, with a reduction in weight alone from 242d. to just 243d. to the Tower Pound.

69 In 1335, Edward III reduced the penny's weight from 243d. to 253d. per Tower Pound; in July 1344, to 266d.; in 1345, to 268d.; in 1346, to 270d.; and finally in 1351, to 300d. per Tower Pound. Thus, over this 16 year period, he raised the silver *traite* from 20s. 3d. to 25s. 0d. per Tower Pound. Feavearyear, *Pound Sterling*, pp. 16-20; and Craig, *The Mint*, pp. 410-1.

70 For Edward III's financial difficulties in these years, see May McKisack, *The Fourteenth Century*, 1307-1399 (Oxford History of England, V, 1959), pp. 154-7, 221-5; George Unwin (ed.), *Finance and Trade Under Edward III* (London, 1918), pp. 93-256; Fryde, 'Public Credit,' *C.E.H.*, III, 459-63. Also, see notes 76, 81, and 85 *infra*.

in 1344, also suffered debasement, a 14 per cent reduction of its original weight by 1351.[71]

The next year Parliament, expressing mounting public discontent, intervened against the king. Even earlier, in 1346, a Commons petition had requested Edward not to debase the coinage without Parliament's consent.[72] Then the Black Death struck England in the years 1348 to 1350, disrupted commerce and agriculture, and carried off perhaps a third of the population. The resulting shortages, especially of labour, produced rapid wage and prices increases; but Edward's debasements, partly responsible to be sure for some of the inflation, received the blame. The baronage led the protest against the debasements and, with mercantile support, forced through Parliament the Statute of Purveyors in 1352. By the statute, the Crown promised that the current coinage 'shall never be worsened, neither in weight nor in fineness (*aloi*).'[73] Not for another sixty years was the English coinage again altered, and then only as a strictly defensive measure that was enacted by Parliament.[74] Again, more than fifty years passed before the next debasement occurred, though in this instance Edward IV apparently ignored Parliament in altering the coinage.[75] Nowhere else did a similar institution exercise so effectively its 'power of the purse' over the monarch's rule.

The chief consequence of this parliamentary ban on debasement was that the Crown instead resorted to foreign trade controls designed to extract a portion of export receipts as bullion for the mints and to prevent the export of all specie. Thus, in strong contrast to the bullionist practices in the Low Countries and elsewhere, medieval English bullionism developed into a prototype of later mercantilist balance-of-trade policies. Edward III had already experimented with bullionist trade regulations during a monetary crisis that

---

71 Reddaway, 'King's Mint,' *Eng. Hist. Rev.*, pp. 1-3; Feavearyear, *Pound Sterling*, pp. 302. The first gold coin, the *florin*, introduced in 1343, proved to be a failure. The gold *noble* of 1344 was pure gold, with 39½ cut to the Tower Pound and a traite of £13.3s.4d. per Tower Pound. In 1346, Edward III reduced its weight to 42 to the Tower Pound and then, in 1351, to 45 to the Tower Pound, giving it a traite of £15.0.0.

72 *Rot. Parl.*, II, 160 (See note 67 *supra*).

73 Stat. 25 Edwardi III, stat. 5, c. 13, in *S.R.*, I, 322.

74 On the 1411 debasement, see chapter 2 *infra*, pp. 61-2. During those intervening years, the English mint officials were fully aware that foreign mints and monetary policies were attracting bullion from England, thus periodically rendering the English mints inactive. But they fully shared, or fully respected, Parliament's deep aversion to debasement; and so the only solution to this problem of Gresham's Law that they would recommend was a strictly enforced ban on the importation of foreign debased coins. See for example *Rot. Parl.*, III, 126: no. 1 (1381).

75 On his debasement of 1464, see chapter 6 *infra*, pp. 161-2.

accompanied the early years of the war with France. Between 1337 and 1342, Edward III had spent the greater part of a million pounds sterling abroad in financing his armies in France and subsidizing his continental allies.[76] That represented a considerable drainage of specie and, to remedy 'the great dearth of money,' the 1340 Parliament required merchants to bring two marks (26s. 8d.) in silver plate to the London mint for every sack of wool they shipped.[77] Parliament renewed the statute in 1341 and 1343, and by the second renewal extended these bullion requirements to other exports.[78]

This first bullionist export regulation failed, however, as did virtually all its successors, because of combined Flemish and domestic resistance. As the chief wool-buyers, the Flemish would have had to furnish most of the required bullion. Fortunately for the Flemish drapery towns, Edward III had recently (in 1340) made Bruges the official overseas staple for English wool in reward for their support in the war against France.[79] Having gained possession of the staple, the Flemish simply refused to pay in bullion for their wools and strengthened the controls against bullion exports. For these reasons, a Commons petitioner in 1348 requested repeal of the law as quite unenforceable, and further declared that merchants no longer dared to ship wool, since they had to supply security for the required bullion. The king rather naively replied that he would ask his Flemish allies to reconsider,[80] but apparently he did permit the law to lapse for the time being. Unhappily for relations with the Low Countries, how-

---

76 Feavearyear, *Pound Sterling*, p. 16. See E.B. Fryde, 'Financial Resources of Edward III in the Netherlands, 1337-1340,' *Revue belge de philologie et d'histoire*, XL (1962), 1168-87, XIV (1967), 1142-1216.

77 14 Ed. III, stat. 1, c. 21, in *S.R.*, I, 289. This statute was evidently based on a Commons petition of 1339 which asked that wool-merchants bring 40s. of silver bullion to the mint for each sack exported. The petitioner confidently predicted that within a short time the realm would have 'graunte plente de Monoie.' *Rot. Parl.*, II, 105.

78 For 1341, *S.R.*, I, 291; for 1343, *Rot. Parl.*, II, 138: nos. 15-7, and *S.R.*, I, 299. The list included lead, tin, hides, and cheese. This statute of 17 Ed. III also required the royal agents 'faire la serche qe nul argent soit portez hors du Roialme, en Monoie n'autrement' and 'qe nul soit si hardy de porter fausse et malveis Monoie en Roialme, sur peyne de forfaiture de vie et de membre.'

79 I.L.A. Diegerick (ed.), *Inventaire analytique et chronologique des chartes et documents appartenant aux archives de la ville d'Ypres*, II (Bruges, 1853), 115-8, nos. 115-8. See also J. De Sturler, *Les relations politiques et les échanges commerciaux entre le duché de Brabant et l'Angleterre au moyen âge* (Paris, 1936), pp. 410-24.

80 *Rot. Parl.*, II, 202: no. 15: 'pur quele charge Marchantz n'osent achatre Leines, par cause q'ils ne poount plat d'argent en les parties de dela trover, et sur ce les gentz de Flaundres ont defenduz qe nul plat passe hors du pays, sur peyne de forfaiture ... Par quoi le Roi sera parler as Messages de Flaundres, q'ils soeffrent la plat venir en Engleterre, saunz destourbance, selonc l'ordenance.'

ever, Edward III himself, his successor Richard II, and later Henry VI and finally Edward IV all resurrected this measure, with more elaborate controls, in a vain attempt to make the wool trade their chief supplier of bullion.

Edward III, meanwhile, had been making the lucrative wool trade serve as an increased source of tax revenue to alleviate his mounting financial distress.[81] In September 1336, just prior to the declaration of war, Edward had forced an Assembly of Merchants (or Great Council) to grant him a '*maltôte*' on wool exports — a vast increase in the customs from 6s.8d. a sack to 40s. (later 50s.) a sack.[82] Parliament angrily demanded its abolition, but in 1340 reluctantly permitted its temporary collection; at the same time, it increased the customs on wool exported by the more vulnerable aliens, to 60s. a sack.[83] Although Parliament continued to oppose this '*maltôte*', for native merchants at least, it succeeded only in gaining the right to supervise the levy of the taxes (1362). The export duties, varying from 40s. to 50s. a sack for native merchants (*denizens*), became a permanent feature of the wool trade and the very foundation of royal finance.[84]

Especially during the years of his military campaigns, Edward sought to extract as much financing as possible from the wool trade. First, in the late 1330s, he borrowed immense sums from Florentine bankers and English merchants on the security of special wool-export grants. Then, after bankrupting the Florentines, Edward farmed the wool customs to various syndicates of English financier-merchants, between 1343 and 1350, and granted them a complete monopoly on exports. The large cash payments he received helped to finance his victory at Crécy and the conquest of Calais in 1346-7.[85] By 1350, however, this syndicate-system had proved inefficient both in marketing the wool and in furnishing the required funds. Worse, it had provoked strong public hostility

81 By October 1339, Edward III's debts amounted to £300,000 sterling when his normal, peace-time revenues had been only £30,000 a year. Fryde, 'Public Credit,' *C.E.H.*, III, 458-60.
82 On the origins of the *maltôte*, see Eileen Power, *The Wool Trade in English Medieval History* (London, 1941), pp. 80-1; McKisack, *Fourteenth Century*, pp. 156-63; and F.R. Barnes, 'The Taxation of Wool, 1327-1348,' in Unwin, *Finance and Trade*, pp. 143-4. According to Barnes, the merchants had granted a subsidy of only 20s. a sack, and an additional loan, if required; but by 1338, the grant had become a straight levy of 40s. a sack.
83 *S.R.*, I, 289-91.
84 On the complex subject of the wool-customs and subsidies, their varying rates over the fourteenth century, and parliamentary opposition to them, see: Power, *Wool Trade*, pp. 63-85; Barnes, 'Taxation of Wool,' pp. 137-77; McKisack, *Fourteenth Century*, pp. 222-5; and Carus-Wilson, *England's Export Trade*, pp. 196-7.
85 See Fryde, 'Financial Resources of Edward III,' *Revue belge de phil. et d'hist.*, XIV (1967), 1142-1216; De Sturler, *Relations*, pp. 321-76. For the conduct of the wool trade in this period, see George Unwin, 'The Estate of the Merchants, 1336-1365,' in *Finance and Trade*, pp. 179-255.

that threatened the wool trade itself. The syndicates' monopoly not only excluded the bulk of the wool merchants but enabled the financiers to pass part of the heavy tax incidence on to the growers, in the form of lower purchase prices. Finally, the combined opposition of growers and merchants succeeded in forcing the abolition of the syndicate monopolies in 1351. The next experiment proved no more successful: the Ordinance of the Staple (1353), which reserved the export trade to aliens alone in order to subject sales to the higher alien export duties. Again, the hostility of excluded English merchants undermined the system, so that Parliament had to revoke the alien monopoly in 1362.[86]

That same year, Edward III at last devised a system that satisfied growers and merchants — if not the foreign buyers — and worked reasonably well for the Crown's financial needs. First, the king organized the wool merchants into a chartered or 'regulated' Company of the Staple, invested its government in the hands of twenty-six merchants and a Mayor, and granted the new Company a virtual monopoly on wool sales to the Continent. To effect this control, Edward on 1 March 1363 made the recently conquered French port of Calais the compulsory 'staple' for all wool sales abroad.[87] Calais was a good choice as a staple port: by this time thoroughly Anglicized, it lay very near to the chief wool markets in the Low Countries. The new Staple Company, eventually composed of some two hundred independent merchants, was far more broadly based than its monopoly-syndicate predecessors. That composition made the growers reasonably content, since the larger number of merchants competing for wool could not force down the purchase price of wools. Finally, the Crown later made a concession to the more important alien merchants. In 1378, Richard II's first parliament exempted Italian and Spanish merchants from the Staple obligations, provided that they exported their wool by sea directly to the Mediterranean.[88] That exemption, however, did not prove to be much of a limitation to the Staplers' trade: for wool exports by aliens fell from 34 per cent of the total in the 1370s to just 10 per cent by the early 1400s and rarely exceeded that proportion of total exports during the fifteenth century.[89] Obvi-

---

86 Power, *Wool Trade*, pp. 84-100; McKisack, *Fourteenth Century*, pp. 350-4.

87 See Power, pp. 86-103; McKisack, pp. 352-5; and Dorothy Greaves, 'Calais Under Edward III,' in *Finance and Trade*, pp. 322-31. The customs on exported wool were still to be collected in England - at thirteen official ports by the royal Customers; but the Customers 'cocketted' all wool destined for Calais, to ensure that they were shipped only to the Staple. A petition for the establishment of the Staple at Calais, 'par cause que les leines du Roialme sont mis a petit value,' dated October 1362, is in *Rot. Parl.*, II, 268.

88 2 Ric. II, c. 3, in *S.R.*, II, 8.

89 From the 1360s, when exports by aliens were clearly separated in the accounts from those by

ously the exceptionally high alien export duties were discouraging the foreigners' trade and for that reason the new Company was able to exclude all such alien merchants from the Calais Staple.

By its control of the Staple, the Company was able to act as a cartelized monopoly in selling wool and thus to pass the heavy tax incidence almost wholly on to the foreign buyers — so long as their demand for English wool remained inelastic.[90] Occasionally, however, the Staplers' cartel was thwarted by the Crown's sale of special export licences that exempted the purchaser from the Staple. For the most part, the Crown sold these licences because of a desperate need for cash; but the threat of issuing licences also proved useful in co-ercing the Staplers to follow Crown policy.

In general, the Company of the Staple, once fully established, continued to control the wool trade until the loss of Calais to France in 1558. As a permanent trading company operating under royal charter, the Staplers became the Crown's chief fiscal agent. The king not only taxed the Company's monopoly profits in customs duties but raised heavy loans from the Staplers, granting them the customs as security.[91]

The Crown almost immediately required the Staplers to act also as its bullionist agent, by re-imposing the 1340 bullion laws on the wool trade. Difficulty of enforcing recent mint ordinances helps to explain the restoration of these laws. In February 1363, just prior to placing the official wool staple at Calais, Edward established a mint there for the new trade. Shortly after, in May, he decreed that only money coined at Calais might be current there and that all foreign coins brought to the Staple were to be reminted.[92] A chief purpose of this decree was apparently to prevent the importation of debased foreign coins,

denizens, the average annual share of the total wool exports accounted for by aliens was as follows :

1360-9	29.4 %	1430-9	15.4 %*
1370-9	34.3 %	1440-9	11.9 %
1380-9	20.3 %	1450-9	12.7 %
1390-9	20.7 %	1460-9	8.9 %
1400-9	9.9 %	1470-9	10.8 %
1410-9	7.2 %	1480-9	10.8 %
1420-9	6.3 %	1490-9	7.3 %

(* when the Anglo-Burgundian war of 1436-9 severely disrupted the Staplers' wool trade.) Estimated from Carus-Wilson, *England's Export Trade*, pp. 48-70. The bulk of the alien shipments was apparently by Italians.

90 Power, *Wool Trade*, pp. 86-103.
91 See Power, *Wool Trade*, pp. 99-103; McKisack, *Fourteenth Century*, pp. 353-65; Lipson, *Economic History of England*, I (*The Middle Ages*, London, 1937), 550 et seq.
92 Thomas Rymer (ed.), *Foedera*, III: 2, 699. On the founding of the Calais mint, see Stanley Walker, 'The Calais Mint, 1347-1470,' *British Numismatic Journal*, 2nd ser., VI (1922), 81; Greaves, 'Calais Under Edward III,' *Finance and Trade*, pp. 333-6.

possibly Flemish, which merchants maintained were defrauding them by as much as one third. Since the decree stated that foreign debasements were responsible for an outflow of specie, the complementary aim was thus to force foreign bullion to the royal mint.[93] These coinage regulations, however, seem to have obstructed commerce by tying up the merchants' working-capital at the Calais mint, for they avoided coinage transactions as much as possible and resorted to an increased use of credit. Edward countered this evasion of his mint by issuing a decree, in March 1364, that strongly condemned all credit sales and required merchants to furnish the Calais mint with bullion.[94] This time, all merchants buying wool at the Staple had to supply as bullion three ounces Tower weight of fine gold, or equivalent silver, for each sack purchased. The Staplers protested so strongly against this ordinance, however, that Edward agreed to let them modify it.[95] While the lack of any further references may suggest that the law simply lapsed, the Calais mint did coin substantial amounts of bullion in the 1360s and early 1370s.[96]

For the remaining thirteen years of Edward's reign there is no record of any further monetary or bullionist legislation, nor of any significant change in the organization of the wool trade. Yet it is significant that both the English coinage output and the volume of wool exports had seriously declined by the end of

93 The Commons petition of 1362 for the establishment of the wool staple at Calais had argued that English jurisdiction over sales abroad would force foreign merchants to pay in good English coin, thus avoiding losses presently caused by 'Eschange des monoies et feblece d'ycelles.' *Rot. Parl.*, II, 268. The same complaint was voiced more explicitly in March 1364: 'que les monoies que feurent receuse ... estoient si febles que les dites leines et marchandise ne poent estre venduz au pris convenable.' The Crown also feared that 'coment les monoies dor et dargent, que sont molt meillours que les monoies dautre paiis, sont de jour en jour en autre treet et porte hors de nostre roialme, par cause de gayn des marchantz, et, si nulle bilioun dor et dargent ne soit porte a nos nostre dit roialme serra destitut deinz breve des monnoies...' Rymer, *Foedera*, III: 2, 725-6. The Crown's bullionist concern may have been provoked by the Flemish debasements of this period. (For these debasements, see Hans Van Werveke, *De Muntslag in Vlaanderen Onder Lodewijk van Male*, in *Mededelingen van de Koninklijke Vlaamse Academie voor Wetenschappen, Letteren, en Schone Kunsten van België, Klasse der Letteren*, Vol. XI: 5, Brussels, 1949, pp. 5-8, 17-27; or his 'Currency Manipulation,' *T.R.H.S.*, pp. 119-21).

94 Rymer, Foedera, *ubi supra*: 'que les dites leines et marchandise par vous et autres marchantz ... sont venduz par voi d'apprest, sanz rien paiere dor ou dargent, que rien purra estre apporte a nos Coignages.' In 1364, Parliament again banned the export of all bullion and coin. 38 Ed. III, stat. 1, c. 1, in *S.R.*, I, 383.

95 For a discussion of this episode, see L. Deschamps de Pas, 'Etude sur les monnaies de Calais,' *Revue de la numismatique belge*, XXXIX (1883), 185-6.

96 Crump and Johnson, 'Tables of Bullion Coined,' *N.C.*, pp. 243-5. The maximum gold coinage, in 1365-6, was 7,597 Tower Pounds, or 10,863.7 marcs.

his reign in 1377.[97] The European-wide depression, apparently quite severe in the 1370s, may account for part of these declines in volume. Edward's heavy export duties and the monopolistic organization of the Staple were undoubtedly also to blame for the wool trade's problems. The other major factors, perhaps the most important ones, responsible for England's steadily diminishing mint activity were competition by foreign mints — French and Flemish -[98] and the progressive deterioration of the English coinage. Edward III found no effective solution for this problem, but in his reign English monetary policy had nevertheless become fixed for several generations to come: in place of coinage-manipulation, to secure bullion for the mint and the royal coffers by banning its export and by requisitioning specie from foreign trade receipts. Both the tax and the bullionist impositions on wool exports were hardly conducive to good relations with England's best customer, the Low Countries, which shortly after Edward's death fell under the domination of the powerful French ducal house of Burgundy. The English Crown had subjected the wool trade to these burdens because it was so very lucrative and because its market was seemingly guaranteed. But it was not an inexhaustible gold mine. As events would demonstrate by the next century, the Crown's policies could serve only to strangle the wool trade and the luxury draperies of the Low Countries.

97 From 1360-9 to 1370-9, the average annual gold coinage output of the London mint fell from 5,730 marcs to 1,083 marcs; of the silver coinage, from 5,180 marcs to 1,510 marcs (computed from Craig, *The Mint*, Appendix II). The Calais mint output also fell sharply after 1373; and between May 1381 and January 1384, the last issue recorded, the Calais mint coined only 8.6 gold marcs. (Crump and Johnson, *ubi supra*). From 1350-9 to 1370-9, the average annual wool exports had fallen from 31,500 sacks to just 22,870 sacks. (Carus-Wilson, *England's Export Trade*, pp. 47-51).

98 For a comparison of English, French, and Flemish mint activity in this period, see Harry Miskimin, *Money, Prices, and Foreign Exchange*, pp. 100-16; and 'Le problème de l'argent au moyen âge,' *Annales*, VI (1962), 1125-30.

CHAPTER TWO

THE WAR OF THE GOLD 'NOBLES': ANGLO-BURGUNDIAN MINT COMPETITION, 1384-1415

Serious monetary conflict between England and the Burgundian Lowlands first broke out during the reigns of King Richard II (1377-1399) and Duke Philip the Bold (1363-1404). The Burgundian duke, who acquired the county of Flanders by marriage, in 1384, undoubtedly provoked the conflict by his aggressive debasement policies. But Richard's own particular fiscal and monetary problems made him perhaps more sensitive to foreign mint competition than Edward III, and also more intransigent in maintaining the re-imposed bullion laws. This first Anglo-Burgundian monetary war, which Richard lost, was chiefly significant as a rehearsal for the far more prolonged and disastrous monetary strife of the fifteenth century. At the same time, Richard's reign also marked some important innovations and refinements in the development of English bullionism as the precursor of mercantilism.

Twice prior to the actual outbreak of the Anglo-Burgundian monetary war in the 1390s, Richard's parliaments had re-instituted Edward III's bullion laws, but only as temporary measures. The Crown's policy can perhaps be explained by the rising costs of the stalemated war in France and, at the same time, by chronic shortages of coin. Thus when the young Richard assumed the throne of an exhausted England in 1377, a resurgent France had renewed the war with bright hopes of victory.[1] The next year, a Commons report declared

---

1 Edouard Perroy, *The Hundred Years' War* (trans. D. Douglas, London, 1959), pp. 168-70, 180-3.

that the defences of Calais, now a crucial gateway to France, were costing more than £24,000 a year and that more money had to be found soon for Buckingham's raids through northern France.[2] Fearful of royal bankruptcy,[3] the following Parliament of 1379 enacted the first of those infamous Poll Taxes. A petitioner of the same Parliament, moreover, complained that 'for lack of good laws' the country was suffering a continuous drainage of specie, so that only 'feeble' coins remained in circulation. The obvious, sensible remedy would have been a defensive debasement, had not memories of Edward III's mint manipulation remained so strong. Demanding 'that the coinage be not changed in any point,' the petitioner advocated instead measures to encourage bullion imports.[4] Parliament responded with a statute, valid for one year, that required all merchants exporting wool and hides and also those importing luxuries — cloths of gold and silver, silks, furs, and jewels — to supply the mint with one shilling's worth of bullion for each pound sterling in the value of the goods concerned.[5]

Although this statute was not renewed, the coinage problem subsequently became so serious that Parliament established a special commission to resolve it.[6] This committee of Tower Mint officials, reporting to the 1381 Parliament, again rejected all proposals for debasement 'because of the universal damage which would occur' and instead offered a solution in a series of mercantilist regulations to control the balance of trade. The report of one Richard Aylesbury is, in fact, the first recorded enunciation of the famous Balance of Trade theory.[7] While the officials were all agreed that a surplus of exports over im-

---

2 *Rot. Parl.*, III, 34: no. 15. The cost of maintaining Brest, it noted, was £8,000 a year.

3 *Ibid.*, III, 88: no. 4. Parliament declared that the king 'est issint outrageousement endettez et ses Joialx en point d'estre perduz.'

4 *Ibid.*, III, 64: no. 39. The London mint's gold coinage output between 1375 and 1379 had fallen from 993 *marcs* to 465 *marcs*; silver output, from 4,601 *marcs* to 1,395 *marcs*. Craig, *The Mint*, Appendix II.

5 *Rot. Parl.*, III, 66: no. 54. See also *Calendar of Close Rolls 1377-81*, p. 193, for evidence that the statute was enforced.

6 See *Rot. Parl.*, III, 126: no. 1, for the Commons petition complaining 'qe en la Tour de Londres n'est fait monnoye d'or ne d'argent... Et les causes sont, pur ceo qe les Monnoiez d'or et d'argent par dela la meer sont pluis febles qe les Monoiez d'Engleterre pur qoi les Merchantz ne purront aporter la bullion en Engleterre a lour profit, ne au profit du Roialme... Item, par cause qe l'or d'Engleterre est si bon et fort, et le Money par dela le meer est feble, les Nobles qi venent a Caleys s'en vont en Flandres, et les autres Nobles qi sont en Engleterre s'en vont par dela le meer, a graunt profit a ceux qi les amenent par dela le meer, et damage au Roi.'

7 *Rot. Parl.*, III, 126-7: no. 2. Aylesbury stated that 'qi si la marchandise qi va hors d'Engleterre soit bon et justement governe la monoie qi est en Engleterre demurra, et graunt pleinte de monoie vendra de partie dela, c'est assavoir qe plus de merchandise estraunge ne veigne deinz le Roialme qe la value n'est del merchandise deniszeins q'est issant par dehors le Roial-

ports was the only efficacious method of increasing the kingdom's bullion supply, they did not at this time convince Parliament of the best means to achieve that favourable balance. Some officials recommended that luxury imports be curbed; others that foreign merchants be required to export their earnings in goods alone. One mint official, named Crantren, advocated a ban on all bills-of-exchange transactions.[8] That recommendation Parliament did accept, at least in part, by forbidding the export of specie for either the settlement of bills made payable abroad or papal tax remittances; the same statute also required pilgrims leaving the country to be searched for bullion.[9]

The offending bill-of-exchange was introduced into England, probably by Florentine merchant-bankers, around the mid-fourteenth century, certainly after its introduction into Flanders. For a long time the commercially less sophisticated English remained hostile to its use, as a threat to their bullionist policies. Crantren, by his report, evidently feared that such foreign exchange transactions would restrict imports of specie and also that foreign merchants collecting bills in England would export specie rather than merchandise. A ban on bills-of-exchange might better control the balance of trade, moreover, by forcing English merchants to limit their imports to the amount that could be purchased from their export receipts. Finally, and perhaps most important, the fact that the bill-of-exchange was a credit instrument, generally unsecured, made it immediately suspect as a sinister device that would lead to large outflows of funds in debt repayment. But its other function, as a transfer instrument, was to obviate the necessity of shipping specie in trade; and it may be argued that the actual effect of all the other measures restricting bullion exports would be instead to promote the use of bills-of-exchange in conducting foreign trade.[10] Bullionism indeed proved to be its best foster-father.

me.' Similarly, Richard Leye argued that 'chescun Marchant apportant marchandise en Engleterre emporte horz dez Comoditees de la terre atant come amontera sa marchandise avant dite; ... et einsi moi semble qe la monoie q'est en Engleterre demourra et graunt quantite de monoie et de bilion vendra des parties de par dela.' (Also, see *supra*, chapter 1, p. 12 and n. 4.)

8 *Ibid.*: 'Item, qe eschaunges ou autres paiements par lettre ne soient faitz hors de Flaundres ne autres parties de par dela, pour paier en Engleterre a cause d'ascun Marchandise.' John Hoo similarly argued against Papal tax remittance, stating 'qe null Clerk null Provisor ne soyt suffert de amesner null argent ne or ne de feace null eschaunge pour estre auvances en la Court de Rome.'

9 *Rot. Parl.*, III, 119-20: no. 107; S.R., II, 17: 'Soit defenduz ... qe nullui del Roialme, n'autre persone quelconque apporte Monoie du Roialme ... ne auxi par eschaunge faite en Engleterre, en nule parte, pur estre resceu par dela ...'

10 On the bill-of-exchange, see Raymond De Roover, 'The Organization of Trade,' *C.E.H.*, III, 41-6, 95-8, 116-8; *Gresham on Foreign Exchange*, pp. 75-85; and *L'évolution de la lettre de change, XIVᵉ-XVIIIᵉ siècles* (Paris, 1953).

The other recommendations of the 1381 Tower Mint Commission were left in abeyance until 1390, when Parliament agreed to enact the chief ones in the first of a long series of 'Employment Acts.' This particular statute required all alien merchants to 'employ' at least one half of their import receipts in the purchase of English goods for export.[11] Despite these merchants' constant and vigorous opposition, the 'Employment Acts' in their various, subsequent forms became a permanent feature of English bullionism. The following Parliament of 1391 complemented this innovation by re-imposing the old bullion law on the wool trade: this time, it required merchants to bring one ounce of gold to the Tower Mint for every sack of wool exported. The statute was to be valid until June 1392 and apparently it was not then renewed.[12]

Possibly the Crown had enacted this last measure as a defence against the mint-policies of Duke Philip the Bold. The debasements of his predecessor, Count Louis de Mäle of Flanders, had already annoyed the English;[13] those of Duke Philip would subsequently cause much greater alarm. Even at this time, England's bullion scarcity does not seem surprising in view of the Flemish mint activity: in the first five years of Duke Philip's rule, from 1384 to 1388, he had debased the gold coinage by 58 per cent and the silver by 51 per cent.[14] For that initial period, however, Philip's drastic debasements were directed not so much against England as against Brabant, in what Henri Laurent has described as a *guerre monétaire* with Duchess Joanna, a war Philip also ultimately won.[15]

11 *Rot. Parl.*, III, 278: no. 7; S.R., II, 76 (14 Ric. II, c. 1). Another act of the same Parliament (c. 2) required all merchants 'making exchange' in Rome, or elsewhere abroad, to buy English goods 'to the full value of the sum so exchanged,' within three months. While modifying the previous ban on such bill-of-exchange transactions, this statute obviously intended to maintain the 'balance of trade' policy by strictly regulating the use of such bills.

12 *Rot. Parl.*, III, 285: no. 7. The same act had temporarily removed the Staple from Calais to the English Home Ports; on 24 June 1392, the Staple 'et la dite Bullion' (mint) were to be restored to Calais. There is no record of further minting at Calais after 1384.

13 For the debasements see Van Werveke, *De Muntslag in Vlaanderen onder Lodewijk van Male*, pp. 5-8, 17-27. For evidence that the Flemish debasements had already annoyed the English, see the 1381 parliamentary mint inquiry, in *Rot. Parl.*, III, 126-7: no. 2: 'qe toutes maneres des monnoies si bien de Flandres, Escoce ... soient deffendues qe elles n'eint nul cours en Engleterre.'

14 See Appendix I, Table C *infra*, and L. Deschamps de Pas, 'L'histoire monétaire des comtes de Flandre de la maison de Bourgogne,' *Revue numismatique*, 2nd ser., VI (1861), 106-39.

15 *La loi de Gresham*, pp. 20-170. Undoubtedly Count Louis de Mäle's debasements had provoked Duchess Joanna's first debasement of 1381. Count Louis' last debasement took place in September 1383, shortly before his death. The next year, on 6 May 1384, his successor Duke Philip the Bold reached a monetary accord with Duchess Joanna: to terminate the mint competition, they agreed to strike a common coinage, with reciprocal rights of circulation, at Malines (for Flanders) and at Louvain (for Brabant). The agreement, similar to a previous one reached in 1339, was to last for five years. (Copy in A.G.R., C. de C., carton 65: bis 1).

At the same time, the duke's involvements in several costly enterprises during this period undoubtedly provided an added incentive for continuing the mint-policies of his predecessor, Count Louis: the bloody suppression of the Ghent revolt and of the English invasion in aid of the rebels; the projected invasion of England — a French expedition under his leadership, involving a fleet of a thousand vessels; his intervention in Brabantine politics and the Guelders war; and, later, the disastrous Crusade of Nikopolis.[16]

The debasement that concerned England the most was Philip's last, the counterfeit issues of the much prized English gold *noble* which he had struck in his mints between 1388 and 1402. The *casus belli* or at least Philip's excuse for his new monetary war with England was the Crown's recently-imposed payment regulations at the Calais Staple. Perhaps the conflict would have begun earlier had not the English, fearing French military activities against Calais, temporarily removed the Staple to Middleburg in 1383.[17] Upon the restoration of the Staple to Calais in 1388, the Crown immediately resurrected old regulations of Edward III that required the Staplers to accept only English gold *nobles* in payment for wool.[18] As with Edward's regulations of 1364, this payment order was intended both to regain the nobles lost to Flanders by trade and to supply the mint with bullion. The Flemish, however, devised a scheme to thwart the Staple regulation. On 8 March 1388, the Ghent *échevins* formally requested Duke Philip to strike gold nobles 'in imitation' of the English coin.[19]

In July, Philip began striking the new coinage, whose silver issues were 11 per cent stronger than the last of Louis de Mäle's. (L. Gilliodts-van Severen (ed.), *Inventaire des archives de la ville de Bruges*, IV, 122, no. 916.) The agreement subsequently broke down, however, and Philip began to debase his coinage in April 1386. The Flemish-Brabantine monetary war ended with a new agreement, signed in June 1389. See *infra*, note 26.

16 See Perroy, *Hundred Years' War*, p. 190; J. Calmette, *Les grands ducs de Bourgogne* (Paris, 1949), pp. 59-88; and especially Richard Vaughan, *Philip the Bold: the Formation of the Burgundian State* (London, 1962), pp. 16-38, 47-51, 95-100. On Philip's finances, see *Ibid.*, pp. 173-8, 226-36; and Michel Mollat, 'Recherches sur les finances des ducs Valois de Bourgogne,' *Revue historique*, CCXIX (1958), 290-307; and A. Van Nieuwenhuysen, 'Le transport et le change des espèces dans la recette générale de toutes les finances de Philippe le Hardi,' *Revue belge de philologie et d'histoire*, XXXV (1957), 55-65.

17 F. Miller, 'The Middelburg Staple, 1383-1388,' *Cambridge Historical Journal*, II: 1 (1926), 63-5.

18 See *Rot. Parl.*, III, 369: no. 80: 'Qe les ditz suppliantz ne resceivent au dit lieu de Caleys pur leur Merchandises illoeques venduz autre Monoie de vostre coigne.' In 1388, a Commons petition requesting the restoration of the Staple to Calais also asked for the re-establishment of the mint there (*Ibid.*, p. 250: no. 41); but there is no evidence that it was restored before 1422. For Edward's payment regulations, see chapter 1 *supra* notes 93-5.

19 Archives Départementales du Nord, Série B. 632/14,534. Précis in L. Deschamps de Pas, *Histoire monétaire des comtes de Flandre de la maison de Bourgogne* (rev. ed., Paris, 1863), p. cxi, no. 7.

MONETARY GRAPH I (1385-1401)
Coinage of pure gold and silver *marcs* in Flanders and England

FLEMISH MINTS:

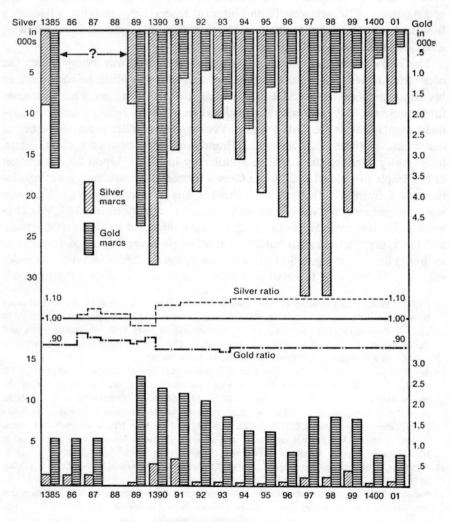

ENGLISH MINTS (London)

SOURCES: See Appendix I, Tables A-D.

Philip readily agreed — if he had really needed any encouragement — and on 1 October he ordered his Flemish mints to strike nobles that would profit both his wool-buying subjects and himself.[20]

Philip's mint indenture, however, required several adjustments before the scheme proved fully successful. To be sure, as the accompanying graph shows, his Ghent mint did coin a great quantity of these nobles in the first year, 1388-1389, but that largely represented a forced recoinage of previous issues.[21] Despite his noble's intrinsic inferiority to the English coin — by (officially) .125 carat and .05 gram weight — his mint price did not offer merchants enough nobles per gold *marc* of bullion. Philip's large profits from the high seignorage fees (5.26 per cent) were thus short-lived and, when the mint output fell sharply, he was forced to reduce his seignorage charges in order to compete with, in particular, the English mints; but, as the correspondence with his monetary officials shows, he did so most reluctantly.[22] Finally, by January 1393, Philip had set the optimum price to benefit both the merchants and himself. In sum, if a merchant took one gold *marc* of English fineness to the London mint, he would receive 30.975 'good nobles' in return (= 43 1/4 nobles for a Tower Pound); but from the Ghent mint he would obtain 31.163 imitation nobles, for a possible gain of almost 1/5th of a noble per *marc*.[23] A profit of roughly

20 A.D.N., B. 632/14,534. Philip replied on 8 Mar. that it 'est son intencion de eulz faire un denier dor *semblable au noble d'Angleterre* de tel pois et aloy et aussi bon ou milleur que les dis nobles sont et ... tel pris comme la noble comme dessus, lequel denier s'il est ordonné par la manière dessus dicte ferait un grant ouvraige et metteront au néant toutes monnoies estrainges.' Ordinance of 1 Oct. 1388 in Bartier and Van Nieuwenhuysen, *Ordonnances de Philippe le Hardi*, I, 292-4, no. 193.

21 *Ibid.*, I, 231-2, no. 147; 292-4, no. 193; Gilliodts-van Severen, *Archives de Bruges*, III, 136.

22 On 10 Jan. 1389, Philip's *maître général de la monnaie* complained that because of 'le petit pris' given to merchants for their bullion, 'l'en en y apporte si peu que l'on n'y a de quoy ouvrer.' Bartier and Van Nieuwenhuysen, *Ordonnances de Philippe le Hardi*, I, 309-11, no. 203. For increases in the mint-prices for bullion until Jan. 1393, see *Ibid.*, 311-2, 335-6, 535-7, nos. 204-5, 223, 332-3; A.D.N., B. 623-4. On 23 Nov. 1392, Philip was about to authorize his final increase in the gold bullion price, to 31 nobles per marc (of 23 3/4 carats), 'pour eschever les inconveniens qui se peussent ensuir se les marchans qui devroient porter le buillon à noz monnoies le portoient à Calais; *combien que en noz dites lettres n'aions pas voulu ceste cause estre exprimée.*' But he first ordered his officials to verify that the Calais mint officials 'donnent XXXI nobles d'Angleterre pour marc d'or ainsi qu'il nous a esté affermé.' (*Ordonnances de Philippe le Hardi*, I, 536-7, no. 333). Apparently this final price did not go into effect until 20 January 1393.

23 See Appendix I, Table C *infra*. The English noble, as struck from 1351, had a fineness of 23 7/8 carats, the English standard for fine gold, and a weight of 7.775 grams, equal to a *taille* of 31.5 nobles to the *marc de Troyes*. The Flemish nobles struck by Duke Philip had a fineness of 23 3/4 carats and a *taille* of 31 2/3 to the *marc* (7.727 grams). For proof of the

1s.3d. sterling per *marc* may seem small, but not compared to the daily wage of 5d. for a skilled building craftsmen or of 6d. for a mounted English archer in this period.[24] When that gain is calculated in terms of buying hundreds or thousands of wool sacks at Calais, it became significant. The merchants, of course, could realize their profit only if they successfully passed the Flemish *nobles* for English ones at the same value of 6s.8d. sterling. English complaints suggest that they did.[25]

Duke Philip had also profited from manipulating his silver coinage. By his drastic silver debasements in the years 1386 to 1388, he evidently succeeded in defeating the Brabantine (and English) mints. His victory over Duchess Joanna of Brabant was marked by a new monetary accord, signed in June 1389, which obligated her to close her mints.[26] In December 1389, he instituted an equally drastic monetary reform, strengthening the silver coinage by 32 per cent, and he then ordered a general recoinage.[27] But at the same time Philip altered the Flemish mint ratios and subsequently raised the mint price to 'favour' silver even more strongly than before. The accompanying graph, which

weight relationships, see A.G.R., C. de C., no. 1158, fo. 11 ro. For the calculations above: (a) from June 1361, the English mint price for gold was £14.15s. 0d. sterling; at 6s. 8d. per noble, the mint price = 44.25 nobles to the Tower Pound = 44.25/1.429 = 30.975 nobles to the *marc*; (b) the Flemish mint price for gold was 31 nobles for a *marc* of 23 3/4 carats fineness = 31.163 nobles at 23 7/8 carats English fineness. (See the previous note.)

24 E.H. Phelps Brown and Sheila V. Hopkins, 'Seven Centuries of Building Wages,' and Nora Ritchie, 'Labour Conditions in Essex in the Reign of Richard II,' in E. Carus-Wilson (ed.), *Essays in Economic History*, II (London, 1962), 177, and 104-7 respectively; McKisack, *Fourteenth Century*, p. 240.

25 See *infra*, pp. 53-4, 60.

26 Bartier and Van Nieuwenhuysen, *Ordonnances de Philippe le Hardi*, I, 327-9, nos. 217-8. The agreement also required her to direct all bullion to the Flemish mints and to permit the circulation of only those coins authorized in Flanders; in return, the duchess was to receive one half of the Flemish mint's 'proufiz et des esmolumens.' But this agreement later broke down and Joanna was permitted to resume minting in May 1392, on condition that she give Philip one-half of her mint profits, and not strike any coins similar to the Flemish (*Ibid.*, I, 467-8, no. 306). Joanna debased her coinage five times and then, finally, in 1399 also returned to a strong coinage. See Laurent, *Loi de Gresham*, pp. 61 et seq.; Van der Wee, *Growth of the Antwerp Market*, I, 126-7 (Table XV); and Hans Van Werveke, 'De Vlaamse Munthervorming van 1389-90,' *Miscellanea Mediaevalia*, pp. 268-90.

27 Text in Bartier and Van Nieuwenhuysen, *Ordonnances*, I, 345-8, no. 231; and of supplementary ordinance of Jan. 1390, pp. 358-61, no. 239. It also decreed the unusually severe penalty of 10 years banishment for exporting bullion. See also Raymond De Roover, *The Bruges Money Market Around 1400* (Brussels, 1968), pp. 39-40; L. Deschamps de Pas, 'Histoire monétaire des comtes de Flandre,' *Revue numismatique*, 2nd ser., VI (1861), 135-9; and Van Werveke, 'Vlaamse Munthervorming,' pp. 278-9. Correcting Deschamps de Pas, he dates the effective commencement of the reform as 23 Jan. 1390.

records these adjustments in the mint ratios,[28] demonstrates how much higher a price for silver bullion Philip's mints offered than did the English, especially after the final mint adjustment of January 1393. Philip's success was striking. Even apart from the large, forced recoinage of 1390, the Flemish mints continually coined vastly greater quantities of silver than did the London Tower mint. Admittedly, such factors as trade balances, dishoardings, and military prizes also helped to determine the absolute volumes and fluctuations in output.

Philip's success in gold minting, despite the conversely more 'unfavourable' mint-ratio for that metal, seems equally impressive. In the eighteen months following his final mint price, Flemish gold coinage output more than doubled. Apparently, therefore, the profit from distributing the counterfeit *nobles* did outweigh the even more adverse mint-ratio for gold. Perhaps that adverse ratio was actually beneficial to Philip's gold minting, since merchants could have their gold minted into Flemish *nobles* and then profit even further by spending

---

28 The two ratios on this and the following monetary graphs represent the *relative* mint ratios for gold and silver, as constructed from both the English and Flemish mint prices; they thus indicate which of the two countries' mints had the greater advantage in attracting each of the metals. For the Years 1393-1404, the two ratios are calculated as follows, with the English mint ratio as the denominator and the Flemish ratio as the numerator :

(a) 'Gold' ratio :

Ratio of Flemish mint-price for gold bullion to silver traite
———————————————————————————————
Ratio of English mint-price for gold bullion to silver traite

$$= \frac{£9.349 \text{ gros}}{£.950 \text{ gros}} \quad . \quad \frac{£14.750 \text{ sterl.}}{£1.295 \text{ sterl.}} = \frac{9.84}{11.39} = .86$$

(b) 'Silver' ratio:

Ratio of Flemish mint-price for silver bullion to gold traite
———————————————————————————————
Ratio of English mint-price for silver bullion to gold traite

$$= \frac{1}{£9.550/£.875 \text{ gros}} \quad . \quad \frac{1}{£15.000/£1.252 \text{ sterl.}}$$

$$= \frac{1}{10.91} \quad . \quad \frac{1}{11.98} = \frac{11.98}{10.91} = 1.10$$

If the relative ratios equalled 1.00, then both countries would have had the same mint ratios and neither country would have had any advantage in attracting gold or silver to its mints. The graphs are so constructed that: a movement of the relative ratio for silver or for gold *above* 1.00, into the top or 'Flemish' half of the graph, indicates that silver or gold, respectively, should have been attracted to the Flemish mints; similarly, a movement of the relative ratios for silver or gold *below* 1.00 indicates that the corresponding metal should have been attracted to the English mints. The graph, however, obviously cannot take account of other factors that would have influenced the flow of bullion into or between the two countries; balances of trade, taxes, war-booty and ransoms, papal remittances, and other foreign expenditures. I am indebted to Prof. Harry Miskimin of Yale University for his suggestions in the method of constructing these graphs.

them in England, where gold was worth relatively more in terms of silver. There is no evidence that an exodus of Flemish *nobles* to England caused Duke Philip any concern — so long as he acquired his seignorage on minting them. He seems to have achieved, so to speak, the best of both monetary worlds. The following table, a record of his mint profits during this reign, however, will help to place the duke's success in better perspective.

TABLE I

Seignorage Revenues from Gold and Silver
Coinage at the Mints of Malines, Ghent, Bruges, and Fauquemont
1384-5 to 1401-02
in livres gros of Flanders

Michaelmas Years	Seignorage on Silver Coinage in £ gros	Seignorage on Gold Coinage in £ gros	Total Seignorage in £ gros
1384-5	£689.18	£1,268.13	£1,957.31
1385-8*	— missing —		
1388-9	264.15	2,497.44	2,761.59
1390-1	375.69	164.42	540.11
1391-2	177.98	143.58	321.56
1392-3	482.65	205.20	687.85
1393-4	254.52	117.18	371.70
1394-5	323.27	78.77	402.04
1395-6	364.72	78.32	443.04
1396-7	534.20	109.26	643.46
1397-8	542.10	75.22	617.32
1398-9	319.88	38.71	358.59
1399-1400	270.99	33.68	304.67
1400-1	143.14	19.04	162.18
1401-2	101.39	13.48	114.87

* From 4 Dec. 1385 to 2 May 1386 'chauma la Monnoie.' An estimate of the share of the seignorage receipts for the latter period of the first Malines account, from 30 Sept.-4 Dec. 1385 would be £105.5s.0d. for silver and £27.8s.0d. for gold. The next available mint account, for Ghent, commences on 10 Oct. 1388.

SOURCES: A.G.R. Chambre des Comptes, comptes en rouleaux, nos. 2142-3, 2145-46, and registres nos. 48,976-7 (Malines); comptes en rouleaux nos. 824-6, (Ghent); comptes en rouleaux nos. 776-87 (Bruges); comptes en rouleaux nos. 2586-7 (Fauquemont).

Since the mint accounts from 2 May 1386 to September 1388, the most active period of coinage debasement, are unfortunately missing, the profitability of Duke Philip's *guerre monétaire* with Brabant can be estimated only for the first and last years. In that final year, 1388-89, when Philip ceased competing for silver with the Brabantine mints to launch his *guerre monétaire* against

England, his mints produced relatively little seignorage from the silver coinage but an impressive amount from the issue of counterfeit nobles. Neither that year's seignorage receipts, however, nor those of 1384-5, likely accounted for a significantly large proportion of the duke's total revenues (for which the complete records are not extant).[29] They would probably not compare with Van Werveke's estimates of Count Louis de Mâle's mint profits, nor, for example, with the £5,473 *gros* seignorage that Duke Philip the Good gained in 1433.[30] Philip the Bold's seignorage revenues never again approached those of 1388-9, as the table shows, perhaps because of his return to a 'strong' and stable coinage in December 1389. Indeed, if his mints were to attract bullion, despite the advantages offered by the counterfeit nobles and the high mint-ratio for silver, the duke could no longer continue exacting high seignorages and was several times forced to reduce them on both metals in order to raise the mint prices.[31]

Philip's monetary policies seem to have been successful, however, in injuring English minting after 1389. As the graph shows, the Tower Mint coined barely any silver from 1391 to 1397 and, despite a mint ratio strongly favouring gold, the coining of nobles dropped to less than one third by 1396. To attribute that decline between those years to unfavourable trade balances would not be convincing, however, because England enjoyed a significant export boom between 1389 and 1395.[32] If England had 'lost' gold bullion to Flemish mints, it evidently reappeared in English circulation as Flemish nobles. According to Richard's officials, merchants were importing great quantities of these nobles, 'whose stamp resembles the king's, but which are of less weight and value,' and were spending them 'as though they were nobles of England, to the destruction of the king's money.'[33] Eventually those receiving these nobles at par would suffer, of course, when some merchants detected them as counterfeits. So would the king, in receiving the nobles in taxes and customs receipts. A large circula-

29 On Duke Philip's finances, see note 16 *supra*. Philip's receipts have been partially estimated as ranging from £185,000 *tournois* in 1384 to about £600,000 *tournois* in 1396.
30 See chapter 1 *supra*, p. 22 and chapter 4, p. 98 *infra*.
31 See Appendix I, Table F.
32 Carus-Wilson, *England's Export Trade*, pp. 52-4, 83-5. Between 1387-9 and 1393-5, average annual wool exports rose from 18,900 sacks to 20,400 sacks; broadcloth exports, from 24,170 pieces to 41,530 pieces.
33 *Cal. Close Rolls 1392-96*, p. 110 (Dec. 1392). That the configuration of the Flemish noble was in fact almost identical to that of the English may be seen from the photographs in J.D.A. Thompson, 'Continental Imitations of the Rose Noble,' *British Numismatic Journal*, XXV (1949), 184 and plate A: 1; and Charles Oman, *The Coinage of England* (Oxford, 1931), plates XIX: 1, 4.

tion of these nobles, moreover, would reduce the 'premium' on English coinage and help explain, along with Philip's competition, the scarcity of bullion in the Tower Mint. In vain, the king and then Parliament several times tried to ban the 'deceitful counterfeits' and to have them reminted, on pain of forfeiture, fine, and imprisonment.[34]

By January 1397, when the Tower Mint output was the smallest in many years, serious financial difficulties further aggravated Richard's monetary crisis. His lavish wedding to the French princess Isabella that month was very costly and, by the wedding contract, he had promised the French considerable aid in fighting the duke of Milan. A hostile Parliament refused the king any funds for this unsavoury alliance.[35] But the January Parliament did at least permit Richard the now traditional remedy for his monetary problems and readily enacted the '*Ordinance de la Bullion*.' Again the bullion law required all merchants, foreign and domestic, to supply the Tower Mint with one ounce of gold in 'foreign coin' for each woolsack, 240 woolfells, and half last of hides exported, within six months of shipping. But this time, to ensure compliance, the statute required exporting merchants to place surety with the King's Customers and to pay fines if they failed to bring the required gold to the mint.[36]

Since previous experience had shown that the bullion regulations were unworkable without the wool merchants' co-operation, Richard also enlisted the Staple Company's agreement to enforce them. In return, the Staplers demanded a complete monopoly on all wool exports to northern Europe. They supposedly enjoyed this monopoly already; but Richard, finding that the sale of special export licences was a handy fiscal expedient, had undermined it. In the Commons, the Staplers had angrily complained that merchants possessing these licences were underselling them in their chief markets. The king therefore solemnly bound himself to revoke all such licences and Parliament enacted new

---

34 *C.C.R. 1385-89*, p. 647 (2 Feb. 1389); *C.C.R. 1392-96*, p. 110 (2 Dec. 1392); *Rot. Parl.*, III, 320: no. 38 (Jan. 1394).

35 In desperation, Richard in August 1397 exacted the largest forced loan of his reign (Rymer, *Foedera*, VIII, 8-9). On Richard's financial difficulties, see McKisack, *Fourteenth Century*, pp. 475-6; and for the decline in Exchequer receipts, A. Steel, *Receipt of the Exchequer, 1377-1485* (Cambridge, 1954), pp. 427-8.

36 Text in *Rot. Parl.*, III, 340: no. 19. On 20 Feb. 1397 the statute's provisions were delivered to the King's Customers in fourteen ports. *Cal. Close Rolls 1396-99*, pp. 37-8. One ounce of gold was worth £1.7s.3d. sterl., about 22-5 per cent of the wool price. The fine for not supplying gold for minting was 13s.4d. (one 'mark') per sarpler of wool, considerably more than the merchant's cost in mintage fees and shipping. For other views, see Schanz, *Englische Handelspolitik*, I, 496; and Eileen Power, 'The Wool Trade in the Fifteenth Century,' in Power and Postan (eds.), *Studies in English Trade in the Fifteenth Century* (London, 1933), p. 80.

legislation for the stricter enforcement of all the Staple's monopoly privileges.[37] Richard apparently hoped to make the Staplers the Crown's permanent bullion supplier — as Edward III had planned to do — since the *Ordinance de la Bullion* had no expiry date. As the accompanying graph suggests, his scheme enjoyed at least initial success; for the Tower Mint's gold coinage more than doubled between 1396 and 1397, and continued to be very substantial until 1399. At the same time, significantly, the Flemish gold minting began to fall steeply from 1397. But the Staplers, despite their renewed monopoly powers, soon found that Burgundian resistance to the bullion exactions made their role as royal mint agents a most difficult one.

Duke Philip could have had little doubt that the *Ordinance de la Bullion* was a retaliatory measure directed solely against him. Obviously Flanders as the chief wool market would have to bear the burden of supplying most of the bullion. Moreover, the statute's reference to gold in 'foreign coin' implicitly meant that the Flemish counterfeit *nobles* were to be surrendered as bullion to the Tower Mint;[38] and that forced reminting would eliminate the incentive to supply any gold to the Flemish mints. But worst of all, the timing of Richard's ordinance was singularly inopportune for Duke Philip, because he then required large sums in gold to ransom his feckless son John 'the Fearless' and other Burgundian nobles whom the Turks had captured in the disastrous Nikopolis Crusade. Flanders itself was obligated to provide some 100,000 gold nobles;[39] and perhaps the loss of so much gold at one time explains Philip's reactions to the bullionist demands of the English. In October 1397, Philip did retaliate: he banned the circulation of English *nobles* and ordered their confiscation as '*billon*.'[40] He thus sought to thwart Richard II and protect his sei-

---

37 *Rot. Parl.*, III, 370: no. 82; S.R., II, 108 (21 Ric. II, c. 17).

38 Later references were only to 'unam unciam auri de cuneo extranes pro quolibet sacco lane.' Public Record Office, C76/84, m. 16. See note 36 *supra*.

39 Prevenier, *Handelingen van de Leden*, p. 140, no. 384; see also nos. 375-80, pp. 136-9. On the Crusade and Philip's financial difficulties, see Vaughan, *Philip the Bold*, pp. 59-78. The grant of 100,000 gold nobles (for two years) equals 3,130 gold marcs; that may help to explain why the Flemish gold minting was so high in 1396-7.

40 Deschamps de Pas, *Histoire monétaire des comtes de Flandre*, p. xvi, doc. no. 78; F. Priem (ed.), *Précis analytique des archives de la Flandre-Occidentale: comptes du Franc*, II: 2 (Bruges, 1844), 12; and Prevenier, *Handelingen van de Leden*, p. 142, no. 389. The ordinance stated that the ban was in retaliation against a similar ban on Flemish nobles at Calais and in England. In this period, the word *billon* (Fl. *billoen*) meant demonetized or 'decried' coinage that might neither be circulated nor exported but had to be reminted; in a more general sense, it meant 'bullion' - not petty or heavily alloyed coins, as in modern French. For confiscations of English *nobles* as billon, see A.G.R., C. de C., comptes en rouleaux, no. 783-b (Bruges mint account, 1397); and Gilliodts-van Severen, *Estaple de Bruges*, I, 403, no. 482 (1398).

gnorage by forcing merchants to remint their English *nobles* into the Flemish counterfeits and to use them in place of the former. At the same time, Philip's ban might have encouraged some diversion of gold bullion itself to the Flemish mints. Philip also took severe measures against the export of bullion to Calais; as an incentive for enforcement, he offered one fifth of the metal seized to those who aided in its confiscation.[41]

Philip's retaliatory measures were ultimately successful in thwarting the *Ordinance de la Bullion,* despite Richard's initial success. Even by the end of the statute's first year, late in 1397, a group of Staplers in Parliament had demanded its revocation on the grounds that the payment regulations were too onerous and costly for them. They complained that the duke of Burgundy, 'perceiving your said ordinance,' was preventing them from acquiring any bullion at the Staple and, furthermore, that the duke's hostile actions were seriously injuring their wool sales. So strict were the Burgundian officials in searching for bullion, 'on every road and passage from his country, that no merchant dares to take his money to your Staple for fear of losing it.'[42] Furthermore, they maintained that, even when they did manage to receive bullion payments, they suffered considerable hardship and expense in taking the gold directly to London and in waiting there while the Tower Mint coined it, 'by which they spend all the gains of their merchandise or more.' Finally, in requesting an immediate release from the bullion obligations, they pointed out that fear of fines for non-compliance, as well as all the hindrances, had discouraged merchants from shipping wool, so that prices had slumped. Richard, however, refused to answer their petition directly, stating only that he would request Duke Philip to remove his restrictions on bullion exports to Calais.

Growing domestic opposition to Richard's rule and then a *coup d'état,* however, finally resolved the bullionist crisis. Just fifteen months later Henry of Lancaster overthrew Richard II. As the new king, anxiously seeking mercantile support, Henry IV readily instructed his first parliament of October 1399 to accept 'the special request of the Staple Mayor' and annul the *Ordinance de la Bullion.*[43] The same parliament also reconfirmed the Staplers' monopoly privi-

---

41 Deschamps de Pas, *Histoire monétaire des comtes de Flandre,* p. xvi, doc. no. 78.

42 *Rot. Parl.,* III, 369-70: no. 480. Moreover, they maintained that 'sovent foitz de ceux qi aventurent illoeqes parmy la dite Pais de Flaundres, tant bien estranges come voz lieges, lour Or est pris come forfait par les Ministres suis ditz, si qe les ditz suppliantz ne purront nullement acquere Bullion pur perfourner vostre dite Ordenance.'

43 *Rot. Parl.,* III, 429: no. 86. The ordinance in fact merely ordered that the 'Exchange' be placed at Calais and that the bullion obligations be annulled until the next Parliament. But that same Parliament also revoked all statutes of 21 Richardi II and the bullion law was not restored by Henry IV. (*Ibid.,* p. 425: no. 66). See also Henry's instructions of 16 Nov. 1399 to the Royal Customers in P.R.O., C76/84, m. 16: 'Nos... pardonamam et relagamimam

leges;[44] but the statute provided an apparently minor exemption that later proved to be most objectionable to the Staplers: permission for Berwick-on-Tweed to export the coarser, cheap wools of Northern England and Scotland free of the Staple.[45] Subsequently the Staplers complained that under the guise of this exemption merchants were shipping the very best English wools directly to the Low Countries, selling them there for far lower prices.

But at the same time, to almost everybody's consternation, the Staplers' victory seemed even more hollow when the revocation of the bullion law failed to produce any reciprocal concessions from Duke Philip. He kept on minting his Flemish counterfeit nobles, and stubbornly refused to remove his ban on the English noble, even despite the strong opposition he was receiving from his own subjects as well. The Flemish drapery towns had, in fact, continuously protested against the ban from the very date of its proclamation.[46] As the mint indentures show, merchants would have lost money in mintage fees by having English nobles reminted, and could only profit from the Flemish nobles by having them coined from bullion.[47] Evidently merchants were also experiencing too great a risk in trying to pass the Flemish counterfeits at the Calais Staple; and after the collapse of the *Ordinance de la Bullion,* English officials were perhaps even more vigilant in their coinage inspections.[48] Thus, from October 1399, the Flemish towns begged Philip more and more insistently to restore the English noble to legal tender and to permit its export 'in view of the fact that all the inhabitants of this land depend upon the drapery industry and trade, and for this they must have English wools, the which they cannot obtain without

eisdem maiori et mercatoribus et eorum cuius libet transgressionem, contemptuum, et mesprisionem quos fecerunt vel aliquis eorum fecit in non apportando unam unciam auri de cuneo extranes ad bullionem praedictam in Turii praed. juxta ordinacionis inde facere a tempore confeccionis...'

44 *Rot. Parl.,* III, 429: no. 87; P.R.O., C76/84, m. 14-6.
45 *Rot. Parl.,* III, 429: no. 87 and *S.R.,* II, 112 (1 Hen. IV, c. 3). That statute also reconfirmed the Italians and Spaniards' 'Straits of Marrock' privilege of 1378, to export wool free of the Staple directly to the Mediterranean. The statute also suggests that Berwick's privilege had already been granted in 1378 as well.
46 See the meetings of the Four Members (Bruges, Ypres, Ghent, and the Franc de Bruges) from 27 Oct. 1397 to 5 May 1398, and then from 19 Oct. 1399 to 23 Feb. 1400 in Prevenier, *Handelingen van de Leden,* pp. 142-5, nos. 389-92, 395-9, 401-5, 409; and pp. 179-85, nos. 463, 465-7, 472-5.
47 One *marc* of fine gold in English nobles consisted of 31.500 nobles; the mint price for those nobles as *billon* was only 31.163 nobles. Thus the merchant would have lost the equivalent of .337 noble per marc, on the average. See note 23 *supra.*
48 The Calais Staple regulations requiring payment in English nobles alone were still in force; but apparently many Flemish counterfeits were still being passed there and reaching England. See *infra,* p. 60.

the said English nobles.'[49] In rejecting their appeal (December 1399), Duke Philip stated that he would give it consideration 'only when the English shall agree to permit the circulation of Flemish nobles in England and at Calais, and cease considering them as *billon*.'[50] The mint accounts show that Philip's officials continued to be zealous in confiscating English nobles.[51] But the Flemish towns, undaunted, finally exerted so much pressure on Philip that, on 31 July 1400, he agreed to restore the English noble to circulation — granting it the same value as his counterfeit nobles.[52] He kept on minting these coins, but in sharply diminishing amounts. Since his silver mintage fared little better, he was at last forced to close his one remaining mint at Bruges, on 16 June 1402.[53]

This drastic decline in Flemish mint output, shown on graph I from 1397, may explain why Philip had taken such a stubborn stance in the 'war of the nobles'. If English bullionism can no longer be blamed, after 1399, there are two other possible explanations for this mint slump: debasements in neighbouring principalities, which Philip claimed himself were victimizing his coinage;[54] and an apparently severe scarcity of specie in North-Western Europe

49 A.D.N., B. 630/14.238: 'pourquoy leur convient avoir laines d'Angleterre, lesquelles ilz ne peuvent avoir sanz nobles dicellui Angleterre.' They also argued that, since these nobles were banned, their merchants had to purchase them 'par manière de change aux marchans qui leur font bailler nobles d'Angleterre à Calais ou en Angleterre quatre ou cinq gros de Flandres oultre le noble de Flandre.' (See also note 46 *supra*).

50 A.D.N., B. 630/14.238. And in conclusion: 'et oultre que se ses ordonnances de ses monnoies sont bien gardéz il conviendra necessairement que les Angloiz achatent les nobles de Flandres aussi comme les Flamens achatent les nobles d'Angleterre.'

51 On confiscations of English nobles as billon in 1397-8, see n. 40 *supra*; for confiscations from 1398 to 1400, see A.G.R., C. de C., comptes en rouleaux, no. 786, and reg. no. 13.925, fo. 4-5.

52 Deschamps de Pas, *Histoire monétaire des comtes de Flandre*, p. xx, doc. no. 100. On 26 Sept. 1401, Duke Philip ordered his bailiffs not to hinder the export of English nobles. *Ibid.*, p. xx, doc. no. 112. Nevertheless, there are some references to confiscations of English nobles after that date. In Jan. 1402, Ypres lodged a complaint against the confiscation of such nobles from merchants going to Calais, 'mids dat onse gheduchte heere gheconsenteirt hadde voortijts dat men de Inghelsche nobele voeren mochte te Ingheland...' Prevenier, *Handelingen van de Leden*, p. 222, no. 542. See also Gilliodts-van Severen, *Archives de Bruges*, III, 462.

53 A.G.R., C. de C., comptes en rouleaux, no. 787. See also note 55 *infra*.

54 Between 1392 and 1399 Brabant had been one of the chief offenders, but in that year Duchess Joanna also returned to a strong coinage (see n. 26 *supra*). In Sept. 1399 Philip complained that foreign coins, especially gold, 'de mauvais aloy se moulteplient si fort' in Flanders and that merchants 'envoient de jour en jour dehors a autres monnoies que a la nostre grant quantite de billon d'or et d'argent.' (A.D.N., B. 630/14.138; and also B. 630/14.238, 26 Dec. 1399). In June 1398, he had encountered such difficulty in farming the Bruges mint that he was finally forced to grant the new mint-master 300 nobles for two years to meet those expenses that could not be covered by the brassage. Cockshaw, 'Le fonctionnement des ateliers,' p. 25.

MONETARY GRAPH II (1400-1416)
Coinage of pure gold and silver *marcs* in Flanders and England

FLEMISH MINTS:

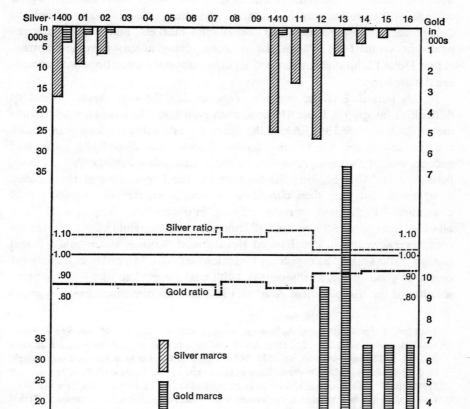

ENGLISH MINTS (London):

SOURCES: See Appendix I, Tables A-D.

during this period, perhaps related to a general trade contraction from the late 1390s.[55] A significant indication of this scarcity is a Flemish ordinance of October 1399 which required all bills-of-exchange to be paid henceforth in coin rather than in bank-transfers. Then, in February 1400, another ordinance went even further in demanding that future payments be made entirely in gold coinage (still undervalued). Not surprisingly, these ordinances served only to disrupt the Flemish money- and commercial markets, and were finally repealed in August 1401.[56] What may seem surprising, at least to some theorists, is that Duke Philip did not respond to these monetary conditions with a coinage debasement.

In this period, England was also experiencing the same severe monetary difficulties: as graphs I and II show, both gold and silver minting had plummeted sharply after 1399. Again the operation of Gresham's Law was clearly a major cause; and the Flemish nobles, despite their diminishing issue, had become one of the chief offenders by their accumulated influx. A Commons petitioner in 1401, blaming the Staplers for the importation of these coins, complained that they then constituted almost a quarter of England's gold circulation.[57] Parliament, in reply, once again ordered the Flemish nobles and all other foreign coins to be 'voided' from the realm or reminted;[58] and over the next several years, it also banned the debased Scottish silver 'mailles' and foreign 'galley-pence' as especially obnoxious culprits.[59] In order to remedy the dearth of good specie, Parliament in 1402 next resorted to its tried if not true solution of the 'Employment Acts' and this time required merchants to spend

---

55 See Flemish complaints about the coinage shortage, in Prevenier, *Handelingen van de Leden van Vlaanderen*, p. 212, no. 524 (May 1401); and their appeals to keep the Bruges mint open in 1402, p. 221, no. 544; also, nos. 539, 545-6, 669, 671. For northern Europe's silver supply in this period, see Andrew Watson, 'Back to Gold - and Silver.' *Econ. Hist. Rev.*, 2nd ser., XX (1967), p. 20. He argues that silver was being shipped to Islamic mints, which were offering a higher price for that metal. On the current trade contraction, see E. Carus-Wilson, 'Trends in the Export of English Woollens in the Fourteenth Century,' *Medieval Merchant Venturers* (London, 1954), pp. 255-6.

56 Raymond De Roover, *The Bruges Money Market Around 1400* (Brussels, 1968), pp. 54-62, 94.

57 *Rot. Parl.*, III, 470: no. 61: '... queux current icy si pleintinouses qe hommes ne prendra la somme de c s. qi ne ferra iii ou iiii tielx Nobles de Flandres, et chescun pece est pire et pluis feble qe le Noble Engleys par iid.' See the Flemish nobles listed in the Westbury hoard of this period, in J.D.A. Thompson, *Inventory of British Coin Hoards* (Oxford, 1956), p. 146 and xlv. From various coin hoards, Peter Spufford estimates that from 10 to 20 per cent of the circulating gold coin was in Flemish nobles, 'Continental Coins in Late Medieval England,' *British Numismatic Journal*, XXXII (1963), 130-1.

58 *S.R.*, II, 122 (2 Hen. IV, c. 6). In particular, the Calais Staplers were ordered to have all Flemish nobles and foreign silver coins reminted by the following Christmas.

59 See *Rot. Parl.*, III, 498, and 600; *S.R.*, II, 163.

their *entire* import receipts on domestic goods for export.[60] But the Tower Mint's bullion supply continued to fall, especially of silver: by 1408, it coined a meagre nine silver *marcs* and for the next three years, apparently none at all.

Finally, therefore, the connected problems 'of the great scarcity of money and several other mischiefs and causes notable' forced Henry IV and Parliament to adopt, in November 1411, a long overdue defensive debasement.[61] With no recoinage since 1351, moreover, the coins in circulation were undoubtedly much underweight from physical attrition, as well as from the export of good coins and their replacement by debased ones. By the statute, Henry IV reduced the weight of his silver coins by 17 per cent and of the gold *noble* by 10 per cent, while retaining the traditional purity of both. At the same time, he correspondingly raised the mint prices for both metals; in fact, he slightly reduced the mintage costs to make the bullion price more attractive.[62] This combination of weight reductions, moreover, altered the English mint ratio somewhat more in favour of silver than it was before. The king evidently hoped that these mint adjustments would overcome the problems of both the silver famine and the circulation of debased coins, such as the Flemish *noble*. In fact, since Henry's new *noble* had a weight equal to a *taille* of 35 to the *marc*, the now heavier Flemish *noble* (31 2/3 to the *marc*) should finally have been driven out of circulation. By clinging so obstinately to 'sound money' the English had taken a long time — some 23 years — to defeat the Flemish.[63]

The 1411 statute, however, had revealed Parliament's significant misgivings about the debasement by requiring the act to be reviewed in two years. But the

---

60 *Rot. Parl.*, III, 502: no. 61, 510: no. 105; *S.R.*, II 138 (4 Hen. IV, c. 15). Merchants were again strictly forbidden to export any coin or plate (except for 'costages raisonables'), and were also forbidden to export 'par Eschaunge fait deinz le dit Roialme d'Engleterre.'

61 *Rot. Parl.*, III, 658-9: no. 28. See also Feavearyear, *Pound Sterling*, pp. 37-9; Oman, *Coinage of England*, pp. 199-200.

62 For the details of this alteration see Appendix I, Table D. Possibly Duke John the Fearless' successful debasement of 1409 (after the abortive attempt of 1407), which produced a coinage output of 25,600 pure silver marcs by 1411-2, was another factor in the English decision to debase the coinage in 1411.

63 In August 1409, Duke John of Burgundy had ordered his father's nobles to be restruck, again at 23 3/4 car. and a *taille* of 31 2/3 to the *marc*, and also a gold *double écu* (23 3/4 car. and 54 *taille*). But only *écus* and no nobles were actually minted. (A.G.R., C. de C., carton 65: bis 1; comptes en rouleaux, no. 827; Acquits de Lille, no. 936: 1). Then, in Dec. 1416, Duke John issued another imitation noble, of 23 1/2 car. and a *taille* of 36 to the *marc*. But this new noble was apparently too inferior to be passed successfully, and only 1,711 nobles (= 47.5 *marcs*) were minted in 1417. (A.G.R., C. de C., comptes en rouleaux, no. 830). Nevertheless, on 5 April 1417, an English royal proclamation did order the banning of the 'burgoigne nobles, newly wrought of less value than the nobles of England.' (*Cal. Close Rolls 1413-19*, p. 427).

recoinage, commencing in April 1412, proved to be very successful in both metals, as graph II suggests. In the five years following 1411, the Tower Mint coined more silver than it had since the early 1360s. Some of that silver coinage output, however, may have resulted from booty acquired in the Normandy campaigns; and even so, the total English silver coinage was 25 per cent less than the amount of silver coined at the Flemish mints following Duke John the Fearless' debasement of 1409.[64] One reason for the difference in the silver minting is the fact that Flanders maintained, until 1426, a mint-price ratio for silver more 'favourable' than England's. The ratio was conversely less favourable for gold, of course; and, as the graph shows, the English correspondingly minted enormous amounts of gold after 1411, while the Flemish coined only negligible amounts. On balance, Parliament had no real cause to quarrel with Henry's debasement and recoinage − unless it would have preferred to have more silver in place of gold. The new coinage as Parliament had decreed it remained unaltered for another fifty years, despite the far more serious challenges that came from the Burgundian mints in the 1420s and 1430s.

No positive, final conclusions can be made about the commercial consequences of the bullionist conflict between Richard II and Duke Philip the Bold. The Commons petitioner of 1397 may have been correct in charging that the bullion ordinances had injured the wool trade, for the customs account do show a decline in exports. From 1393-95, before the implementation of the bullion law, to 1397-99, average annual exports fell from 20,400 sacks to 16,560 sacks. Exports continued to decline, however, even after the end of the monetary war, so that in the decade 1400-09 average annual wool exports were only 14,200 sacks. At the same time, English broadcloth exports also fell: from an annual average of 38,600 pieces in 1390-99 to one of 32,900 pieces in 1400-9.[65] Certainly that decline was not the result of the monetary conflict, since the English cloth trade was free of the bullion obligations − clearly it could never have borne them − and was already banned from the Flemish market.[66] The cloth trade, on the contrary, stood only to gain from the conflict: from injuries to the wool trade that might, one would suppose, divert wool from the Low Countries' draperies into domestic manufacturing.

In sum, the evidence for this period suggests that the decline in wool-exports was largely, if not entirely, due to the contraction of international trade that had

---

64 On Duke John the Fearless' monetary policies, especially between 1407 and 1409, see De Roover, *Bruges Money Market*, pp. 40-1, 67-75; and Hermann Van der Wee, 'L'échec de la réforme monétaire de 1407 en Flandre, vu par les marchands italiens de Bruges,' in *Studii in Onore di Amintore Fanfani*, III (Milan, 1962), 579-89.

65 Carus-Wilson, *England's Export Trade*, pp. 53-5, 86-8.

66 See *supra*, Introduction, pp. 7-8.

affected northern Europe in general. There were also some particular factors that disturbed Anglo-Flemish trade in the early fifteenth century: the mounting tensions of the Anglo-French conflict — and the increased English and Breton piracy. For the Flemish towns, their chief concern was to obtain a secure treaty of neutrality from England that would guarantee their wool supply in the event of renewed, full-scale war. Both Duke Philip and his successor John the Fearless were sympathetic to this demand, and Duke John did attempt to secure English support, especially in his struggle against the Armagnacs.[67] Finally, after the formation of the Anglo-Burgundian alliance in 1419 and the allies' apparent victory in France, trade did recover and expanded significantly.

Nevertheless, even if Richard II's bullion policy apparently caused no serious, lasting injury to Anglo-Flemish trade, it did leave a harmful legacy. The Staplers' — and Duke Philip's — overthrow of the *Ordinance de la Bullion* in no way dissuaded the Crown from pursuing this self-defeating policy in the future. Nor did the Burgundians learn from the 'war of the nobles' that debasements were bound to provoke English retaliation in their mutual struggle for bullion. They were, so to speak, 'Bourbons' all. The only lesson that both seemed to have learned was to pursue their conflicting policies with greater skill, artifice, and determination.

---

67 See Perroy, *Hundred Years' War*, pp. 209-44; Vaughan, *Philip the Bold*, pp. 183-5; and his *John the Fearless: the Growth of Burgundian Power* (London, 1966), pp. 15, 20-1, 91-2, 201-15, 250.

CHAPTER THREE

THE QUEST FOR THE GOLDEN FLEECE: FROM THE BATTLE
OF AGINCOURT TO THE CALAIS BULLION LAWS, 1415-1429

> Though Jason's Fleece was fam'd of old,
> The British wool is growing gold.[1]

The next most important phase of Anglo-Burgundian commercial relations
began with the Battle of Agincourt, 25 October 1415. The consequences of
Henry V's victory led, directly or indirectly, to the formation of an unstable
political alliance between the two countries, the expansion of Burgundian
power into the Low Countries, conflict over the wool and cloth trades, and a
renewal of monetary warfare in a struggle for bullion more bitter than before.
Of these developments, the duke of Burgundy's role in the Hundred Years'
War and the political, military, and diplomatic aspects of the Anglo-Burgundian alliance (1420-1435) have naturally received the most attention from
historians.[2] The only aspects of this period's diplomatic history that need to be

1 Dryden, 'King Arthur,' as cited in E. Lipson, *Economic History of England*, I, 544.
2 See Paul Bonenfant, *Du meurtre de Montereau au traité de Troyes* (Brussels, 1958) and *Philippe le Bon* (Brussels, 1955); Marie-Rose Thielemans, *Bourgogne et Angleterre: relations politiques et économiques entre les Pays-Bas bourguignons et l'Angleterre, 1435-1467* (Brussels,
1966); C.A.J. Armstrong, 'La double monarchie France-Angleterre et la maison de Bourgogne, 1420-1435: le déclin d'une alliance,' *Annales de Bourgogne*, XXXVII (1965), 81-112;
J.G. Dickinson, *The Congress of Arras, 1435: a Study in Medieval Diplomacy* (Oxford, 1955);
E.F. Jacob, *The Fifteenth Century, 1399-1486* (Oxford History of England, Vol. VI, 1961),
pp. 161-263; Edouard Perroy, *The Hundred Years' War* (London, 1959), pp. 235-96. Richard
Vaughan, *Philip the Good: the Apogee of Burgundy* (London, 1970).

examined, therefore, are those which help to clarify the basic changes in Anglo-Burgundian commercial and monetary relations over the fifteenth century. That the political events cannot be quantified does not make them any the less relevant to economic history.

Henry V's invasion of France did not itself produce any political agreements with Duke John the Fearless of Burgundy, who had chosen to remain neutral, though outwardly loyal to the French monarchy. But the Battle of Agincourt did benefit Duke John by eliminating his chief Armagnac opponents. Later, Henry's second invasion, in 1417, diverted enough royal troops to permit John's seizure of Paris from the Armagnacs. Still, John had no intention of serving the Lancastrian cause as a puppet. Now that the Armagnac remnants posed no threat to his domination of the French court, he sought a reconciliation and alliance with the Dauphin Charles to oppose the English conquest.[3] But during a meeting with the Dauphin on 19 September 1419, at Montereau, Duke John was murdered by Armagnac agents. His son and heir, Philip the Good, immediately made contact with Henry V. Their respective emissaries met at Mantes on 26 October.

That conference of Mantes drew Philip into a perhaps unwilling alliance with the English. Henry's emissaries announced the king's plans for gaining the French crown and bluntly told the Burgundians that, if Philip refused to co-operate, Henry would wage war on him. But if the duke agreed, Henry would punish the murderers and arrange a marriage alliance between the duke of Bedford and Philip's sister. Philip was undoubtedly bitterly determined to avenge his father's assassination at any cost. At the same time, his fear of either a total English victory that would exclude him from all power, or of a hostile Anglo-Dauphinist settlement directed against him left the duke little choice but to accept the English terms. Finally, on 21 May 1420, Henry V and Philip the Good contracted a formal political and military alliance in the Treaty of Troyes. The aged, senile Charles VI, no more than a Burgundian puppet, was forced to adhere to this treaty, sign away his kingdom, and disinherit the Dauphin. The treaty recognized Henry V, conqueror of Normany, as heir to the French throne. Both parties agreed to rule France jointly and to extend their conquests against the Dauphin, now a refugee at Bourges.[4] Then, on 22 August 1422, Henry V died and his scheme for a double, Anglo-French monarchy was left to his brother, John Duke of Bedford, to fulfill.

---

3 Vaughan, *John the Fearless*, pp. 205-15, 222-3, 250; Perroy, *Hundred Years' War*, pp. 236-44.
4 See especially Bonenfant, *Du meurtre de Montereau* and his *Philippe le Bon*, pp. 33-5; Vaughan, *Philip the Good*, pp. 3-6, 16-19; Perroy, *Hundred Years' War*, pp. 242-58.

If Philip entertained hopes of dominating the alliance and thus the governance of France, the goal of his two predecessors, the duke of Bedford soon thwarted any such designs and so, in effect, encouraged him to concentrate his energies upon expanding Burgundian power in the neighbouring Low Countries.[5] Philip undoubtedly required little encouragement. He had already purchased the county of Namur in 1421 from his childless cousin John of Flanders, and much more extensive territorial ambitions had in fact long been evident in the skilfull marriage alliances arranged by his father and grandfather. By the first, Philip the Bold had secured the great duchy of Brabant-Limburg for his younger son Anthony (1405-15). By the second marriage, between Anthony's son Duke John IV (1415-27) and Jacqueline of Bavaria in March 1418, John the Fearless evidently hoped to extend Burgundian influence over the three counties to which Jacqueline had just fallen heir: Hainaut, Holland, and Zealand. The succession to these counties, however, was disputed by her uncle John of Bavaria. Though the Hainaut Estates immediately recognized Jacqueline, John managed to provoke a civil war in Holland-Zealand: between the town-centred Kabiljauw party which pronounced for him, and the noble Hoek party which supported Jacqueline. Then, early in 1419, Philip the Good intervened (in his father's name); by his arbitration John of Bavaria was recognized as regent of Holland-Zealand. John IV of Brabant readily accepted this agreement, but Jacqueline did not. The next year she deserted her indolent husband and fled to England where, in October 1422, she married Humphrey Duke of Gloucester, Henry V's impetuous younger brother.

Gloucester himself had territorial designs upon the Low Countries and it was his intervention that afforded Philip the Good the opportunity of seizing the three disputed counties. To restore his new wife's inheritances, Gloucester invaded Hainaut in 1424, only to suffer defeat and Jacqueline's capture by Philip's troops. The next year, however, Jacqueline escaped to Holland, rallying support from the Hoeks. By that time, John of Bavaria had died and Philip had secured John IV's agreement to claim the regency. Invading Holland, he allied himself with the Kabiljauws, who opened the town gates to his forces. Gloucester sent another army to aid Jacqueline but was so decisively beaten (Brouwershaven, 1426) that he ungallantly deserted her cause. Finally, by the Treaty of Delft of July 1428, Jacqueline accepted defeat and agreed to recognize Philip as *ruwaert* and successor to her three counties.[6] Two years

5 See Armstrong, 'La double monarchie,' pp. 81-112, and especially Vaughan, *Philip the Good*, pp. 16-28, who strongly maintains that Philip 'had never been seriously interested in French affairs' and that his political ambitions had always lain in the Low Countries.

6 Vaughan, *Philip the Good*, pp. 31-50; Pirenne, *Histoire de Belgique*, II, 373-8. Duke Philip formally secured title to the three counties in April 1433, after Jacqueline had re-married, in violation of the Delft Treaty.

later Philip also acquired Brabant, but by a more peaceful inheritance: his cousin Philip of St. Pol, who had succeeded John IV in 1427, himself died childless in August 1430.[7]

Although the duke of Gloucester's escapades in the Low Countries had placed a severe strain upon the recently-achieved Anglo-Burgundian alliance, their outcome had clearly benefited Duke Philip. Furthermore, the duke of Bedford, Gloucester's brother, had averted a rupture by marrying Philip's sister and awarding the Burgundian duke more French territory.[8] Thus ultimately more significant than these specific political events in disturbing the alliance were the commercial implications of Duke Philip's acquisitions in the Low Countries. By the 1420s Holland, Zealand, and Brabant had become important markets for both English wool and cloths; the Dutch and Brabantine drapery towns had for some time, in fact, been rivalling the Flemish as chief customers at the Calais Staple. At the same time, the Merchants Adventurers of London had recently (1421) established their headquarters for their cloth export trade at Antwerp, while still maintaining Middelburg in Zealand as an active market and transhipping centre.[9] Dutch shippers were also increasing their cargoes of English cloth from both London and the fairs of Antwerp and Bergen-op-Zoom.

As noted earlier, the Dutch and Brabantine drapery towns at this time were demanding protection from the growing competition of the English cloth trade. During 1427 and 1428, these towns met several times to discuss imposing a cloth ban.[10] Then, on 25 July 1428, Duke Philip the Good formally banned from Holland and Zealand all English cloth imports, which the ordinance maintained were threatening the destruction of the drapery industry.[11] A month

---

7 Vaughan, *Philip the Good*, pp. 51-3; Bonenfant, *Philippe le Bon*, pp. 52-4. Duke Anthony, second son of Philip the Bold, died at Agincourt in 1415 and was succeeded by his son, John IV (husband of Jacqueline); on his death in 1427, his brother Philip of St. Pol succeeded him.

8 Vaughan, *Philip the Good*, pp. 20-1, 47; Bonenfant, *Philippe le Bon*, pp. 44-5. Perroy, however, considers Gloucester's intervention to have had more serious consequences. *Hundred Years' War*, pp. 271-2.

9 E. Carus-Wilson, 'Origins and Early Development of the Merchant Adventurers' Organization in London,' in *Medieval Merchant Venturers* (London, 1954), pp. 143-82.

10 The town delegates met at Malines, Haarlem, Leyden, and Antwerp. See N.W. Posthumus (ed.), *Bronnen tot de Geschiedenis van de Leidsche Textielnijverheid, 1333-1795*, I (*De Middeleeuwen*, The Hague, 1910), 116-8, no. 102; and K. Höhlbaum, K. Kunze (eds.), *Hansisches Urkundenbuch*, VI (Leipzig, 1907), 413, no. 767.

11 Frans van Mieris (ed.), *Groot Charterboek der Graaven van Holland, van Zeeland, en Heeren van Vriesland*, IV (Leyden, 1756), 923-4: 'want bi den Ingelschen gewande ende wollen garen dat men vast veel gewone is te brengen in die voirsc. lande van Hollant, van Zeelant ende van Vriesland, die steden der selven landen, die welke meest staen ende gefondeert syn op draperie hoir coepmanscepe ende neringe, vast veel verloren hebben ende noch meer gescapen waren

later, on 25 August 1428, his cousin and protegé, Philip of St. Pol, also banned English cloth from Brabant, on virtually the same grounds.[12] The circumstances of the recent Dutch civil war and the signing of the Delft Treaty in the same month as the cloth ban suggest that Philip the Good granted the ban in order to solidify his support from the drapery towns of the Kabiljauw party as the new ruler. He may also have done so in retaliation against Gloucester's military support of Jacqueline and the Hoeks. The Holland-Zealand ban, however, soon encountered bitter opposition from those Dutch commercial and industrial interests dealing in English cloth, and was soon allowed to lapse.[13] By at least April 1430, the Middelburg magistrates were again permitting the sale of English cloth in that port.[14] The Brabantine authorities maintained a stricter enforcement of their cloth ban;[15] but it also ultimately failed, particularly because of the pressures exerted by English and Hanse merchants.[16] Finally, after the Cologne Hanse had boycotted the Brabantine fairs, Philip the Good as the new duke of Brabant repealed the ban in March 1431.[17]

te verliesen, ende bi langheden van tyden mit allen te nieten te gaen...' Total English broadcloth exports had, in fact, risen sharply: from an annual average of 28,800 pieces in 1415-9 to one of 41,510 pieces in 1425-9. (Carus-Wilson, *England's Export Trade*, pp. 91-3).

12 E. Van Even (ed.), *Inventaire des chartes et autres documents appartenant aux archives de la ville de Louvain, 1125-1793* (Louvain, 1873), p. 125, no. 174.

13 See Middelburg's protests (Dec. 1429) in H.J. Smit (ed.), *Bronnen tot de Geschiedenis van den Handel met Engeland, Schotland, en Ierland, 1150-1485*, II (The Hague, 1928), 625, no. 1012.

14 *Ibid.*, II, 627, n. 1; 635, no. 1024.

15 The Rentmeester of the Iersekeroord Toll complained that, during 1429 and 1430, his revenues 'seere ghearght is overmids dat ... die Inghelsche lakenen verboden sijn.' W.S. Unger (ed.), *De Tol van Iersekeroord: Documenten en Rekeningen, 1321-1572* (The Hague, 1939), p. 154; and Smit, *Bronnen Handel*, II, 631, no. 1019.

16 See the complaints of the Cologne Hanse to the Antwerp magistrates in Nov. 1428, demanding the removal of the cloth ban, 'as dat ir die keuperliche vriiheit ind ouch die vriiheit van urme marte unverbrocken halden willen.' K. Koppman (ed.), *Die Recesse und Andere Akten der Hansetäge von 1236 bis 1430*, VIII (Leipzig, 1897), 365-6, no. 558. Negotiations to restore freedom of the English cloth trade at Antwerp ended in deadlock in July 1429; then, in March 1430, the Cologne Hanse forbade its merchants to visit the Antwerp fairs. (Bruno Kuske (ed.), *Quellen zur Geschichte des Kölner Handels*, I (Bonn, 1923), 270, no. 791; 276, no. 800). In July 1430, the English King's Council, acting on a petition of the Merchants Adventurers, also banned trade with Antwerp 'until merchants are assured their safety in goods and merchandises' (including also a dispute over the linen trade). N.H. Nicolas (ed.), *Proceedings and Ordinances of the Privy Council of England*, IV (London, 1836), 55; and *Calendar of Patent Rolls 1429-36*, p. 26.

17 E.R. Daenell, *Die Blütezeit der deutschen Hanse*, I (Berlin, 1905), 389; R. Van Uytven, 'La Flandre et le Brabant: 'terres de promission' sous les ducs de Bourgogne?' *Revue du Nord*, XLIII (1961), 288.

The Dutch and Brabantine drapery towns had failed in trying to emulate Flanders' protectionist policy essentially because they lacked the overwhelming political and economic dominance of their Flemish counterparts, who had never encountered serious resistance to their own cloth ban.[18] Thus the English cloth trade, having been denied the Flemish market from the beginning, had developed too powerfully in Holland, Zealand, and Brabant to be so easily excluded. As suggested in the Introduction, there is no evidence that Duke Philip the Good, now the ruler of all these territories, favoured such a policy of protection. Even if he had, his rule over these recently acquired lands, which had long traditions of municipal independence, was not yet strong and centralized enough to impose such a policy successfully. Nevertheless − despite the lessons of the 1428 bans − Duke Philip subsequently resorted three times to total prohibition of English cloth from Burgundian territory in economic wars with both the Lancastrian and Yorkist governments. Philip's acquisition of his new territories perhaps made commercial conflict with England more likely. They certainly made his rule more vulnerable to English economic pressures; at the same time, they also made England more vulnerable to Burgundian retaliation. Again, the issue that provoked the economic conflicts of the fifteenth century was not so much competition in the cloth trade as the English Crown's re-imposition of the bullion laws on the vital wool trade.

In large part, the resumption and intensification of bullionist competition resulted from the English invasions and ravaging of France, a country already debilitated by civil war. The numismatist Jean Lafaurie has shown that the Armagnac-Burgundian struggle and the conquest of Normandy produced the most serious coinage debasements in France since the mid-fourteenth century.[19] By the time of the Burgundian seizure of Paris, France had become divided into three competitive minting areas: Henry V's Normandy, the duke of Burgundy's duchy and northern France, and the Dauphin's lands south of the Loire. To help finance their campaigns, all three combatants quickly debased their coinages − the silver coinages by almost 75 per cent in two years. After the Treaty of Troyes in 1420, Henry V and Duke Philip the Good (in France) returned to 'strong' coinages, but the refugee and impecunious Dauphin continued his debasements with a dizzying series of ever-inferior coins. By June 1422, his '*gros tournois*' contained only a meagre 2.7 per cent of the silver in the 1417

---

18 See *supra, Introduction,* pp. 7-8. In effect, the duke of Burgundy (as count) and the Four Members shared the governance of Flanders.

19 Jean Lafaurie, *Les monnaies des rois de France: Hughes Capet à Louis XII* (Paris, 1951), pp. 68-9. For a survey of France's economic plight at this time, see Perroy, *Hundred Years' War,* pp. 249-65.

MONETARY GRAPH III (1417-1433)

Coinage of pure gold and silver *marcs* in the Burgundian Lowlands and England

BURGUNDIAN MINTS:

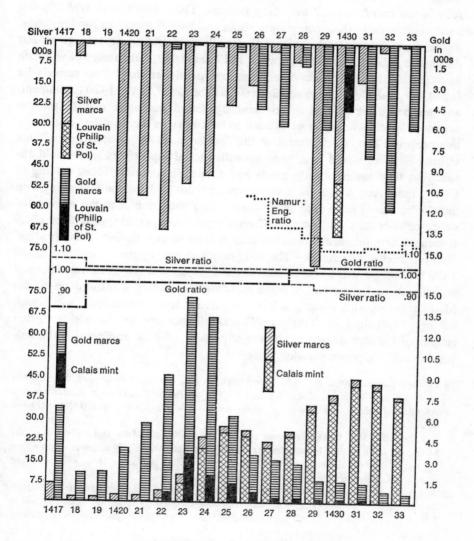

ENGLISH MINTS (London and Calais):

SOURCES: See Appendix I, Tables A-D.

issues.[20] At the end of the year, the Dauphin similarly restored a 'strong' coinage; but very soon military and financial necessity forced him to resume his debasements, though in not quite so drastic a fashion.

The effects of this first period of French debasements upon the English and Burgundian mints cannot be accurately measured, but some reactions can be seen in the two countries' monetary policies. The English were typically the most vociferous in their complaints about the loss of specie to foreign lands. To be sure, graph III shows that England's gold and silver coinage output declined by about two-thirds between 1417 and 1419, but surely not so much as to justify the complaints of a Commons petitioner that 'if no remedy be found, very shortly all the remaining coin will be lost.'[21] In the 1420 Parliament, another petitioner offered a new and significant bullionist remedy for the supposed specie scarcity in what came to be known as the 'hosting system.' By this proposed law, a refinement of the Employment Acts, foreign merchants visiting England would have to lodge with special supervisors who would ensure that they exported only goods and no precious metal. Those trading at Calais, moreover, would have to surrender their gold bullion and coins to a 'host' who would have such metal coined into good nobles at the merchants' expense.[22] For the time being, the Crown ignored this petition, with its cumbersome and harmful regulations; but later it tried several times to foist 'hosting' laws on foreign merchants.[23] The only major monetary statute enacted in the 1420 Parliament was a new version of the 1397 bullion laws, this time imposed on only those Italian and Spanish merchants exporting wool and tin to the Mediterranean. This statute, in fact, remained in force throughout the fifteenth century.[24] But since the Treaty of Troyes' alliance had just been signed, that session of Parliament was hardly the opportune time for re-imposing the bullion laws on Burgundian trade.

20 Lafaurie, *Les monnaies,* pp. 68-72. The Dauphin's *gros tournois* was debased from a *traite* of £10 t. in 1417 to one of £370 t. in 1422. For the Burgundian mints in France, see also Anatole Barthelamy, *Essai sur les monnaies des ducs de Bourgogne* (Dijon, 1850), pp. 65 et seq.

21 *Rot. Parl.,* IV, 118 (1419). Parliament accepted the petitioner's advice that military subsidies be shipped to Normandy in goods rather than in coin. The declining mint output might reflect the end of the 1412 recoinage and the Crown's own minting in Normandy, as well as the loss of bullion to the various mints engaged in debasements.

22 *Rot. Parl.,* IV, 125-6: no. 14; 126: no. 21. The petitioner also advocated that the Staplers should sell their wool at high fixed prices and then immediately return the cash proceeds in full to England. That particular request re-appeared in the Calais Staple Partition and Bullion Ordinances of 1429. See *infra,* pp. 84-6.

23 See Feavearyear, *Pound Sterling,* pp. 35-6 for a discussion of this system.

24 *Rot. Parl.,* IV, 126: no. 15, and *S.R.,* II, 203 (8 Hen. V, c. 2). One ounce of gold or equivalent silver per woolsack or three pieces of tin exported.

Of more direct concern to the Burgundians was a statute in the following year (1421) for the re-establishment of the Calais mint, dormant since 1384.[25] The statute itself was in response to a Stapler petition, which is most indicative of current monetary policy. Apparently the Crown was once more requiring the Staplers to pay all their wool duties and subsidies to the Calais Treasurer in English coin alone. The petitioner maintained, however, that a currently severe shortage of English *nobles* at Calais prevented them from complying; moreover, since they were no longer permitted to accept Rhenish and Burgundian 'florins' for their wool-sales 'debts,' the Flemish were finding it difficult to buy wool. But the Staplers, instead of seeking the revocation of this obstructive payment regulation, requested a mint at Calais for coining the required *nobles* from foreign gold.[26] After the mint had been put into operation, Parliament strictly forbade the export of all English coin on the grounds that, 'if nobles were not so plentifully sold in Flanders, a great amount of bullion would come to the said mint' at Calais.[27] This mint was perhaps necessary for supplying the base and garrison at Calais. But its establishment was also a necessary prerequisite for the Crown's subsequent bullion policies.

The Calais mint, commencing operations in July 1422,[28] soon became a great success and allayed Parliament's bullionist anxiety for the present. The London mint similarly increased its output greatly. As graph III shows, the total volume of English minting mounted rapidly in the early 1420s, reaching a level not achieved since the middle of Edward III's reign. Part of that large coinage volume was due to a mintage-free recoinage ordered by Parliament in 1421;[29]

25 *S.R.*, II, 206 (9 Hen. V, stat. 1, c. 6).
26 *Rot. Parl.*, IV, 146: no. 27; and more fully in a Stapler letter to the Staple Mayor in Nov. 1421: 'Unqore la petit quantite de monoie que vient de pardeca ou que nous pourrons rescei-vre en les parties susditz pour noz debtes en graunde peyne, cest de florenes de Geldre et dautres seigneurs deca la Reen et aussi de Holand, lesquelz le vitaillier de Calais nautres aiantz, noz obligacions de coustume nont volue nullement accepter ne receivre; ains vueillant avoir tout en nobles Dengleterre que nest pas en nostre puissance de le faire.' Scott and Gilliodts-van Severen, *Cotton Manuscrit Galba*, pp. 411-2, no. 169. See also Leyden's complaints about these payment regulations in Posthumus, *Bronnen Textielnijverheid*, I, 108, no. 91.
27 *Rot. Parl.*, IV, 252: no. 42: 'En tant qe on trouvera a Bruges journelment si graunt quantite des nobles d'Engleterre a vendre en les mains des chaungeours qe merveille est; la quelle chose s'il ne soit remedie, serra destruction au dit Mynt.' The Staplers themselves could not control the supply and disposal of English nobles in Bruges because 'ils ne sount comunes acchateurs des marchandises en Flaundres.' For the statute, 2 Hen. VI, c. 6, see *S.R.*, II, 219-20.
28 *Cal. Pat. Rolls 1422-29*, p. 337. On 4 May 1422, Henry V appointed Richard Bokeland, then Calais Treasurer, as the Mint-Keeper. Nicolas, *P.P.C.*, II, 332.
29 Parliament ordered the recoinage because it was disturbed by the number of underweight coins in circulation (9 Hen. V, stat. 1, c. 11, in *S.R.*, II, 208). A reduction of the *brassage* on gold, raising the mint price from £16.7s.6d. sterl. to £16.8s.4d. sterl. a Tower Pound, on 26 July 1421, probably also helped to attract bullion. See Appendix I, Tables A-B, and D.

some, to French booty, ransoms, and the minting of plate for military expenditures. But undoubtedly a good proportion of the minting reflected the trade boom which followed upon the Treaty of Troyes and its restoration of full, unimpeded commercial relations with the Low Countries and northern France. Thus, average annual broadcloth exports climbed 50 per cent and the wool exports, though affected by the expanding English cloth production, declined only slightly.[30] During these golden years of large coinage volumes, there was no further monetary legislation in England.[31] But when the mint output fell in the later 1420s, the King's Council became gravely concerned and summoned Parliament for drastic remedies.

Meanwhile, in the Low Countries, the duke of Burgundy had also reacted, and in kind, to the French debasements that followed the Agincourt disaster. Duke John the Fearless, specifically blaming these debasements for his current mint inactivity, ordered new coins of lesser weight and fineness to be struck in December 1416.[32] But, as graph III suggests, he did not increase the mint price sufficiently to attract bullion. Not until his son Philip issued a new ordinance in June 1418 was Flemish minting fully restored. Acting in Duke John's name, Philip took severe measures against the circulation of foreign debased coins and then himself debased the Flemish gold coinage by 21 per cent, the silver by 13 per cent.[33] But by this time, the Flemish towns had become alarmed about

---

30 For the boom in English cloth exports, see note 11 *supra*. Wool exports declined only slightly over this period: from an annual average of 14,705 sacks in 1415-9 to one of 14,180 sacks in 1425-9. Carus-Wilson, *England's Export Trade*, pp. 57-8.

31 Much more gold was then being minted, however, than silver, undoubtedly because the English mint ratio 'favoured' gold and discouraged silver (see *infra*, pp. 75-82). Thus in 1423 Parliament expressed its concern about 'the grete scarcite of Whit money' and charged that silver bullion was being sold in the market at 32s. a Troy pound, above the current mint price. Parliament thus forbade silver to be sold above 30s. a Troy pound. *Rot. Parl.*, IV, 256: no. 54; and *S.R.*, II, 223-4 (2 Hen. VI, c. 16).

32 Text in Deschamps de Pas, 'Histoire monétaire des comtes de Flandre,' *Revue numismatique*, 2nd ser., VI (1861), 223-4: 'l'ouvrage desquelles monnoyes ... ait convenu cesser et n'y ait ou peu ouvrer ne forgier ja longtemps ... pour les diminutions et empirances des monnoyes de monseigneur le Roy faite depuis nos dites ordonnances, et aussi pour les diminutions des monnoyes de plusieurs seigneurs voisins de nos dits pays ... et par ce la plus grand partie de nostre dit monnoye, qui estoit de plus fort aloy, a este vuidee et portee fondre esdites monnoyes voisins.' By his ordinance, Duke John debased the gold coinage by 11 per cent, and the silver by 18 per cent. See Appendix I, Table C.

33 Philip's ordinance provided the same rendition of Gresham's Law as his father's previous decree: 'pour obvier a ce que les estranges monnoyes de divers pays, par lesquelles ... les monnoyes d'or se sont moult haulchees.' A.G.R., C. de C., no. 580, fo. 41-7. (Excerpts in Deschamps de Pas, 'Histoire monétaire des comtes de Flandre,' pp. 228-31). The provisions of the ordinance may be found in Appendix I, Table C. Note the drastic reduction in the sei-

the danger that monetary instability might damage their commerce. They consented to this latest debasement decree only after extracting from Philip the promise not to alter the coinage again for fifteen years.[34]

During the fifteen years following Philip's formal succession to the county of Flanders in September 1419, he faced three critical monetary (and fiscal) problems. First, he soon had to meet the challenge of further debasements by the Dauphin Charles and other neighbouring princes, whose inferior coins seemed to flood unceasingly into Flanders. Second, he was going to require a vast amount of coinage and as much seignorage revenue as his mints could muster to wage his several military campaigns in Holland and France (1425-33). As he later commented, the 'burdensome and murderous' Dutch war, the first and major one of his reign, 'had cost me, besides all the heavy expenses that I incurred throughout this period in the French war, over a million gold *saluts,* which at first I was extremely ill-prepared to find.'[34a] Above all, he needed gold coins, since Flemish silver coins were not so acceptable abroad; and before the wars his mints, while coining considerable quantities of silver, had attracted very little gold bullion. That situation undoubtedly reflected an unfavourable mint-ratio for gold, as graph III suggests. Before he could meet these two problems, he had to resolve the third: the Flemish yoke on his minting policy, almost akin to a fifteen-year tax moratorium. Philip's territorial acquisitions in the Lowlands, however, permitted him to evade that minting restriction. By the same contract for purchasing Namur, he also acquired the count's mint with two-thirds of the seignorage.[35] Four years later (1425) his alliance with the

gnorage rates: from 3.9 per cent to 1.0 per cent on gold, and from 6.7 per cent to 1.5 per cent on silver. Philip ordered confiscations, fines, and three years' banishment from Flanders for those accepting illegal foreign coins, accepting legal tender coins for more than the official rates, and for exporting *billon.* Foreign coins accorded legal tender rights were French couronnes, francs, moutons, and écus; English nobles; Genoese and Venetian ducats; Florentine, Hungarian, and Bohemian florins; Imperial écus; and Brabantine pieters. As previously argued in chapter 1, Burgundian monetary policy was much more liberal than the English.

34 A committee of the Flemish towns in March 1418 had originally requested that 'dese munte sal ghedeurch zijn zonder angheven ofte veranderen xl jaer;' but that period was reduced to 15 years in the final ordinance. (A.G.R., C. de C., no. 1158, fo. 7 vo.) When Philip became count in his own name, the Four Members required him to re-affirm this promise. Gilliodts-van Severen, *Estaple de Bruges,* I, 526, no. 630.

34a Cited in Vaughan, *Philip the Good,* pp. 307-8 (from *Dagboek van Gent,* I, 57-8: speech to the Ghent *échevins,* Jan. 1447). On Philip's finances, see Vaughan, pp. 17-8, 259-63.

35 A.G.R., C. de C., no. 18, 203. Minting commenced for 'monseigneur le duc de Bourgogne' on 23 Oct. 1421. Philip gained the entire seignorage on Count John's death in 1429 (*ubi supra*). On the purchase of Namur, see Vaughan, *Philip the Good,* pp. 29-31.

Kabiljauws provided him another mint, at Dordrecht in Holland.[36] Finally, in 1430 he gained the large and important Brabantine mints of Louvain and Brussels.[37]

With these new mints, especially the Namur mint close to France, Philip the Good was fully prepared to engage in a minting competition with the Dauphin (now King Charles VII). In 1422 Charles had earnestly tried, to be sure, to restore a strong coinage. But more and more he approached virtual bankruptcy: one half of his kingdom lost to the conquerors, the other half financially exhausted from the depradations of *routiers,* bandits, and corrupt officials. Faced also with almost certain military defeat, the hapless 'King of Bourges' again resorted to debasements to finance his dwindling armies.[38] Duke Philip followed suit in 1425, the year of his involvement in the Dutch civil war.[39] The complex series of Burgundian and French debasements that ensued may be seen from the following two tables:

36 Minting commenced on 23 Nov. 1425. P.O. Van der Chijs, *De Munten der Voormalige Graaf-schappen Holland en Zeeland* (Haarlem, 1858), pp. 369-75, and Algemeen Rijksarchief van Nederland, Rekenkamer no. 4937: I. The Dordrecht mint apparently closed on 24 Dec. 1427, after having coined only gold. The second account, for both gold and silver coinage, covers the period 12 Dec. 1429 - 20. Feb. 1433; the Dutch mint was then located at Zevenbergen, though later it may have been restored to Dordrecht. (A.R.A., Rek. no. 4937: II-III; see also Van der Chijs, pp. 379-86.) The Lille Chambre de Comptes contains a special Zevenbergen mint account for 15 Apr. 1430, which records the coining of 412.8 gold *marcs,* from an English subsidy of 14,565 nobles, into Dutch *clinquaerts.* (A.D.N., B. 639/15,567, fo. 1 vo.-3 ro.). This coinage may, or may not, be included in the second Dutch account for Zevenbergen/Dordrecht.

37 A.G.R., C. de C., no. 18,067, and 17,986. Minting for Philip the Good at Louvain commenced on 4 Oct. 1430; at Brussels, not until Sept. 1434.

38 Charles began debasing his gold coinage in March 1423, but not his silver coinage until May 1426. On Charles' economic straits, see Perroy, *Hundred Years' War,* pp. 262-3. While the area under his control contained more fiscal resources than that under the Anglo-Burgundians, it nevertheless produced less revenue. The Estates of Chinon in 1428 refused to grant Charles further taxes until he had again restored the currency, but Charles continued to find debasement profitable until the military tide turned in his favour after 1434.

39 On 2 May 1423, two months after Charles had debased his gold *écu,* Duke Philip ordered Charles' coins to be seized as *billon* and reminted. (Deschamps de Pas, 'Histoire monétaire des comtes de Flandre,' pp. 460-1.) Philip's debasements of his gold coinage began with the striking of the *clinquaert* in Holland in Nov. 1425. It contained 33 per cent less gold per *livre gros* of Flanders than the Flemish gold coinage of 1418. Over the following years, the series of continuously inferier issues of *clinquaerts,* at Dordrecht-Zevenbergen, Namur, and Ghent, accounted for the bulk of Philip's gold coinage output.

TABLE I

French and Burgundian Debasements of Gold Coinage, 1423-1433

| Date of ordinance | Charles VII | | Philip the Good | | Gold *Traite* per marc |
	Ecu	Tournay Crown	Clinquaert	Pieter	
June 1418					£11.6s.8d.
Jan. 1423	23 7/8 carats 64 taille				
Mar. 1423	23 7/8 carats 68 taille				
Aug. 1424	23 carats 70 taille				
			(Dordrecht)		
Nov. 1425			17 carats 67 taille		£15.15s.3d
			(Namur & Ghent)		
July — Aug. 1426	22 carats 70 taille		17 carats 67 taille		£15.15s.3d
May 1427		23 carats 67 taille			
Nov. 1427	21 carats 70 taille				
Jun.-Jul. 1428	20 carats 70 taille	22 carats 67 taille	16 carats 67 1/2 taille		£15.3s.9 1/2d.
Jan.-Feb. 1429	18 carats 70 taille		15 1/2 carats 67 1/2 taille		£15.13s.7d.
Jun. 1429			— the same —		£16.2s.2 1/4d.
Aug. 1429		21 carats 67 taille			
	Royal				
Oct. 1429	23 7/8 carats 64 taille				
May 1430				*(Louvain)* 21 carats 68 1/2 taille	£15.16s.10d.
			(Dordrecht)		
Aug. 1430			15 1/2 carats 67 1/2 taille		£16.11s.0d.
Sept. 1430		20 1/2 carats 67 taille			

Date of ordinance	Ecu	Tournay Crown	Clinquaert	Pieter	Gold *Traite* per marc
			(*Namur*)		
Dec. 1430		20 1/2 carats 67 1/2 taille	16 carats 68 taille		£16.3s.0d.
Apr. 1431	?* 64 taille		15 7/8 carats 68 taille		£16.5s.7d.
Sept. 1431	?* 70 taille	17 1/2 carats 67 1/2 taille	15 3/4 carats 68 taille		£16.8s.2d.
				(*Namur & Louvain*)	
Dec. 1431			15 carats 68 taille	20 carats 68 taille	£17.4s.7d.
Dec. 1432		16 carats 68 taille		19 carats 68 taille	£17.17s.10d.
May 1433				18 carats 68 taille	£18.17s.10d.

SOURCES: A.G.R., Chambre de Comptes, nos. 580, fo. 93-4; 18, 203; Algemeen Rijksarchief Nederland, Rekenkamer no. 4937:I-II; Lafaurie, *Les monnaies des rois de France*, I, 97-102; Marcel Hoc, *Histoire monétaire de Tournai*, pp. 95-116.

* During this period the *royal* was officially 23 7/8 car. fineness, but Lafaurie believes it was debased in fineness as well as in weight.

TABLE II

French and Burgundian Debasements of Silver Coinage, 1423-1433

	Charles VII				Philip the Good		
Date	'Blanc'	Silver Traite in livres tournois	Tournay Plaque	Silver Traite in livres gros (& tournois)	Namur 'Double Gros'	Flemish 'Double Gros'	Silver Traite in livres gros
Aug. 1423					5 deniers* 50 taille	[6 den. 68 taille June 1418]	£1.0.0. gros
Nov. 1423	5 den.* 80 taille	£8.0.0. tournois					
July 1425		£10.0.0.			5 den. 53 taille		£1.1s.2 1/2d.
May 1426	4 den. 80 taille	£11.0.0.					
Jul.-Aug. 1426	3 den. 7 1/2 gr. 80 taille	£13.0.0.			4 den. 22 1/4 gr. 53 taille		£1.1s.5 1/4d.
Nov. 1426	3 den. 81 taille	£8.0.0.					
Dec. 1426	4 den. 11 gr. 61 taille	£10.0.0.			4 den. 23 gr. 54 taille		£1.1s.7 1/4d.
Aug. 1427	4 den. 80 taille	£11.0.0.				6 den. 68 taille	£1.2s.8d.
Nov.-Dec. 1427	3 den. 7 1/2 gr. 80 taille	£13.10.0d.	6 den. 1 gr. 67 taille	(£8.0.0.t)			
Jun.-Jul. 1428	3 den. 81 taille				4 den. 12 gr. 54 taille		£1.4s.0d.
Nov. 1428						5 den. 8 gr. 68 1/2 taille	£1.5s.8 1/4
Jan. 1429	2 den. 7 1/2 gr. 84 taille	£18.0.0.			4 den. 4 gr. 54 taille		£1.6s.0d.

Date	'Blanc'	Silver *Traite* in *livres tournois*	Tournay *Plaque*	Silver *Traite* in *livres gros* (& *tournois*)	Namur 'Double Gros'	Flemish 'Double Gros'	Silver *Traite* in *livres gros*
March 1429	2 den. 84 taille	£21.0.0.					
April 1429	1 den. 18 gr. 84 taille	£24.0.0.	5 den. 8 gr. 68 taille	£1.5s.6d.gr. (£8.17.6d.) tournois			
June 1429	1 den. 12 gr. 84 taille	£28.0.0d.			4 den. 54 taille		£1.7s.0d.
Oct. 1429	5 den. 80 taille	£8.0.0d.					
Sept. 1430			5 den. 4 gr. 68 taille	£1.6s.4d. (£9.4s.0d.)			
June 1431			5 den. 68 taille	£1.7s.2d. (£9.10.0.)			
Aug. 1431			4 den. 20 gr. 68 taille	£1.8.1 1/2d. (£9.16.6d.)			
Sept. 1431	4 den. 80 taille	£10.0.0.					
Dec. 1431	5 den. 80 taille	£8.0.0d.			3 den. 18 gr. 54 taille		£1.8s.9 1/2d.
Jan. 1432			4 den. 18 gr. 68 taille	£1.8s.7 1/2d. (£10.0.0.)			
Sept. 1432			4 den. 16 gr. 68 taille	£1.9s.2d. (£10.5s.0d.)			
May 1433					6 den. 70 taille (2 2/3d. gros)		£1.11s.1 1/3d.
Aug. 1433					6 den. 70 taille		£1.3s.4d.

* Fineness measured out of 12 *deniers argent-le-roy*, with 24 grains to each *denier*.
SOURCES: See Table I.

As can be seen from these tables, the period of greatest debasement activity by both rulers began in 1428, with the renewal of heavy fighting in France that culminated in the siege of Orléans. From June 1428 to June 1429, for example, Charles debased his 'blanc' five times, reducing its original silver content by 70 per cent. The French coinage issue of greatest concern to Philip, however, were those struck in the bishopric of Tournay, a Dauphinist French enclave within the Burgundian Lowlands. From 1428 Charles used the Tournay Mint to strike, in particular, inferior counterfeits of the Flemish silver *'double gros'* and drastically debased these coins, as well as the Tournay gold *'couronnes'* over the next seven years. By that time, Philip's silver minting in Flanders, where the Tournay imitations were widely circulated, had ceased entirely.[40]

In Flanders, Philip's pledge of 1418 prevented him from retaliating effectively with counter-debasements to eliminate the Dauphin's coins. Nevertheless, in 1428 Philip had violated both the spirit and the letter of his promise, with some significance for England. First, after several unsuccessful attempts, his Ghent mint struck an effective imitation of the English gold *noble* and coined a large number of them by 1430.[41] Second, by the same ordinance of November 1428, Philip debased the ten-year old silver coinage of Flanders. Although this debasement was comparatively modest at 13 per cent, the Ghent mint's silver coinage of 1429 was by far the largest of Philip's reign − and far larger also than any of England's.[42] Thereafter, Philip did not again alter his Flemish coin-

---

40 See Table IV *infra*, p. 88. On 26 June 1428, Duke Philip had extracted from the échevins of Tournay a promise not to permit any minting within their jurisdiction (A.D.N., B. 638); but Tournay's minting for Charles VII continued unhindered until 25 Oct. 1433. See Le Comte de Castellane, 'Les monnaies d'argent du système flamand frappées à Tournai au nom de Charles VII,' *Revue numismatique*, 2nd ser., IV: 2 (1898), 103-15; Marcel Hoc, *Histoire monétaire de Tournai* (Brussels, 1970), pp. 95-116; Spufford, *Monetary Problems*, pp. 89-93.

41 In June 1425, both the Ghent and Namur mints had struck imitation *nobles* of 23 1/4 carats fineness and 35 1/2 *taille* to the *marc*, compared to the English *noble's* fineness of 23 7/8 carats and a *taille* of 35 to the *marc*. Apparently Philip's *nobles* were too inferior to pass successfully, and few were then struck. Then, in September 1427, the Ghent mint issued a much stronger noble, 'aussi bon en poix et en aloy comme ceulx que l'en forge a present en Engleterre,' of 23 7/8 car. and a *taille* of 35 1/4 to the *marc*. But these nobles offered merchants too small a financial advantage to attract much bullion to the mint. The third, and finally successful, noble of November 1428 had the same *taille* of 35 1/4 to the *marc* but a reduced fineness of 23 1/2 carats: its official price also represented a 20 per cent debasement from the 1418 standard. Between 10 Nov. 1428 and 25 Feb. 1430, the Ghent mint struck 4,577 *marcs* of pure gold in these nobles. (A.G.R., C. de C., Acquits de Lille, no. 937). See the monetary ordinances in Deschamps de Pas, 'Histoire monétaire des comtes de Flandres,' *Revue numismatique*, 2nd ser., VI (1861), 462-5, 468-71. Finally, Philip had also attempted to mint the gold *clinquaert* at Ghent in November 1426, but was forced to cease issuing it two months later. A.G.R., C. de C., Acquits de Lille, no. 937-7.

42 72,461 marcs of pure silver in 1428-9; 34,992 marcs in 1429-30. See Appendix I, Table B.

age until he was legally free to do in 1433. Instead, he relied upon his other, neighbouring mints for the increased tempo of his debasement policy after 1428.

Well before Philip's debasements reached their maximum intensity, in fact the very next year, the English Crown reacted to them strongly. As graph III and Table III clearly show, the value of England's coinage output between 1425 and 1429 had suffered a drastic decline of 45 per cent, while the (real) value of Burgundian minting in the same period had increased more than fivefold. Evidently Philip's debasement policy had succeeded in attracting large volumes of bullion — and in increasing his mint profits more than proportionately. Although the sources of this bullion cannot be determined, undoubtedly some of it at least had been lured away from the English mints. Thus particularly striking is the catastrophic fall in English gold minting and the correspondingly impressive surge in the Burgundian. Significantly, the graph also shows that by July 1426, for the first time in the history of the Low Countries, Duke Philip had altered the mint ratios to 'favour' gold over silver more strongly than the English ratio.[43] From then until October 1433, when Philip's mint ratios were again adjusted to 'favour' silver, his gold coinage output was the largest of the Burgundian era. At the same time, silver minting declined at the Burgundian mints (except for the Ghent debasement of 1428), in accordance with the altered ratios, and rose at the English mints[44] — but obviously not enough to reduce by very much the great difference between the two countries' total minting values. That difference, to be sure, may also have reflected variations in the bullion supplies from trade revenues, tax and subsidy receipts in plate, booty, and ransoms from the war.[45] The mint policies of Charles VII and of other princes, moreover, probably affected both countries' minting as well — especially England's, with its obdurate policy of not altering the coinage. But, despite these other reasons for a minting slump, the English Crown seemingly

43 The Namur mint-ratio was adjusted to 'favour' gold in July 1426; the Ghent mint-ratio, in September 1427. The fall in the Namur mint-ratio for gold - but never enough to discourage seriously the supply of that metal - reflects: first, the reduction in both the official price of the *clinquaert* and of the high seignorage on gold; and second, the debasement of silver at Namur in 1428-9. See Appendix I, Tables E-F.

44 Between 1423 and 1429 English silver minting almost quadrupled, chiefly at Calais. Apparently Flemish, Dutch, and other foreign merchants trading at the Staple chose to pay in silver, or to have their silver bullion coined there, rather than pay in gold. In 1428-9, the Calais mint coined only 148.1 gold *marcs,* only 4.4 per cent as much gold as it had coined in its first full year, 1422-3.

45 The balance-of-trade argument, however, is not very convincing because, as previously noted, the period 1425-9 was one of a trade boom for England, with the highest combined total of wool and cloth exports in the fifteenth century. See notes 11, 30 *supra.*

believed itself justified in demanding from its Burgundian ally the bullion 'robbed' from England at this most critical moment of the French war.

TABLE III

Combined Value of Gold and Silver Minting and of Mint Seignorages,
in Pounds Sterling, for England and the Burgundian Lowlands, 1420-1439

| Michaelmas Years | English Mints: London and Calais | | Burgundian Mints: Ghent, Namur, Dordrecht, Louvain, and Brussels | | |
	Total value of coinage in £ sterling	Total Seignorage in £ sterling	Total value of coinage in £ st. (a)	Total Seignorage in £ st. (a)	Total value of seignorage in £ *gros* Flemish
1419-20	£ 45,533	£ 473	£ 62,944	£ 925	£ 965
1420-1	67,865	708	60,681	890	928
1421-2	110,930	1,155	77,490	1,126	1,173
1422-3	182,196	1,889	54,991	817	850
1423-4	179,671	1,832	53,785	800	831
1424-5	102,580	1,012	30,057	427	457
1425-6	67,196	649	69,039	1,924	2,383
1426-7	59,244	571	69,484	2,915	3,809
1427-8	58,335	552	24,235	648	815
1428-9	57,398	519	157,175	2,937	3,582
1429-30	60,261	540	129,672b	1,340	1,667
1430-1	65,292	580	109,942	1,448	1,939
1431-2	57,898	506	141,749	3,525	5,143
1432-3	50,462	438	71,200	3,677	5,473
1433-4	38,553	344	121,494c	779	879
1434-5	27,160	241	132,127	897	1,018
1435-6	17,495	157	124,493	815	928
1436-7	6,478	66	61,587	444	502
1437-8	7,467	74	32,210	216	327
1438-9	13,342	127	24,843	157	177

(a) The Burgundian statistics, as estimated in pound sterling (English) value, were calculated by multiplying the mint-outputs in *marcs de Troyes* and the seignorages, as percentages of output, by the following: £11.658 st. per *marc* for gold, and £1.087 per *marc* for silver. Since the value of English gold and silver coinage in pounds sterling was constant between 1411 and 1464, these statistics provide a reasonably valid comparison between English and Burgundian mintings. The final column gives the actual seignorage receipts in *livres gros* of Flanders, as recorded in the mint-accounts. (See Appendix I, Tables H-I.)

(b) The total value of Burgundian coinage in 1429-30 includes 3,347.0 gold *marcs* and 19,467.7 silver *marcs* struck for Duke Philip of St. Pol of Brabant at Louvain. The seignorage from that year's Louvain minting, however, is not included in the total seignorage receipts (for Philip the Good).

(c) Not included in the total Burgundian minting and seignorage for 1433-4 is the output of the Valenciennes mint, since the following accounts are missing. Between Nov. 1433 and Apr. 1434, the Valenciennes mint struck 371.0 gold *marcs* and 8,519.4 silver *marcs*, producing a total seignorage of £99.0 *gros*.

SOURCES: See Appendix I, Tables A-B and H-I for the sources of the mint-accounts, and the method of computing the estimates of annual minting and seignorage in this table.

In the Parliament of 1429, the Crown took the first steps to prevent the loss of gold, in particular, to foreign mints. A Commons petitioner in September had complained that foreign merchants were refusing to accept silver for their goods but only gold bullion and English *nobles,* which they took abroad for minting into foreign coin, 'so that thai wynne in the aloy of each noble 20d. ... to the great prejudice of the Kynge.'[46] Those coins were likely Philip's debased *nobles* and *clinquaerts,* and also Charles' *écus* and *couronnes.* In reply, Parliament forbade merchants to force English subjects 'by pact, covenant, or oath' to make payments in gold or to refuse payments in silver on the pain of double forfeit.[47]

But the most significant monetary legislation of that 1429 Parliament was the series of statutes known as the Calais Staple Partition and Bullion Ordinances, a revival of the 1397 laws in far more rigorous form. Apparently, these statutes constituted a series of regulations recently devised by the Crown and the Staple government together. Parliament confirmed them as law ostensibly in response to a petitioner's charges about serious evasions of the Calais Staple. According to the petition, merchants were shipping such large quantities of wool directly to the Low Countries, under 'colour of exceptions' and of royal licences, that 'youre mynte at Calais is like to stande voide, dissolate, and be distrued.'[48] Parliament's solution for increasing the Calais mint output was to impose upon all Stapler merchants three regulations: to 'putte to more encrese and avauntage' the price of wools; to sell only for ready cash 'in hand,' permitting no credit; and, most important, to deliver one-third of the wool price in bullion to the Calais mint after each sale.[49] To enforce the ban on credit sales, the statute also demanded from the Staplers sealed pledges 'to th'entent that no merchaunt seller sal not leen agayn to no merchaunt no manere money of hym receyved' but shall instead take all the money directly to England.[50]

The Crown was well aware that the failure of the previous bullions laws in the fourteenth century was due largely to the opposition of the Staplers them-

---

46 *Rot. Parl.,* IV, 360-1: no. 66.

47 *S.R.,* II, 257 (8 Hen. VI, c. 24).

48 *Rot. Parl.,* IV, 358-9: no. 59.

49 *Rot. Parl.,* IV, n. 359: no. 60; *S.R.,* II, 254-6 (8 Hen. VI, c. 18). The requirement works out to approximately one-third of the price in bullion: 'That ye Bullyon be brought into ye mynte at Caleys... for ech sarpler of Wolle, of which the sak weyght is sold for xii marcs, £vi; x marcs, £v... to be forged into the Kynges coigne.' A 'marc' was worth 13s.4d. sterling, or two-thirds of a pound; a wool sarpler weighed on the average 2.25 sacks. Thus the requirement in bullion for the sale of a wool sarpler selling at 12 marks per sack was £6 (= 2.25 × £8/3), or one-third.

50 *Rot. Parl.,* IV, 359: 'that the hool paiement be made in hand for ye said Wolle, Wollefelle, and Tynne, in gold and silver, withouten any subtilite or collusion.'

selves, who had found Flemish resistance so injurious to their wool sales. To obtain better results this time the King's Council secured support not from the whole Company but a small group of the wealthiest, leading Staplers. Again the Council agreed not to sell any more wool-export licences, but, more important, it gave this small group full control over the Staple's government and trade.[51] The chief mechanism for granting these monopoly powers was the complementary Partition Ordinance, which required merchants to divide or 'partition' all of their receipts, not according to their individual sales, but to the amount of wool that each had brought to the Staple.[52] According to subsequent Dutch accounts, the 'partition' system forced out of business those lesser merchants who had depended upon a rapid turnover of small stocks and upon the proceeds from these quick sales to buy new wool stocks. First, they received proportionately less for their sales in the initial partition of receipts than did merchants with large stocks. Second, they had insufficient working-capital and credit for maintaining their trade over that long period of several successive 'partitions' necessary to produce their final sales receipts. Consequently, the few surviving large merchants – later estimated to be only 20 or 30 in number – were collectively able to monopolize the trade, fix the prices at high levels, and enforce the bullion laws on wool sales.[53] The Calais Staple Partition and

51 On 23 Feb. 1430, just when the Calais Ordinances took effect, the Crown extended for two years John Reynewell's term of office as Staple Mayor, despite the Staple regulations on electing mayors for limited terms and 'aliquo statuo vel ordinancione in contrarium factis non obstante.' Public Record Office, C76/113, m. 12. John Reynewell later figured prominently in the Anglo-Burgundian negotiations of the 1430s, when he acted as the chief Stapler official defending the Calais ordinances.

52 *Rot. Parl.*, IV, 359, and *S.R.*, II, 255 (in 8 Hen. VI, c. 18): 'That every man that selleth or doth selle any Wolle or Wollefelle at the said Staple at Caleys make true and even partition of the money thereof with hem that have Wolle or Felles of the same Contrees that his Wolle of Fells is of and that he is adjoined and associed.' See also Eileen Power, 'The Wool Trade in the Fifteenth Century,' *Studies in English Trade*, pp. 82-3 for a discussion of this system.

53 The Dutch accounts, also discussed by Eileen Power, are in Smit, *Bronnen Handel*, II, 697-9, nos. 1126-7. Prof. Power, while saying that the statutes' 'origin and objects are obscure,' believed that a Stapler clique had initiated them and that the bullion requirements were merely its bribe to obtain a wool monopoly from the Crown. The evidence suggests on the contrary that the Crown had initiated the laws and was forced to bribe the Stapler leaders to gain their support. The higher wool prices would not only compensate these Staplers for any losses in wool sales by the new system, but would provide them with the higher rate of interest required for the longer period of capital-turnover in the Partition scheme. Prof. Power's views were largely based on: Michael Postan, 'Credit in Medieval Trade,' *Economic History Review*, 1st ser., I (1928), 240-55, and Georg Schanz, *Englische Handelspolitik gegen Ende des Mittelalters*, I (Leipzig, 1881), 481-90. The most recent account largely repeats the views of Power, Postan, and Schanz: M.R. Thielemans, *Bourgogne et Angleterre*, pp. 170-5.

Bullion ordinances were to enter in force in February 1430 and initially, to endure for three years, until March 1433. Later, the Crown sought to make permanent this 'good politique governaunce of the Staple.'

Finally, the Crown cemented the Staplers' commitment to its bullionist policy by enacting unusually severe laws to tighten their wool monopoly. One statute imposed a penalty of two years' imprisonment and double forfeit of goods for those merchants found guilty of evading the Calais Staple; it also empowered the Staplers to inspect ships and ensure that wools were not being concealed or shipped elsewhere.[54] Another statute abolished the special wool-export privileges of the ports of Berwick and Newcastle.[55] While these two ports had been licenced to export only the coarser, cheaper northern wools, the Staplers had long accused them of shipping the higher quality wools of Yorkshire and Lincolnshire 'under colour of exceptions' directly to Flanders and Zealand, as previously noted; significantly, the Staplers had this time also charged them with 'bringing no gold or silver into the realm.'[56] Obviously the purpose of such strict guarantees for the Staplers monopoly was not only to ensure enforcement of the bullion regulations but also to prevent the Low Countries from obtaining their wool tax- and bullion-free.

The Burgundian reaction to the Calais Ordinances was almost universally hostile, for it was clear that they were directed primarily against the Low Countries. Philip understandably felt threatened by this assault upon his mints, his seignorage revenues, and the 'wealth' of his lands at a time when he himself was actively seeking bullion. This threat became even graver, moreover, with

---

54 *Rot. Parl.*, IV, 359: no. 61; *S.R.*, II, 254 (8 Hen. VI, c. 17). This statute, however, confirmed the exemptions of those Italian and Spanish merchants exporting wool to the Mediterranean; but statute 8 Hen. V, c. 2 (1420) had already imposed the bullion requirements on them. (*Supra*, note 24). Another of the 1429 statutes forbade local Calais residents to sell any wool on the grounds that they had been trading directly with foreign merchants, and 'for thair singuler lucre ymagyn be subtille meenys to brynge downe the pris of the Commodite of this Roiaume.' *Rot. Parl.*, IV, 360: no. 62; *S.R.*, II, 256 (8 Hen. VI, c. 20).

55 *Rot. Parl.*, IV, 360: no. 63; *S.R.*, II, 256 (8 Hen. VI, c. 21). Berwick's privileges had been granted in 1399, or perhaps as early as 1378 (see chapter 2, note 45). In July 1423 and in July 1427, the King's Council had granted Newcastle a licence similar to Berwick's to ship wools of Scotland, Northumberland, Westmoreland, Cumberland, and Durham directly to Middelburg and Bruges, for six years. See Nicolas, *P.P.C.*, III, 115 (1423), and 355-6 (1427). For other licences to Berwick, see *Ibid.*, III, 39; Smit, *Bronnen Handel*, II, 611, no. 988; and *Cal. Pat. Rolls 1422-29*, p. 82.

56 *Rot. Parl.*, IV, 360: no. 63: 'as moch as thai have been solde fore in Flaundres and in other places whar thai repaire, to be paied at reasonable terms, in gold and silver to be brought in to this Roiaume, whereas by hem ther commyth nowe no peny.' Berwick and Newcastle could have undersold the Staplers easily, because they paid the lower customs duty of 13s.4d. a sack.

the increasing frequency of foreign debasements at this very time. Graph III shows a serious slump in Philip's mint output in 1430 and 1431 which likely reflects a drainage of bullion to neighbouring mints, as well as to the Calais Staple.[57] For example, the Louvain mint in the neighbouring Duchy of Brabant struck new debased coinage from September 1429 and, by the following September, had coined three times as much gold as Philip's mints.[58] Fortunately for Philip, his acquisition of Brabant in that month (1430) also gained him the offending Louvain mint. More damaging competition, however, came from the mints of the Rhinelander princes and of Charles VII, as Philip himself saw in the Louvain mintmaster's report of December 1430. That report listed some ten different foreign coins struck as counterfeit imitations of Burgundian coins; compared the intrinsic metal contents of the counterfeits with those of Philip's; and calculated the profits from their fraudulent distribution. Such gains were as much as 60 per cent on the silver coins and 35 per cent on the gold, easily enough to warrent reminting the Burgundian coins at the countefeiting mints.[59] One of the worst offenders was Charles VII's Tournay mint, whose issues of debased gold and silver coins have been noted in Tables I and II. The accompanying Table IV demonstrates the catastrophic effect that Charles' debasements of his imitation of the Flemish *double gros* had upon Philip's silver minting in this period.

57 Some of that minting slump was probably due also to the completion of domestic recoinages
- of the old, outstanding issues. For an estimate of the flow of bullion to Calais, see chapter 4, Table II, p. 96.

58 A.G.R., C. de C., no. 18,065; and also the ordinance in C. de C., no. 131, fo. 85-8r, no. 580, fo. 67-8r. Duke Philip of St. Pol had justified his debasements also in terms of Gresham's Law: 'overmits alre hande vremde munten, die in onse voirsc. lande zeer hoege boven hoere werde gegaen hebben, metten welcken tgout ende tselver uten selven onsen lande zeer getogen.'

59 A.G.R., C. de C., carton 65: bis 1 and 65: 2; Flemish version partly in C. de C., no. 580, fo. 92r. (See Appendix II for this report). The Louvain mint-master named the Rhenish lordships of Rummen-Wesemal and Reckheim-Sombreffe, the bishoprics of Liège and Tournay, and the duchy of Guelders; and complaints about coins from Utrecht, Cologne, and Jülich are also noted. Thus, 'les éscus que on forge presentement audit Liège contrefaictes apres ceulx de mondit seigneur;' and 'munte te Dornyck [Tournay] gecontrefayt naer die van s'hertogen slage hebbende in stede van Leuven.' The next year, in September 1431, Duke Philip the Good ordered the Namur mint to reduce the gold content of the *clinquaert*, because 'en ladite Monnoye de Namur n'a à present peu ou néant d'ouvrage par aucune autre monnoie qui donnent plus hault pris que on ne peut faire en nostre dit monnoie.' On 24 November he ordered that money-changers be paid the same price for gold and silver bullion as given at the mints of Tournay and Germany. Deschamps de Pas, *Histoire monétaire des comtes de Flandre*, p. xxxix, doc. nos. 195-6.

TABLE IV

Silver coinage output at the mints of Tournay, Ghent, and Louvain,
in marcs de Troyes of pure silver
1 Oct. 1429 to 25 Oct. 1433

Years (1 Oct.-30 Sept.)	Tournay	Ghent	Louvain
1429-30	13,527 *marcs*	34,992 *marcs*	19,468 *marcs**
1430-1	12,824	5,585	2,728
1431-2	15,948	111	360
1432-3	17,668	-nil-	-nil-
1 Oct.-25 Oct. 1433**	1,237	-nil-	-nil-

* Struck for Duke Philip of St. Pol (Brabant).
** New coinage issue from 20 October, 1433.
SOURCES: A.G.R., Chambre de Comptes, nos. 18,065-8; A.G.R., C. de C., Acquits de Lille, liasse no. 937; Comte de Castellone, 'Les monnaies d'argent du système flamand frappées à Tournai au nom de Charles VII,' *Revue numismatique*, 2nd ser., IV:2 (1898), 103-15.

Philip nevertheless pursued his mint policy of debasing and 'favouring' gold. But the Calais Ordinances, if effectively enforced, threatened to eliminate any profit from passing debased Burgundian gold coins, such as the imitation *nobles,* in England.[60] The evidence does suggest that the English bullion laws, as in 1397, were designed in part to force the reminting of Burgundian coins at Calais. Philip undoubtedly viewed this check to his debasement policy as an additional attack upon his mints' bullion supply.[61]

The Calais Ordinances threatened even greater disaster for Philip's cloth-making subjects of Flanders, Brabant, and Holland. Their wool was already so expensive that further price increases might leave the market fully to the Eng-

60 Although no *specific* complaints against Burgundian coins of this period have been recorded, Philip's gold noble of 1428, struck at Ghent, appears to have been an excellent imitation of the English noble. (See note 41 *supra*.) In 1436, the author of the *Libelle of Englysche Polycye* wrote: 'Shall any prince ... wheche hathe nobles moche lyche to ours, Be lorde of see and Flemmynges to our blame?' (ed. G. Warner, Oxford, 1926, p. 3, lines 42-5.) Plate III in *Ibid.*, p. 1, moreover, does show a striking resemblance between the two coins. See also Thompson, 'Continental Imitations of the Rose Noble,' *British Numismatic Journal*, XXV (1949), 185.
61 In an ordinance of Feb. 1428 Duke Philip had decreed that Flemish merchants were to use his coinage 'even if the payment shall take place abroad.' Diegerick, *Archives de la ville d'Ypres*, III, 127, no. 855. It is perhaps significant, moreover, that the Ghent mint coined the last of Philip's nobles on 25 Feb. 1430, just three weeks after the Calais Ordinances entered into force. A.G.R., Acquits de Lille, liasse no. 937.

lish cloth trade. Meeting the bullion requirement itself was also costly for the wool-buyers: in evading the traditional ban on bullion exports that was soon to be rigidly enforced, in bidding up the market price of metals, and in paying the Calais mintage fees.[62] Quite clearly, the Calais laws prevented the Staplers from accepting foreign coins as legal tender, as they had previously been doing. Many complaints, in fact, suggest that the Staplers arbitrarily and 'unfairly' undervalued the bullion contents of Burgundian coins.[63] But the most harmful consequence of the Calais Ordinances was the disruption of the credit-financing system upon which the wool trade, cloth manufacturing, and marketing so vitally depended. Most drapers lacked sufficient working-capital to make the whole payment in cash and they would have found it prohibitive to borrow the necessary funds — if available — in English coins and bullion.

The noted English historians Michael Postan and Eileen Power have already shown that the wool trade functioned essentially upon a chain of credit that ran 'from the wool grower in the Cotswolds to the buyer of Dutch cloth in Poland or Spain.'[64] In general, throughout this chain, the buyer paid one-third in cash at the time of purchase and arranged payment for the remainder in two 'bills' or promissory notes over a year. Obviously drapers and merchants could only obtain funds to redeem their bills when they themselves had received payment from their own customers and debtors. Just as the sales-credit chain

---

62 The bullion requirement would have proven costly if ingots were supplied and the wool-buyers' demand raised the price of the metal above the official mint price; or, if coins were supplied as bullion for reminting, thus necessitating a double mintage fee. As subsequently to be noted, the Staplers had apparently always required a cash down-payment of at least one third, though, legally or not, they had generally been willing to accept foreign coins as legal tender. See the following note and note 69.

63 The Crown's previous attempts to prevent payments in foreign coin have already been noted, as has the Burgundians' more liberal policy of accepting certain foreign coins as legal tender, granting them a slight premium above their bullion contents. Subsequently, Duke Philip complained that the Staplers refused to sell wool 'ten sy billoen van goude of van silvere, sonder te willen ontfangen gancbair munte.' (Charles Piot (ed.), *Inventaire des chartes de la ville de Léau*, Brussels, 1879, p. 27, no. 8.) In 1436, the Sovereign Bailiff of Flanders also charged that merchants were required to sell their Burgundian gold *rijders* at Calais at the rate of two *rijders* per English gold *noble*. On the average, two *rijders* contained 3.3 per cent more gold than the English *noble*; and the Calais mintage fee was then 1.5 per cent. See F. Morand (ed.), *Chronique de Jean le Fèvre de St. Remy*, II (Paris, 1876), 378.

64 Michael Postan, 'Credit in Medieval Trade,' *Econ. Hist. Rev.*, 1st ser., I (1928), 240-4; and Power, 'Wool Trade in the Fifteenth Century,' *Studies in English Trade*, pp. 49-72. A contemporary and quite hostile reference to sales credit at Calais may be found in the *Libelle of Englysche Polycye* of the 1430s: 'Whan they borrowed at the town of Caleys, as they were wonte, ther wolle that was hem lente.' (G. Warner ed., p. 23). For examples of credit contracts made at the Staple, see Posthumus, *Bronnen Textielnijverheid*, I, 184, no. 161, and H.E. Malden (ed.), *The Cely Papers*, I (Camden R.H.S., 3rd ser., 1900), *passim*.

ended with the final retail sales of cloth, so a reverse chain of debt settlements commenced with the cash obtained from these final cloth sales. This credit system therefore economized on the use of coin by using, *in effect,* that same cash in a (diminishing) flow through the chain back to the wool growers. In these debt settlements, merchants further economized on coin by using bills-of-exchange, which obviated specie shipments between two countries. For example, the Flemish, Brabantine and Dutch wool-buyers paid their 'Calais bills' at the semi-annual fairs of Bruges, Middelburg, Antwerp, and Bergen-op-Zoom, and did so in Flemish currency. The simplest and most profitable way for the Staplers to transfer these receipts to London was to sell a bill-of-exchange or 'lend' these Flemish funds to the London Mercers, the chief English importers of goods from the Low Countries. That bill would be 'drawn' on the Mercers' London office, to be repaid there at a later date in sterling (with the interest disguised in the exchange rate). Thus the Mercers used Flemish funds to import goods from the Low Countries and then their English sales receipts to redeem the bills held by the Staplers.[65]

The Crown's reason for prohibiting credit sales through its Calais ordinances — just as it had earlier tried to ban bills-of-exchange — was, therefore, simply the fact that credit transactions did reduce the flow of specie into the country.[66] By another statute of the 1429 Parliament, moreover, the Crown had demonstrated its hostility towards all credit in general. This act, an extreme version of the old 'Employment' laws, forbade the granting of 'loans' to all foreign merchants and required full payment from foreigners in 'ready money' or in merchandise at the time of sale.[67] Within two years, however, that law had proved so impractical and harmful that Parliament was forced to relax its provisions. A Commons petitioner complained in January 1431 that the credit

---

65 In these bills, the Staplers charged a hidden interest by adjusting the exchange rates between the English and Flemish currencies in their own favour, and varied the interest rates according to the due-dates of the bills. For examples, see Power, 'The Wool Trade in the Fifteenth Century,' pp. 65-6. The Staplers themselves were not 'communes acchateurs des Merchandises en Flandres' (*Rot. Parl.*, IV, 252), and so had to employ the Mercers for the re-exchange of funds to England.

66 For an example of the continuing English hostility against all credit operations in the sixteenth century, see 'A Treatise Concerning the Staple,' in R.H. Tawney and E. Power (eds.), *Tudor Economic Documents*, III (London, 1924), 93-4. The author maintained (ca. 1520) that, as a result of the Staplers' credit transactions, 'the mynt in Caleis desolyved.'

67 *S.R.*, II, 257 (8 Hen. VI, c. 24) and *Rot. Parl.*, IV, 360-1: no. 66: 'Consideryng that thorowe the gret apprestes that has been made hem in this Roiaume, that have ful gretly and avaunced her merchandises and broght doune to noght the pris of the Commodite of this Roiaume [wool], making hem riche and us pouere, that is shame and abusion.' There is no doubt that this hostile view reflected the general opinion of the Commons as well as of the Crown.

ban had prevented English merchants from selling their cloth. Since the English cloth trade had no captive markets, Parliament had no hope of enforcing the law and so, in reply, permitted cloth sales to foreigners on six months credit.[68] While no such relief was granted to the wool merchants, the Crown ought to have realized that credit was just as important for the wool trade. Several times previously Stapler officials had informed the Crown that their customers were unable to buy wool for ready cash and, indeed, that England's wool had no value unless they 'lent' it to the Lowlander buyers.[69] One can only assume, therefore, that the leading Staplers' shortsighted lust for monopoly profits overrode their better judgement in supporting these destructive payment regulations.

At the same time, the Crown's failure to appreciate the consequences of its bullionist policy seems remarkable. Its implementation soon produced a twofold disaster for England in the 1430s: a precipitous decline in wool sales, which thus undermined the very foundations of royal finance; and second, from the injured Low Countries, growing hostility and then economic retaliation, which severely strained and finally ruptured the vital Anglo-Burgundian alliance. Both calamities struck the English at the very time when their power in France was beginning to collapse in the face of Charles VII's attempts to regain his kingdom, with the aid of the Maid of Orléans.

The strength of that French military challenge, however, helps to explain why the English Crown was so desperate and why it re-imposed the old bullionist policy in such a rigorous form. Its current policy, moreover, was due not just to a severe monetary crisis, magnified by those traditional fears that equated bullion losses with national weakness. Apparently also responsible for the enactment of the Calais Ordinances was the Crown's current fiscal crisis, its first serious Treasury deficits, as more and more money was sent to bolster the English armies in France.[70] But most of all, the Crown became greatly concerned about financing the Calais garrison, which it had just enlarged fol-

---

68 *S.R.*, II, 263-4 (9 Hen. VI, c. 2): 'par apprest de paiement affaire en monoye ou en marchandise de vi moys apres tielx achatz et bargaignez faitz.' The petition is in *Rot. Parl.*, IV, 377: no. 31: 'par cause de qele ordinaunce, les Marchantz Englis n'ount ny venduz, ne poient vendre ne outer lour Drapz as Marchantz alienz.'

69 Scott and Gilliodts-van Severen, *Cotton Manuscrit Galba*, pp. 308-11, no. 135 (10 June 1411). The Stapler letter, pleading for a renewal of the Anglo-Burgundian truce, stated that 'les Merchantz en fesantz deliveraunce de lours leins illoeques pour argent comptant, ceo ne poet estre; qar tous ceulx que ont accustumey daccheter leins ne les poevent acchater par argent comptant;' and, 'que les leins ne purront estre deliverez a nulle value sanz estre apprestez...' Other references to credit in nos. 101, 127, 133, 168.

70 Jacob, *Fifteenth Century*, pp. 255-6; Steel, *Receipt of the Exchequer, 1377-1485*, pp. 430-1. Full expenditure accounts are not available; but the doubling of loans and receipts from 1428

lowing the Orléans defeat of May 1429.[71] Calais had long been a costly burden,[72] but its preservation was vital in maintaining the lucrative Staple trade and especially in keeping open the chief gateway to France. In order to pay the wages and ensure the loyalty of the larger number of troops, the Crown badly needed ready cash — as much coin as it could exact from the wool trade in customs duties, loans, and seignorage, as quickly as possible.[73] Already the soldiers at Calais had grumbled about receiving their pay in 'tallies,' or promissory Exchequer notes; and subsequent revolts of the garrison ensured that the Crown would not relent in enforcing the Calais Ordinances. More and more, also, the King's Council became dependent upon loans from the leading Staplers to finance the garrison.[74] But the Crown needed more than just gold to secure Calais and meet the growing threat from Charles VII's armies — it needed the Burgundians.

to 1431 indicates the severity of the crisis. See also Nicolas, *P.P.C.*, IV, xxi-xxii for other details on the financial crisis of 1430-1, especially the lack of money to pay the soldiers in France.

71 Since July 1426, Parliament had been assigning 13s.4d. per woolsack from the customs to the maintenance of Calais; in September 1429, it enlarged the Calais garrison and assigned 10,000 marks to the Calais Treasurer 'pro vadiis certorum hominem ad arma et sagittariorum.' *Rot. Parl.*, IV, 340: no. 24 and P.R.O., C76/112, m. 24 (20 Dec. 1429).

72 For example, a complete financial record for 1421 shows that Calais then accounted for 37 per cent of the Crown's total expenditures: £19,120 out of £52,236. Rymer, *Foedera*, X, 113-4.

73 In 1429, Parliament also provided for 'commodium et proficium de cunagio nostro ibiden' for meeting Calais payments. P.R.O., C76/112, m. 24.

74 For Stapler loans in 1429-30, see *Cal. Pat. Rolls 1429-36*, pp. 111, 120; Nicolas, *P.P.C.*, IV, 52 (£2,333.6s.8d. for payments of the Calais garrison's wages, June 1430). On the use of tallies, see Steel, *Receipt of the Exchequer*, pp. 430-60.

CHAPTER FOUR

THE BURGUNDIAN REACTION: THE BAN ON ENGLISH CLOTH AND THE ANGLO-BURGUNDIAN WAR, 1430-1442

Burgundian opposition to the Calais Ordinances, implemented in February 1430, united Philip the Good and his drapery town subjects as no previous issue had. These traditionally independent towns looked to the duke for leadership and he looked to them for active support in quashing these injurious regulations. Initially, they relied on negotiations with the English to seek relief. In December 1430 Philip sent his first Flemish mission to Calais, where it held several inconclusive meetings with the Staplers and Henry Cardinal Beaufort, then leader of the King's Council and probable author of the ordinances.[1] Six months and several missions later, in June 1431, Philip's councillors convoked a formal conference of the Flemish towns and the Staplers at Bruges. Apparently Philip hoped to resolve the problem of wool purchases 'without being required to furnish gold and silver bullion,' but the English were obdurate.[2] They also refused the representations of a subsequent Flemish delegation to Calais, sent to protest the damages inflicted upon their drapery industry.[3]

1 A.G.R., C. de C., no. 32.485, fo. 57 vo. (Bruges): 'an de Cardinal van Inglant ende andere Staple van Calais ... vander coopmanscepe vander wulle.' Subsequent meetings with Cardinal Beaufort, to May 1431, are noted in Nicolas, *P.P.C.*, IV, 18.
2 A.G.R., C. de C., no. 42.549, fo. 28 vo. (Franc de Bruges); 'omme te sprekene metten cooplieden van Ingheland omme weghen te vindene daer bi dat men Inghelsche wulle zoude moghen ghecrighen zonder billoen van goude of van zelver daer over te moeten leverne.'
3 A.G.R., C. de C., no. 32.485, fo. 63 vo. (Bruges, 26 June 1431), no. 38.655, fo. 13 ro. (Ypres, 28 June 1431).

Rebuffed, Duke Philip then appealed to the estates of his realms to devise 'remedies against these prejudicial ordinances.'[4] On 14 September 1431, an historic assembly met at Antwerp, the first 'Estates General' or parliament of the Burgundian Lowlands, with deputies from Flanders, Brabant, Holland, and Zealand under the direction of Philip himself and his councillors.[5] During October and November Philip summoned two further such Estates General at Malines and Brussels. They apparently explored the possibility of a general retaliatory ban on English cloth, a proposal further discussed by the Flemish towns in December.[6] But this flurry of anti-Calais activity then ceased and was not openly resumed for another eighteen months.

The possible reasons for Philip's delay in directly retaliating against the Calais Ordinances are worth examining, if only to understand the full dimensions of the problems he faced. First, in view of later developments, the proposal to ban English cloth probably encountered strong resistance from the Dutch and Brabantine merchants, especially since the two cloth bans of 1428 had just been lifted.[7] Second, one might argue that the Calais Ordinances were impossible to enforce fully for long, and thus that the Burgundians no longer considered the Staple issue to be as critical as it had first appeared. Quite possibly, as a Commons petitioner maintained in May 1432, the Low Countries' draperies were obtaining some of their wool free of the Staple, either smuggled or exported on licences. The petition charged that, with such light penalties for evading the Staple, merchants were daily exporting large quantities of wool directly to the Low Countries and selling it there 'so goode chepe' that the Calais Staple was losing its customers.[8] Although Parliament did re-enforce

4 A.G.R., C. de C., no. 42.549, fo. 45 vo. (Franc de Bruges): 'up de prejudiciable ordenancen ghemaect bi die van den Staple van Caleys up t' fait vander Inghelscher wulle die daer ghe-cocht worde, raed ende advijs te hebbene ende weghen van remeden daer jeghen te vindene.' Also, no. 38.655, fo. 15 vo. (Ypres).

5 Various accounts in Joseph Cuvelier (ed.), *Actes des Etats Généraux des anciens Pays Bas, 1427-1477* (Brussels, 1948), pp. 8-11; see also Hermann Vander Linden (ed.), *Itinéraires de Philippe le Bon, duc de Bourgogne, et de Charles, comte de Charolais* (Brussels, 1940), p. 95. A prior assembly of the Burgundian Low Countries took place in May 1427, but it involved only Flanders and Hainaut on the governance of the latter county.

6 Cuvelier, *Actes*, pp. 9-11; A.G.R., C. de C., no. 32.486, fo. 57 vo., 58 vo. (Bruges). On 12 December, the Flemish towns met at Ghent 'omme te sprekene up tstic vanden Inghel-schen lakene.' *Ibid.*, fo. 58 vo.

7 See chapter 3 *supra*, pp. 68-9.

8 *Rot. Parl.*, IV, 410: no. 51: 'And also by the seid Wolles and merchandises so caried into the parties aforesaid, commes no money into this Royalme ageyn, ne the Roialme therby is nothing encresed, ne the mynt at Calais sustened.' The previous year, the King's Council had sent officials into the northern counties of Northumberland, Cumberland, Westmoreland, and Durham - after Newcastle had petitioned for the restoration of its export licence - to investi-

the Staplers' monopoly privileges, it significantly exempted from the Staple all wools shipped on royal licences.[9] That November the Crown also restored Newcastle's licence to ship northern wools to Flanders.[10] Apparently the Crown found its financial straits serious enough to resume the sale of these export permits.

TABLE I

Wool and Coinage at Calais:
English Woolsacks exported to Calais, and the Output of the Calais Mint
1420-1440

Michaelmas	Woolsacks shipped to Calais	Silver marcs coined	Gold marcs coined	Total value of coinage in £ st.
1419-20	11,384	—	—	—
1420-1	11,832	—	—	—
1421-2	13,402	1,323.4	656.9	9,098
1422-3	14,476	6,513.3	3,372.6	46,398
1423-4	15,913	19,314.1	1,962.5	43,874
1424-5	11,195	25,469.3	1,262.3	42,402
1425-6	12,247	21,514.6	702.3	31,575
1426-7	16,083	19,655.0	389.2	25,903
1427-8	15,351	24,074.1	191.2	28,398
1428-9	11,398	32,923.5	148.1	37,516
1429-30	7,066	36,584.6	164.6	41,687
1430-1	10,433	42,321.2	173.2	48,023
1431-2	10,540	41,193.3	—	44,778
1432-3	8,663	37,724.0	—	41,007
1433-4	838	24,951.7	—	27,123
1434-5	12,923	18,199.5	—	19,783
1435-6	2,531	8,936.2	—	10,119
1436-7	66	—	—	—
1437-8	156	—	—	—
1438-9	505	537.7	—	584
1439-40	17,731	—	—	—

SOURCES: E. Carus-Wilson and O. Coleman, *England's Export Trade, 1275-1547* (Oxford 1963), calculated from tables in pp. 57-65.

P.R.O. (L.T.R.), E 364/59, 61-63, 65-66, 69, 72; (K.R.) E 101/192-93; C.P.R. 1422-1429, pp. 337-338, 520; C.P.R. 1429-1436, pp. 256-7, 259.

gate illegal shipments of wools 'from diverse harbours and creeks.' (*Cal. Pat. Rolls 1429-36*, pp. 131-2). See also Power, 'The Wool Trade in the Fifteenth Century,' *Studies in English Trade*, pp. 84-7. She doubts that the Staple regulations were rigidly enforced in terms of the credit and bullion requirements, but all the evidence provides the contrary impression.

9 *S.R.*, II, 276 (10 Hen. VI, c. 7).

10 P.R.O., C76/114, m. 2 (20 Nov. 1432). The customs accounts show no wool exported from Newcastle between Michaelmas 1429 and August 1432; but 512 sacks from then until Michaelmas (29 Sept.) 1433. Carus-Wilson, *England's Export Trade*, pp. 58-60.

TABLE II

*Prices of Flemish Woollens Purchased Annually
for the Civil Officials of Ypres and Bruges in livres parisis*,
1425-1434*

Year	Bruges: Fine White Cloths Purchased for the *Buerch-meesters*	Ypres: Dyed Cloths Purchased for the *Hooch bailliu* and *Schepenen*	Ypres: Dyed Cloths Purchased for the Four *Hoofmannen*
1425	£54.0.0	£67. 4.0	£58. 4.0
1426	54.0.0	—	58.16.0
1427	54.0.0	58.16.0	61. 8.0
1428	54.0.0	56. 8.0	60. 0.0
1429	54.0.0	—	55. 4.0
1430	60.0.0	—	—
1431	60.0.0	72. 0.0	66. 0.0
1432	66.0.0	72. 0.0	64.16.0
1433	62.8.0	72. 0.0	66. 0.0
1434	69.0.0	72. 0.0	66. 0.0

* 1 *livre parisis* = 20d. (1s.8d.) *gros*.

SOURCES: A.G.R., C. de C., nos. 32,479-88 (Bruges) and 38,650-8 (Ypres). The size of the Bruges cloths was 36 ells by 9 quarters; of Ypres cloths, apparently 30 ells by 10 quarters.

But it is still doubtful that the draperies of the Low Countries were able to ignore the Staple for the bulk of their wool supply. Table I suggests that the Calais Ordinances likely were effective in acquiring bullion for the Calais mint — and also in damaging the wool trade. For the four years following the enactment of the laws, in the years 1430-3, the annual average of the Calais mint output was 42 per cent *above* that of 1426-9, while the annual average of wool shipments to Calais was 32 per cent *below* the 1426-29 average. Moreover, for the corresponding periods, the average annual number of drapers' stalls rented in Ypres' *ghemijnghede lakenhalle,* where apparently the most expensive luxury woollens were traded, fell from 215 to 166, a sizeable drop of 30 per cent that probably reflects the inability of the smaller weaver-drapers to survive the costs of the Calais ordinances.[11] Equally significant is the sudden jump in the prices

11 A.G.R., C. de C., nos. 38.651-7 (Ypres). Two other categories of stalls were those rented to *upzetters* in the *ghemijnghede halle,* and those to drapers in the *blaeuwe halle*: the former were generally wealthier entrepreneurs and merchants who came from the finishers' guild; the latter probably handled less costly woollens, since their stalls rented for only 8s. *parisis,* compared to 15s. for *ghemijnghede halle* stalls. Their average number of stalls rented remained roughly stable in these two periods, but after 1435 all three categories showed a precipitous and relentless decline in the number rented. See *infra,* pp. 181-2. The significance of the Ypres' drapery statistics (1406-1500) will be analyzed more thoroughly in the sequel to this study.

MONETARY GRAPH IV (1428-1444)

Coinage of pure gold and silver marcs in the
Burgundian Lowlands and England

BURGUNDIAN MINTS:

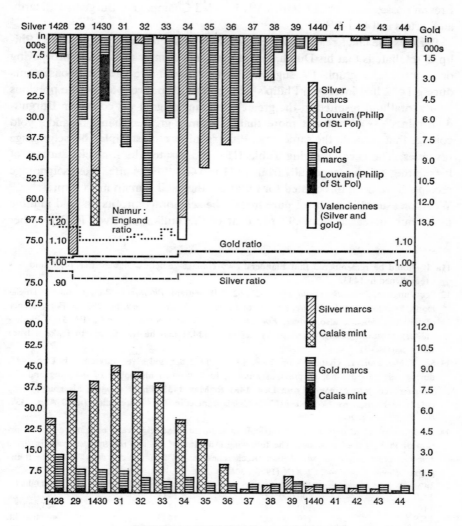

ENGLISH MINTS (London and Calais):

SOURCES: See Appendix I, Tables A-D.

of Flemish cloths immediately after 1429, as shown in Table II.[11a] Apparently therefore, the Staple's bullion ordinances remained a real problem for Duke Philip and his subjects, though for the duke not yet sufficiently serious to warrant a rupture of the Anglo-Burgundian alliance. Philip was still dependent upon English subsidies, and he especially needed their support to maintain his French possessions when Charles VII invaded Champagne, Burgundy, Picardy and Artois in 1430-1.[12]

Perhaps the chief reason why English bullionism had not yet provoked Philip to retaliate is that his Dutch, Brabantine, and Namur mints were prospering once more. As graph IV suggests, further and more drastic debasements during 1432 had increased Philip's mint output 20 per cent above the previous year's total and resulted in the greatest amount of gold yet coined in Burgundian mints[13] – an amount more than ten times greater than England's gold coinage that year. At the same time, Philip's mints almost tripled his seignorage revenues. The accompanying Table III demonstrates the financial success of his minting policies, especially from 1431 to 1433.[14] Even after these seignorage receipts have been discounted for inflation, they still remain most impressive.[15] When measured in terms of pure metal, the seignorage profits on gold minting at Namur increased from .97 per cent of the bullion received in September

---

11a It should be remembered that Flanders' own coinage remained stable after 1428, and was strengthened in 1433.

12 See Vaughan, *Philip the Good*, pp. 17-27, 62-6; Bonenfant, *Philippe le Bon*, pp. 48-58; Thiele-mans, *Bourgogne et Angleterre*, pp. 49-56; Jacob, *Fifteenth Century*, pp. 250-60. For evidence of the subsidies, see also Rymer, *Foedera*, X, 454-5; and Nicolas, *P.P.C.*, IV, 31-2. Philip's military position greatly worsened by September 1431 and he was forced to make a truce with Charles VII.

13 See Tables I and II, chapter 3, pp. 77-80 *supra*. Philip debased silver only once, in Dec. 1431, during this period; and, as previously noted, he continued his policy of debasing and 'favouring' the gold coinage. From Dec. 1431 to May 1433, Philip debased his gold *pieters*, chiefly at Namur, by 13 per cent. The Calais mint coined no more gold after 3 Aug. 1431. *Cal. Pat. Rolls* 1429-36, p. 259.

14 Again, insufficient data makes it difficult to estimate these seignorage revenues as a proportion of Philip's total revenues. The following estimates of Philip's *recettes générales* in *livres tournois* are taken from M. Mollat, 'Recherches sur les finances des ducs Valois de Bourgogne,' *Revue historique*, CCXIX (1958), 306-7.

1426	405,000 l.t.	1430	190,000 l.t.
1427	100,000 l.t.	1431	190,000 l.t.
1428	190,000 l.t.	1432	315,000 l.t.
1429	190,000 l.t.	1433	440,000 l.t.

See also Vaughan, *Philip the Good*, pp. 259-63.

15 See Table III, chapter 3, p. 83 *supra*, where the total Burgundian seignorage receipts have been discounted in terms of the stable pound sterling. Between June 1418 and May 1433, the overall Burgundian debasement of gold was 39 per cent, of silver 28 per cent.

1431 to a substantial 5.40 per cent of the bullion in May 1433. Again, as in previous years, the profitability of gold debasement more than made up for the (consequent) decline in silver minting. Most of that gold, as the table shows, was struck at the Namur mint, the only one which Philip was then free to manipulate at will. Its purchase in 1421 proved to be one of his best investments.

TABLE III

Seignorage on Gold and Silver Coinage from the Burgundian Mints
at Ghent, Namur, Dordrecht, and Louvain, in livres gros of Flanders,
and in pure marcs de Troyes, from Michaelmas 1423-4 to 1432-3

Michaelmas Years	Silver Seignorage from all mints		Gold Seignorage in livres gros		Gold Seignorage from all mints	Total Seignorage receipts
	in livres gros	in pure marcs	Namur	All mints	in pure marcs	in livres gros
1423-4	£807.9	715.1		£22.7	2.0	£830.6
1424-5	353.3	312.4		103.2	7.5	456.5
1425-6	226.5	202.5	£1,146.1	2,156.2	146.1	2,382.7
1426-7	47.6	44.8	1,041.8	3,761.3	245.9	3,808.9
1427-8	122.9	106.8	452.8	691.5	45.6	814.4
1428-9	2,034.8	1,587.1	769.8	1,547.3	104.0	3,582.1
1429-30	1,316.1	1,003.5	286.5	351.5	21.4	1,667.6
1430-1*	283.1	217.4	553.7	1,656.1	103.9	1,939.2
1431-2*	54.8	39.7	4,266.8	5,087.5	298.6	5,142.3
1432-3	14.1	9.1	5,242.3	5,459.2	314.5	5,473.3

* Louvain mint: seignorages paid to Philip the Good from October 1430 included (but not the seignorage paid to Duke Philip of St. Pol in 1429-30).

SOURCES: A.G.R., C. de C., nos. 18,203; 18,065-8; A.G.R., C. de C., Acquits de Lille, liasse no. 937; A.R.A. (N.), Rekenkamer no. 4937:I-II.

During 1433, however, Philip's fortunes changed, so that both the Staple and the monetary issues finally forced the Burgundians to strike against the Calais Laws. First, the English dashed any hopes that these laws would be permitted to lapse with their expiry in March. Instead, the Parliament of July 1433 re-enacted them in full for an indefinite term, with specific reiterations of the credit ban, the bullion exactions, and the 'partition' regulations.[16] The same

---

16 *Rot. Parl.,* IV, 454: no. 63; *S.R.,* II, 287 (11 Hen. VI, c. 13). Although the petitioner asked
   that the Calais laws be extended for only three years, the Crown replied: 'Salvant toutz foitz
   au Roi poiair et auctorite de modifier mesme lestatut quant loy plerra, par advis de son Coun-

statute also reconfirmed the Staplers' monopoly on wool exports, again costing Newcastle its export licence. This extension and tightening of the Staple ordinances likely reflected fears that England was again losing bullion to the active mints of the Burgundian Lowlands. As graph IV shows, the boom in English minting that followed the initial implementation of the Calais laws ended in 1432 and minting then slumped some 23 per cent in total value by mid-1433. At the same time, the worsening Treasury deficits — for a total unsecured debt of £165,00 — and the mounting costs of the Calais garrison had undoubtedly stiffened the Council's determination to maintain its bullionist policy.[17] Perhaps as decisive a factor as any in its decision was the mutiny of the Calais garrison that April, a bloody revolt over the long arrears in wages.[18]

This extension of the Calais ordinances was singularly inopportune for Duke Philip, because by mid-summer — at a time of rising military expenditures — his mints also were no longer attracting much bullion.[19] Apparently, the ex-

seill, selon qe ceo qe meulx luy semblera pur le profet de luy et de son roialme.' In fact, by this clause, the extension was made indefinite. The Council had also already 'modified' the bullion regulations imposed on the 'Straits of Marrock' merchants (of 8 Hen V, c. 2). In February 1433, the Council permitted them 'respite of brynging yn thair said sommes to the Bullione as betwix him and thaim shal mowe be accordede, taking of thaim sufficeante seurte.' (Nicolas, *P.P.C.*, IV, 145). On 20 July 1433, five Genoese merchants were granted one year to bring back the bullion for their wool and tin exports, on the surety of £5,000 sterl. (*Cal. Pat. Rolls 1429-36*, pp. 289-90.) These grants do at least indicate that the Crown was still trying to exact bullion from export receipts.

17 Jacobs, *Fifteenth Century*, p. 255. Of that total debt, the Calais defences accounted for £45,100 or 24 per cent. The annual deficit was then £21,447, after accounting for the wool customs and subsidies of £20,307. For the account presented to Parliament, see *Rot. Parl.*, IV, 434-5. Significantly, the Exchequer receipts had slumped from £168,751 in 1431 to almost half, £85,578, in 1433. See Steel, *Receipt of the Exchequer*, pp. 430-1.

18 On 19 Dec. 1432 the Council had urgently requested the Lord Treasurer to furnish the Calais garrison with £2,666 'for asmuche as the Kyng considereth well the grete povertee and indigence that the saide souldeours long have sufferede and yit standen yn.' (Nicolas, *P.P.C.*, IV, 139). Then on 21 Feb. 1433 the Council appointed a commission to investigate the conditions of the Calais garrison and 'certes dissensiones et discordie inter locumtenentum et alios officiarios nostros ibidem et soldarios eiusdem ville ut informamur sint ex orte ad eo quod bonnum regimen dicto ville et salva custodia eiusdem...' (P.R.O., C76/115, m. 10). For the ensuing April revolt, which Gloucester suppressed with summary executions, see J.H. Ramsay, *Lancaster and York*, I (Oxford, 1892), 449. Nevertheless, the wages were still not paid, and in Parliament a petitioner again asked 'to th'entent for to have restitucion of thair wages.' (*Rot. Parl.*, IV, 473: no. 20). In reply, Parliament requested a loan from Hamo Sutton, the current Staple Mayor, Richard Bokeland, the Calais Treasurer, and other 'marchauntz de le Staple.' (*Rot. Parl.*, IV, 474: no. 22).

19 Only the Namur mint was operating at this time and most of its coinage was struck by 30 May 1433. A.G.R., C. de C., nos. 18.202-3. On Philip's financial problems in this period, see Bonenfant, *Philippe le Bon*, pp. 58-9, and Vaughan, *Philip the Good*, pp. 26-66.

cessive degree of his recent debasements and the consequent inflation had caused a ruinous distrust of his coinage. To worsen his monetary problems, a flood of debased foreign coins and counterfeits was inundating his lands, and Philip tacitly admitted that his mints could no longer compete with these foreign debasements.[20] His only solution for ridding the Lowlands of these coins, reviving his mints, and restoring monetary confidence was a 'strengthening' and deflation of the coinage.[21] This step was also necessary, of course, to protect his own revenues against inflation. That year, moreover, marked the termination of his fifteen-year pledge not to alter the Flemish coinage, so that he was now free to displace the various coinage systems of his Lowlander provinces with a unified coinage. The resulting monetary reform of October 1433 did provide the Burgundian Lowlands with its first common coinage in the *gros vierlander* system, essentially based upon the former Flemish coinage.[22] By this reform Philip had considerably deflated the value of the new coinage: compared to

20 On 25 May 1433, Philip issued the last of this series of decrees to debase the coinage, 'pour obvier aux cours de plusieurs estranges monnoies d'or et d'argent de divers seigneurs d'Alemaigne et autres forgees a Tournay [Charles VII], en forteresses et ailleurs, lesquelles ont eu cours et este de petite valeur et non suffisant, apportees, mises et haulces a plus grant pris que ne valent en nos dits pais; et encore sont les dictz monnaies estrainges journellement empirees, et soubs umbre de ce que les pluisieurs d'icelles sont faictes et forgees a la facon des nostres si pres, que la difference ne s'en peut bonnement congnoistre, si non par les gens qui se meslent de fait de monnoies, elles sont journelement princes et receues en nos dits pais, dont plusieurs fraudes et inconveniens sur le fait de la marchandise se commettent de jour en jour.' Full text in Renier Chalon, *Recherches sur les monnaies des comtes de Hainaut* (Brussels, 1818), 208-11, no. 15. This document provides perhaps the best contemporary description of the economics of debasement; it also describes well the malpractices of Burgundian monetary policies. In the same decree, Duke Philip also promised to strengthen the coinage in the near future and, as a first step, to 'call down' his coins by 25 per cent on 15 Aug. 1433. But there is no evidence that he did in fact take this arbitary measure. (*Ibid.*, pp. 210-11).

21 On the economics of *renforcement*, see chapter 1, pp. 28-9 *supra*. Philip's plans for altering and strengthening the coinage apparently took shape from January 1432. From then until mid-1433, his councillors met with the Four Members of Flanders on the new coinage and in August 1432, he sent his Namur mint officials into Brabant and Holland-Zealand to discuss this coinage. See A.G.R., C. de C., nos. 32,486, fo. 59 r. (Jan. 1432); fo. 61 r. (April), fo. 62 r. (May), fo. 64 r. (July); and no. 32,487, fo. 64 r. (December), fo. 64 vo. (Jan. 1433), fo. 71 r. (August 1433).

22 Full text in Deschamps de Pas, 'Histoire monétaire des comtes de Flandre,' *Revue numismatique*, 2nd ser., VI (1861), 471-2. The ordinance began with the same complaint about debased foreign coins, so that 'en brief temps nul bon or ne aussi blanche monnoye ne seroit trouvee' in his lands. Minting of the new coins commenced at Ghent on 30 Oct. 1433, at Valenciennes on 26 Nov. 1433, at Dordrecht after 23 Jan. 1434, but at Brussels not until 4 Sept. 1434. (Appendix I *infra*). On the reform, see Spufford, *Monetary Problems*, pp. 4-6, 30-1; and H.E. Van Gelder and M. Hoc, *Les monnaies des Pays-Bas bourguignons* (Amsterdam, 1960), pp. 9-11.

his last Namur coinage of May, the new, virtually pure gold coins were 39.2 per cent stronger; the silver, 30.0 per cent stronger. (Compared, however, to the last Flemish coinage of November 1428, the new gold coinage was only 6.1 per cent stronger and the silver, 7.0 per cent stronger).[23] In order to achieve this monetary unification, Philip had to secure the agreement of all his provincial Estates, apparently with difficulty from some of them. They in turn extracted from Philip his promise to maintain the stability of the new coinage for at least twenty years; and since their collective consent was necessary for any changes, they were able to make Philip respect that pledge in full.[24]

The monetary reform, however, presented a problem for the Burgundian mints. Obviously, a strengthening of the coinage, even with the inducement of stable monetary values, would not itself attract as much bullion to the mints as would a debasement. To make the mint price more attractive for merchants, Philip had to reduce his seignorage charges to the barest minimum, under 1 per cent. That proved ineffective and, in November, the duke's mint officials and Flemish civic officials met at Ghent 'to seek remedies for the fact that so little new money had been minted.'[25] Philip's drastic solution was to 'decry' most of his former coins and order them reminted at fixed prices, a measure which provoked a near revolt in Ghent.[26] At the same time he imposed a strict ban on all bullion exports, including for the first time any bullion trans-shipped through his lands by foreign merchants. That export ban Philip harshly enforced – as

---

23 Appendix I, Tables C, E, F. His new gold *Philippus* or *rijder* was worth 4s. *gros*, with a fineness of 23 13/16 carats and a *taille* of 67.5 to the *marc*; the *double gros* (2d.) had a fineness of 6 *deniers argent-le-roy* and a *taille* of 72 to the *marc*. Note from the graph that the new Burgundian mint ratio still 'favoured' gold more than did the Flemish ordinance of June 1418, and also more than the current English mint ratio. For the ordinance prescribing new exchange rates on those foreign coins with legal tender, see A.G.R., C. de C., carton 65: 1 and no. 580, fo. 85 r-89 r.

24 Van Duyse and De Busscher, *Archives de la ville de Gand*, p. 192, no. 552 (18 Jan. 1434). See Spufford, 'Coinage, Taxation, and the Estates General of the Burgundian Netherlands,' pp. 74-5; and *Monetary Problems*, pp. 145-53.

25 A.G.R., C. de C., no. 32,488, fo. 65 vo. (Bruges).

26 See J.J. De Smedt (ed.), 'Kronyk van Jan van Dixmude,' in *Corpus Chronicorum Flandriae*, III (Brussels, 1856), 42-3: '... doe was in Vlaenderen groote beroerte omme de nieuwe munte, ende zonderlinghe in Ghend, omme dat gheordonnert was by s' princen rade ... dat men in dat goud zoude verliesen den daerden penninc, ende hieromme was in Ghend groote murmuracie...' The Hanse *kontor* at Bruges also referred to this 'grote zwaer ordinancie van eener nyer munte,' which Philip proclaimed on 11 November, 'umme dat hiir gheen nye ghelt off tomale cleyne was geslaghen;' the Hanseatic official reported that at the end of two months 'so sal alle [decried] ghelt over billoen gereckent wesen und dat sal men in de wessel brenghen;' and he listed the mint prices for the decried coins. G. Von der Ropp (ed.), *Hanserecesse 1431-1476*, I (Leipzig, 1876), 196-7, no. 317.

far as possible – for many years, to the consternation and anger of English and German merchants.[27] As graph IV shows, the new coinage shortly thereafter did prove successful, so that very large amounts of both gold and silver were minted from 1434 to 1437. The monetary reform apparently also foiled the foreign counterfeiters; assisted by Philip's forceful persuasion, it at least finally halted the competing mint production at Tournay.[28] In the meantime, to ensure the success of his mints, Philip set about to check the Staple's exaction of bullion payments.

Simultaneously with the proclamation of his monetary reform, Philip renewed his attack upon the Calais Ordinances by soliciting active support from his Estates-General. Reviving its proposal of late 1431, he requested, and then demanded general consent to a retaliatory ban on English cloth imports. In early October, his councillors met with delegates from the Flemish and Brabantine towns but Brabantine objections to the ban prevented them from reaching any agreement. Philip then ordered these delegates and those from the Holland-Zealand towns to hold a session of the Estates the next month at Lier (Brabant) and, hopefully, 'to reach a *final* conclusion on the aforesaid matter.'[29] The fact that from then until June 1434 Philip had to convoke no fewer than seven more sessions of the Estates and town conferences demonstrates how strong and determined was the opposition of the Brabantine and Dutch cloth-importing interests.[30]

27 Philip's ban on bullion exports of 10 November offered his officials 20 per cent of all that they seized. Deschamps de Pas, 'Histoire monétaire des comtes de Flandre,' *Revue numismatique*, 2nd. ser., VII (1862), 117. His monetary ordinance of October had already prescribed confiscation and three years' banishment as penalties for exporting bullion, for not taking it directly to the mint, for buying or keeping forbidden coins (*billon*), and for not respecting the legal exchange rates.

28 See notes 20 and 22 *supra*. Charles VII ceased minting his imitation *cromstaerts* at Tournay almost immediately, on 25 Oct. 1433 (See chapter 3, Table IV, *supra*, p. 88). Though Tournay did mint some *patards* of the same weight and fineness as Philip's *double gros*, between Nov. 1433 and June 1434, it did not debase them. On 10 Feb. 1434, Philip extracted from the Tournay *échevins* an agreement to cease minting for six years, in return for his promise to respect their neutrality (A.G.R., Trésor de Flandres I, 2368). The Tournay mint formally closed on 21 Sept. 1435 and did not re-open until 24 June 1440, thereafter minting only French royal coins. See Hoc, *Histoire monétaire de Tournay*, pp. 97-101, 110-3; Spufford, *Monetary Problems*, pp. 93-5.

29 From Philip's letter to the Dutch leaders, in Raimond van Marle, *Le comté de Hollande sous Philippe le Bon* (The Hague, 1908), pp. viii-ix, no. 7; excerpts in Smit, *Bronnen Handel*, I, 1054, no. 1054.

30 From 29 Oct. to 15 Nov. 1433, meetings were held at Lier, Ghent, Antwerp, Malines, and Brussels 'vanden Inghelschen lakene te verdrevine ute ons gheduchts heeren landen.' A.G.R., C. de C., nos. 42,552, fo. 28; 32,488, fo. 64 vo.) Between 14 Jan. and 29 Jan. 1434, the Four Members of Flanders and the duke's officials conferred in preparation for a meeting of the

Meanwhile, in co-operation with the duke, the Flemish drapery towns embarked on diplomatic negotiations abroad. After conferring together in October 1433, the 'Four Members' of Flanders decided to make a final attempt at negotiations with the English and also to approach the Hanseatic merchant colony in Bruges.[31] In early December, a Flemish mission headed by Philip's personal envoy met with the King's Council at Westminster 'to beseech for annulment or some moderation of the ordinances imposed on the wool trade.'[32] The protracted discussions, lasting until March 1434, proved only the futility of such diplomacy and the need for more positive action.

The Flemish negotiations with the Hanseatic League, then the largest dealers in both English and Flemish cloth, were considerably more promising. The Four Members secured the full support of the Hanse *kontor* at Bruges and, in late October, they both sent similar letters to solicit support from the Hanse Diet at Lübeck. They informed the Diet that the Flemish-Hanseatic cloth trade was in severe difficulties, because 'the English at Calais in recent years have made extensive, sharp, strict, and unreasonable ordinance on wool, which they further stiffen from year to year, so that wool can only be obtained at great and heavy cost.'[33] The *kontor* mayor maintained, with some exaggeration, that 'by the costliness of wool more than half the drapery industry has perished.' The Flemish pointed out that the higher wool costs had also harmed the Hanseatic merchants by sharply raising the prices that they had to pay for Flemish cloth. Both then announced − prematurely − the agreement of the duke and the Estates of Flanders, Brabant, Holland-Zealand, and Hainaut to ban the import of all English cloth, 'as a remedy so that the English might be pressured into revoking these unreasonable ordinances and selling wool as they used to do.'

Estates which was held at Ghent from 7 March to 23 March, and then from 6 May to 15 May, with delegates from Flanders, Brabant, Holland, and Zealand. A final and successful session of the Estates (*infra*; pp. 106-7) was held at Bruges in June. (A.G.R., C. de C., nos. 32,488, fo. 67 vo., 69 r. 71 vo., 83 r.; 42,552, fo. 22 vo., 31 r.; and Cuvelier, *Actes*, pp. 12-6).

31 A.G.R., C. de C., no. 32,488, fo. 64 r. (Bruges).

32 A.G.R., C. de C., no. 32,488, fo. 65 r. (Bruges): 'ten parlemente aldaer ghehouden omme te verzoukene dat de ordenancie ghehouden te Calais up de wulle te nieuten ghedaen, of ghemodereirt mochte woorden;' and no. 42,552, fo. 29 r. (Franc de Bruges): 'omme te versoukene dat zekere statute ghemaect van nieux inden Staple te Calays aengaende den uutvoerne vander wulle ende vachten, de welke grotelike prejudisch de ghemeene coopmanscepe, ende specialeke den lande van Vlaenderen, te nieuten ghedaen worde, met vele redenen ... ciii daghen.'

33 Von der Ropp, *Hanserecesse*, I, 133, no. 191 (20 October). The letter of the kontor mayor is in *Ibid.*, I, 135, no. 192 (22 October). He stated virtually the same: 'so hebben de Engelschen langhe tijt herwaert to Callis grote zwaer ordinancien up de Engelsche wulle upgesat und gemaket, und bezwaert de wulle van tyden to tyden also zeere, dat se nymand van daer krygen en mach, daer lakene af te makende ... daerute dat de neringhe van der draperie, daer dit land und ander lande hiir umme gelegen by staen, zeer medde to nichte gheet.'

Finally, the *kontor* mayor argued that, if the proposed ban proved successful, 'we might again purchase more cloth at better prices' and thus that the whole League should co-operate in the ban by temporarily foregoing its commercial privileges in the Low Countries.[34] The League was asked, at the very least, to find alternative routes for shipping English cloth.[35]

Although the often arrogant Hanseatic League might normally have objected to such restrictions on its commerce, its own current conflict with England over the Baltic trade assisted the Burgundian cause. The Prussian Hanse resented English competition in trading directly with Danzig's hinterland; London merchants long resented the Hanse's special tax privileges in England and the lack of reciprocal rights in Baltic ports. Open conflict flared in late 1433 when the Prussians seized English goods at Danzig; in retaliation, the English confiscated Hanse goods and threatened to cancel their privileges.[36] The general Hanseatic hostility towards England undoubtedly explains why the Diet of Elbing, in February 1434, raised no objections to the proposed Burgundian cloth ban and thus to the suspension of the Hanse's right to ship English cloth through the Lowlands.[37] The Anglo-Hanseatic dispute subsequently became so inflamed that on 5 June the League Diet at Lübeck imposed its own ban on the English cloth trade.[38] At that time, Duke Philip had just prorogued a session of the

---

34 *Ibid.*: 'ordinancien up to makende unde vorsenichheit to hebbende, waermedde de Engelschen wedder mochten gedrunghen werden van de vorscreven unredeliken ordinancien to latende und de wulle to verkopende also men van alden tiiden plach to doende ... daerby dat de neringhe van der draperie wedder verbredet worde und dat wy wedderumme de lakene betters kopes mochten kopen.'

35 In 1359, the Hanseatic League had extracted from the Flemish a partial exemption from the ban against English cloth: permission to transship English cloth via Bruges, provided that the cloth remained packed and bound in bales and directly re-exported. (*Supra*, Introduction, p. 7 and note 28). It was this transshipment privilege in particular that the Flemish wished the Hanseatic merchants to forgo: 'dat uwe copliede enigher Inglescher lakenen te doene hebben, zij zullen die woil gecryghen by anderen weghen, dan duer de voirscreven landen die to bringhende.' Von der Ropp, *Hanserecesse*, I, 134, no. 191.

36 Michael Postan, 'Economic and Political Relations of England with the Hanse, 1400-1475,' in Postan and Power, *Studies in English Trade*, pp. 105-16. English cloth merchants had begun their invasion of the Hanse's Baltic preserves in the 1370s, and conflict had been chronic since that time. The *casus belli* of the 1433 conflict was Parliament's attempt to increase the duties on Hanse imports (1431) and the Prussians' retaliation, by trying to evict the English from Danzig.

37 Von der Ropp, *Hanserecesse*, I, 173, no. 268.

38 *Ibid.*, I, 202, no. 321: 'Ok en schal men denne in nyner Henzestad jenige Engelsche laken nich lakene van Engelscher wulle gemaked sliten by vorlust der lakene under by xx marken sulvers [of Lübeck]; unde men schal denne ok scriven in Vlanderen, Holland, Braband, Zeeland ... dat se also daner lakene in de Henzestede nicht en bringen by vorlust der lakene.' (Despite these provisions, this ban does not in fact seem to have affected those cloths made

Estates-General at Bruges, which had made no definite resolution on banning English cloth.[39] But, with the League's apparent closure of England's chief alternative market, he now rushed to force through his long-sought ban. Dutch and Brabantine resistance to his retaliatory policy might be weakened, moreover, if the important German merchants would no longer trade in English cloth at the Brabant Fairs.

On 15 June, Philip's councillors met with the Flemish, Brabantine, and Dutch delegates to obtain their formal consent to the ban.[40] Only the Zealanders, dominated by their shipping towns, obstinately refused to co-operate. Nevertheless, the decree that Philip signed on 19 June 1434, affected all the Burgundian Lowlands and all foreign merchants trading there.[41] The long, detailed text of the decree leaves no doubt about Philip's motives and should end the common argument that this ban — and succeeding ones — was only

from English wool in the Burgundian Lowlands.) To increase the pressure upon England, the Grand Master of the Teutonic Order agreed to expel the English from Prussia; and the Hanse Diet issued an ultimatum to the English: to confirm all Hanse privileges and to make full restitution, or the League would embargo all trade with England. For the ensuing 'Vorrath' negotiations, see Postan, pp. 116-26.

39 Cuvelier, *Actes*, pp. 15-6; Vander Linden, *Itineraires*, p. 121 (7 May - 15 May).

40 A.G.R., C. de C., no. 32,488, fo. 71 vo; Posthumus, *Bronnen Leidsche Textielnijverheid*, I, 130, no. 113; Smit, *Bronnen Handel*, I, 661, no. 1065. (Only the last source makes any reference to the presence of Zealander delegates).

41 Charles Piot (ed.), *Inventaire des chartes de la ville de Léau* (Brussels, 1879), pp. 26-8, no. 8 (complete text): 'dat van nu voertan tot ewelic durende, die voirscr. lakenen ende gaerne gemaict ende gewracht in den ryke van Ingeland syn ende selen worden gebannen uut onsen landen van Brabant, Lymborch, Vlaenderen, Artois, Henegouwe, Hollant, Zeelant, Namen, marcsgrefscap des Heiligen ryx, onse steden ende heerlicheden van Vrieslant ende van Mechelen ende landen van Overmaze, ende allen anderen onsen landen ende heerlicheden van heerweerts over, ende datter meer geen inne gevuert, vercocht, och gedistribueert en selen worden ... noch oic dair mede en trecken of lyden by onsen landen om die tot anderen te vuren.' Thus the ban definitely did affect the Hanseatic privileges. The ban was supposedly issued at the request and advice of Brabant, Flanders, and Holland; no mention was made of the Zealanders. The terms of the ban were as follows: (1) foreign merchants, 'sonder alleen in onsen lande van Vlaenderen, daer die Inghelsche lakenen *van ouden tyden gebannen ende verboden geweest syn,*' were otherwise given forty days to dispose of this cloth; (2) all English cloth confiscated would be burnt; (3) all those contravening the ordinance, beyond suffering confiscation of the cloth, would be fined 16s.8d. gros for each cloth they had imported, and £4.3s.2d. gros for each cloth they had bought or sold - about triple forfeit; (4) every merchant carrying or delivering packages was required to swear that no English cloth was contained in them; and if such cloths were found on them, the merchants would suffer double the fine; (5) to encourage enforcement, Duke Philip offered one-third of the fines to those discovering and apprehending the offenders. Partial texts and précis are given in Smit, *Bronnen Handel*, I, 660-1, no. 1065; Schanz, *Englische Handelspolitik*, II, 657-9, no. 171; Van Duyse and De Busscher, *Archives de la ville de Gand*, p. 196, no. 563.

'protectionist.'[42] The introduction, to be sure, maintains that recently large increases in English cloth imports had damaged and 'seriously diminished' the drapery industries of the Low Countries.[43] Yet the real culprits are clearly identified as the Staplers, who 'have greatly raised their wool prices, and fixed them at excessive levels.' With some exaggeration, the text then maintains that the Staplers 'furthermore will sell wool only for gold and silver bullion and will not accept current coin, so that all the bullion of our lands is being taken to England, leaving our lands hardly any, thereby causing them great damage and injuries.'[44]

The bullionist emphasis of the decree, while evidently the most important consideration, does not make the protectionist issue irrelevant. One cannot dismiss the role of the drapery towns in advocating this ban, since the increased wool costs from the Staple regulations did place them at a serious competitive

---

42 For the protectionist argument, see Henri Pirenne, *Histoire de Belgique*, II (Brussels, 1908), 417-8; Hans Van Werveke, 'Economic Policies of Governments: the Low Countries,' *Cambridge Economic History*, III, 325-6; J.A. Van Houtte, 'La genèse du grand marché international d'Anvers,' *Revue belge de philologie et d'histoire*, XIX (1940), 109-14; H. Van der Wee, *Growth of the Antwerp Market*, II, 45-9. But see also Georg Schanz, *Englische Handelspolitik*, I, 442-3; Power, 'The Wool Trade,' in *Studies in English Trade*, p. 84; N.J.M. Kerling, *Commercial Relations of Holland and Zealand with England*, pp. 80-90; and Thielemans, *Bourgogne et Angleterre*, pp. 60-1, who link this cloth ban with the Staple question, but stress only the protectionist aspect, as a reaction against the increased costs of wool.

43 Piot, *Chartes de Léau, ubi supra*: 'Dat men in den ryke van Ingelant, van sekeren tyden herwaerts, grote menichten van wollen lakenen ende gaerne gemaict heeft ... ende veel meer dan men van ouds geplogen heeft, welke lakenen ende gaerne men gevuert heeft ende noch dagelix vuert bynnen onsen landen van Brabant, Vlaenderen, Hollant, Zeelant, ende anderen onsen landen en heerlicheden voirsc., die selve onse landen, die sonderlinghen gefondeert syn upten neringe van der drapperie, zeer beschiedet ende gehindert geweest hebben ende noch syn, ende die neringe van der drapperie aldaer grotelic vermindert ende te nyete gescepen is te gaen.' Total English cloth exports increased from an annual average of 28,830 pieces in 1415-9 to one of 40,860 pieces in 1430-4; exports by the London Merchants Adventurers, from an annual average of 3,500 cloths in 1415-9 to one of 10,690 cloths in 1430-4. Carus-Wilson, *England's Export Trade*, pp. 92-4.

44 *Ibid.*: 'die coipman ende luyde van den selven coninckricke, die haer wolle plegen te vercoepen ende te setten tot redenlyken prise den onderseten van onsen voirscr. landen binnen corten tyden herweert, hebben die selve ... zeere verhoecht ende geset tot meerdere weerden ende prise; ende dair toe en willen sy die selven wolle onsen onderseten niet vercoepen, ten sy by billoen van goude of van silvere, sonder te willen ontfangen gancbair munte, dair by dat alle 't billoen van onsen voirsc. landen van Brabant, Vlaenderen, Hollant ende anderen getogen wordt in voirsc. rijke van Engelant, ende dieselve onse landen dair af naict gemaict worde, ende noch meer andere grote schade ende inconvenienten om deser saken wille dagelix lyden ende noch meer geschepen weren te lyden; en worde haestelic dair niet in versien, ons ontmoedelic biddende ende versuekende dat ... die selven lakene ende gaerne gemaict ende gewracht in Ingelant gemeenlic te bannen uut allen onsen landen...'

disadvantage in the cloth trade. There is no doubt, moreover, that English cloth shipments to Holland-Zealand and Brabant had substantially increased since the abortive bans of 1428.[45] At the same time, the standard interpretation of Philip's role in issuing the ban — that he merely acceded to the drapers' demand for protection — is quite misleading. One must also recognize the vital importance of his own bullionist concern about the Calais payment laws.[46] It is equally clear that Philip personally supervised most of the diplomatic missions and sessions of the Estates, and that he himself sought the cloth ban as a purely retaliatory measure for forcing the revocation of those laws.

The Burgundian ban did not, however, hurt England enough to achieve this aim. Woollen cloth, to be sure, was by then England's most important export, having recently surpassed wool exports in value;[47] unemployment in the cloth industry and trade would probably have affected a large enough number of persons to embarrass the government.[48] The English cloth trade was certainly vulnerable to a *combined* Burgundian and Hanseatic ban, but not to a Burgundian ban alone. As Table III shows, the Hanse were clearly not adhering

---

45 See note 43 *supra*. Flanders, of course, remained excluded as a market for English cloth. (See the text of the ban in note 41 *supra*, and also the Introduction, pp. 7-8 *supra*). As evidence that the Flemish ban was still in force during this period, the Bailiff of Ecluse's account for Jan. - May 1431 records the confiscation of seven English *kerseys*, 'lesquelz draps ledit bailly calenga et print comme fourfais envers monditseigneur, pour ce que tous draps d'Engleterre sont baniz du pays de Flandres, excepte que les marchans dudit Alemaigne les peuvent amener oudit Flandres en fardeaux et ramener hors sans les y despacquiers ou vendre et non autrement.' (A.G.R., C. de C., no. 13,296, fo. 5 vo.) It is surely significant that Flanders, already fully protected against English cloth, was the province that most vigorously sought the cloth ban.

46 Vociferous Hanse complaints suggest that Philip's stern measures to prevent the export of bullion, including bullion that was transshipped through the Low Countries, were proving effective. In July and again in December, the Hanseatic merchants demanded 'dat de voirsc. sodaene gelt, golt under ander sulver, alse se hir int land bringen, und ok hir int land van erer kopmanschape maken, dat se dat wedder vrii mogen utvoren.' In June 1435, the Flemish replied: 'als van den golde ende zelvere, billoen wesende, buten lande ne mogen voren, hopen de lede, dat de vorsc. sendeboden dat uterlik niet en souden willen begeren, want het waere de *bedervenesse* van den lande van Vlaanderen ende der coepmanschepe int geheele.' That reply was evidently dictated by Philip's councillors. Von der Ropp, *Hanserecesse*, I, 233, 322, 332-3, nos. 357, 397-8.

47 In the years 1430-4, the average annual value of cloth exported was approximately £87,400 sterl.; of wool, £73,630 (including £16,900 in customs). These values are calculated on the basis of £2 a broadcloth exported by denizens and Hansards and £2.5 a cloth by other aliens; for wool, £9 a sack exported by denizens and £9.65 a sack by aliens (including customs). See H.L. Gray, 'English Foreign Trade, 1446-1482,' in *Studies in English Trade*, pp. 9, 12-3; Carus-Wilson, *England's Export Trade*, pp. 92-3.

48 After the 1447 cloth ban, such unemployment did cause protests in Parliament and considerable embarrassment to the government. See chapter 5, pp. 141-2 *infra*.

to their own ban and, in fact, markedly increased their exports of English cloth in 1434 and 1435.[49]

TABLE IV

Exports of English Cloth, 1432-1439

Michaelmas Year	London Denizens	By Total English Denizens	By Total Hansards	By Total Other Aliens	Total English Cloth Exports
1432	13,334	27,095	2,397	9,115	38,607
1433	12,719	26,193	3,674	8,171	38,038
1434	9,890	26,454	5,302	11,214	42,970
1435	8,699	20,585	5,857	12,557	39,000
1436	2,084	10,963	2,368	12,017	25,348
1437	3,449	16,377	12,064	11,418	39,859
1438	8,879	31,480	11,324	14,656	57,460
1439	8,848	26,938	9,406	16,477	52,821

SOURCE: Carus-Wilson and Coleman, *England's Export Trade*; calculated and estimated from tables, pp. 92-94.

In addition to the large German and Baltic markets served by both English and Hanse merchants, England also had outlets for its cloth in France, Gascony, Spain and Portugal, the Mediterranean littoral, Norway and Iceland.[50] Finally, Philip evidently experienced difficulty in enforcing his own cloth ban. Records show that Cologne merchants were still shipping English cloth through the Lowlands and that Zealanders were selling it in Middelburg.[51] The customs accounts, in sum, show little success for the Burgundian cloth ban in its first year: while English *denizen* exports had fallen 22 per cent by Michaelmas 1435, foreign merchants increased their cloth exports, so that the total decline was only 9 per cent. Similarly, as Table I shows, an apparent boycott of wool at Calais during 1434 was also a failure. Despite the harshness of the payment

---

49 See Postan, 'Economic and Political Relations of England and the Hanse,' *Studies in English Trade*, pp. 116-20.

50 *Ibid.*, pp. 138-53; E. Carus-Wilson, 'The Overseas Trade of Bristol in the Fifteenth Century,' and 'The Iceland Venture,' and 'The Origins and Early Development of the Merchant Adventurers' Organization in London,' in *Medieval Merchant Venturers*, pp. 1-182. Italian merchants, exporting from Southampton, monopolized most of the cloth exports to the Mediterranean; Bristol merchants served chiefly Gascony and Iceland; the North-East ports of England, Scandinavia and the Baltic; London, the Low Countries and northern France.

51 Gilliodts-van Severen, *Archives de la ville de Bruges*, V, 223, no. 1017; Höhlbaum, *Hansisches Urkundenbuch*, VII, 48-52, nos. 95-6, 103. Some of these cloths were confiscated by Philip's Rentmeester of the Bewester Schelde.

regulations, the Low Countries could not long forgo English wool.[52] Thus, the chief result of the Staple conflict and cloth ban was to create new tensions between England and Burgundy and further the disintegration of their alliance. The shattering of that alliance shortly after and the ensuing Anglo-Burgundian war wrecked the real havoc on both countries' commercial economies.

The precise date when Duke Philip resolved to desert the alliance is not certain. He had not done so in 1431 by his truce with Charles VII, forced upon him after several defeats in France — defeats he attributed to the English failure to send him the promised funds and troops.[53] When Charles VII broke that truce by invading the duchy of Burgundy and Champagne in early 1433, Philip was again left without any English aid. In vain, he sought English consent to a general truce but even this rebuff and Philip's more precarious military position did not result in a Burgundian withdrawal from the war.[54] Apparently the crucial decision for peace came only in mid-1434. Philip's reaction to the Calais bullion laws and his retaliatory ban of that June indicate what little faith he then had in his English ally. In that same month, the prospects for a favourable separate peace with Charles VII greatly improved when the pro-Burgundian Comte de Richemont replaced Philip's bitter enemy, La Tremöille, as the French king's chief councillor.[55] Some months later, in January 1435, Philip met personally with the Comte de Richemont and French ambassadors at Nevers to negotiate the basic terms of the subsequent peace treaty.[56] After concluding their negotiations on 6 February, Philip and de Richemont invited

---

52 The English were well aware of how dependent the Burgundian Lowlands were on their wool. As the author of the *Libelle of Englysche Polycye* (ed. Warner, p. 6) wrote in 1436:
'Thane, yf Englande wolds hys wolle restrayne
From Flaundres, thys foloweth in certayne,
Flaundres of nede muste wyth us have pease
Or ellis he is destroyde wythoughten lees.'

53 Joseph Stevenson (ed.), *Letters and Papers Illustrative of the Wars of the English in France During the Reign of Henri VI*, II (London, 1864), 196. Philip's letter of 12 Dec. 1431 to Henry VI's Council.

54 Jacob, *Fifteenth Century*, p. 257; Bonenfant, *Philippe le Bon*, p. 57; Vaughan, *Philip the Good*, p. 62-8.

55 The Emperor Sigismund's alliance with Charles VII in May 1434 undoubtedly also encouraged him to seek a separate peace. Arthur, known to the French as the 'Comte de Richemont,' was the brother of Duke John V of Brittany, and brother-in-law of Philip the Good. He had originally served the English, but deserted to Charles VII in 1424, serving him as Constable until his overthrow in 1427. Vaughan, *Philip the Good*, pp. 9, 68-72; Bonenfant, *Philippe le Bon*, p. 57; Perroy, *Hundred Years' War*, pp. 268-70, 273-4, 291-5.

56 J.G. Dickinson, *The Congress of Arras, 1435: a Study in Medieval Diplomacy* (Oxford, 1955), pp. 69-72, 163-5. The two parties agreed that if a general peace was not secured, Philip would ally himself with Charles and in return receive the Somme towns.

English and papal representatives to attend a general Peace conference at Arras later in the summer.

Although the English were apparently unaware of Duke Philip's decision for a separate peace with the French, the King's Council was sufficiently concerned by the Nevers conference to seek reconciliation with the Burgundians. On 13 February, the Council for the first time authorized negotiations on the Staple dispute and granted its ambassadors full power to make any 'moderation or modification' of the Calais ordinances deemed necessary. In the instructions to its ambassadorial mission, the Council officially admitted that the Burgundians had found these laws 'highly prejudicial, excessive, and oppressive' and had 'on many occasions pleaded for the complete repeal or modification of the ordinances to permit an increase in trade.'[57] But the negotiations of this English mission and also of a subsequent mission in July were failures.[58] That mission of July was headed by England's staunchest advocate of the bullionist policy, Henry Cardinal Beaufort, and evidently his proposals for modifying the laws were unacceptable to Duke Philip and his Flemish ambassadors.

Nor were the prospects for a general peace in France any more promising. English ambassadors, again headed by Cardinal Beaufort, did attend the Congress of Arras in August. They stubbornly refused to renounce young Henry VI's claim to the French crown, however, and angrily quit the conference on 1 September.[59] The rest was anti-climax. On 21 September, Duke Philip and King Charles VII signed the Treaty of Arras, rightly described by Miss Dickinson as a 'triumph for Burgundy, a disaster for England, and a humiliation for France.' Philip kept most of his conquests and obtained from Charles the Somme towns, exemption from homage and military obligations – virtual recognition of independence – and promises of aid should the English attack

---

57 P.R.O., C76/117, m. 7; Rymer, *Foedera*, X, 605-6: 'plenam potestatem et mandatum ... de et super modificacione et moderacione renovabili ordinancionum et statutorum ... quae quidem ordinationes Ducis Burgundie et Quator Membrorum Flandriae saepimus informati sumus praejudicium non modicum tendunt et gravamen...' and which 'cum magna instantia creberime supplicantum ut aut ordinationes penitus cassare et adnullare aut ipsorum moderatione et modificatione pro gratiosori mercandisarum.' The ambassadors included Hamo Sutton, the Staple Mayor, and Richard Bokeland, the Calais Treasurer. A Flemish mission under the comte d'Estampes had requested the negotiations. See Nicolas, *P.P.C.*, IV, 298.

58 P.R.O., C76/117, m. 3; Rymer, *Foedera*, X, 619-20.

59 The only terms the English would consider were a truce, recognition of Charles VII's sovereignty over those areas he then controlled, and a marriage alliance. These terms the French summarily rejected. The English delegation to Arras was under the leadership of Archbishop Kemp of York, but Beaufort played the main role. John Duke of Bedford had undoubtedly established the English terms, but at the time of the conference he laying dying at Rouen, expiring on 14 Sept. See Jacob, *Fifteenth Century*, pp. 260-1; Perroy, *Hundred Years' War*, pp. 293-5; Dickinson, *Congress of Arras*, pp. 132-5. Vaughan, *Philip the Good*, pp. 99-100.

'because of this present agreement.'[60] Immediately following the signing of the treaty, Philip sent Henry VI's Council a final Franco-Burgundian peace offer.

The English reaction to this Burgundian desertion, which placed the greater part of northern France under Valois control and made their defeat almost inevitable, was quite predictable. The faction-riven Council quickly united in rebuffing Philip's peace overtures. It publicly berated him as a traitorous villain and so aroused the London mobs that they massacred numerous Flemish merchants.[61] Philip's bitterest enemy on the Council and the chief advocate of war with Burgundy, Humphrey Duke of Gloucester, was then appointed commander of an expeditionary force and sent to Calais to prepare an invasion of Flanders. Under his direction, English pirates in increasing numbers attacked all along the Flemish coast.[62] Shortly after, in December, the Council sent the Holland-Zealand towns letters of 'friendship' in a heavy-handed and unsuccessful attempt to win them away from their Burgundian allegiance.[63] The Dutch turned these letters over to Philip, who, roused to fury and encouraged by his Francophile councillors, responded in February with a virtual declaration of war upon the English. In a letter to the King's Councillors, he harshly accused

---

60 Dickinson, *Congress of Arras*, pp. 160-98; Bonenfant, *Philippe le Bon*, pp. 58-65; Thielemans, *Bourgogne et Angleterre*, pp. 66-72; Vaughan, *Philip the Good*, pp. 100-2. Complete text of the treaty in L. Douet-D'Arcq (ed.), *Chronique d'Enguerran de Monstrelet*, V (Paris, 1861), 151-83. While Philip lost Champagne and Brie, he did retain the counties of Mâconnais, Auxerre, Ponthieu, and Boulogne. The Somme Towns of Saint-Quentin, Amiens, Péronne, Corbie, and St. Riquier were granted to Philip for the protection of Artois against English attacks; but the French Crown retained the right to redeem them for 400,000 *écus* (as Louis XI later did). Charles also promised to punish the murderers of John the Fearless and to make expiations for that crime. (Vaughan's interpretation of these events is much more favourable to Charles, whom he maintains 'duped' Philip, than the other sources cited). Philip also acquired the Somme mints of Amiens and St. Quentin: but he struck only French royal coins in them, their output was not significant, and their ownership disputed with Charles VII. See Spufford, *Monetary Problems*, pp. 77-89.

61 Thielemans, *Bourgogne et Angleterre*, pp. 66-7. See an account of these events in *Chronique de Monstrelet*, V, 190-5. An anonymous political poem of this time refers to the duke as 'thou, Phellippe, founder of new falshede, distourbur of pees, capiteine of cowardice.' Thomas Wright (ed.), *Political Poems and Songs Relating to English History, 1327-1485*, II (London, 1861), 148.

62 Thielemans, pp. 75-6; Bonenfant, *Philippe le Bon*, pp. 64-5; Vaughan, *Philip the Good*, pp. 74-5; *Chronique de Monstrelet*, V, 195-212.

63 *Ibid.*, V, 206-9; and text of the letters in Scott and Gilliodts-van Severen, *Cotton Manuscrit Galba*, pp. 428-9, no. 177. The Council asked for the support of the Dutch towns, 'desirans pour ce de tout nostre cuer icelles amitiez estre continuees ... estimans que quelconque nouvelle confederacion nest a preferer a lancienne.' That the English sent the same letter to Jacqueline of Bavaria, the former countess of Holland-Zeeland, deposed by Philip, must surely have infuriated the Burgundians.

them of inciting piracy attacks and border incursions, directing German princes into a hostile alliance against him, and fomenting a Dutch revolt.[64] The Burgundian war-council then made plans for laying siege to Calais.

The decision to attack Calais proved to be rash, but seemed logical at the time. Seizure of Calais would remove a serious threat to the Flemish southern flank and might cripple the English supply-line to northern France. Philip evidently hoped, moreover, that Burgundian control of the Staple would finally force the English to abolish the hated Calais Ordinances, which Parliament had pointedly re-affirmed the previous October.[65] At an assembly of Flemish town leaders that March in Ghent, Philip's councillors indeed made a strong issue of this grievance in order to enlist their support for the war.[66] Bitterly assailing the Staple's pricing system and bullion requirements, 'which other countries have never made at all,' they maintained that these regulations 'threaten to deprive our lord's lands of all money and livelihood.'[67] Their long harangues were apparently successful in gaining Philip the Flemish funds and troops he re-

---

64 Douet-D'Arcq, *Chronique de Monstrelet*, V, 211-2; Thielemans, *Bourgogne et Angleterre*, pp. 78-9. See also A.G.R., C. de C., no. 32,490, fo. 42 r. for reports of English pirate attacks. On 17 March 1436, Henry VI himself replied, denying all Philip's accusations and proclaiming his desire for peace. Scott and Gilliodts-van Severen, *Cotton Manuscrit Galba*, pp. 431-5, no. 178.

65 *Rot. Parl.*, IV, 490: no. 19; S.R., II, 289, 291 (14 Hen. VI, c. 2 and 5). The purpose of the act was to prevent evasion of the Staple and of the Bullion-Partition regulations.

66 One English account of this time states that the Flemish agreed to support the siege of Calais on condition 'that the townes of Flaundres have the wollys of Calys departid among them' and 'that non Englishman shal be suffred to selle non English cloth at non market withinne the lordshippes of the seid Duyk.' Another report also maintained that the Flemish were 'so glad and fayne that they shulde lay seege to Caleis, and wynne the wulles of the Staple of Caleis.' From G.B., Historical Manuscripts Commission, *Various Collections*, IV, 197-8 and F.W.D. Brie (ed.), *The Brut*, II (London, 1908), 572, respectively. If Duke Philip's object was to force the revocation of the Calais laws, he had a precedent in the fate of Edward III's bullion law of 1340. As previously noted in chapter 1 (pp. 35-6 *supra*), the Flemish refused to comply with the bullion demands once the Staple was placed at Bruges, under their direct control, and so caused Parliament to repeal the law.

67 The speech of Collard de Commines, Sovereign Bailiff of Flanders, has been recorded in F. Morand (ed.), *Chronique de Jean Le Fèvre de St. Remy*, II, 378: 'que la laine d'Angleterre est mise si hault que les marchans n'y peuvent prouffiter, et que, plus estre, il fault payer ung tiers de buillon et baillier deux Phelippes [Burgundian gold coin] pour ung noble. Par lesquelles institucions et ordonnances la monnoie de nostre tres redoubté seigneur seroit en voye de aller à neant et son pays estre sans gaignage.' A similar version is given in Douet-D'Arcq, *Chronique de Monstrelet*, V, 215: 'qu'ilz voulsissent aidier à reconquerre ycelle ville de Calais ... parce que les laines, estain, plont et fromage et aultres marchandises que ceulx de Flandres y achetoient on ne povoit payer de quelque monnoye, tant fust de bon aloy, a leur plaisir. Et leur convenoit baillier or ou argent fondu et affiné, ce que ne fesoient point les aultres pays.' Philip himself attended the Ghent conference. See Vander Linden, *Itinéraires*, p. 152.

quested.[68] But he received no such aid from the Dutch and Brabantine towns, who were not enthusiastic about Philip's proposed war. When Philip issued a complete ban on English trade in May, they opposed it and then ignored it.[69] Only the Flemish participated in the coming campaign and they paid a heavy price.

The July siege of Calais produced the most ignominious defeat of Philip's reign. His fleet and French auxiliaries failed to arrive on time; worse, the badly organized Flemish militias could not defend themselves against English forays from Calais. In both disgust and despair, they mutinied and fled. Gloucester then counter-attacked and laid waste to South-West Flanders; his fleet, at the same time, ravaged the coast unopposed up to Bruges.[70] Though Philip had lost the war in less than a week, he refused to recognize reality and let the hostilities, in the form of piracy, drag on for almost three years.

Philip was not even willing to admit that the war was severely damaging the economy of the Low Countries. He ignored the pleas for peace by his Anglophile councillor, Hugh of Lannoy, whose long memorandum of September 1436 vividly detailed Flanders' desperate plight: the soaring costs of a war which was destroying the very financial resources to pay for it, resentment against extra taxes, the disruption of vital commerce, growing unemployment in the towns, and the imminent danger of general rebellion. He warned especially that if the Flemish were to continue being deprived of their commerce

68 Morand, *Chronique de Jean le Fèvre,* II, 381; A.G.R., C. de C., no. 32,490, fo. 45 r. According to the chronicler Jan van Dixmude, 'die van Ghend consenteerden den hertoghe ... met ziele ende met live, ende met haren goede met den prince te Calays te varende ende te belegghen-ne.' De Smedt, *Corpus Chronicorum Flandriae,* III, 45-6. An English report stated that the Flemish volunteered 60,000 troops, surely an exaggeration. Hist. Man. Commission, *Various Collections,* IV, 198.

69 On 17 May 1436 and again on 4 June and 23 July Philip forbade all trade with England, ordered the confiscation of English goods, and declared that those violating the ban would be considered traitors. Smit, *Bronnen Handel,* II, 672, 675, nos. 1084, 1089; Höhlbaum, *Hansisches Urkundenbuch,* VII, 98, no. 198. On 27 May Burgundian officials were also sent to the Holland-Zealand towns 'dat sij souden doen verkundigen mijns genadichs heren brieven van den Engelsche lakenen' and 'te verbannen uuyt alle die landen van Hollant ende van Zeelant die Engelsche lakenen.' Smit, *Bronnen Handel,* II, 678-9, nos. 1095-6. Dutch and Brabantine opposition to the war have been discussed in Thielemans, *Bourgogne et Angleterre,* pp. 82-6, and G.A. Holmes, 'The Libel of English Policy,' *English Historical Review,* LXXVI (1961), 196-7. (The Dutch had in fact promised 100 ships and 60,000 gold 'ridders' but Philip never received them).

70 See 'On the Siege of Calais,' in Wright, *Political Poems,* II, 151-6; *Chronique de Monstrelet,* V, 238-65; Thielemans, *Bourgogne et Angleterre,* pp. 80-107; Vaughan, *Philip the Good,* pp. 74-83. On 30 July 1436 Henry VI formally declared the 'so-called' duke of Burgundy a traitor and transferred his 'fief' of Flanders to Duke Humphrey of Gloucester. Rymer, *Foedera,* X, 651-3.

and drapery industry, while seeing the Dutch trade with the English, they would undoubtedly attempt to make a separate peace 'without your leave and permission.'[71] The war, in fact, caused the most serious disruption of the wool trade in its entire history, so that only a mere 66 sacks were shipped to Calais in 1436-7.[72] Worse, universally bad harvests in northern Europe, combined with the English blockade, caused grain prices to soar astronomically in 1436-1438.[72a] According to the chronicler Monstrelet, mass unemployment, famine, and its inevitable consequence, the plague, struck the Flemish drapery towns in 1437-8 and provoked insurrections of their citizenry.[73] But in vain did Bruges, Ypres and Ghent beg the duke for an end to the war.[74]

Dutch opposition to Philip's war was equally strong. Directly encouraged by the King's Council, the Holland-Zealand towns continued their English trade and foiled most of Philip's attempts to suppress it.[75] In July 1436, for example, when the duke's officials tried to confiscate English cloth found in Middelburg,

71 Text in Kervyn de Lettenhove (ed.), 'Programme d'un gouvernement constitutionnel en Belgique au quinzième siècle,' *Bulletin de l'Académie Royale des sciences, des lettres, et des beaux-arts de Belgique*, 2nd ser., XIV (1862), 224-50: And also: 'se le pays demeure longuement sans fere marchandise ne draperie, il ne faut doubter que grant inconvient ne s'en ensieve.' (p. 226); 'vous véez comment votre peuple de Flandres s'est esmeu et une partie d'eulx en rebellion et en armes' (p. 225). This memorandum has been discussed at length in Thielemans, *Bourgogne et Angleterre*, pp. 111-2, and Vaughan, *Philip the Good*, pp. 102-7 (with partial translation).

72 See Table I *supra*, p. 95. The Ypres treasurer's account for 1436 records that no stalls were rented in the Wool-Hall 'bij daer gheen wulle was...' A.G.R., C. de C., no. 38,660, fo. 6 ro. The war also shut down the Calais mint almost immediately. P.R.O., (LTR) E 364/72, m. 49. In 1436, the farmer of the Damme-Ecluse toll lamented that the war had so drastically reduced revenues that he had been 'de tous poins destruis et mis à povreté.' Gilliodts-van Severen (ed.), *Cartulaire de l'ancien grand tonlieu de Bruges*, V (Bruges, 1904), 66-7, no. 2673.

72a Van der Wee, *Antwerp Market*, I, 176 (Table I); II, 61-5, 294-5.

73 Douet-d'Arcq, *Chronique de Monstrelet*, V, 321-3: 'ilz n'avoient plus de laines d'Angleterre, par quoy pluseurs ne scavoient en quoy employer leur temps pour gaigner leur povre vie... et par ce estoient plusieurs esmeus et rioteux.' Bruges and Ghent had already revolted in Sept. 1436, following the Calais débâcle. Not until Feb. 1438 was order restored. See Vaughan, *Philip the Good*, pp. 85-92.

74 A.G.R., C. de C., no. 32,491, fo. 91 (Bruges, April 1437: 'vanden traitete vanden bestande van Inghelandt.'); Thielemans, *Bourgogne et Angleterre*, pp. 115-6.

75 Smit, *Bronnen Handel*, II, 667-8, 675-8, 680, nos. 1076, 1090-4, 1097; W.S. Unger (ed.), *Bronnen tot de Geschiedenis van Middelburg*, II (The Hague, 1931), 80, no. 163. Entries for ships from Arnemuiden, Zierikzee, Middelburg, and Dordrecht continue to be found in the English customs accounts. See Holmes, 'Libel of English Policy', pp. 196-7, and Thielemans, *Bourgogne et Angleterre*, pp. 111-7. While the King's Council eagerly promoted Dutch trade, it banned all trade with Flanders. Rymer, *Foedera*, X, 654-5 (8 Sept. 1436), *Cal. Close Rolls 1435-41*, pp. 96-7; Von der Ropp, *Hanserecesse*, II, 17-8, no. 22.

the citizenry murdered them and restored the cloth to its owners.[76] Philip's anger against this Dutch treason mounted. In March 1437, his *stadhouder* convoked an assembly of the Holland-Zealand towns and harshly condemned them for giving the duke virtually no aid in the war, trading with England and carrying English cargoes. The Dutch leaders replied to these charges by pleading poverty from the war-damages to their economy, especially to their cloth industry. They maintained, moreover, that they saw no need to defend their coasts, since they were not enemies of the English.[77]

The Dutch leaders in fact were then most anxious to be entirely free of Philip's war so that they might concentrate upon fighting their Hanseatic competitors in the Baltic trade. Like the English, the Dutch towns had been encroaching more and more upon the Hanse's Baltic trading preserves and, since the 1420s, had fought several naval battles with Lübeck and the Wendish towns. At Flemish insistence, the Dutch towns had reluctantly agreed upon a truce in 1435.[78] By 1438, the Dutch towns were not only chafing under the restrictions imposed by the truce; they also feared that the Wendish Hanse were making military preparations to exclude them permanently from the Baltic. The previous year, the Hanseatic League itself had been forced to terminate its unpopular commercial war with England, because too many of its members had been violating the League embargo for their own private advantage; and early in 1437, the League leaders finally agreed to sign the Vorrath Treaty, which conceded reciprocal rights for English trade in the Baltic.[79] To the Dutch, that treaty portended ill, for they undoubtedly saw the danger that the English might steal a stroke on them in the race for the Baltic and Prussian

---

76 Smit, *Bronnen Handel*, II, 674-5 and n. 2, no. 1089. In August, Philip sent an army to subdue the rebellious town. See Kerling, *Commercial Relations of Holland and Zealand*, p. 76.

77 Van Marle, *Le comté de Hollande sous Philippe le Bon*, pp. x-xiv, no. 9: 'te kennen gegeven hebben den Rade voirsc. die groete armoede die overal in den land is, overmits die groete zware bede die lange gestaen heeft ende vermeeret is ende dat hoire gemejnte neringeloys sitten sonder draperie te hebben, dair sy vele by leven moeten; voirt, dat groote verlies, schade, ende achterdeel dat ze van de water gehat hebben...' The *stadhouder* also scornfully repeated Philip's refusal to permit Middelburg and other Dutch towns to renew their English trade. (For the Dutch requests, see Smit, *Bronnen Handel*, II, 686, no. 1110; Unger, *Bronnen Middelburg*, II, 316-7, no. 224). However, references to English cloth imports into Haarlem and Arnemuiden during 1437-8 are listed in Smit, *Bronnen Handel*, II, 800, no. 1259; *Cal. Pat. Rolls, 1436-41*, pp. 310-1.

78 T.S. Jansma, 'Philippe le Bon et la guerre hollando-wende,' *Revue du Nord*, XLII (1960), 5-9; Daenell, *Die Blütezeit der deutschen Hanse*, I, 221-61, 275-85; F. Ketner, *Handel en Scheepvaart van Amsterdam in de Vijftiende Eeuw* (Leyden, 1946), 16-20.

79 Postan, 'Economic and Political Relations of England and the Hanse,' *Studies in English Trade*, pp. 116-9. Hanseatic exports of English cloth almost tripled after the treaty was signed. Carus-Wilson, *England's Export Trade*, pp. 93-5.

trades. Worse, they realized that the Hanse would now surely be unwilling to permit any further challenges to its Baltic supremacy and would seek to crush the Dutch. Especially ominous to the Dutch was the threat that Lübeck would soon intervene in the rebellion against their staunch ally, King Erik of Denmark, and thereby seize control of the Danish Sund, the only naval entrance to the Baltic – a threat fully realized just a few months later. The Dutch thus had no choice but to act immediately. In April 1438, they unilaterally deserted Philip's war and, acting quite independently of the duke, broke the truce with the Hanse to begin their assaults upon German shipping.[80] Under those circumstances, Philip had no alternative but to permit the Dutch, in May, to begin negotiations with the English on a peace and trade treaty.[81]

The Dutch desertion seriously undermined Philip's attempts, already forlorn, to continue the war. Then, at the very time the Dutch mission left for England, the community of foreign merchants in Bruges presented the duke with an ultimatum to make peace with the English. These merchants, having suffered commercial losses by the war, bluntly warned Philip that they would otherwise quit Flanders and boycott its trade.[82] Following urgent demands for peace from the Flemish and Brabantine towns, Philip finally agreed to negotiations in June.[83] In Henry VI's Council, however, hatred of the 'so-called duke of Burgundy' was so intense that not until November did the peace faction, ironically led by Beaufort, prevail. Even so, the Council would agree to treat only with Philip's wife, the Duchess Isabella. A long series of Anglo-Burgundian treaty conferences began the next month.[84] Fairly quickly, both sides agreed upon a

---

80 Van Marle, *Le comté de Hollande*, pp. xxv-xxxiii, nos. 13-4. The ensuing naval war itself was inconclusive; but ironically King Christopher, Lübeck's protégé, soon decided to adopt his predecessor's anti-Wendish policies and greatly assisted the Dutch in gaining their decisive victory by the Treaty of Copenhagen in 1441, which guaranteed them free and full access to the Baltic trade. See Daenell, I, 292-6, 301-22, 424-7; Ketner, pp. 19-21, 115-20; Jansma, pp. 9-18; and Vaughan, *Philip the Good*, pp. 92-4. On the Flemish opposition to this war, which hurt their trade, see Gilliodts-van Severen, *Archives de Bruges*, V, 199-202.

81 Smit, *Bronnen Handel*, II, 691, 694, nos. 1118, 1125; Nicolas, *P.P.C.*, V, 95. The Dutch delegation was headed by Hughes de Lannoy and Hendrik Utenhove. See Thielemans, *Bourgogne et Angleterre*, pp. 116-20, on the activities of this delegation.

82 Gilliodts-van Severen, *Archives de la ville de Bruges*, V, 190; Scott and Gilliodts-van Severen, *Cotton Manuscrit Galba*, p. 440.

83 A.G.R., C. de C., no. 32,491, fo. 102 r., 105 vo. (Bruges, 26 Mar. and 29 June). For a different view, see Thielemans, *Bourgogne et Angleterre*, pp. 116-8.

84 The duke of Gloucester argued strenuously against any negotiations, but lost out to Cardinal Beaufort - who was the uncle of Duchess Isabella. For a reference to Duke Philip as 'ille notorius proditor inimicus et rebellis noster qui se ducem Burgundiae et comitem Flandriae vulgariter nominat,' see Rymer, *Foedera*, X, 654. On 23 Nov. 1438 the Council appointed

military truce, but negotiations over reparation demands and the commercial disputes proved difficult. Again the English rejected all requests for moderation of the Staple ordinances; they retorted with a demand that Philip remove his prohibition on transhipments of foreign bullion through the Lowlands.[85] But finally, on 29 September 1439, the Duchess Isabella and delegates from Flanders, Brabant, and Malines agreed to sign a peace and commercial treaty with England.[86] Later Anglo-Burgundian conferences extended the duration of this treaty to November 1447.[87]

The English had clearly won the peace, for the Flemish had to pay heavy reparations,[88] and the treaty nowhere refers to the Calais Ordinances and the bullion problems. Duke Philip was also forced to admit the failure of his retaliatory cloth ban and permit the legal resumption of the English cloth trade in its former markets in the Low Countries. Flanders, to be sure, remained barred to the English cloth trade and, on 1 December, Philip re-affirmed the

ambassadors to negotiate with Duchess Isabella; among them were John Rynewell, the Staple Mayor, and Robert Whittington, a former mayor and currently Calais Treasurer. Cardinal Beaufort again led the English delegation. P.R.O., C76/121, m. 17; Rymer, *Foedera*, X, 713-4. The negotiations began in December 1438 at Gravelines, a Flemish coastal town near Calais. For the Anglo-Burgundian negotiations, see Scott and Gilliodts-van Severen, *Cotton Manuscrit Galba*, pp. 440-1, 451-2; Smit, *Bronnen Handel*, II, 710-1, nos. 1142-4; Douet-D'Arcq, *Chronique de Monstrelet*, V, 352-4; Thielemans, *Bourgogne et Angleterre*, pp. 119-30; Bonenfant, *Philippe le Bon*, pp. 67-9; Vaughan, *Philip the Good*, pp. 107-9; and C.T. Allmand, 'The Anglo-French Negotiations, 1439,' *Bulletin of the Institute of Historical Research*, XL (1967), 1-33.

85 Flemish delegation under Pierre Mathys sent to London in March-April 1439, in Scott and Gilliodts-van Severen, *Cotton Manuscrit Galba*, pp. 440-1; A.G.R., C. de C., no. 32,492, fo. 76 r. (Bruges); F. Priem (ed), *Précis analytique des documents des archives de la Flandre-Occidentale à Bruges; comptes du Franc*, 2me série, II (Bruges, 1844), 52-3. The English also demanded reparations for the siège of Calais.

86 Full text of the treaty in Emile Varenbergh, *Histoire des relations diplomatiques entre le comté de Flandre et l'Angleterre au moyen âge* (Brussels, 1874), pp. 579-95, no. IV: 7. Instructions for the execution of the treaty in Rymer, *Foedera*, X, 736-7; *Cal. Close Rolls, 1435-41*, pp. 357-8; Scott and Gilliodts-van Severen, *Cotton Manuscrit Galba*, pp. 445-6, no. 181. For the negotiations between June and September 1439, see Nicolas, *P.P.C.*, V, 335-403; *Cotton Manuscrit Galba*, p. 441; Gilliodts-van Severen, *Archives de la ville de Bruges*, V, 190-2; Thielemans, *Bourgogne et Angleterre*, pp. 127-31.

87 Originally the treaty was to last three years; on 23 Dec. 1439 Henry VI and the Burgundians ratified it to last for eight years. Rymer, *Foedera*, X, 750. The treaty itself went into effect on 23 Nov. 1439.

88 Flanders was required to pay heavy indemnities for the damages inflicted on English subjects between 'the said day of Arras' and the formal declaration of war in 1436. Later, on 15 June 1440, the Four Members agreed to pay the English £6,400 *gros* in gold. Rymer, *Foedera*, X, 791-3; Gilliodts-van Severen, *Estaple de Bruges*, I, 627, no. 768.

century-old Flemish prohibition.[89] But the English had not contested this Flemish ban for years,[90] Philip's decree made no mention of a ban for the rest of the Lowlands, and the Anglo-Burgundian treaty itself specified the restoration of 'free-trade' as it had *customarily* existed.[91] As a result of trade restoration, both wool and cloth exports from England jumped significantly after 1439: wool exports to Calais, from an annual average of 3,240 sacks in 1435-39 to one of 9,760 sacks in 1440-44; total English cloth exports, from an annual average of 42,900 pieces in 1435-39 to one of 56,940 pieces in 1440-44.[92] While wool exports never again approached the pre-1430 averages, English cloth exports during the early 1440s were the largest they had ever been.

The Dutch leaders had meanwhile been negotiating separately with the English and refused to sign a similar commercial treaty until April 1445.[93] Since the Dutch had not considered themselves to have been enemies of the English, they stubbornly resisted the English terms, particularly the reparation claims for alleged piracy. The Dutch also tried to obtain some modification of the Calais Staple regulations but the arguments of two special missions, in 1438 and again in 1441, no more moved the English than had the pleas of Duchess Isabella's

---

89 Gilliodts-van Severen, *Archives de la ville de Bruges*, V, 189-90, no. 1015: 'nous a este expose et remonstre que jasoit ce que danciennete certaines ordonnances et deffenses aient este faictes en nostre dit pays de Flandres que aucuns draps d'Angleterre ne feussent amenez en icellui nostre pays ne y venduz ne distribuez...'

90 See Introduction *supra*, p. 8 and notes 30-1.

91 In June 1438, delegates from Flanders, Brabant, Holland, and Zealand had met at Ghent 'up 't stic van den Engelschen gewande, om dat te verdrijven uuyt den landen voirseit.' (Smit, *Bronnen Handel*, II, 707-8, no. 1141). Evidently the main question was whether or not to maintain the ban in view of the current negotiations of the Dutch mission, sent to London that May. There are no further references to the cloth ban in Holland-Zealand and Brabant after November 1439; and the 1439 treaty, which included Brabant and Malines in its terms, specified that all English merchants might freely import and sell 'toutes manieres de marchandises, tant vivres comme autres, excepte armeures, artilleries ... et autres choses semblables et invasibles;' and that English merchants were to enjoy all rights 'comme ils ont joy en quelque temps depuis cinquante ans enca.' Otherwise, the treaty merely guaranteed the safety and privileges of both parties' merchants, and their protection against losses from brigandage and piracy. Finally, as evidence that the treaty did restore the English cloth trade to its former markets, several documents refer to the legal sale of English cloth in Holland, Zealand, and Brabant after 1439: *Cal. Pat. Rolls, 1436-41*, p. 370; Smit, *Bronnen Handel*, II, 730, 733-4, nos. 1177, 1183.

92 Exports of cloth by non-Hansard aliens, a group including many Dutch merchants, rose from an annual average of 13,425 pieces in 1435-9 to one of 19,230 pieces in 1440-4. Carus-Wilson, *England's Export Trade*, pp. 60-1, 94-6.

93 Smit, *Bronnen Handel*, II, 832-8, nos. 1295-6. On the Dutch negotiations, see Thielemans, *Bourgogne et Angleterre*, pp. 139-45.

ambassadors.[94] Nevertheless, the absence of a formal treaty did not prevent the Dutch merchants from partaking fully in the English cloth trade boom following the Anglo-Burgundian treaty of 1439.

That treaty was signed a full decade after the enactment of the Calais ordinances, a decade of mutual disasters. Despite the severe damages which the bullionist conflict had inflicted upon England's chief export trades, the King's Council still showed no willingness to relax the Staple regulations.[95] Its one and only concession was to restore, somewhat later, Berwick's and Newcastle's licences for exporting the coarse northern wools.[96] Nor was Philip willing to relax his opposition to the Calais ordinances. His lands' current economic distress, to be sure, prevented any further attempts to retaliate against the vital English commerce. But in November 1439 he issued stronger instructions for confiscating all bullion being transported to the Calais Staple.[97] A decade had passed, in sum, with no apparent hope of resolving this destructive conflict.

Despite all the possible explanations and excuses for both English and Burgundian bullionism, the results clearly did not justify maintaining these mone-

---

94 The Dutch mission of May-June 1438 is discussed later in this chapter, pp. 123-4. For the mission of August 1441, see Smit, *Bronnen Handel,* II, 762, no. 1299: 'quod per graciam specialem celsitudo regia provideat, ut libere valeant emere lanas et vellera in stapula, ordinacione stapule non obstante.'

95 In Nov. 1439, Parliament strengthened the Staplers' monopoly powers, this time making evasion of the Staple a felony offence. *Rot. Parl.,* V, 30: no. 54; *S.R.,* II, 311-2 (18 Hen. VI, c. 6).

96 Berwick received a three-year licence on 18 Jan. 1440, later renewed for three more years. (*Cal. Pat. Rolls, 1436-41,* pp. 379-80; Nicolas, *P.P.C.,* V, 227); Newcastle received a two-year licence on 15 July 1441, to ship northern wools to Bruges and Middelburg, and that licence was also renewed for three years (Smit, *Bronnen Handel,* II, 756-7, no. 1224; Nicolas, *P.P.C.,* V, 227). Over the eight year period 1440-8, Berwick and Newcastle officially exported an average of 465 sacks a year, about 6 per cent of the total denizen wool exports. Carus-Wilson, *England's Export Trade,* pp. 60-1.

97 Deschamps de Pas, *Histoire monétaire des comtes de Flandres,* p. xlvi, doc. no. 233 (7 Nov. 1439). Philip's officials proved over-zealous, however, and on 2 Dec. the duke had to order them to inspect merchants only in the towns, instead of stopping and searching them for bullion on every road. (Van Duyse and De Busscher, *Archives de la ville de Gand,* p. 202, no. 579). In the same month on November, Philip levied a tax of one English noble per sack of wool coming from Calais via Gravelines. Mme. Thielemans states convincingly, however, that this Gravelines Toll was levied by the consent of the Flemish Estates to help pay the ransom of the duke of Orléans, and was not originally designed to interfere with the Staple trade. When Philip subsequently tried to raise the tax, the Flemish Estates purchased its abolition for an *aide* of 350,000 gold *saluts.* (*Bourgogne et Angleterre,* pp. 175-6). Philip did abolish the toll on 23 Sept. 1440 (Gilliodts-van Severen, *Estaple de Bruges,* I, 628, no. 771); but he later restored the toll, this time apparently in order to exert pressure on the Staple. See chapter 5 *infra,* pp. 142, 150.

tary policies so tenaciously. In the Burgundian Lowlands, it appears that increasingly hostile opposition to debasement had forced Duke Philip, in 1433, to restore a strong and stable coinage. Possibly, also, the Burgundian officials came to realize during the 1430s that the diminution in tax and excise revenues from trade offset the prior gains from bullion inflows and seignorage profits. In England, unquestionably the representations of many merchants had fully and clearly informed the King's Council that the Calais ordinances were costing it considerably more in lost revenues from the wool trade than could possibly be gained from the bullion exactions. The growing power of that mercantile opposition, domestic and foreign, finally produced the first major setback to the Crown's bullionist policies.

The Crown had first aroused the Commons' ire by granting some leading Staplers priority in selling Staple wools and freedom from the bullion regulations, in return for large loans. In October 1435, a merchant petitioner in the Commons charged that some Staplers 'in destruction of ye gode ordenaunce ... purchasen licences for their singuler availle to shippe Wolles to Caleys and been not bounden neither to kepe the pris, ne to receive no Bullion, ne to make partition ne distribution of thaire moneye.'[98] A royal licence issued in December 1435 proves that the Crown ignored this complaint: it granted the Staple Mayor, Hamo Sutton, and two others these very same privileges to permit their recovery of a £5,333 loan to the Council.[99] Undoubtedly the Crown's

---

98 *Rot. Parl.*, IV, 490: no. 19. Besides complaining about the sale of such licences, the petitioner charged that 'diverses personnes havyng no drede of the Statut aforsaid' were shipping 'notable substance of Wolle and Wollefelles and theym caryen and leden into Flaundres, Holand, Zeland, Brabant, and Normandye' in evasion of the Staple. In reply the Crown and Parliament declared that all staple goods shipped contrary to the statute should be forfeit and later that surety should be placed with the Customers to ensure export to Calais; but the statutes nevertheless did not forbid the sale of licences. *S.R.*, II, 291, 300 (14 Hen. VI, c. 5; 15 Hen. VI, c. 8).

99 P.R.O., C76/118, m. 19 (2 Dec. 1435). Licence to William Estfeld, Hamo Sutton, and Hugh Dyke: 'quod ipsi in vendicione lanarum suarum apud villam Cales ad valorem summo praedicto [octo milium marcarum] per omnibus alius mercatoribus ibidem preferantam ... vendere et summa ad inde provenientes penes se retinere valeant licite et impune absque aliqua restriccione vel particione inde in Stapula Cales inter mercatores eiusdem faciendi, aliquo statuto vel ordinacione in contrarium editer non obstante.' In early 1436, a Council note refers to 'mandant de une lettera majoris Stapule ville Cales de 10,000 li. de prima vendicione lanarum...' F. Palgrave (ed.), *Kalendars and Inventories of the Treasury of His Majesty's Exchequer*, II (London, 1836), 158. In December 1440, the Crown issued a similar licence to Nicholas Bedford for selling wool at the Staple without any 'particione inde stapula Cales inter mercatores eiusdem ... statutes vel ordinacionibus in contrarium factis non obstanter.' P.R.O., C76/123, m. 30. In November 1441, however, the Staple Mayor protested against a licence issued to William Cantelowe for selling wool at Calais 'without departison ayenst th'ordenance of th'estaple' on the grounds that this licence would hinder the Staple leaders'

currently serious financial straits explain its policy of selling licences to exempt creditors from the bullion laws.[100] But this policy was foolish, for the unfair advantages granted to wealthy Stapler creditors soon provoked the lesser merchants into attacking the Calais Ordinances in their entirety.

The wool merchants' assault against the ordinances began in the Commons of 1437. A petitioner charged that their wool sales had been severely hindered both 'by specialle Licences graunted to private persones apart' and also 'by streitnes of an Ordenance as touching receit of Bullion late made amonges other in the saide Staple.' He maintained in particular that their inability to meet the terms of friendly Dutch merchants for purchasing wool, 'because of the Statut aforesaid,' had kept these important buyers away from the Staple. The Crown, however, rejected the petitioner's solution 'for the redyer utteraunce' of wool to Dutch merchants 'to modere the said Ordenaunce of Billion' and to let the Staplers 'liefully receyve alle manere payement, such as partition may be made of, answeryng to the paiement in England.'[101]

own sales of wool and thus prevent them from recovering their loan of £10,000 sterl. to the Crown. The Crown had permitted them to do so by taking four nobles from the subsidy for each sack sold. Nicolas, *P.P.C.*, V, 168.

100 The Crown was still greatly concerned about financing the Calais garrison, particularly because of the Anglo-Burgundian war. In 1436, Parliament had again granted 13s.4d. in customs per wool sack for the defence of Calais. The Crown, 'ad supplicacionem' of the garrison, allocated 10s. per sack from this grant 'circa solucionem et contentacionem soldariorum.' P.R.O., (K.R.) E101/192-2; C76/118, m. 3 (5 Mar. 1436). The following year, 1437, it was reported in Parliament that the garrison leaders 'amonges your self haven communed of the Subsidee of Wolle and Wollefelles, xx s. of every Sacke weght, to be hadde and employed unto the paiement of the wages of the Soudeours of the said Toune.' *Rot. Parl.*, IV, 499: no. 18. See also Nicolas, *P.P.C.*, V, 38. For a series of Stapler loans from May 1435 to July 1437, to be used for the defence of Calais, see *Cal. Pat. Rolls 1429-36*, pp. 466-7; Nicolas, *P.P.C.*, V, 26.

101 *Rot. Parl.*, IV, 508-9: no. 37. He maintained that 'where certeins Merchauntz of Leyden, Amsterdamme and other parties of Holland and Seland ... come thider to have boght a gret part of the said Wolles and Wolfell, offring suffisant contentement, plein agrement, and redy paiement therefore; the pore Merchaunts of this Royalme than beyng there might ner durst not enclyne therto, be cause of the Statut aforesaid.' He also advocated an amendment to the Employment Acts so that if any Dutch merchant who sold his goods in England 'likett to leve his said money here in this Roialme not employed and sette seurtee' could thereby 'bye and employe within covenable tyme the value thereof in Woll and Wolfell beyng at Caleys.' It is not clear, however, that this petitioner really favoured - or rather, dared favour - credit sales, for he also requested confirmation of a previous law forbidding all Englishmen except cloth merchants to sell goods for anything 'but oonly for redy money or Merchandise for Merchandise to be paied and contented in hande.' He also criticized the trade of the Lombards in England, who 'byen notable substance of godes to apprest and to long dayes.' (But perhaps the implication was that English merchants should be given the same privileges).

The following May, the Dutch merchant leaders themselves presented very detailed and impressive arguments to show the King's Council the financial folly of its Staple policies.[102] While they argued in vain, their conference records are important for providing the clearest available analysis of the Staple operations both before and after the implementation of the ordinances. In essence, the Dutch demand was that the Staple restore the 'free commerce' and the 'old customs' of the early 1420s.[103] According to their account, the wool merchants were then 'free to sell their goods high or low, without fixing prices, and each sold his goods as dearly as he could, and each man paid the [wool] merchant as he wished, so long as the other was contented.' But the buyers never had to pay more than £10 down in cash for a wool-sarpler, were permitted to pay that in current coin, and the rest later *'up lange dage.'*[104] They maintained that the currently harsh regulations harmed not only the Dutch buyers but also the smaller Stapler merchants. In particular, they charged that the Staple government had added to the Partition scheme 'special ordinances' that effectively eliminated the lesser merchants' trade: arrangements to distribute partition-receipts in such a way that merchants had to wait three or four years 'to receive the last penny on their goods,' and limitations on the amount of wool to be brought to the Staple and sold in each partition-lot. As a result, 'the wool trade is controlled by only twenty or thirty merchants,' who had fixed and raised prices at will to about one-third higher than before. The Dutch ambassadors then pointed out that the Calais Ordinances had caused wool sales to fall by more than one-half; and in conclusion they sarcastically remarked: 'We think that the King of England must be extremely disturbed to know that merchants no longer respect the Staple ... whereby the King is losing his customs revenues.'[105]

102 This was the Dutch mission sent to London in May 1438, referred to earlier (note 81 *supra*). Led by Philip's chief councillor, Hughes de Lannoy, the delegates were from the drapery towns of Leyden, Delft, and Haarlem.

103 Smit, *Bronnen Handel*, II, 699, no. 1128: 'dat alle comanscippen sullen also vry wesen in den stapel als zij waeren over xiv off xvi jair na ouder custumen, als up die tijt waeren, te betalen mit reden gelde;' and 'te spreken van den belliene ende payemente, dair die voirnoemde coopluyde menichwerff gemoeyt hebben geweest.'

104 *Ibid.*, II, 698, no. 1127: 'alle coopluyden binnen Calays waeren vry hoir goede te vercoepen hoge off lage, sonder hoir goet te setten up enigen prijs, ende elc man gaff sijn goet also duyer als hij mochte, ende men betaelde den coopman tot sijnen wille, so als hij tevreden was; alle wolle ende velle coste men up die tijt den derden of den vierden penninc min dan men nu ter tijt doet; noichtan en plach men niet meer reet te geven up elc scerpelier wollen thien pont [£10 sterl.] ende 't ander up lange dage.'

105 *Ibid.*, II, 697-8, no. 1126: The receipts were partitioned not according to sales but 'dat deylen zij al gemeyne, also wael die gene die niet en vercoept also die gene die vercoept, elc na die groote van der wollen ende vachten die hij in den stapel heefft, sodat die coopman

The mercantile opposition did not manage to thwart the Crown's bullionist policy until 1442, when both domestic and foreign merchants adamantly refused to abide further by the Staple laws. By that time, so many former Staplers were engaged in wool smuggling that Parliament became sufficiently concerned to listen to those merchants hostile to the Staple government. In January, some Commons' members, 'enforced to leve their merchandises of Woll because they may not be rulers of their owen goodes,' succeeded in having at least the Partition Ordinance repealed. The King's Council itself now apparently agreed that the partition system was partly to blame for the serious decline in customs revenue, 'as it apperith sufficiently of record in your Excheqier.'[106] But the petitioners were not so successful in attacking the bullion requirements. Despite their charge that Duke Philip's 'grevous and streite serch uppon Bullion' made the law unworkable,[107] the Crown insisted that merchants continue to exact one third of the price in bullion. The only concession it granted was

die alre eerst vercoept binnen drie of vier jairen den lesten penninc van sijnen goede niet gecrijgen en kan, ende dairom moeten zij hoir goet veel te hogen setten, want sii plagen hoir goet twee warff tsjairs te vercoepen ende hoir gelt dairof te ontfangen.' The amount of wool placed in each partition was limited 'so en mach gheen coopman wolle offe vachten meer te stapel brengen om te vercopen voir die tijt dat die voirnoemde particie geheellic ende al berooft is, dat leste mitten eersten.' Thus, 'hebben xx of xxx coopluyde die comanscip alleen ende setten dat goet den derden of vierden pennick hoger den pleecht te doen;' moreover, the wool stands so long before it is finally sold by this partition scheme that 'wordt sij verderfflic ende rottet ende mottet.' The Dutch estimated that wool sales had fallen from 7,000-8,000 sarplers to only 3,000-4,000 sarplers (see Table I), 'vierbij verliest die coninc sijn costume.' See also chapter 3 *supra*, pp. 84-5 and Power, 'The Wool Trade in the Fifteenth Century,' *Studies in English Trade*, pp. 83-4.

106 *Rot. Parl.*, V, 64: no. 38. That petitioner asked that all wool at the Staple 'be putte to sale by the oweners of the saide Wolles' at prices the Staple would decree and 'as ofte and when somever it shall like to the same merchauntes;' furthermore, that all coin and bullion received should be delivered to the merchant 'owners' of the wool, 'without any partition of the money that shall come of the said Bullion, or eny paiement of the other parties, or the value of the said Wolles and Wollefelles, to be hadde or made.' Parliament ordered the Staplers to reform the laws among themselves 'accordant a le dit petition' before 1 August 1442, and to maintain the reform for seven years; otherwise, the Crown would enforce the petition as it stood. *S.R.*, II, 324-5 (20 Hen. VI, c. 12).

107 *Rot. Parl.*, *ubi supra*. The petitioner maintained that 'the saide streite rule hath caused Merchantz Estraungers to labour unto their Lordes of their partie, to make so grevous and streite serch uppon Bullion commyng unto your Mynt at Caleys, so that men of divers Countries in conveyeng of Bullion hath bene gretely hyndered aswell in theire persones as in theire goodes, so that the seide Mynt is fallen into grete decay.' From the sources cited in Table I (*supra*, p. 95), there is no evidence that Calais' minting revived with the wool sales after 1439 treaty. Such is also the opinion of Spufford, *Monetary Problems*, p. 103. See also *Ibid.*, p. 102, n. 2 for evidence of bullion seizures by Duke Philip's officials on the road to Calais in the years 1440-2.

to delete the requirement for the entire payment in ready money, thus implicitly permitting credit for the remainder of the wool price.[108]

Nevertheless, repeal of the Partition Ordinance itself served to undermine the Crown's bullionist policy, because the new law permitted a re-organization of the Staple government. Shortly after, the lesser wool merchants combined to overthrow the rule of those monopolists who alone had supported the payment laws. Unfortunately for the Crown, moreover, it then desperately needed substantial loans from the new Staple government to stave off impending financial disaster, from the reverses in the French war.[109] Particularly ominous was yet another revolt of the Calais garrison in August, over arrears in wages.[110] The Crown's position was thus very weak when the newly elected Staple Mayor appeared before the Council that October. But the Council was still shocked when he adamantly refused to grant any further loans until the bullion law was fully annulled. Cardinal Beaufort stubbornly rejected this ultimatum, saying that 'the Flemynges have now that thei wolde have' in Parliament's recent concessions. He argued, moreover, that if 'thei coude feel that the Kyng for this his necessitee sholde thus dispense with th' estatut of bringing in of bullion etc. he shulde never hereafter by constreint make hem bringe in any bullion.'[111] The old cardinal failed to realize that he no longer had the power to

---

108 Statute 20 Hen. VI c. 12 required that 'la tierce partie de la price et value pur toutz tielx lains et pealx lanutz a le dit estaple, en apres a vendiers, a le temps de la vende et devant le livera diceux... soit apporte et eu en bullion dargent a le Mynt du Roy a Calays.' (*S.R.*, II, 325). The stipulation for silver bullion may have been a recognition of the fact that the Staplers could not exact payment in gold, for which the English mint-ratio was still unfavourable. (See graph IV). On these petitions, see also Power, 'The Wool Trade in the Fifteenth Century,' pp. 88-9; and Postan, 'Credit in Medieval Trade,' *Econ. Hist. Review*, 1st ser. I (1928), 242; and Schanz, *Englische Handelspolitik*, I, 503-4.

109 In 1441-2, the fighting in Gascony had cost the English vast sums of money. In Oct. 1442 Henry VI complained that 'us nedethe in haste greet and notable sommes of moneye whereof we be not as now purveied, nother can not be, withoute chevissaunce of oure subgettes, or sale, or departyng from us of parcelle of our joialx.' Twice before, in May and February, he had authorized the Exchequer to sell or coin as much of his jewels and plate as was necessary. Stevenson, *Letters and Papers*, I, 431; Nicolas, *P.P.C.*, V, 132, 207. The preceding Nov. 1441, the Stapler leaders had lent the Crown £10,000 'in this the Kynges grete necessitee.' *Ibid.*, V, 163-4.

110 In February the Crown had commissioned several officials to inspect the Calais defences and to investigate the garrison's complaints 'de vadiis et stipendiis suis remanet non solutum.' P.R.O., C76/124, m. 16. But on 26 August the Captain of Calais reported to the Council that 'the souldeours of Caleis maade a restraintte of wolls for that that is due for theire wages.' Nicolas, *P.P.C.*, V, 203-4, 207.

111 Nicolas, *P.P.C.*, V, 216-7 (12 Oct. 1442). The Staple Mayor also demanded that the garrison be paid to guarantee the safety of the wools, and that they be repaid their former loans out of the customs.

influence events and the Staplers' decisions.[112]

The following week the Staple officials bluntly informed the Council that 'thei of their owne auctoritee' had revoked the payment regulations. The Staple mayor explained that, in view of Duke Philip's rigorous searches and confiscations, 'it is impossible, it cannot be done to bringe in the iiide part in bullion.' He then reminded the Council that 'there is nothing whereof monnoie sholde grow for the said necessitees but by shipping of wolles' and threatened an embargo on exports unless the statute was 'dispensed wit.' Henry VI and his councillors had no choice but to accept the Staplers' unilateral action. Yet the king gave his consent 'oonly for this tyme' and begged the Staplers to bring in 'as moche bullyone as ye shall mowe godely get.'[113]

Thus, despite the Burgundian defeat in the 1439 treaty, Duke Philip appeared to have won after all. But Philip's stringent ban on bullion exports was less responsible for this victory than was the inherent vulnerability of the Calais Ordinances themselves, which had so strongly antagonized the majority of the wool merchants. These merchants clearly saw that the payment regulations provoked foreign resistance that prevented them from selling their wool. That their opposition counted the most seems evident if only because Philip failed to unite his subjects in effective retaliation in the 1430s. This Burgundian victory was nevertheless short-lived. Henry VI had never promised complete surrender in the Crown's bullionist policy and Parliament in fact did not repeal the bullion statutes.[114] When the partitionist faction again managed to gain control of the Staple, the Anglo-Burgundian conflict had to be fought once more.

112 Henry Cardinal Beaufort, who had lent the Crown a total of £200,000, lost out in the conflict with the Yorkist faction in the Council and shortly thereafter withdrew from active participation in royal affairs. See Jacob, *Fifteenth Century*, pp. 442, 467.

113 Nicolas, *P.P.C.*, V, 219-22 (18 Oct. 1442). In a letter to the Staplers, the king also wrote: 'The whiche ordinance as we have conceived by you is in manere an impossible thing to do, considered the inhibicions and grete cerches that he hath called hym Duc of Bourgoigne hath ordeined and made as well by land as by water in his landes and lordshippes by cause whereof no bullyon may be broughte through his lordshippes to Calais.' The king agreed that, in view of the 'grete hurte' that would be caused by 'noune shipping and noune sale of wolles,' and in view also of 'the grete charges that daily rennen upon us as for paiment of our souldeours of Caleys,' the Staplers might therefore ship and sell wool at Calais 'without that ye bring therefore in the iiide part in bullion as the said ordenance wolde; and also withowte that ye shall renne to any daunger of the said ordinance.'

114 Both Michael Postan in 'Credit in Medieval Trade,' p. 242, and Eileen Power in 'The Wool Trade in the Fifteenth Century,' p. 89, stated that the Calais Ordinances were inoperative, null and void, after 1442. But nothing in the Council's minutes or in Henry VI's letter, cited in the previous note, suggests any complete and final annulment of the bullion law. The phrase 'only for this tyme of shipping' seems to suggest the contrary; and evidence that the bullion laws were shortly thereafter restored will be found in the next chapter.

CHAPTER FIVE

THE RENEWAL OF THE STAPLE CONFLICT AND THE SECOND BURGUNDIAN CLOTH BAN, 1443-1460

Although the 1442 Parliament had specifically obligated the Crown to terminate the Partition system and to reform the Staple's administration, the Council's subsequent defeat over its bullionist policy made it unwilling to accept the newly elected Staple government. Fragmentary evidence suggests that the Crown succeeded in restoring the former 'Partitionist' faction to power in late 1443 or early 1444, for by that time one of the chief Partitionists, Hamo Sutton, again occupied the office of Staple Mayor. A wealthy wool merchant and long a prominent Crown creditor, Sutton had previously governed the Staple from 1433 to 1436, the very years when the Calais Partition and Bullion Ordinances were in full force.[1]

The first evidence for a renewed Crown-Partitionist alliance may be found in two letters patent which Henry VI issued to Hamo Sutton in February 1444. By the first, King Henry pledged for seven years not to grant any licences for exporting wool independently of the Staple. As security for that pledge, so often

---

1 P.R.O., C76/126, m. 13 (Feb. 1444). See *Rot. Parl.*, IV, 474, and P.R.O., C76/115, m. 7 (24 May 1433) for references to Hamo Sutton as both Staple Mayor and Crown creditor in 1433; P.R.O., C76/117, m. 7 and 3, Rymer, *Foedera*, X, 605-6, 619-20, for his participation as Staple Mayor in the Anglo-Burgundian negotiations on the Staple issues, during February and July 1435; P.R.O., C76/118, m. 19, for a licence of Dec. 1435 by which the Crown granted Sutton, again as Mayor, the right to sell wool at Calais free from the bullion and partition regulations in order to receive repayment of loans to the Council.

broken in the past, the king authorized the Staplers to ship their wool customs-free should any such licences be issued.[2] Obviously the Crown would hardly have made so generous a contract unless the Staplers had provided either substantial loans or renewed support for the bullion regulations. Sutton's support for enforcing the Crown's policies seems implicit in the second letter of 8 February in which King Henry ratified and reconfirmed the Staplers' 'franchises, ordinances, and liberties, as were in force *before this present time.*' The royal grant did not specify, however, the ordinances to be restored, probably to avoid a direct and illegal contravention of the 1442 statute. But, significantly, Henry VI justified a change in regulations by contending that recently wool prices had 'greatly deteriorated and diminished because of defects in the [Staple] government and in ordinances which were supposedly made for the restoration and increase of the said commodities' price.' Furthermore, the king explicitly protected Hamo Sutton and his lieutenants against possible charges of illegality by empowering them to execute and enforce the restored ordinances, 'notwithstanding any other statutes, ordinances, provisions, or any of our grants made to the contrary.'[3]

Subsequent testimony from some Leyden merchants suggest that these restored ordinances again required the Staplers to sell wool at higher fixed prices and for ready cash. These Dutch merchants had, in fact, refrained from buying wool in the vain hope that 'the ordenaunce made at the Staple shulde be bro-

---

2 P.R.O., C76/126, m. 13 (3 Feb. 1444). There are subsequent grants of wool licences on this roll, but they were for wool exports to Calais, granting exemptions from customs duties as a means of providing repayment of loans to the Crown. See for example a licence granted in Jan. 1445 to William Cantelowe for shipping wool to Calais free of customs, up to the sum of a £290 loan to the Crown; but the condition was 'semper quod lano praedicto ad dictam villam nostram Cales venientes sint ibidem sub regimine, ordinacionibus generalium in dicta stapula.' P.R.O., C76/127, m. 9. See the following note 3 for its significance.

3 P.R.O., C76/126, m. 13: 'iamtarde pretium magne commoditatis lanarum et pellium lanutarum tam ad dictam stapulam nostram Cales quam in regno nostro praedictus deterioratum excitit et diminutum et causa pro defectis gubernacione et ordinaciones sit supponitam existit que pro reformaciones et incremento pretii eiusdem commoditates fieri potuissent.' The letter ended by granting 'eisdem maiori, constabularis et societate eiusdem stapule et successoribus suis quod bene licebit eis omnia huiusmodi statuta, ordinaciones et provisiones ponere in execucionem et eis uti occupare et gaudere ad proficium nostrum istine regni et dictus stapule nostrorum aliquibis statutes, ordinacionibus, provisionibus sive actubus factis et nobis pertinentibus sive spectantibus in contrarium factis non obstantis.' Eileen Power's interpretation of what is apparently this same document is a contrary one: that 'this grant, together with the act of 20 Henry VI c. 12 marks the end of the partition ordinance.' ('Wool Trade in the Fifteenth Century,' *Studies in English Trade*, p. 89). Her view does not seem justified by the full text of the letter, especially in view of the special concessions to Hamo Sutton himself, nor by the fact that the statute was enacted two years before this grant.

MONETARY GRAPH V (1443-1459)

*Coinage of pure gold and silver marcs
in the Burgundian Lowlands and England*

BURGUNDIAN MINTS:

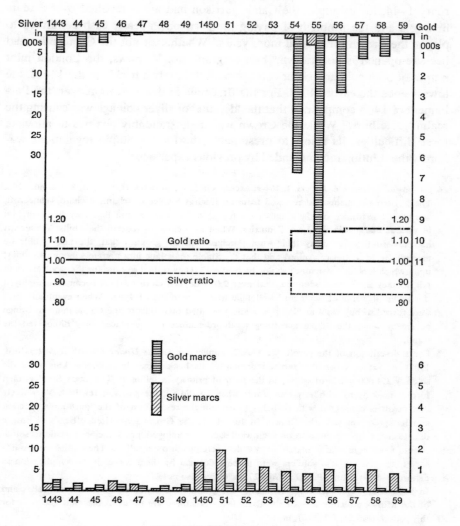

ENGLISH MINTS (London):

SOURCES: See Appendix I, Tables A-D.

kene and that thei shulde withynne short tyme have better chepe wolle.' They were mistaken in believing that the king would rescind the regulations in return for substantial Staple loans, but not in describing the Crown's financial difficulties.[4] The growing fiscal and monetary crisis may indeed explain the Crown's apparent determination to re-impose the payment regulations. Early in February 1444, for example, the Calais garrison had again revolted over arrears in wages and the problem of paying the garrison in ready cash continued to plague the Crown for several more years.[5] Whether or not the Calais mint had been re-opened is not known,[6] but, as graph no. V shows, the London mint output of both gold and silver coinage sank to barely a trickle in the 1440s, the lowest since the early 1400s. For the first time in decades, moreover, the Parliament of 1445 complained that the 'defaute' of silver coinage was causing the realm 'grete hurt.'[7] While the Crown was understandably anxious to alleviate these difficulties, its resort to presumably the former Staple regulations was hardly the solution recommended by previous experience.

4 Stevenson, *Letters and Papers,* I, 464-9; excerpts in Smit, *Bronnen Handel,* II, 831-2, no. 1293. The Leyden merchants had received from an English Stapler merchant, Richard Whitecroft, worthless bills drawn on the Calais mint for £30,000 sterl., a sum that they had lent him in various markets in the Low Countries. When they came to redeem their bills, Whitecroft had advised them to delay their wool purchases on the grounds that 'the king shulde be mariede [to Margaret of Anjou] and that the Staple must lene him a grete somme of money, upon which lene th'ordenaunce shulde be brokene.' They waited so long for the wool prices to fall, as they themselves admitted, that over 2,000 Leyden cloth workers became unemployed 'for lakke of werke of wolle and wollefelle to erne with their lyvyng.' When eventually they were forced to buy wool at high prices and presented their bills to the Calais mint 'to bringe payemente unto the Staple according to th'ordenaunce of the place,' they discovered the fraud.

5 For a description of the revolt, see C.A.C. Sandeman, *Calais Under English Rule* (Oxford, 1908), pp. 25-6. When the garrison demanded its back wages in cash, the king gave the soldiers £4,000 worth of wool and the right of priority in selling it. The angry Staplers then forced the king to withdraw this grant; when he did so, the garrison revolted. Very likely that revolt is connected with or helps to explain the restoration of the 'partitionist' faction and its agreement with the Crown. In July 1445, the Crown authorized officials to ensure that 13s.6d. from the customs on each wool sack be employed 'pro soluciones, vadiores soldariorum nostrorum ville et marchiarum Cales, percipiendi omni tali ...' The 'tallies' or promissory notes given to the soldiers were to be redeemed by them for cash 'ad supplicacionem dictorum soldariorum.' P.R.O., C76/127, m. 6. See also note 10.

6 In September 1445, one Giles Seintlowe was granted the office of Controller of Calais and of the Mint - probably also of the Exchange - but there are no available mint accounts for this period. (P.R.O., C76/127, m. 12).

7 *Rot. Parl.,* VI, 108-9: no. 36: 'which scarcite and wantyng of Half Penyes and Ferthings hath falle be cause that for their grete Weight and their finesse of Allay, thei be daily tried and molte and putte into other use.' From Feb. 1445 to Oct. 1447 the Tower Mint struck lighter half-pence and farthings at 33s. instead of 30s. to the Tower Pound, to help relieve this short-

As in the past, the Crown's manipulation of the Staple provoked opposition from the lesser wool merchants and the Commons. A Commons petition of the 1445 Parliament is particularly enlightening about the current organization of the Staple government. It charged that a faction of wool merchants had fraudulently admitted a number of outsiders into the Staple and used their votes to elect a mayor and two constables who would promote that faction's interests.[8] According to the petitioner, these new members were not engaged in the wool trade and thus, 'as it is thought, would not hede ne tender gretely' the general welfare of the merchants. In order to prevent 'the inconveniens which myght ensue to the said Staple,' he requested that subsequent elections be conducted according to Edward III's Staple charter, so that only those persons having at least ten woolsacks at the Staple be permitted to vote. The king, however, refused to consider the petition.

The Staple government remained unchanged until, three years later, another revolt of the Calais garrison revealed considerable mismanagement and forced the Crown to promise reforms. Apparently, a sharp decline in wool revenues had prevented the Staple officers from paying the Calais garrison's wages;[9] the soldiers then attempted to recover their arrears by seizing the wool-stocks and placing them on sale at high prices. As a result, the Staplers refused to ship more wool to Calais until the Crown had regained control of the Staple and satisfied the mutinous garrison.[10] The king's subsequent report on the garrison's revolt publicly criticized the Staple administration for 'the several disputes and dissensions that have recently arisen' and for 'the harmful and unsound ideas

---

age. (See Craig, *The Mint*, pp. 87-8). As the graph shows, the Burgundian mints also coined very little silver in this period. In France, however, Charles VII, after having maintained a stable coinage since 1436, resumed his debasements in 1445 and reduced the precious metal contents of his gold and silver coins by about 5 per cent between then and 1450. See Lafaurie, *Monnaies des rois de France*, pp. 108-11.

8 *Rot. Parl.*, V, 105: no. 29: 'by multitude of voyces of divers persones made free of the saide Staple and not havyng Goodes nor Merchaundises under the rules of the same Staple, at tymes of such Election ... but procurryed by divers menes to be ther at the said tymes to geve thaire voyces as they were stered unto, which persones of lykelyhed as it is thought would not hede ne tender gretely the wele of the said Merchantz and Staple...'

9 Wool exports to Calais in 1446-7 were only 2,154 sacks, compared to 16,153 sacks in the previous year. Carus-Wilson, *England's Export Trade*, pp. 66-7; Appendix III *infra*.

10 P.R.O., C76/130, m. 11 (9 March 1448); also printed in Georges Daumet, *Calais sous la domination anglaise* (Arras, 1902), pp. 176-9, no. 18: 'Soldarii ... pro vadiis suis sibi ut asserverunt aretio existentes insoluter super mercandisas in dicta stapula existentes districtionesque ac restrictiones multociens fecerunt... sic que mercandise in eadem stapula existentes ad vendicionem et explicasionem rarius et parcius exponuntur...' On 20 Aug. 1448 Henry VI issued a formal pardon to Humphrey Duke of Buckingham, Captain of Calais, for the garrison's confiscation of wool stocks. P.R.O., C76/130, m. 9.

on both the regulations for selling wool and the manner of electing the Staple mayor;' it charged that these conditions had resulted in 'excessive and oppressive costs of Staple goods' and in 'severe damages, injuries, and losses' for the king, the realm, and the wool merchants.[11] The king's explanation for this misrule is, however, not convincing: that the Staple leaders had unwisely delegated their powers during frequent absences to their agents and attorneys, who had 'few goods or none at all at the Staple.' The king was also imprecise in stating what 'remedies for these improprieties' he intended by the appointment of William Earl of Suffolk (a Beaufort adherent) as special governor of the Staple for five years. Suffolk was granted full powers to provide 'good ordinances and sound government,' but he was to do so *only* on the advice of 'the most notable merchants.'[12] A significant indication of royal policy is the fact that the Burgundians, who had already retaliated against the Staple payment regulations, continued their protests long after Suffolk took office as governor.

The first recorded Burgundian reaction to the current Staple regulations is to be found in the negotiations for the Anglo-Dutch trade treaty of April 1445, when Duke Philip's ambassadors unsuccessfully attempted to secure measures for the 'maintenance' (*handhaving*) of the wool trade.[13] Two months later, in June, the Four Members of Flanders formally requested Duke Philip to re-

11 P.R.O., C76/130, m. 11: 'unde nonulle varietates, discordie, ac diverse et insalubres opiniones inter mercatores predictas mote et exorte extiterunt et existunt, tam in ordinacionibus pro exposicione et vendicione lanarum et pellium lanutarum in dicta stapula faciendis, quam in electione majorum eiusdem stapule, qui ibiden propter multitudinem vocum diversarum personarum nullam substanciam bonorum in dicta stapula tempore huiusmodi electionum habencium electi fuerunt ... quarumquidem varietatum, discordiarum, opinionum ac electionum occasione, graves et excessive expense bonorum dicte stapule, dampna quoque, incommoda, inconvenience et alia deperdita non modicum ... evenerunt.' Note that this description of the Staple elections substantiates the charges of the petitioner in the 1445 Parliament. (See note 8 *supra*).

12 P.R.O., C76/130, m. 11: 'pro remediis inconvenienciarum predictarum ac aliorum premissorem ac pro bonis ordinacionibus et salubri gubernacione eorumdem ac mercandisarum suarum in eadem stapula existencium...' The king also granted Suffolk the power to punish all persons 'transgredientes suis ordinacionibus predictus in eadem stapula inobedientes...' In the introduction, the king noted that 'maior et mercatores Stapule praedictus habeant potestatem faciendi et ordinandi inter eos tales ordinaciones pro bone regimine eorundem et mercandisarum suarum,' with apparent references to his charter of February 1444 to Hamo Sutton. That the Staple Mayor's right to make regulations was now to be subordinated to Suffolk's powers is clear in the king's conclusion: 'aliquibus concessionibus maiori et mercatoribus stapule predicte ante hoc tempore factis aut aliquibus aliis statutis, ordinacionibus et provisionibus incontrarium factis non obstantibus.'

13 Smit, *Bronnen Handel*, II, 832, no. 1295. The treaty of 10 April 1445 makes no reference to the wool trade. (*Ibid.*, II, 832-8, no. 1296; Rymer, *Foedera*, XI, 82.) See *supra* chapter 4, pp. 119-20 for the circumstances of this treaty.

impose the ban on English cloth (in Brabant, Holland, Zealand, Hainault, Namur, Artois and Picardy); and it is quite possible that their petition was connected with the Staple issue. In any event, Philip promised only to consider imposing the ban 'by the best and most acceptable means that we, our great-council, the Four Members and the subjects of our other lands having an interest therein shall advise and find to be [both] possible to do and conducive to the public welfare.'[14] For the moment, Philip's councillors chose to pursue discussions with the English, undoubtedly hoping that the strong threat of a renewed cloth ban might facilitate a resolution of the Staple dispute. The best opportunity afforded to them was the following year's negotiations, from March to August 1446, for the renewal of the Anglo-Burgundian commercial treaty. The English ambassadors had been specifically instructed to discuss the Staple ordinances on wool sales,[15] and numerous times during this period they conferred at Calais with the Four Members and Philip's councillors 'on the manner of conducting the Staple trade.'[15a] The Burgundian appeals for reform were, however, again in vain, and the treaty finally signed on 4 August ignored the issue entirely.[15b] At the same time, Philip was required to sign a supplementary treaty that guaranteed English merchants in Antwerp full commercial rights, explicitly specifying the right to import and sell English cloth in that port.[16]

Nevertheless, neither Philip nor the Flemish had forsaken the idea of retaliating against the English cloth trade. In early August, immediately after the treaty had been signed, and again in early September, the Four Members met at Bruges to discuss the treaty negotiations and the Staple problems.[17] By December, they and Philip had apparently decided that the Staple would make no concessions, for that month the duke convoked at Ghent an assembly of the

14 Stadarchief van Gent, n. 591/431 (9 June). The Flemish gave only one reason for requesting the ban: that again English cloth imports had 'tellement y multipliez que le fait de la draperie généralement... est fortement amenry, diminué et en aucuns lieux presques mis au néant.' See note 23 *infra*.

15 Rymer, *Foedera*, XI, 125-7: 'De aussi entendre... de faire Ordonnances sur le Achat et Vendition de Laines, comme autrement.' (16 Mar. 1446).

15a A.G.R., C. de C., 38.670, fo. 8 ro. (9 Apr. 1446, Ypres accounts). See also fo. 7vo., 10ro-vo; and C. de C. 32,498, fo. 39r., 42vo., 43vo. (Bruges).

15b Rymer, *Foedera*, XI, 140-6. The treaty was renewed until 1459. On the negotiations, see also Thielemans, *Bourgogne et Angleterre*, pp. 150-1.

16 Schanz, *Englische Handelspolitik*, II, 162-70, no. 2; 6 August 1446. The English merchants had complained about customs and toll regulations and had threatened 'deserere ac alia loca visitare, nisi... de remedio providere.' English cloth imports were to be taxed at 24d. *gros* a bale. (See also Unger, *Tol van Iersekeroord*, p. 9.) This charter is especially significant as the first record acknowledging the importance of the English cloth trade at Antwerp.

17 A.G.R., C. de C., no. 42,577, fo. 33ro. (11 Aug. 1446, Franc de Bruges); no. 38,670, fo. 10ro-vo. (9 Aug. and 4 Sept., Ypres).

towns of Flanders, Brabant, Holland, and Zealand to discuss implementation of the cloth ban.[18] This time, there was no protracted debate nor strong opposition to Philip's retaliatory policy and shortly after, on 12 January 1447, the duke formally re-issued the prohibition against English cloth.[19]

Since the text of this decree is virtually identical with that of the 1434 ban, it is difficult to tell specifically which issues and grievances this time predominated in the Burgundian decision. If the current Staple payment regulations were as severely bullionist as those of the 1430s, evidence is lacking to *prove* a significant drainage of specie from the Low Countries to Calais. Nevertheless, the Burgundian Lowlands, like England, for some time had been suffering from a scarcity of bullion. The duke's officials had been concerned in particular about the rising market prices for gold and the increasing influx of debased, fraudulent coins from neighbouring principalities in the eastern Netherlands and the Rhineland.[19a] From October 1440, Duke Philip had convoked numerous assemblies of the provincial Estates and the towns to find a solution to these problems of the gold coinage. The Estates, however, held Duke Philip to his promise not to alter the coinage and instead demanded stricter enforcement of the coinage rates prescribed in the 1433 ordinance.[20] Finally, in January 1443, they made one concession in permitting a slight increase in the official

18 A.G.R., C. de C., no. 42,558, fo. 21vo-22ro. (Franc de Bruges): 'up 't fait vanden Inghelschen lakene te verbiedene ute alle ons gheduchts heeren landen;' C. de C., no. 38,670, fo. 12vo. (Ypres). Other records of the Ghent assembly, from 15 Dec. to 31 Dec. 1446, are given in Cuvelier, *Actes*, p. 40; and Smit, *Bronnen Handel*, II, 850, no. 1313. Duke Philip's personal presence there is verified by Vander Linden, *Itinéraires*, p. 246.

19 A.G.R., C. de C., no. 132, fo. 123-6; slightly different version printed in Van Marle, *Le comté de Hollande sous Philippe le Bon*, pp. xcvii-cx, no. 37, but misdated 1446. Excerpts in Smit, *Bronnen Handel*, II, 848-9, no. 1311. To the conditions of the previous ban (1434), Duke Philip added one stricter provision: the offending merchant would suffer not only fines and confiscation of the cloth, but also forfeit of all goods accompanying the cloth. Zealand is once again ommitted from the list of those provinces requesting the cloth ban.

19a See Spufford, *Monetary Problems*, pp. 106-16, for the competitive debasements by first the Rhenish Electoral mints and then by the mints of Utrecht, Liège, Guelders, and various Rhinelander principalities. On 30 Nov. 1441, Philip again issued a decree to enforce the coinage rates 'pour ce que les pièces d'or esoient hauchiéz au prejudice de ladite Monnoie.' Deschamps de Pas, *Histoire monétaire*, p. xivii, doc. no. 240.

20 Meetings of the Brabant Estates from 6 Oct. 1440 and again from 18 Jan. 1440, at Brussels (A.G.R., Trésor de Flandres I, 2371-73a); of the Estates-General at Antwerp, 23-28 Apr. 1441, and at Brussels, 28 Nov.-7 Dec. 1441 (Cuvelier, *Actes*, pp. 31-4); of the towns at Ghent and Brussels during Nov. 1442 (A.G.R., C. de C., no. 32,495, fo. 42ro., 45vo.), and of the Estates-General at Ghent, 15-22 Jan. 1443 (Cuvelier, *Actes*, pp. 35-9). For the meeting of the Brabant Estates in Jan. 1441, the nobles suggested an increased price for the Rhenish florin; but the towns refused, stating that, if the coinage rates were not maintained in the Lowlands, that would be 'la totale destruction dicelluy pays.' (A.G.R., Trésor de Flandres I, 2372).

price of the Burgundian gold *rijder,* from 48d. to 50d. gros.[20a] As graph V suggests, this increase, and the public proclamations on gold rates, did little to assist the Burgundian mints:[20b] only small amounts of gold were coined in the early 1440s, and after October 1445 none at all for almost ten years. Nor were the mints much more successful in coining silver, which also ceased after April 1447.[21]

Under such circumstances, Duke Philip understandably would have reacted harshly to any Staple regulations that were even moderately bullionist – though more for monetary than fiscal reasons. There is little doubt that the Staple's sales regulations, at the very least, had again angered the Burgundians; quite possibly the Staple by that time had also adopted the policy of exacting cash 'fines' in lieu of bullion, a policy that later appeared to be customary.[22] But for the Burgundians, the most serious consequence of the Staple regulations was to render their drapery industries dangerously uncompetitive at the very time when English cloth exports had soared to the highest volume yet attained, about 60,000 pieces a year at the maximum.[22a] Significantly, the average number of drapers' stalls in the Ypres *ghemijnghede halle* had fallen from 215 in 1425-9 to just 90 in 1445-9; the average combined total of drapers', dyers', and *upzetters'* stalls in the two halls, from 372 to 159.[22b] The gravity of the threat posed by this English competition was indeed strongly emphasized in a special passage of the cloth ban decree which Philip appended to the old

---

20a A.G.R., C. de C., no. 32,495, fo. 47 ro., 98 vo., (partially printed in Gilliodts-van Severen, *Archives de Bruges,* V, 384, no. 1066). To take effect on 15 Mar. 1443. The ordinance, however, commanded that the current market rates of 8s.4d. for the English noble and 40d. for the Rhenish *gulden* (florin) be reduced to 8s.0d. and 38d. respectively. On the role of the Estates, see Spufford, *Monetary Problems,* pp. 114-7, 156-7.

20b During June-August 1445 Philip's officials issued warnings against accepting the debased French royal *couronnes* (note 7 *supra*) and again forbade the *postulat guldenen* of Cologne and Utrecht. (A.G.R., C. de C., no. 32,497, fo. 47r., 49r., no. 42,556, fo. 35). Spufford notes that the Rhenish electoral mints were all closed for lack of bullion by 1443 (pp. 55-6, 116). Significantly, the Genoese gold to silver ratio had also risen strongly, from 10.4: 1 in 1438 to 11.35: 1 in 1447. Jacques Heers, *Gênes au XV* siècle* (Paris, 1961), p. 618.

21 A.G.R., Acquits de Lille, no. 937:26. The Ghent mint closed on 5 April 1447; minting in the Burgundian Lowlands was not resumed until Philip debased the gold coinage in Jan. 1454.

22 During the Anglo-Burgundian negotiations of 1467, the Burgundian ambassadors maintained that the Staplers required 'que partie du pris sera billon, et se l'acheteur ne peult finer de billon ilz se recompensent et prendent de l'acheteur au lieu de tel billon, quelque somme environ d'un noble pour sarplier.' Thielemans, *Bourgogne et Angleterre,* p. 471, doc. no. 8.

22a Average annual English cloth exports in total had risen from 42,900 pieces in 1435-9 to 56,950 pieces in 1440-4, an average not again attained until the 1490s. Carus-Wilson, *England's Export Trade,* pp. 94-5.

22b A.G.R., C. de C., nos. 38,650-73. See Table III in chapter 6, *infra,* p. 181.

(1434) text.[23] He subsequently made clear to the English, however, that the remedy sought was a thorough reform of the Staple regulations rather than the permanent exclusion of English cloth from his lands.[24]

Since the previous cloth ban had proven too ineffective to force any concessions from the English, Philip ordered his officials to enforce this second ban much more ruthlessly.[25] To be sure, much evidence again shows that the Dutch mercantile towns were violating the cloth ban, but the records of cloth confiscations also suggest that this time the duke's officials were commendably vigilant.[26] The Zealand towns of Middelburg, Arnemuiden, and Zierikzee suffered the greatest number of police raids and apparently ended their defiance of the ban in late 1449, after Philip had personally punished them for cloth smuggling.[27] Philip was equally determined to deny the English cloth trade its

23 A.G.R., C. de C., no. 132, fo. 125v-6r.: 'die voirsc. laken ende gaerne van Engelant van dage te dage anwassen ende vermeerdenen ende dat men die vuert ende distribueert in veel meerder getale binnen denselven onsen landen dan men te doen plach, tot grooten verliese ende schaede van onsen landen ende ondersaten ende tot achterdeele ende vermindernisse van de neringe van de draperije derselver onsen landen, dat die meeste ende principaelste ondersaten voirsc. hem mede generen ende behelpen ende tot meerdere schade geschepen waeren te commen en worde bij ons dair in niet versien.'

24 Several historians, including Schanz, *Englische Handelspolitik*, I, 443, Pirenne, *Histoire de Belgique*, II, 417-8, Kerling, *Commercial Relations*, p. 77, and Thielemans, *Bourgogne et Angleterre*, pp. 151-7, have stated that this ban was specifically 'protectionist' and intended to exclude English cloths permanently from the Burgundian Lowlands. If that were so, it would be puzzling that Duke Philip should have signed the treaty with the English merchants in Antwerp just five months previously. Subsequent evidence will suggest that the 1447 ban, like the one of 1434, was a retaliatory measure against the Calais Staple ordinances.

25 Piot, *Chartes de Léau*, pp. 28-31, nos. 84-5. Philip's instructions of 16 Jan. 1447 to his officials and to magistrates of the towns of Brabant, Limburg, and the 'Outre-Meuse' on the enforcement of the cloth ban.

26 Suggestions that smuggling was being carried on can be seen in Philip's 'open mandemente… roerende 't verbot van den Engelschen lakenen,' sent to Leyden, Haarlem, Amsterdam, Rotterdam, and ten other Dutch towns in Sept. 1447 (Smit, *Bronnen Handel*, II, 860, no. 1331). Again, in April 1449, Philip ordered the officials of the Geervliet and Iersekeroord Tolls and the Zealand Rentmeesters 'te arresteren alle de Engelssche lakenen, die sij vonden elcx binnen sinen bedrijve.' (*Ibid.*, II, 876, no. 1335). Records of the Geervliet Toll, off Dordrecht, and of the Gorkum Toll of South Holland, between 1448 and 1451, refer several times to the seizures of concealed English cloth on ships bound for Holland and Brabant. (*Ibid.*, II, 926, no. 1503). See also the following note.

27 The strong opposition of the Zealand towns to the cloth ban can be seen from the several meetings which they held on this matter in 1448 (Smit, *Bronnen Handel*, II, 862, no. 1336). Around this time, the duke's officials confiscated a large number of English cloths in Zealand and deposited them for safe-keeping in Vander Goes; the Middelburg authorities then 'met gewapenderhant opgesat ende mit machte van volcke getrocken hebben in onse haverne van der Goes ende aldair opgenomen zeyn zekere menichte van Inghelschen lakenen, die daer ge-

access routes through the Low Countries to the large German markets, particularly through Antwerp, and his ban on transhipping cloth by that port soon produced strong protests from the Hanseatic merchants.[28] But, even though the Flemish tried to secure restoration of the Hanse charter privileges, for fear of suffering the League's commercial retaliation, Philip refused to relent.[29] The registers of the Iersekeroord and Gorkum Tolls attest to Philip's success in preventing English cloth from reaching Antwerp; indeed, the toll farmers' complaints about their 'impoverishment' forced Philip to compensate them for the tax revenues lost through the ban.[30] The major test of the ban's effectiveness, however, was the damage it inflicted on English cloth exports. As the accompanying Table I shows, English cloth exports from 1447 to 1449 fell by almost one half.

arresteirt waren ... ende dieselve lakenen hebben ontslagen ende ute voirsc. arrest geset.' Unger, *Bronnen tot de Geschiedenis van Middelburg*, II, 40-1, no. 32. In November 1449, the Rentmeester of Zealand, acting on behalf of Middelburg, begged Duke Philip to let that town's merchants 'gepriviligiert te sijne te mogen copen, vercopen, ende vertieren sonder eenige boete of verbuerte die Engelsche lakenen, niettegenstaende 't verbot.' Philip curtly rejected their demands and ordered the Rentmeester to prevent any such cloth imports. (Unger, *Bronnen Middelburg*, III, 96, no. 194; Smit, *Bronnen Handel*, II, 888, no. 1376). His suspicions aroused, he ordered his officials to search out and confiscate English cloth in Zealand; in December, he ordered the deputies of Middelburg, Arnemuiden, and Zierikzee to appear before him and account for the English cloth found in their towns. (Smit, *Bronnen Handel*, II, 877-8, no. 1356, and Unger, *Bronnen Middelburg*, II, 336, no. 235). There are no further references to violations of the cloth ban in Zealand; but from May to September 1450, the Middelburg authorities held several meetings with English merchants and other Dutch towns on the cloth trade question. (Smit, *Bronnen Handel*, II, 881, no. 1362; Unger, *Bronnen Middelburg*, II, 338, no. 236).

28 Von der Ropp, *Hanserecesse*, III, 202, no. 299. Letter of the Bruges *kontor* to Cologne, 10 July 1447: 'In Antworper market lest leden openbaerlike is utgheropen ... dat de here hertoghe van Bourgongen na den terminiine daerto ghestelt ghene Engelsche lakene doer ziine jurisdictie und ghebiede to watere noch to lande en zullen ghevoert noch ghebracht werden, de lakene en zullen verboert ziin mytgaders der groten bote ... welk groetlich bejeghent und contrarie is des ghemen copmans van der Duitschen Hanze privilegie und vriiheiden.' The letter states that the only concession that Duke Philip would grant was to permit the Hanse to ship their remaining cloths via Middelburg and Antwerp up to 11 Nov. without penalty. See also Bruno Kuske, *Quellen zur Geschichte des Kölner Handels*, I, 408, no. 1164.

29 Von der Ropp, *Hanserecesse*, III, 298, no. 345:79. The Hanseatic Diet had appealed to the Four Members of Flanders to secure the full restoration of Hanse trading privileges. On 6 April 1448, the Four Members replied that they had asked Duke Philip 'dat de coopmanne de Engelsche lakene in corden mochten dor zyn land, stede, und gebede voren ... dat dat den coopmanne nicht hinderen en solde.' Subsequent Hanse protests about cloth confiscations are recorded for the period August to December 1449, in *Ibid.*, VII, 826-7, no. 518.

30 Smit, *Bronnen Handel*, II, 860-1, no. 1332 (6 Mar. 1448): 'dat de Inghelsche lakenen, die Inghelsche coypluden ende anderen in den mercten ... niet gheweest en hebben.'

TABLE I

English Cloth Exports, 1444-1451

Year	London Denizens' Exports (Merchants Adv.)	Total London Exports	Total Exports from England
1444-45	13,140	22,895	56,912
1445-46	6,847	16,086	48,542
1446-47	8,673	20,947	60,291
1447-48	4,555	12,215	50,197
1448-49	5,157	10,301	31,299
1449-50	6,548	11,598	38,714
1450-51	8,048	17,487	40,224

SOURCE: Calculated or estimated from Carus-Wilson, *England's Export Trade*, pp. 95-96.

While the Burgundian cloth ban may explain the sharp fall in London's exports, directed chiefly towards the Low Countries, it was not entirely responsible for the total decline in England's cloth exports. Beginning in 1449, serious disruptions and dislocations in other markets also damaged the cloth trade and over the next twenty years reduced the volume of exports by about 30 per cent: the renewal of the war in France, which quickly resulted in the loss of Normandy and then of Bordeaux; then, a revival of conflict with the Hanseatic League and also with Denmark, which together injured English trading rights in the Baltic, Scandinavia and Iceland.[31] These other set-backs to the cloth trade, therefore, made the Burgundian ban that much more alarming than the ban of the 1430s had been. Maintaining the welfare of the cloth trade, moreover, was of considerably greater importance this time, because by the 1440s woollen cloth had become even more decisively England's most valuable export and was then providing the largest employment in manufacturing industry as well.[32] Thus the increased threat to the cloth trade aroused Parliament in 1449

31 H.L. Gray, 'English Foreign Trade from 1446 to 1482,' M. Postan, 'Economic and Political Relations of England and the Hanse,' E. Carus-Wilson, 'The Iceland Trade,' and 'The Overseas Trade of Bristol,' in *Studies in English Trade*, pp. 2-3, 25-9, 120-31, 177-82, 210-2.

32 For the years 1440-4, average annual wool exports were 11,080 sacks, at an estimated value of £100,590; average annual cloth exports were 56,945 pieces, at an estimated value of £123,510. In 1448, wool exports were 10,128 sacks, worth approximately £91,545; cloth exports were 50,197 pieces, worth approximately £106,950. These export values are based on

to demand retaliation against the Burgundian Lowlands. Parliament's strong stand enabled the Crown to be more aggressive in dealing with the Burgundians than it had been during the desultory negotiations of the previous year;[33] but, as England's commercial crisis worsened in 1449, the Crown was soon obliged to become more conciliatory and, for the first time, to negotiate earnestly the grievances over the Staple regulations.

Initially, neither the Crown nor the first Parliament of 1449, which met in February, was willing to make any concessions and together they enacted three measures harmful to the economic interests of the Burgundian Lowlands. Their attitude reflects not only the commercial crisis but also the recurrence of financial and monetary difficulties, which made this Parliament the most severely bullionist since those of the 1420s. Enacting a much strengthened version of the old, and apparently unenforced Employment Laws, Parliament required all importing merchants to 'employ' the *full* amount of their sales receipts on English goods and held the royal customers liable for any bullion or coin exported.[34] The worsened slump in both gold and silver minting would certainly explain the grave concern about a supposed drainage of bullion, but so might the realm's fiscal inability to check French aggression against Normandy.[35] In that Parliament, the Council Lords complained that the royal indebtedness was then

H.L. Gray's estimates of £9 a sack (including customs) exported by the Staplers and £9.65 a sack exported by aliens; for cloth, of £2 a broadcloth exported by English and Hansard merchants and £2.5 a broadcloth exported by other aliens (also including customs). These values for wool and cloth exports are at the point of export only; the sales values in European markets and the profits from the export trades cannot be accurately estimated. See Gray, 'English Foreign Trade,' pp. 9, 12-3; Carus-Wilson, *England's Export Trade*, pp. 60-6, 95-6.

33 English and Burgundian delegates conducted negotiations at Calais during February, March, April, June, and November-December 1448, as noted in P.R.O., C76/130; Rymer, *Foedera*, XI, 220-1; Smit, *Bronnen Handel*, II, 862-3, no. 1336; A.G.R., C. de C., no. 32,500, fo. 32vo., 33vo. (Bruges), and no. 42,559, fo. 43vo.: 'Te kennene te ghevene zeker valscheden ende andre ghebreken die men daghelix vint in Inghelsche vulle;' (Franc de Bruges, April 1448). Further references are in Thielemans, *Bourgogne et Angleterre*, p. 156. Subsequent English reports refer to fruitless attempts to secure a revocation of the cloth ban in that year. *Rot. Parl.*, V, 150: no. 20; Nicolas, *P.P.C.*, VI, 69-70.

34 *S.R.*, II, 349-50 (27 Hen. VI, c. 3); *Rot. Parl.*, V, 155: no. 4: 'saunz emporter ovesque eux ascune ore ou argent en coigne, plate, ou masse, hors du dit roialme.' The petitioner had maintained that evasion of the Employment Acts had resulted in 'the grete hurte and em-poverishyng of this Land and anientesyng of the Coigne of the seid Kyng.' The statute required surety to be taken of all foreign merchants selling goods in England.

35 W.I. Haward, 'The Financial Transactions Between the Lancastrian Government and the Merchants of the Staple from 1449 to 1461,' in Power and Postan (eds), *Studies in English Trade in the Fifteenth Century* (London, 1933), pp. 294-5; Jacob, *Fifteenth Century*, pp. 501-502.

'grete and grevous;'[36] the Crown, moreover, had already beseeched the Calais garrison to be patient once more in awaiting its wages and had then appealed to the Staplers for financial assistance.[37] The Stapler leaders agreed to provide a series of large loans, but only on condition that their monopoly privileges be strictly enforced. Parliament, in its second major statute of that session, complied by cancelling almost all wool-export licences, revoking the right of Berwick and Newcastle to ship wool directly to the Lowlands, increasing the penalties on smuggling, and, for the first time, granting the Staplers the power to sue illegal wool shippers.[38] Finally, the statute restored the Staple government's authority to 'do execution of all maner things and matiers whereof the knowledge to theyme longeth or apperteynth,' presumably referring to those powers reserved the previous year to Suffolk as Governor of the Staple.[39] Although the king later maintained that this article of the statute was supposedly intended to permit a 'reform' of the Staple, there is no evidence that either the Crown or the Staple mayor then wished to relax the payment regulations.

36 *Rot. Parl.*, V, 183. The royal debt then stood at £372,00. That Parliament voted the king large subsidies and more taxes, but the Commons had become restive about the financial burdens.

37 Sandeman, *Calais Under English Rule*, p. 25; see Haward, 'Financial Transactions,' pp. 293-301 for a discussion of Stapler loans to the Crown.

38 *S.R.*, II, 347-9 (27 Hen. VI, c. 2); *Rot. Parl.*, V, 149: no. 19. The statute excepted from the ban on licences those for exporting wool to the Mediterranean, which had never contravened the Staplers' privileges, and those recently granted to the Queen, the Duke of Suffolk, and five other persons. Anyone convicted of illegally shipping wools would suffer forfeit of all his moveable goods and chattels to the Staple; the Staplers were also given the right to seize wools shipped on illegal licences. The loss of Berwick's and Newcastle's privileges to export the cheap northern wools directly to the Low Countries is confirmed by Council minutes in Nicolas, *P.P.C.*, VI, 117. The customs accounts in Carus-Wilson, *England's Export Trade*, p. 61 show no wool exports from Berwick and Newcastle between 1449 and 1451. The Staplers' desire to have these two ports' licences cancelled may be seen in their complaint about the fraudulent use of licences 'in shipping more nombre and weight and coloring by new feyned names, as Morlings and Shorlings.' (Lamb's wool and wool sheared from dead sheep, considered to have been inferior.)

39 *Rot. Parl., ubi supra.* In requesting this statute, the Stapler petitioner maintained that the wool customs revenues had declined from £68,000 in the reign of Edward III to only £12,000 because of the excessive issue and misuse of licences and the 'diverse restreintes of merchandise in Calais, aswell by werres, as by Soudeours for thaire wages, and many other causes wherein the Merchants of the saide Staple have not ben cherished, ner of power to rejoys thaire Libertes and Fraunchises of olde tyme used and accustumed,' so that the Staplers were 'gretely amennyshed bothe in nombre and goodes.' There are no records of Suffolk's activities as Staple Governor from the time of his appointment in March 1448 to his murder in April 1450.

The decision of this Parliament of 1449 which most seriously concerned the Burgundians, however, was its statute for imposing retaliatory measures against Duke Philip's cloth ban. A petitioner informed the Commons that negotiations for removal of this ban, 'streitly kept in the parties of Brabant, Holland, and Zealand,' had proved fruitless, and maintained, furthermore, that this ban was causing England 'right intollerable hurt' and much unemployment, both to the drapery artisans and the merchants.[40] Undoubtedly the Crown was also concerned about the falling customs revenues. Parliament therefore authorized the following ultimatum: that unless the duke of Burgundy provided 'due contynuell reformation' by the next Michaelmas, to permit the free importation and sale of English cloth in Holland, Zealand and Brabant, then no merchandise of any kind from the Burgundian territories was to be imported, on pain of forfeiture.[41]

Shortly after, on 17 March, King Henry sent two ambassadors to Philip's wife, the Duchess Isabella, with instructions to protest vigorously against the cloth ban as a violation of the standing treaties. They were to warn the Burgundians that a ban on cloth might very well lead to prohibitions against other goods and 'so to alle, and by that means alle marchandise ceese.' That threat was to be made explicitly clear by presenting the details of Parliament's recent ultimatum. King Henry realized, however, that the Burgundians were unlikely to surrender without some concessions. He thus advised the ambassadors to speak 'as colourably as they can' about the selling of Staple wools and to state that 'thay doubte not but that the King wol on his behalf so ordeine that it shal be to the plesir of the saide Duchesse and profite to hir people.' If necessary, the ambassadors were to arrange further negotiations between the Staplers, the 'Four Members' of Flanders, and Burgundian councillors.[42] But no such nego-

---

40 *Rot. Parl.*, V, 150: no. 20. He stated that the king 'hath often herebifore this tyme do write his letters requisitoire and sende his messages for due reformation to have be hadde in this behalve, whereof as yet no due redresse is hadde, unto the right intollerable hurt of alle the Commenes of this Reame, be cause that many Clothmakers, men Wevers, Fullers, Diers, and women Kembers, Carders, and Spynners, and other Biers and Sellers therof ... such of theym as can not do noon other occupations, become as ydell pepull, whiche provoketh them to synne and myschevous lyvyng.' Various meetings of English and Burgundian delegations were held at Calais during 1448, with the Staple problem as the one issue discussed. A.G.R., C. de C., no. 42,559, fo. 43vo. (Franc de Bruges); Smit, *Bronnen Handel*, II, 862-3, no. 1336.

41 *S.R.*, II, 345-6 (27 Hen. VI, c. 1). No demand was made to permit the sale of English cloth in Flanders. This statute was to continue in force until the next Parliament.

42 Nicolas, *P.P.C.*, VI, 69-73; Scott and Gilliodts-van Severen, *Cotton Manuscrit Galba*, pp. 384-387 (but misdated as 1418). General commission to ambassadors William Pirton and Edward Grimston in Rymer., *Foedera*, XI, 233-4. Maintaining that 'he mervailleth that shold sture or be the causes or means of such ordenance and prohibicions,' Henry VI stated that 'the saide

tiations took place, apparently because the English were not yet ready to offer any acceptable terms for resolving the Staple dispute.[43]

During the months that followed the king's mission to Isabella, Anglo-Burgundian relations continued to deteriorate. In May, Philip arbitrarily levied a toll at Gravelines on Staple wools, perhaps to force more reasonable terms from the English. This Gravelines Toll, a discriminatory tax of 5 per cent placed only on those wools coming from Calais, angered not only the English but also his own subjects, who finally submitted under great duress.[44] In England, meanwhile, the growing strain of the current grievances can be seen in the spread of rumours about the 'evylle dysposicion and malicious purpos of the Duc of Bourgoigne ... towardys oure towne of Calais.' Passions became so aroused that Henry VI had to place under royal protection the Dutch and Flemish merchants in London, who had 'ben troubled, spoylede, and undewly vexede and cruelly entretede dayly.'[45] That violence in part reflected the Londoners' growing hostility towards all foreign merchants, a climate of xenophobia which members of the King's Council were then exploiting for their political advantage.

ordenance is agenst the custume long tyme observed, for it cannot be remembred, but at alle tymes it hath been sen used English cloth to resorte and have his uttrance in Hollande, Zelland and other places where it is now forboden;' and, furthermore, 'that for the putting doune and to set aside the said ordinance, the king hath many tymes and ofte writen to the saide Duchess...' On the Staple question, the king advised the ambassadors to tell the Duchess that 'if she wolde putte therto hir hande, it might be so purveyed by meanes that by the said uttrance [of wools] great good sholde mowe growe not oonly to the marchantes that uttre their wolle, but also to the beyers therof, the which in greet part be hir subgettes.'

43 See Thielemans, *Bourgogne et Angleterre*, pp. 155-6, and note 251 for references to Anglo-Flemish negotiations during 1448 and 1449. There seems to be no evidence of any Anglo-Flemish negotiations before Henry VI sent a second mission to Duchess Isabella in late July.

44 Smit, *Bronnen Handel*, II, 865, no. 1340 (16 May 1449). The toll was three gold saluts per sarpler of wool, 'een twintichsten' of the price. Philip ordered his officials to stop all ships at Gravelines, near Calais, to collect the tax. For the previous levy of the Gravelines toll, in 1439-40, to raise funds for the ransom of the duke of Orléans, see chapter 4 *supra*, p. 120 and note 97. There is no record specifically of Flemish protests against the resumption of this toll, but several of strong Dutch protests. Leyden merchants refused to pay the toll until February 1451; the town then agreed to pay £500 *gros*; and the Staplers themselves lent Leyden £300 of this amount. Posthumus, *Bronnen Leidsche Textielnijverheid*, I, 275-6, nos. 237-8. See also Schanz, *Englische Handelspolitik*, I, 444. Mme. Thielemans, in *Bourgogne et Angleterre*, pp. 177-8, argues that this toll was imposed purely for revenue purposes and was not designed to hurt the Staple trade. Her argument seems sound for the toll's original imposition in 1440, but not so convincing for its resumption. Certainly the English considered the Gravelines toll to be a retaliatory and discriminatory tax. See *Rot. Parl.*, V, 277: no. 6 (1454) and pp. 150-1 *infra* in this chapter.

45 Nicolas, *P.P.C.*, VI, 74 (Council order of 11 June, 1449).

At that very time, the royal Councillors' anti-foreign measures had provoked another conflict with the Hanseatic League that helped to strengthen the Burgundian position. On 23 May, English privateers off the Isle of Wight captured the Hanseatic 'Bay Fleet' of some 110 ships bound for the salt flats of Bourgneuf; subsequently, despite angry threats from the Hanse, the English government refused to release the German merchandise. The League rightly blamed the King's Council for this outrage, since the pirates had close Council connections and their ships were part of a privateering fleet which the Crown maintained under the guise of the 'Keeping of the Seas Act' (1442). As Prof. Postan has shown, the Council's privateering policy produced a decisive turning point in Anglo-Hanseatic relations: it converted the previously neutral Lübeck, the leader of the Bay Fleets and the Hanse town most vulnerable to English piracy, into an implacable enemy that was more powerful and dangerous than Danzig had been in the 1430s.[46] Ultimately Lübeck and its Wendish League exacted their revenge by excluding English merchants from the Baltic trade. But the more immediate significance of the Bay Fleet capture was the opportunity it afforded Duke Philip to exploit the Hanse's inflamed hostility towards England — precisely as he had done during the earlier conflict of 1434.

Thus, on 23 July 1449, Philip sent an ambassador to the Hanseatic Diet at Bremen to request a general Hanse ban on English cloth. Lübeck, not surprisingly, strongly favoured the proposal and wished to make it a general ban on all English trade. The Prussian League and the Teutonic Order, however, refused to endorse any hostile measures against the English because they considered the trade in English cloth too valuable to sacrifice.[47] Other Hanse towns, moreover, were clearly irritated by the Burgundian ban as a serious infringement on their shipping rights in the Lowlands. Philip's quest seemed hopeless but at least Lübeck had begun to take retaliatory measures. Subsequently, Lübeck succeeded in closing the Danish Sund to English shipping and prohibited English cloth imports into the Baltic.[48]

---

46 See Michael Postan, 'Economic and Political Relations of England and the Hanse,' *Studies in English Trade,* pp. 122-8. Most of the Hanse towns, including Danzig and the Prussian members, had recovered their losses by confiscating English goods in their ports; but Lübeck, who had suffered the greatest loss, had few English merchants in its port and so few goods to confiscate. The Bay Fleet had also included some Dutch and Flemish ships, but these were released in June, after Duke Philip had ordered the confiscation of English goods in the Low Countries. See Thielemans, *Bourgogne et Angleterre,* pp. 154-5.

47 Smit, *Bronnen Handel,* II, 875-6, no. 1335: 'begeerde dat sij die Engelssche lakenen ende gairne in hoiren lande ende bewijnde wouden doen verbieden ende dairuut bannen.' The Diet's discussions are in Vonder Ropp, *Hanserecesse,* III, 412, no. 546:7.

48 Postan, pp. 130-2. The ban on English cloth was imposed in 1451, almost too late for Philip's purposes. Again, Cologne and the Prussian towns evaded this ban.

This Burgundian mission to the Bremen Diet apparently alarmed the English Crown, for on 28 July Henry VI sent more ambassadors to Duchess Isabella and this time included among them the Staple Mayor, Robert White. While the king's private memorandum for the negotiations repeated the threat of retaliation against the Burgundian cloth ban, the king now seemed to realize that a mere repetition of Parliament's ultimatum was not very convincing — particularly since England could ill afford to disrupt her trade with both the Hanse and the Burgundian Lowlands at the same time.[49] King Henry was thus prepared to make some more definite concessions and specifically instructed the ambassadors, in the formal letter-patent, to negotiate a solution to the dispute over the Staple regulations on wool sales and payments.[50] The private memorandum itself makes the enlightening admission that a serious decline in wool sales and customs revenue were 'understande causid by the direccion and reules not most profitable usid in the Staple at Calais.' Since the Staple mayor had obtained from Parliament 'certain articles for the wele and ease of the saide Estaple,' the ambassadors were first to summon the Staple officials and remind them of these provisions and of the promises made on behalf of the Staple Fellowship. Specifically, these promises were that 'the saide Maire and Felishippe shulde be redy to entende to the puttyng aside of such things as lette the said utteraunce [of wool] and to ordeigne and stablisshe good Reules for better utteraunce to be hadde, as it appereth by the letter sent fro the saide Felishippe to thaire Maire.' Those instructions suggest that the Staple Mayor

49 Memorandum to John Dudley and Thomas Kent, 30 July 1449, in Nicolas, *P.P.C.*, VI, 76-85; Scott and Gilliodts-van Severen, *Cotton Manuscrit Galba*, pp. 451-9, no. 185 (misdated 27 March). After repeating Parliament's provisions for retaliation against Burgundian goods, the king instructed the ambassadors to 'desire and requier the saide duchesse that the saide ordenaunce be annulled and revoked in such wise, as the king have no cause to procede to th'execucion of the saide decree.' According to this memorandum, the duchess had informed the king that the cloth ban 'ordenaunce was made by th'avis, wille, or aggrement of the marchauntes of the Staple at Calais.' The king ordered the ambassadors to refute this contention and to state that 'fully the Marchauntes of the Staple had never knowlech therof for thei had in examinacion therin plainly denied [it].' The Staplers might reasonably have been suspect, since their wool sales might have increased had the ban on English cloth imports successfully aided the cloth industries of the Low Countries. Possibly, therefore, the Burgundians had concocted this plausible story to arouse the king's ire against the Staplers and so to undermine their position. The king's misunderstanding of the duchess is perhaps a more likely explanation: she may have maintained that the Staplers, by their 'avis, wille, or aggrement' on the Staple regulations, were the ones really responsible for provoking the cloth ban, as the rest of the memorandum suggests.

50 P.R.O., C76/131, m. 6 (28 July 1449); Rymer, *Foedera*, XI, 233: 'Et specialiter de modo venendi et emendi lanes et pelles lanutas quae ad stapulam nostram praedictam adductae sunt, et in futurum adducentur, ac etiam de et super securitate solutionis per ipsos lanas et pelles lanutas ementes fienda.'

was alone to blame for the ills of the wool trade, but the Crown was hardly likely to confess its own responsibility for the conduct of the Staple.

As soon as the Staplers had revised the regulations, the ambassadors were instructed to arrange negotiations at Calais between the Staple officials and the Four Members of Flanders and ensure that the Staplers 'honestly and frealy commune' with the Flemish and make them 'such offres as thaim shall think expedient.'[51] The ambassadors were empowered to conclude a treaty on the wool trade, based on these negotiations, but no such treaty was signed and for the time being the Staple regulations remained unchanged.[52]

The Burgundian cloth ban also remained fully in force, despite Parliament's stern ultimatum demanding its revocation by Michaelmas. Philip had little to fear by ignoring the deadline. When Parliament next met in November, it quickly retaliated — by enacting a second ultimatum. This time, the Burgundians were given seven months, until 24 June 1450, to lift the cloth ban or from that date suffer a seven year embargo against their goods.[53] Shortly before June, Parliament extended this deadline to the coming Michaelmas.[54] After Philip had again failed to comply, the English Crown still took no action against Burgundian imports. The London Merchants Adventurers, however, had already retaliated on their own initiative. In October 1449, when the futility of their own protests and Parliament's threats had become readily apparent, they boycotted the Antwerp fairs and designated 'another place' to conduct their continental trade.[55] Since the cloth-selling Adventurers were also important purchasers at these fairs for the London Mercers, the chief importers of merchandise from the Low Countries,[56] their boycott was undoubtedly injurious

---

51 Nicolas, *P.P.C., ubi supra.*
52 See Thielemans, *Bourgogne et Angleterre,* p. 156, n. 251 for references to Anglo-Flemish negotiations at Calais during August 1449 (Also: A.G.R., C. de C., no. 42,560). The presence of Dutch delegates at Calais is also attested to by Smit, *Bronnen Handel,* II, 863, no. 1337. None of these sources, however, states the results of the negotiations. While the Staple regulations and the cloth ban issues were clearly the major ones discussed, the Burgundians also demanded reparations for the Bay Fleet seizure; the English, on the other hand, demanded payment of the Dutch indemnities owing to them since the 1445 treaty and the release of English merchants and goods arrested by Philip's officers in reprisal against the Bay Fleet seizure (Nicolas, *P.P.C.,* VI, 76-7). In Sept. 1451, the English paid the Burgundians compensation for the Bay Fleet piracy. Gilliodts-von Severen, *Estaple de Bruges,* I, 719-20, no. 903.
53 *S.R.,* II, 353-4 (28 Hen. VI, c. 1); *Rot. Parl.,* V, 201: no. 57.
54 *Ibid.,* V, 202. Sometime between Whitsun and St. John's Day (24 June) 1450.
55 See Oscar De Smedt, 'De Engelsche Handel te Antwerpen in de Jaren 1305-1515,' *Bijdragen tot de Geschiedenis,* XV (1924), 589-90. The English were also angry because Antwerp was charging them tolls from which the 1446 charter had exempted them. See note 57 *infra.*
56 E. Carus-Wilson, 'Origins and Early Development of the Merchant Adventurers' Organization in London,' in *Medieval Merchant Venturers* (London, 1954), pp. 143-82.

to Antwerp's commerce and to the Burgundian economy in general. Philip tried to force their return by forbidding all merchants in his lands, native and foreign, to trade with the English anywhere except at Antwerp.[57] But the English apparently did not restore their trade to Antwerp until after Duke Philip had removed the cloth ban.

Philip finally terminated his cloth ban in 1452: first in Brabant, sometime after 15 April,[58] and then in Holland-Zealand on 23 June.[59] But, beyond recognizing the opposition of the Dutch merchants to the ban, he offered no explanations for his decisions. Quite possibly, he had agreed with the recent advice of his Brabant *Chambre de Comptes* that the cloth ban was ineffective and served only to deny the duke potential toll revenues[60] – as some other officials had already complained.[61] Certainly the ban was also proving costly in terms of the Merchants Adventurers' boycott of Antwerp. At the same time, the current Hanseatic boycott and blockade of Flemish trade, which the League had im-

---

57 Frederic Verachter (ed.), *Inventaire des anciens chartes et privilèges et autres documents conservés aux archives de la ville d'Anvers* (Antwerp, 1860), p. 128, no. 414. (21 Aug. 1450). They were forbidden to trade with the English during the fair time and for forty days thereafter.

58 On 15 April, Duke Philip granted Antwerp provisional permission to import and sell English cloth, while waiting for a 'general decision' on the cloth ban. Verachter, *Archives de la ville d'Anvers*, p. 131, no. 425. On 27 Sept. 1452, the city council of Antwerp requested the Geervliet toll-keeper not to prevent imports of English cloth, since Duke Philip had permitted such cloth to be sold in the fairs of Antwerp and Bergen-op-Zoom (Smit, *Bronnen Handel*, II, 891-2, no. 1386). In December 1452, magistrates of Bergen-op-Zoom went to Middelburg to inform the English merchants 'dat sij Engelsche lakene souden moghen brenghen te Berghene ende moghen vercopen.' *Ibid.*, II, 892, no. 1389.

59 On 11 June 1452 Duke Philip ordered his officials to restore all confiscated English cloths to their owners on the grounds that 'tot onser voirseide ordinancie ende verbot onser voirseide landen van Hollant, Zeelant, ende Vrieslant *geen consent gegeven en hebben,* ende sonderlinghe dat die voirseide Engelsche laken dagelicx openbairlic gebrocht ende vercoft worden in onsen landen van Brabant ende elwers.' Philip promised to consult the Dutch Estates on a new ordinance by 24 June. Smit, *Bronnen Handel*, II, 890, no. 1382. Subsequently, in May 1459, the Holland-Zealand Rentmeester General reduced fines in several convictions for various cloth-ban violations in the period 1449-52, in the view of the fact that since 23 June 1452 'ende noch jegenwoirdelic die Engelsche lakenen loep hebben gehad ende hebben in Hollant ende Zeelant.' *Ibid.*, II, 956, no. 1503.

60 A.G.R., C. de C., no. 17, fo. 72vo. (15 Jan. 1451). The report stated that 'non obstant les deffenses faites et publiez sur lesdiz draps d'Engleterre le fait de la drapperie es bonnes villes [de] pardeca n'est en riens amendé;' and pointed out that 'les marchans trouve passage par mer jusques à Campen et autres partes sans passer parmy les pays de mondit seigneur, par quoy il a pris grand dommage en ses tonlieux.' It indeed recommended the levy of a special toll on transshipments of English cloths to Germany and Italy to remedy the sharp diminution in toll revenues on English wools transshipped to these countries.

61 See Smit, *Bronnen Handel*, II, 892, no. 1386: 'dwelc den tolnere van Yersicheroirt grotelic gescaet heeft binnen den middelen tijde voirseit.'

posed the previous year to fortify demands for new monopolistic stapling privileges,[62] may equally have forced the duke's hand; for the Burgundians even less than the English could not afford two commercial wars. If that were not enough, Philip was then also faced with the very destructive Ghent rebellion.[62a] Finally, there remains the possibility that the Burgundians had succeeded in gaining some modification of the Staple ordinances in return for revoking the ban. The only recorded evidence of an English concession that year was the royal Council's restoration of Newcastle's licence to ship northern wools directly to Bruges and Middelburg.[63] Subsequent statements in the 1454 Parliament, however, suggest that Philip had won a more substantial victory; for, the Commons debate of that year makes clear that the 'partitionist' faction of the Staple had again been overthrown and that its strict price-fixing and bullionist payment regulations were no longer in force.

When the 1454 Parliament met in March, a group of merchants in the Commons almost succeeded in restoring the 'partition' faction to power in the Staple. First, the merchants petitioned the Crown to re-affirm the 1429 Staple Partition and Bullion Ordinances, though with some modifications. In particular, they asked that *all* wool sellers having stock at the Staple share in the partitioning of receipts and not just Staple members from the same county as the sellers.[64] That seemingly liberal amendment is obviously connected with their next request: that all English subjects might freely sell wool at Calais and enjoy all the privileges of regular Staple members without paying the Company's entrance fees. But the partition faction's ulterior and self-interested motives can be seen from its previous use of non-members' votes to manipulate Staple elections during the 1440s.[65] These petitioners also requested that the

---

62 See Daenell, *Die Blütezeit der deutschen Hanse,* I, 397-424, 437-40. The Hanse did not return until Aug. 1457.

62a See Vaughan, *Philip the Good,* pp. 303-33. It lasted from 1449 until Ghent's defeat at the Battle of Gavere, July 1453.

63 Nicolas, *P.P.C.,* VI, 117-8 (8 Mar. 1452); Smit, *Bronnen Handel,* II, 890, no. 1381. The Council renewed the licence for five years on 19 July 1454 and on 18 July 1459 for a further five years. Unger, *Bronnen Middelburg,* III, 97, no. 199; Carus-Wilson, *England's Export Trade,* pp. 62-4.

64 *Rot. Parl.,* V, 275-7: no. 6. In accordance with the 1429 statutes, the petitioner requested that wool prices be increased and that one third of the sales price be brought in bullion to the Calais mint. But this time the Staplers were to exact not full payment but only half the payment in ready cash. While permitting credit for the other half, even that use of credit was to be controlled: the Staplers were to take surety for the other half and sign pledges 'to th'entent that noo merchaunt shall leene to any Merchaunt straunger any maner of money of him received... but that the same money mowe be brought into this youre Reaume without subtilte or fraude.'

65 *Supra,* pp. 119-20 and note 8.

Staple monopoly be strictly enforced and that the Staple be empowered to fix prices. They were supported by another petitioner, who complained that wool prices had 'gretely decayed' as a result of the 'grete habundance of Wolles' shipped on licences; to check this competition, he more specifically requested that Parliament fix the minimum *export* prices on some 51 varieties of English wool.[66]

The King's Council supported these petitions[67] and, indeed, had very likely arranged for their presentation in support of its bullionist policy. Again, financing the Calais garrison would explain the Crown's policy. Now England's last continental possession, Calais seemed doomed to fall before an imminent French attack when, on 19 March, the Lord Chancellor urgently requested Parliament to vote £40,000 for its defence. The Commons, however, bluntly refused, 'for they kan not, may not, ne dar not make eny moo grauntes, considered the grete povrete and penurie' of the country.[68] In its desperation, the Council apparently turned to the leading Stapler 'partitionists' for assistance and, with their support, counted upon exacting enough bullion and ready cash from the wool trade to pay the garrison's arrears in wages.[69]

Once again, however, the King's Council had underestimated the resistance of the other wool merchants and their elected Staple mayor. The next month, in April, the Mayor and Fellowship of the Staple petitioned Parliament to reject the proposed laws, condemning in particular the Bullion and Partition ordinances 'for divers hurtes and lossez that shuld ensewe therof.' They also demanded that the Crown affirm their right to sell wool freely at the prices they deemed best, guarantee repayment of outstanding loans, issue no more unauthorized export licences, and reduce the wool subsidy to the traditional 33s. 4d. a sack. On these conditions, the Staple Fellowship offered the Council a

66 *Rot. Parl.*, V, 274-5: no. 5. The petitioner maintained that, because of the large volume of illegal wool exports, 'the price of the said Wolles ys so gretely decayed and amenused in the handes of the growers,' and furthermore that cloth making, 'which is the grettest occupacion and lyving of the pore communes of this land, is so anyentysed and nygh destroied by that grete habundance of Wolles' shipped to countries where English cloth was being sold. Total English cloth exports had slumped from an annual average of 56,944 pieces in 1440-4 to one of only 37,380 pieces in 1450-4. Presumably the petitioner was thus seeking support from the cloth-making interests in the Commons, since higher wool-export prices would certainly have benefited cloth exports.

67 *Rot. Parl.*, V, 257: no. 55, section iii.

68 *Rot. Parl.*, V, 240: no. 30. See also Nicolas, *P.P.C.*, VI, 174, for early April : 'the jepart and distresse that oure towne of Calais standeth in, for as we be credibilie enfourmede our adversaries with all the myghte they can make dispose in al haste to besige our said towne.'

69 On the Council's relations with the Staplers at this time, see Haward, 'Financial Transactions,' *Studies in English Trade*, pp. 301-7.

loan of £6,667 to pay the Calais garrison's wages. The Council readily accepted the loan; but it only reluctantly agreed to 'make noon Acte of Parlement,' on the grounds that the partition petition was not in accordance with the 1429 statute, and implied that the bullion ordinance ought to be enforced.[70]

The Council's reversal of its decision was apparently due to the political machinations of Richard Duke of York, who had taken advantage of King Henry VI's suspected fit of insanity to challenge the Beaufort-Somerset faction for control of the kingdom. On 27 March, after the Council's original assent to the Staple laws, Richard secured power as Protector of the Realm and 'chief of the Kynges Counsaill.'[71] But, to remain in power, he needed the support of the Calais garrison, now England's largest standing army, whose loyalty could be ensured only by the immediate payment of its arrears in wages.[72] Thus, in return for the Staplers' loan, Richard was quite willing to offer the Fellowship his support in quashing the Bullion and Partition petitions.[73] The Staplers might have offered the Council the same loan in March, had the Council leaders then not been so derelict in settling the accumulated Crown debts and so insistent upon pursuing their bullionist policy.[74]

The defeat of the proposed bullionist legislation probably averted another serious rupture in Anglo-Burgundian commercial relations, particularly because of Duke Philip's current monetary problems in the Lowlands. Since 1447, constantly rising prices for gold and silver had kept his mints dormant;[75] in part, the rising gold prices reflected the debasement activities of neighbouring mints

---

70 *Rot. Parl.*, V, 256-7: no. 55. The Crown stated that the bullion and partition statutes of 8 Hen. VI (1429) should be maintained 'as it was had and used whan Raynewell was Maire of the Staple.' (1429-34). For the Staplers' loan, see *Ibid.*, V, 249: no. 7; *Cal. Close Rolls 1454-61*, pp. 1-2; P.R.O., (K.R.) E101/195-3, E 364/92, m. 52-3. See chapter 3, note 51 *supra*.

71 Jacob, *Fifteenth Century*, p. 509; G.L. Harriss, 'The Struggle for Calais: an Aspect of the Rivalry Between Lancaster and York,' *English Historical Review*, LXXV (1960), 31-6.

72 In May 1454, before York could take control of Calais and pay the garrison, the soldiers revolted and again seized the wool stocks for their arrears in wages. See *Rot. Parl.*, V, 279: no. 9; Haward, 'Financial Transactions,' p. 302; Harriss, 'Struggle for Calais,' pp. 36-7. See also P.R.O., C76/137, m. 5 and m. 17, for subsequent provisions to pay the garrison's wages by assigning it 20s. in subsidies per wool sack.

73 Harriss, 'Struggle for Calais,' pp. 34-7.

74 Between 1451 and 1454 the Staplers lent the Council £40,943 sterl. For their difficulties in recovering these loans, see Haward, 'Financial Transactions,' pp. 301-7.

75 Philip's last mint, at Ghent, closed in April 1447 (A.G.R., Acquits de Lille, liasse no. 937:26). For the ordinance's complaints, see A.G.R., C. de C., carton 65:1. Thus 'vanden voirsc. gulden penningen die cours gegeven hadden binnen sekeren tyden herwaerts gehoeght in hueren prise...' See also note 20 *supra*. The rising prices for gold affected other parts of Europe as well: the Genoese valuation of gold in terms of silver had risen from 10.4: 1 in 1445 to 12.5: 1 in 1454. Heers, *Gênes au XVe siècle*, p. 618.

elsewhere in the Low Countries and the Rhineland, who were striking counterfeit imitations of Rhenish *florins* and Burgundians *rijders*. The constantly rising flood of these coins, more and more debased with each issue and circulated 'at far higher prices than they are worth,' greatly alarmed the Burgundian officials.[76] Since the 1433 monetary ordinance had prohibited any alteration of the coinage for twenty years, Philip was unable to resolve these two problems before January 1454. Once free to do so and to reactivate his mints, he issued a new ordinance on 18 January for the striking of new gold coins, the '*lions*,' at a slightly reduced fineness (23 carats) and at a *traite* value 11 per cent higher than that placed on his previous gold coins.[77] As graph V shows, the Burgundian mints of Bruges, Malines, Dordrecht, and Valenciennes were successful in coining a vast amount of gold during the next two years. Philip's mints might not have proven quite that successful had the Calais bullion laws then been in full force.

Nevertheless, the conflict over the Staple's payment regulations had not yet been fully resolved. In the same March session of the 1454 Parliament, a Commons petitioner accused Duke Philip of imposing two severe measures designed to undermine the Staple's commerce: the 'outrageous Toll' levied at Gravelines on all wools purchased at Calais 'and upon noon other Wolles comyng into his said Countreys,' and 'a grete penale restreint' on the shipping of *foreign* silver bullion through his lands to Calais, so that the Staplers lacked coined money to pay the wool growers.[78] He maintained that, as a result, large amounts of

---

76 The chief offending coins 'van snoeden gewichte ende alloye' were the *postulaat gulden* of Utrecht and the *florins* of Guelders, Liège, and Cologne. The ordinance maintained that the Utrecht *postulaat* in particular had been debased from a standard of 16 carats and a *taille* of 72 to the *marc* to one of 12 carats and a *taille* of 78 to the *marc*, a loss of 30 per cent of its gold content; and furthermore, that 'onse gulden penningen Philippus geheten Riders [rijders] ende andere goede penningen van goude dien wy cours gelaten hadden in onsen voirsc. landen daer uut worden getogen ende gedragen in anderen vremde landen ende munten ten groten achterdiele ende schade van ons...' A.G.R., C. de C., carton 65: 1. See also Van der Chijs, *Munten van Holland*, pp. 417-20; J. De Chestret de Haneffe, *Numismatique de la principauté de Liège* (Brussels, 1890), p. 190; and, Spufford, *Monetary Problems*, pp. 118-20.

77 See sources cited in the previous note; précis in Deschamps de Pas, 'Histoire monétaire des comtes de Flandre,' *Revue numismatique*, VII (1862), 121-2. The new gold *leeuw* (*lion*) of 23 carats and a *taille* of 57 1/2 to the *marc* was worth 5s. *gros* and thus had a *traite* of £15.0.0d. *gros*. No change was made in the silver coins and thus the gold to silver ratio was raised accordingly from 11.25: 1 to 12.44: 1. In July 1456, Philip increased the mint price for gold by 2s. *gros* a *marc*. See Appendix I, Table C.

78 *Rot. Parl.*, V, 227: no. 6: 'that the said Duk hath made a gret penale restreint upon passage of merchaundise called Bullyon of Silver to pass thurgh eny of his landes aforesaid to come to Caleys, which merchaundise groweth in no land of his, whereof money shuld be coyned in the Kynges mynte atte Caleys, to be caried and sprade in this Reaume, for to pay the growers

wool were being shipped directly to the Low Countries in evasion of the Staple. 'For remedie hereof,' he requested Parliament to prohibit the sale of all wools to Burgundian subjects unless the duke rescinded both the Gravelines toll and his ban on shipping foreign silver to Calais. This petition, however, never received a response, apparently ignored during the turmoil caused by the other bullionist petitions of that session.

Burgundian sources suggest that Duke Philip continued to enforce these two discriminatory measures against the Staple until the English modified the payment regulations to his satisfaction.[79] By the late 1450s, the English Crown finally agreed to meet the Burgundian demands but only after succumbing to the urgent demands of the Staple Fellowship. Greatly concerned about their declining wool sales, the lowest since the troubled 1430s, the Staplers feared that continued friction with the Burgundians could only further injure their trade.[80] They had taken the initiative for a lasting settlement also in the hope of binding both the Crown and Duke Philip to a pact that would guarantee them a full monopoly on wool sales to the Low Countries.

Although the Crown had promised to respect the Staplers' monopoly privileges in the loan agreement of April 1454, the king's continued financial distress left him little choice but to resume the sale of wool export licences the following October. After the king had granted an unusually large number in 1456, the Staplers fortified their protests with threats to deny him further loans. The next year, King Henry reluctantly agreed to issue no further licences, except for a few in his own name.[81] The Staplers could hardly be satisfied with such a weak promise that the king had broken so often in the past. Early the next year, however, King Henry's desperate need for a loan to redeem pressing debts of the Royal Household forced him to meet the Staplers' terms.[82]

As the first step towards a general agreement, King Henry on 19 March 1458 granted the Stapler Fellowship a special charter confirming all their former privileges. In particular, the charter ratified their right to elect freely the Mayor and two constables and to issue their own laws and ordinances on

---

of the said commoditees, the lakke wherof is grete hurt to the commune wele.' (Thus the petitioner apparently accepted Duke Philip's right to ban the export of bullion earned or acquired in the Low Countries). The levy of the Gravelines Toll, 'whiche is grete letting and hurt to the utterance of the said' wools and woolfells also angered Philip's Dutch subjects. (See *supra*, note 44). When Philip lifted the cloth ban for Holland in June 1452, he rejected the Dutch demands for the removal of this toll. Smit, *Bronnen Handel*, II, 891, no. 1383.

79 See *Ibid.*, II, 970-1, no. 1525.

80 Between 1456 and 1459, average annual wool exports to Calais were only 5,633 sacks. Carus-Wilson, *England's Export Trade*, p. 63.

81 Haward, 'Financial Transactions,' in *Studies in English Trade*, pp. 307-8.

82 *Ibid.*, p. 313.

the Staple trade. Somewhat ambiguously, the king noted that several 'harmful' dissensions had arisen between English and Burgundian merchants 'because of the lack of good and sound regulations and government.'[83] While that observation might refer to the Staple regulations on wool sales, other references to 'dissensions and injuries' concerned jurisdictional conflicts between the Staplers and the Merchants Adventurers. The king therefore granted the Staple mayor full powers and complete jurisdiction over Stapler affairs in the Lowlands and forbade the Adventurers to interfere with the Staplers in Antwerp.[84] A month later, in April, Duke Philip similarly forbade the Merchants Adventurers to interfere with the Staplers' trade.[85] Philip's decree may also have marked his willingness to make a permanent settlement with the Staplers, for, in the following months, a series of Anglo-Burgundian conferences were held at Calais and Bruges to discuss the Staple regulations.[86]

Finally, on 11 December 1458, Henry VI announced a proposed agreement on the wool trade, whose provisions would be binding on the Crown, the Staplers, and the duke of Burgundy for four years. Responding to the Staplers' complaints about the direct exports of wool to the Burgundian Lowlands in evasion of the Staple, King Henry solemnly promised to issue no more export licences during this period and to deal harshly with wool smugglers. Furthermore, he accepted the Staplers' nomination of ambassadors to negotiate a treaty on the wool trade with Duke Philip and the Four Members of Flanders and instructed them to secure the duke's promise for a ban on imports of all English wool that had not been stapled at Calais. To gain that concession, the ambassadors were empowered to negotiate with the Burgundians 'for remedies, provisions and ordinances for the secure payment in *money, bullion, or otherwise* for wools and woolfells to be sold at the said Staple.'[87] Finally, in return

83 P.R.O., C76/140, m. 18: 'quod, ob defectum boni et sani regiminis et gubernacionis, diversa dampnia, discensiones, gravamina, et angustie inter mercatores regni sui Anglie ac aliorum diversorum suorum in partibus Holandie, Selandie, Brabancie, Flandrie...' John Thirsk was appointed Staple Mayor, by the election.

84 Verachter, *Archives de la ville d'Anvers*, p. 137, no. 447. See also De Smedt, 'De Engelsche Handel,' p. 590.

85 Schanz, *Englische Handelspolitik*, II, 543-4, no. 17; précis in Verachter, *Archives de la ville d'Anvers*, p. 137, no. 448.

86 See Rymer, *Foedera*, XI, 410-1 (May 1458); 417 (August 1458); A.G.R., C. de C., no. 42,570, fo. 19 (Nov. 1458); James Gairdner (ed.), *The Paston Letters, 1422-1509*, III, 130 (June 1458); P.R.O., C76/140, m. 10-2 (May, July, August 1458). For a discussion of the political background and of the diplomacy in general, see Thielemans, *Bourgogne et Angleterre*, pp. 372-5.

87 *Cal. Pat. Rolls 1452-61*, pp. 500-1; précis in Smit, *Bronnen Handel*, II, 949, no. 1488. But see also Henry VI's instructions of the same date issued to his ambassadors William Pyrton, Thomas Stone, and Henry Sharp in P.R.O., C76/141, m. 11. He was there more explicit in

for the Crown's efforts to protect their wool monopoly, the Staplers agreed to provide a £16,000 loan for the Royal Household, to be issued in instalments of £1,000 every three months. But the Staplers declared that any violations of this agreement or any 'restrictions' placed on their wool sales at Calais would automatically free them from their loan obligations. The king, at the same time, would also be 'free to resume his former liberty,' presumably to resume granting wool export licences.[88]

The Anglo-Burgundian negotiations on the wool trade issues and on the prolongation of the 1439 commercial treaty continued through most of 1459.[89] They apparently reached a successful conclusion by the end of the year, for, in December, Duke Philip formally prohibited the importation of English wools that had not been purchased at Calais.[90] The duke's decree, however, encountered strenuous opposition from the Dutch drapery towns. After several strong protests, these towns in July 1460 threatened to boycott Calais and to refuse the duke a promised loan of 16,000 gold *écus* unless he revoked his ban on non-stapled wools.[91] Philip continued to ignore these threats and protests,[92] but he did satisfy the Dutch demands to reduce the Gravelines Toll.[93] That heavy toll, originally a discriminatory tax on wools purchased at Calais, was now contrary

requesting them to seek agreement on the 'bringing in of bullion:' to negotiate a treaty, for four years from the coming April 1459, 'de et super viis, mediis, modis, et formis emptionem et venditionem huiusmodi lanarum et pellium lanutarum apud eandem stapulam et recepcionem securitatem pro securis solucionibus inde fiendis ac de et *super inductionibus bullionis ad stapulam* predictam pro huiusmodi solucionibus fiendis.'

88 *Cal. Pat. Rolls 1452-61*, p. 501. The Staplers were permitted to recover their loans from the customs on the wools they sold at the Staple. See P.R.O., C76/141, m. 11 (Dec. 1458), m. 10 (March and April 1459).

89 See A.G.R., C. de C., no. 32,511, fo. 30r. (July 1459); no. 32,512, fo. 22r. (Aug. and Sept. 1459), fo. 23vo. (Oct. and Nov. 1459). See Thielemans, *Bourgogne et Angleterre*, pp. 374-81 for the Burgundian involvement in the Yorkist-Lancastrian struggle during these negotiations.

90 P.A.S. van Limburg-Brouwer (ed.), *Boergoensche Charters 1428-1482* (The Hague, 1869), p. 123. This précis states 'laken' (cloth) but it should be wool. See notes 91-3 *infra*, especially the text in note 93.

91 Posthumus, *Bronnen Leidsche Textielnijverheid*, I, 363-4, no. 316: 'der comanscip van der vellen ende wollen, die uut Engelant overquamen hier te lande, ende niet verstapelt en waeren tot Calis, verbuert souden wesen, ende dairtoe soude men verbueren een grote pene, om mijn genadigen heere te onder wysen, dat dat mandemente of ende te niet wesen mochte, wanttet een nuwicheyt ende verderffenisse voir den lande wair.' (no. 7 of 28 Mar. 1460). See also no. 8 (May), no. 9 (June), no. 10 (4 July: 'van den 16,000 scilden niet en consentieren en wouden die saken ende nuwicheden van den mandemente ... moesten eerst afgedaen wesen;'), no. 15 (7 June).

92 *Ibid.*, I, 364-5; Smit, *Bronnen Handel*, II, 957-8, no. 1054.

93 On those same occasions, the Dutch towns had also asked Philip again, in vain, to remove the Gravelines Toll. But finally, on 2 Sept. 1462, Philip's son Charles (as count of Charolais)

to Philip's current agreement with the Staple. While the evidence is not fully conclusive that the bullion regulations had been entirely eliminated, the toll had presumably finished serving its purpose. Nevertheless, Philip's victory over the English Crown did not obligate him to abolish the toll entirely. That he chose to retain it at a reduced levy for the welcome revenues it provided, and agreed to exclude non-Stapled wools, indicates again that Philip's commercial policies reflected more his own bullionist and fiscal concerns than a true consideration of his subjects' economic welfare.

ordered the Gravelines Toll-farmer to limit the tax to the satisfaction of the Dutch towns. He stipulated, however, that the agreement must be 'sonder prejudice van den brieven die mijn ... vader binnen zekeren tijts herwaerts geaccordeert ende geoctroyeert heeft dien van der stapel van Calais, inhoudende verbod van niet te mogen brengen in den voirseiden landen ... enige wolle offe vellen ... tensij dat eerst verstapelt zijn tot Calis.' Smit, *Bronnen Handel*, II, 970-1, no. 1525. The Gravelines toll was still being collected in 1466, then at a rate of 5 per cent ad valorem. In December, Duke Philip noted that many merchants were evading the toll and he ordered his officials to ensure that all merchants passed through Gravelines after leaving Calais. Smit, *Bronnen Handel*, II, 1008, no. 1564.

CHAPTER SIX

THE THIRD BURGUNDIAN CLOTH BAN AND THE END OF THE BULLIONIST CONFLICT, 1460-1478

Duke Philip's settlement of the three-decade old Staple conflict was a short-lived triumph, for within just four years the 1459 Anglo-Burgundian agreement collapsed under the pressures of a renewed and more intense struggle for bullion. Once again the English, under the new Yorkist monarchy of Edward IV, were responsible for reviving the conflict. Facing an imminent fiscal crisis from the protracted civil war and urgently needing ready money to secure his shaky throne, King Edward had little compunction in breaking the agreement undertaken by his discredited Lancastrian predecessor. In a broader perspective, however, the bullionist conflict may have also reflected Europe's growing scarcity of precious metals, a dearth which some historians maintain had become unusually severe by the early 1460s.[1] That scarcity, to be sure, made mining

---

1 See Feavearyear, *Pound Sterling*, pp. 43-5; Renée Gandilhon, *La politique économique de Louis XI* (Paris, 1914), pp. 319-22; J.U. Nef, 'Mining and Metallurgy in Medieval Civilization,' in Postan and Rich (eds.), *Cambridge Economic History*, II, 456-8. More recently, three economic historians have argued that in the 1450s and 1460s Europe was experiencing a drainage of specie to Muslim lands. Both Jacques Heers (*Gênes au XVe siècle*, pp. 64-5) and Harry Miskimin (*Economy of Early Renaissance Europe*, pp. 138-58) maintain that Italian merchants were then exporting large quantities of both gold and silver to Syria and Egypt to sell to Levantine goldsmiths and more especially to pay for increased imports of eastern luxuries. Andrew Watson, on the other hand, argues that Syria's higher valuation of silver caused a drainage of just that metal. He notes that in 1453 Jacques Cœur was accused of shipping thousands of silver *marcs* to Syria for, as Cœur admitted, 'quand il vault 6 escus par deca, il

MONETARY GRAPH VI (1460-1476)

Coinage of pure gold and silver marcs in the Burgundian Lowlands and England

BURGUNDIAN MINTS:

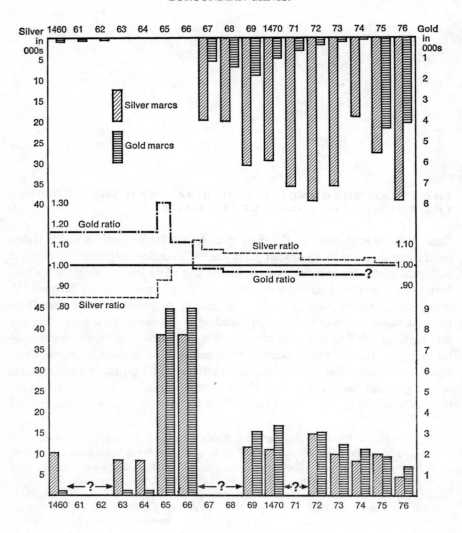

ENGLISH MINTS (London):

SOURCES: See Appendix I, Tables A-D.

once more profitable after a prolonged slump; and with the South German discovery of the method for extracting silver from argentiferous copper ores, a Central European mining boom succeeded by the late 1480s in satisfying much of the hunger for silver.[2] But in the meantime many European rulers looked to the traditional, more expedient remedies of coinage debasement and controls on trade or 'foreign exchange.' As Renée Gandilhon has shown, France's King Louis XI (1461-83) was more sophisticated than most of his contemporaries in adopting a co-ordinated policy of 'Colbertisme' to augment his country's specie supply.[3] To the degree that he succeeded, his policies probably magnified the serious monetary problems of his English and Burgundian neighbours.

In the Burgundian Lowlands, Duke Philip was apparently faring less successfully than King Louis in resolving his bullion scarcity. He had already become disturbed about a steadily declining mint output as early as September 1457, when he accused his licenced money-changers of diverting bullion from his mints to those of Tournay (France) and other principalities that offered them large profits.[4] The accompanying graph VI seems to justify his concern: the Burgundian mints received no silver after 1458 and, after coining a mere 42 gold marcs in 1461-62, they ceased operating entirely for over four years.[5] On the mints' closure in March 1462, the mint-masters informed Philip that the market prices for both metals, but especially for silver, exceeded the official prices for bullion and, moreover, that the circulation of foreign debased coins in his lands was steadily increasing. For these reasons, they argued that they could only resume minting if the coinages were debased sufficiently to raise the mint price for gold by 2.0 per cent and for silver by 12.5 per cent.[6] But Philip

---

en vault 7 par dela.' See 'Back to Gold — and Silver,' *Econ. Hist. Review*, 2nd ser. XX (1967), 30-1.

2 Nef, 'Mining and Metallurgy,' *C.E.H.*, II, 469-73.

3 Gandilhon, *Louis XI*, pp. 319-24.

4 A.G.R., Acquits de Lille, no. 931-3: 'ils ont leur dit billon d'or livré en autres monnoies estranges, comme à Tournay et ailleurs, ou autrement distribué, à leur prouffit.' In response, Duke Philip ordered a fine of 8s. *gros* to be imposed on the changers 'pour chascun marc d'or qu'ilz deffauldront à deliverer.' Later, on 31 Jan. 1459, he again banned the circulation of the debased gold *florins* of Liège, Utrecht, and Guelders. Deschamps de Pas; *Histoire monétaire des comtes de Flandres*, p. li, doc. no. 265. See also Spufford, *Monetary Problems*, pp. 120-1.

5 The Ghent mint, the only one then operating, closed on 16 March 1462, and re-opened on 18 June 1466. A.G.R., C. de C., nos. 18, 196-7.

6 A.G.R., C. de C., carton 65: bis 1. They recommended raising the mint price of silver bullion from 22s.9d. *gros* per *marc* to 26s.0d. *gros* per *marc*; for gold bullion, from £14.16s.0d. *gros* per *marc* to £15.0.0d. *gros* per *marc*, and thus to establish a new ratio more favourable to

had already failed twice, in 1459 and 1461, to obtain consent from his town assemblies for an alteration of the coinage;[7] a subsequent session of the towns in February 1464 once more rejected his proposed monetary ordinance for reviving his mints.[8]

By that time, Duke Philip's quandary had become much graver as a result of Edward IV's strong reactions to his own monetary difficulties. As graph VI shows, the London mint was hardly more productive than the Burgundian mints during the early 1460s and may have been closed in 1461 and 1462. To some extent, that minting slump may reflect economic dislocations from the civil war that plagued England for the three years following Edward's coronation of June 1461. While the extent of these dislocations has long been disputed, the exports of both wool and cloth in this period apparently suffered unusual fluctuations and an overall decline, which likely reduced the influx of bullion.[9] Those monetary difficulties were aggravated, moreover, by the burden of Edward's military expenditures that he required to crush the remnants of the Lancastrian cause.[10]

During this last phase of the Wars of the Roses, the problem of financing the Calais garrison again caused the Crown grave anxiety; for at one point Edward's fate seemed dependent on maintaining the garrison's support. Thus, in April 1462, the deposed but not defeated Queen Margaret fled to France to seek Louis XI's support for a Lancastrian restoration. In desperation, she offered him Calais in return for troops and money. Louis agreed and by June their combined forces were ready to besiege the port. For an easy conquest,

silver ('valudra les xi m. 1 once ii est. d'argent pour chacun d'or fin.') See also A.G.R., C. de C., no. 1158, fo. 23-35, an undated but apparently related Flemish text of the same report, presenting the same proposals. Both reports advocated banning all coins of Liège, Guelders, Cologne, and Utrecht. The latter also recommended that all other foreign gold coins be accepted only 'bij gewichte ... dat men tmarck silvers veel min coopen sal.' (fo. 34-5).

7 A.G.R., C. de C., nos. 32,511, fo. 29r. and 42,570, fo. 43vo. (May 1459, at Antwerp and Brussels); Cuvelier, *Actes*, pp. 41-4; A.G.R., C. de C., no. 32,513, fo. 29r. (Jan. 1461); Cuvelier, *Actes*, pp. 45-8 (Jan.-Feb. 1461 at Brussels), pp. 49-50 (March 1461 at Brussels), pp. 51-2 (April 1461 at Brussels).

8 Cuvelier, *Actes*, pp. 58-95 (Jan.-Feb. 1464 at Bruges).

9 Carus-Wilson, *England's Export Trade*, pp. 64-5, 100-1. Thus, wool exports were only 2,906 sacks in 1461-2; and average annual exports fell from 8,567 sacks in 1455-9 to 5,776 sacks in 1460-4. Over the same periods, average annual cloth exports fell from 37,542 pieces to 30,934 pieces. Even if the fluctuating export statistics reflect the effects of the Wars of the Roses on the ability of the royal Customers to control exports, there was still a decline in customs revenues for the Crown.

10 See Steel, *Receipt of the Exchequer*, pp. 433-4. Most of the accounts of this period are incomplete, but the partial receipt rolls for the early 1460s show lower revenues. For a discussion of Edward's finances in this period, see Jacob, *Fifteenth Century*, pp. 528-44.

they counted upon the disaffection of the Calais garrison troops; reportedly, they were ready to mutiny 'for defaute of their wages' and to open the gates to Margaret's forces upon receipt of her silver. On hearing such disastrous news, the royal Treasurer rightly had 'mych to do for thys cause.'[11] Fortunately for Edward, the Staplers rescued him with a loan of £41,000 for the garrison's wages.[12] Calais was secure, but only so long as the Crown could continue its payments in coined money.

Thus, to resolve both his monetary and fiscal difficulties, the Yorkist victor resorted to the twice-discredited policy of his Lancastrian predecessor: the Crown reconstituted the old alliance with the Staplers and required Parliament to revive the Calais bullion laws. The statute which the Parliament of May 1463 enacted for three years was, however, not so onerous as the 1429 laws. While the statute obliged the Stapler merchants to exact 'redy payment and contentation' before or upon delivery of their wools and other stapled goods, it required that only 'the half part be in lawfell money of England, Plate, or Bullion of Sylver and Gold;' and it did not otherwise specify how much was to be in bullion. Any bullion received was to be coined immediately at the Calais mint and the cash receipts were then to be brought into the realm within three months of the sales transaction.[13] These provisions suggest that the Crown's chief concern was to receive its customs revenues in good English money as quickly as possible, though again another object may have been to prevent an influx of debased coins. The Burgundians thus would likely have found this requirement less obnoxious than the former exactions of one third in bullion; moreover, the wool buyers were implicitly permitted sales credit for 50 per cent of the price. Finally, this statute made no mention of either monopoly price-fixing or of the Partition system, which had undermined the Lancastrian

---

11 James Gairdner (ed.), *The Paston Letters, 1422-1509,* IV (London, 1904), 57.

12 *Cal. Pat. Rolls 1461-7,* pp. 222, 438 (16 Sept. 1462).

13 *Rot. Parl.,* IV, 503: no. 18; *S.R.,* II, 392-4 (3 Ed. IV, c. 1): 'dount la demy part soit en loialle money Dengleterre, plate, ou bullion d'argent ou d'or, et tout mesme la money en cest Roialme duement amesne.' The act was to enter into force on Michaelmas 1463 and endure until Michaelmas 1466. The penalty for evading the bullion law was set at 5 marks (£3.6s.8d. sterl.) per woolsack sold, roughly 50 per cent of the price; the Staplers were also strictly forbidden to sell their merchandises anywhere but at Calais. On this act, see Power, 'The Wool Trade in the Fifteenth Century,' *Studies in English Trade,* p. 89; and Postan, 'Credit in Medieval Trade,' *Econ. Hist. Review,* 1st ser., I (1928), 242-3. Postan's argument that this act permitted full sales credit for three months is not convincing, since that period of grace was clearly granted to permit the Staplers time to have their bullion coined. There is no clear evidence that thereafter the Calais mint was in operation, though F.A. Walters has found some of Edward IV's gold coins which he believes were struck at Calais. 'The Coinage of Edward IV,' *Numismatic Chronicle,* IX (1909), 156.

schemes. But the Crown did grant the Staplers more far-reaching monopoly privileges to secure their support in enforcing the new bullion law — and to subject the whole wool trade to its provisions. Thus, by the same act, Parliament for the first time (since the 1350s) forbade *aliens* to export wool and imposed the harsh penalty of forfeiture and two years' imprisonment for those evading the Calais Staple.[14]

This modified bullion law represented, however, only the first part of Edward's overall monetary-fiscal policy, which could benefit the English only at the expense of the Burgundians. That same May Parliament and the following one of November (1463) next banned the importation of silks, woollen cloths and various finished textiles, and a long list of various 'ready wrought' goods currently competing with English manufactures. Significantly, many of the prohibited goods were Burgundian manufactures which had found one of their chief export markets in England.[15] Parliament also enacted a 'Navigation Act' to prohibit the use of foreign ships when English ships were available, a measure injurious to Zealander shippers.[16] While the ostensible purpose of these acts was to protect employment in the industries and trades concerned, an equally important consideration was surely to curb the outflow of specie — or,

14 *S.R.*, II, *ubi supra*. This anti-alien measure chiefly affected the Italians who exported from Southampton. In the five years prior to the act, aliens exported an average of 603 sacks, 9 per cent of the total; in 1463-4, they exported only 34 sacks, but thereafter resumed their former export volumes. The act exempted the coarser, cheaper wools of the northern counties (exported from Newcastle) from the Staple requirements; but Newcastle was then exporting only about 100 woolsacks a year. (Carus-Wilson, *England's Export Trade*, pp. 63-4). The following year, Parliament further strengthened the Staplers' monopoly powers by reviving their right to sue violaters of their privileges (4 Ed. IV, c. 2, in *S.R.*, II, 408). On the extent of Edward's financial indebtedness to the Staplers by 1464, see Daumet, *Calais sous la domination anglaise*, p. 141; Sandeman, *Calais Under English Rule*, p. 72.

15 In May 1463, Parliament banned all imports of silk manufactures 'et toutz autres choses touchantz mesme les mestiers et occupacions prestes overez.' (3 Ed. IV, c. 3 in *S.R.*, II, 395). In November, it banned imports specifically of woollen caps and cloth, laces, corsets, ribbons, saddles, stirrups, harnesses, spurs, bridles, grid-irons, locks, hammers, tongs, pans, tennis balls, purses, gloves, girdles, shoes, galoshes, corks, knives, bodkins, sheers, scissors, razors, playing cards, pins, pattens, needles, caskets, copper rings, chafing dishes, curtain rings, ladles, brushes, carders, iron thread (3 Ed. IV, c. 4, in *S.R.*, II, 306-7); the next year, another act banned all imports of foreign woollen cloths (4 Ed. IV, c. 1, in *S.R.*, II, 407). For the goods listed then being manufactured in the Burgundian Lowlands and exported to England, see Thielemans, *Bourgogne et Angleterre*, pp. 403, 225-46.

16 *S.R.*, II, 394-5 (3 Ed. IV, c. 1, May 1463, appended to the Calais Bullion law). See also Thielemans, pp. 307-43, 403, on the Zealanders' shipping. Aliens living in England were, however, exempted from this statute, whose subsequent enforcement is very doubtful.

in the modern parlance for justifying mercantilist legislation, 'to conserve foreign exchange.'[17]

The following year, in August 1464, King Edward imposed by royal proclamation his third and final monetary measure: a coinage debasement by which he succeeded where Philip had recently failed in reviving mint production. His new mint indenture ordered a fairly drastic reduction of 20 per cent in the weight of the silver penny and a 25 per cent increase in the value of the gold noble (to 8s.4d.).[18] In view of the steady decline and recent stagnation in coinage output, Edward's justification for the debasement as a purely defensive measure 'by consideracion of the scarcite of money' seems reasonable. Thus, since the English coinage had not been altered for over fifty years, one might assume that the circulating coin had deteriorated in weight and quality and that, with the consequent rise in the market value of bullion, heavier good coins and plate were being exported. Edward himself maintained, moreover, that his mints were receiving no gold or silver because merchants 'may have more for theire bolion in other princes' myntes.'[19] Nevertheless, Edward's refusal to consult Parliament on the alterations, a clear violation of the 1352 statute, leads one to suspect his altruistic concern about defending the realm's money supply. As the mint indenture reveals, his motives were also fiscal: the levy of the unusually high seignorage charges of 11.5 per cent on gold and 9 per cent on silver, mint profits which Parliament would likely have considered outrageous.[20]

17 Statute 4 Ed. IV, c. 4 spoke of 'the evils of importing wares ready wrought' because English industries producing the same goods 'sont graundement empoverez et grevousment endamagez et prejudicez de lour encrece du vivre ... par la graund multitude des diverses chaffares et wares.' (*S.R.*, II, 397). While none of these acts makes any reference to specie outflows, they were clearly in accordance with the English bullionist policy enunciated in the 1380s (see chapter 2 *supra*, pp. 44-6) and with Edward IV's current monetary policy. In January 1465, however, Parliament relaxed those provisions of the last Employment Act which required 'surety' from foreign merchants (*S.R.*, II, 413-4, 4 Ed. IV, c. 6). The Crown evidently found it more expedient to adopt import bans than to continue enforcing the unwieldy Employment legislation.

18 *Cal. Pat. Rolls 1461-7*, pp. 370-1 (mint indenture of 13 August 1464); *Cal. Close Rolls 1461-8*, p. 216. See also Feavearyear, *Pound Sterling*, pp. 39-45; Oman, *Coinage of England*, pp. 217-219; Craig, *The Mint*, pp. 91-2, on the new coinage.

19 Rogers Ruding (ed.), *Annals of the Coinage of Great Britain*, I (London, 1840), 282, citation of patent 4 Ed. IV, pt. 11, m. 16. In April 1464, Louis XI's mint-masters had advocated a debasement of the French coinage on the same grounds: 'en faisant ladite monnoye ... la matière d'or et d'argent de cedit royaume ne s'en pourront tirers hors [du royaume] pour convertir en autres monnoyes.' (Gandilhon, *Louis XI*, pp. 424-6, doc. no. 9). But Louis XI, like Philip the Good, did not then succeed in altering his coinage.

20 Since the 1370s, the seignorage had never exceeded 1 per cent of the *traite*. See Appendix I, Table D for the English mint prices and mintage fees.

In the months following his August indenture, the London mint coined large amounts of the new, lighter silver, despite the high mintage, but little gold. To increase the gold coinage output, Edward in March 1465 decided upon striking new and much lighter coins, the *'ryals'* and *'angels'*. Their official valuation amounted to a further debasement of 8 per cent, but this time Edward also reduced his seignorage by almost two-thirds to 4.1 per cent.[21] Over the next six years, Edward was forced to reduce his seignorage on both gold and silver several more times in order to maintain the mint's bullion supply. By April 1471, both seignorages had been restored to the traditional level of 1 per cent and the mint prices remained fixed for the next twenty years.[22] The mint accounts show that his debasements proved to be very effective: in the years 1464-66, the London mint coined a total of 76,357 silver marcs and 17,712 gold marcs; of the latter, domestic recoinages accounted for not more than 44 per cent.[23] Thus the mint apparently succeeded in attracting a very considerable amount of 'new' gold, perhaps in response to the adjustments of the mint ratio more and more in favour of that metal. Possibly, also, the Staplers were responsible for some of this gold influx from the bullionist exactions on the wool trade.

King Edward's monetary policies, as might be expected, provoked the usual retaliation from the injured Low Countries. Of the three measures that affected the Burgundians, the seemingly mild Calais bullion law of 1463 seems to have caused the greatest hostility. Perhaps Duke Philip's angry reaction may reflect his own current monetary frustrations in failing to restore his mint production. He surely must have been incensed at England's sudden and arbitrary repudiation of his hard-won settlement on the Staple regulations. If subsequent Burgundian charges are to be believed, moreover, the Staple's new payment regulations were more burdensome than the 1463 statute had required. These charges suggest that the old Partition system had been restored, for the Burgundian ambassadors to England maintained (in 1467) that the Staple ordinances required wool merchants to sell their wools at fixed prices and to distribute part of their sales receipts 'to those others who had unsold wool stocks, to each according to the quality of his wool.' The ambassadors further complained

---

21 *Cal. Pat. Rolls 1467-77*, pp. 138-40; full text in C.E. Blunt and C.A. Whitton, 'The Coinages of Edward IV,' *British Numismatic Journal*, V (1948), 53-6. The gold *traite* was raised from £20.16s.8d. sterl. per Tower Pound to £22.10s.0d. sterl.

22 See Appendix I, Table D: on 29 Sept. 1466, 29 Sept. 1467, and 14 Apr. 1471.

23 During the Michaelmas year 1465-6, a total of 137,875 old *nobles* were recoined. If they were of full weight, wihch is highly unlikely, that recoinage would have constituted 3,939 *marcs* or 44 per cent of that year's estimated average mint-output. *Cotton's Abridgement of the Records*, p. 685, cited in David Macpherson, *Annals of Commerce*, I (London, 1805), 684.

that the Staplers were forbidden to extend *any* credit to the buyers or to accept any payments in goods, that they would only accept good coins for less than the official values, that they arbitrarily demanded a portion of the payment in bullion 'when it pleased them,' and that they levied an extra charge of one gold *noble* per sarpler on those wool buyers who could not supply the required bullion.[24] The ambassadors concluded their mission to England, as the Dutch had done some thirty years previously, with the warning that the Staple regulations were killing the goose that laid the golden eggs:

> It is completely certain that, were the above-mentioned burdens to be maintained, the subjects of my lord would have to bear such costs for each sarpler of wool, those exacted by the King, that they would be forced to give up cloth-making in my lord's lands, or else obtain wool from elsewhere and thus forego the said English wools.[25]

That was an option available to the cheaper draperies but not to the traditional luxury draperies, at least not without sacrificing their reputation, as the English well knew.

Duke Philip nevertheless endured the Calais bullion laws for a full year after their enactment before he finally implemented retaliatory measures. In the meantime, his officials may have hoped to secure their revocation during the several Anglo-Burgundian commercial conferences held in 1463 and 1464.[26]

---

24 Thielemans, *Bourgogne et Angleterre*, pp. 469-72, doc. no. 8. Burgundian complaints about commercial relations presented to an English delegation headed by the bishop of Salisbury (1467), no. 7: 'Item ordonnent iceulx de l'estapple ... que nul marchant d'Angleterre ne puist vendre ses laynes aux marchans de par deca, si non en argent comptant, *sans riens laissier à creance*, ne tout ne en partie et sans povoir user de changement ou commutacion à autre denrée, ja feussent les dits Anglois bien contens de croyre jusques à certains terms, en tout ou en partie, ou aussi de changier à aultre denrée ...;' no. 8: 'Item, ordonnent aussi, quand il leur plaist, sur la manière des payemens des laynes, que partie du pris sera billon, et se l'acheteur ne peult finer de billon, ilz se recompensent et prendent de l'acheteur, au lieu de tel billon, quelque somme environ d'un noble pour sarplier.' They also complained about the mixing of good and bad wools and other frauds in packing. See also note 65 *infra*.

25 *Ibid.*, pp. 473-4. See also a royal patent dated 25 March 1464 in *Cal. Close Rolls 1461-8*, pp. 280-1. It suggests that Edward IV was demanding a specified amount of bullion on each woolsack sold and also that the Staplers were again finding it difficult to comply: for, in return for a Stapler loan of £18,741.13s.4d. sterl., Edward agreed to reduce temporarily the bullion requirement to a half-mark of silver (6s.8d.) per sack, 'such statutes notwithstanding and without any impeachment or grievance.' A patent roll of the following year, 24 Mar. 1465, shows that he granted the same reduction of the bullion requirement in return for another Stapler loan of £11,728.19s.2 1/2d. sterl. *Cal. Pat. Rolls 1461-7*, p. 438.

26 On 6 Aug. 1463 Edward IV commissioned ambassadors who extended the 1439 commercial

But, when those negotiations brought no satisfaction, the duke's officials in August 1464 met with the Four Members to discuss the English ordinance 'made to the injury of the land of Flanders.'[27] No more conferences have been recorded and likely no further discussion was necessary after so many precedents. On 26 October Duke Philip thus imposed his third and final ban on all English cloth imports, using almost precisely the same text as in his 1434 decree.[28]

Of his cloth bans, Duke Philip seems to have enforced this one the most successfully. In protest, the London Merchants Adventurers proclaimed a boycott of the Antwerp Fairs and in November removed their trading operations to Utrecht, outside Philip's jurisdiction.[29] While the Utrecht authorities quickly granted the Merchants Adventurers 'free markets' for their cloth trade,[30] London 'denizen' merchants still suffered a calamitous drop of 76 per cent in their cloth exports during the first year of the ban; and as Table I shows, aggregate English cloth exports fell by 35 per cent during 1464-65.

treaty for one year, on 26 Oct. 1463; on 20 Oct. 1464, just before the cloth ban, the treaty was again extended for one year. Rymer, *Foedera*, XI, 507, 536; Dehaisnes and Finot, *Archives du Nord*, I, 377. For the diplomacy of this period, see Thielemans, *Bourgogne et Angleterre*, pp. 382-410.

27 A.G.R., C. de C., no. 32,516, fo. 31r.: 'op de ordonancie die de zelve ghemaect hadden te Londres in bejeghenstede vanden lande van Vlaenderen;' no. 32,517, fo. 23vo. That might also refer to the statutes banning imports of certain Burgundian manufactures. The duke's officials and the Four Members met three times between 21 August and 4 September 1464.

28 Complete text in French in L.P. Gachard (ed.), *Collection de documents inédits concernant l'histoire de la Belgique*, II (Brussels, 1834), 176-82, no. 19; précis in Gilliodts-van Severen, *Estaple de Bruges*, II, 129, no. 1060 (dated 3 Nov. 1464) and in Diegerick, *Archives de la ville d'Ypres*, III, 255-7, no. 991. The only significant change from the wording of the 1434 decree was to include in the ban his duchy and county of Burgundy. (The decree therefore made no mention of the English bans on imported Burgundian manufactures.) Both Schanz (*Englische Handelspolitik*, I, 445) and Oscar De Smedt ('De Engelsche Handel te Antwerpen in de Jaren 1305-1515,' *Bijdragen tot de Geschiedenis*, XXV (1924), 591) provide a purely protectionist explanation for the ban, to halt the competition from English cloths; but this view, also adopted by Pirenne, does not seem warranted by the facts, since English cloth exports in the early 1460s were still lower than they had been in the early 1440s.

29 Smit, *Bronnen Handel*, II, 985-6, no. 1545 (letter of safe-conduct from the Utrecht authorities to William Caxton, Governor of the Merchants Adventurers). On 20 Oct. 1464 Edward IV had commissioned Caxton and others to negotiate an agreement on trade relations with Duke Philip, possibly in anticipation of the cloth ban. See note 26 *supra*.

30 On 27 Dec. 1464 the Utrecht authorities granted the English three 'free markets:' from 6 Jan. to 17 Feb., 21 Apr. to 1 June, and from 20 June to 20 July. Smit, *Bronnen Handel*, II, 986-7, no. 1546; Höhlbaum, *Hansisches Urkundenbuch*, IX, 85, no. 148. In the same month, Zutphen asked Utrecht to permit its merchants to trade there also with the English.

TABLE I

English Cloth Exports, 1461-62 to 1467-68

Year (Michaelmas)	London Cloth Exports			Total	Total Export from England
	Denizens	Hanse	Other Aliens		
1461-62	12,940	8,653	768	22,361	36,785
1462-63	9,893	4,670	487	15,050	27,907
1463-64	12,207	7,407	189	19,803	30,592
1464-65	2,962	4,117	1,046	8,185	19,983
1465-66	9,342	3,816	4,317	17,475	39,237
1466-67	8,133	6,436	1,672	16,241	35,388
1467-68	16,594	6,878	2,449	25,586	41,170

SOURCE: Calculated from tables in Carus-Wilson, *England's Export Trade*, pp. 101-103.

Thanks to the newly acquired Utrecht market, the London Adventurers were able to increase their cloth exports in 1465-66 and 1466-67;[31] but their export volumes during those two years amounted to much less than a full recovery, and only half as much as they would export after the ban's removal in November 1467. During this period, Philip's cloth ban also seems to have injured the trade of the Hanseatic merchants and his Dutch subjects. Both the League Diet and the assembly of Holland-Zealand towns delivered strong protests to the duke, the Dutch several times, but their opposition to the ban succeeded only in causing the duke's officials to stiffen their enforcement of the decree.[32] Again Middelburg proved to be the chief offender and suffered confiscation of large amounts of English cloth in 1465.[33]

31 For English trade at Utrecht in 1466, see Smit, *Bronnen Handel*, II, 1007-8, no. 1563; and W. Stein, 'Die Merchant Adventurers in Utrecht von 1464-1467,' *Hansisches Geschichtsblätter*, XXVII (1899), 179-89.

32 The Holland-Zealand towns first met at the Hague on 28 Nov. 1464, 'om te verhoudene [afsluiten] dat mandement van de Engelsche lakene' and drafted a protest to Duke Philip. Unger, *Bronnen Middelburg*, II, 351, no. 25; Posthumus, *Bronnen Leidsche Textielnijverheid*, I, 402, no. 348:8. They met again at the Hague in March 1465; and representatives held meetings with the duke's officials at Brussels in January and March 1465, 'omme provisie te hebben opt verbot vanden Engelschen lakenen.' *Ibid.*, I, 402; Cuvelier, *Actes*, pp. 102-3, 105-8. In early 1465, the civic authorities of Hoorn requested permission from the *stadhouder* and Council of Holland-Zealand to let merchants sell those English cloths currently in the city, but this request was denied. Smit, *Bronnen Handel*, II, 987, no. 1548; 1000, no. 1566. The Hanseatic Diet at Lübeck issued its protest, at the request of Cologne, on 23 July 1466. Von der Ropp, *Hanserecesse*, V, 586, no. 800:16.

33 Smit, *Bronnen Handel*, II, 988-94, no. 1549: an inventory, dated 18 Mar. 1465, listing several hundred English broadcloths and kerseys which Philip's officials had confiscated in Middelburg. The Middelburg magistrates requested the return of the cloths, pleading 'que en la dite ville a plusieurs bourgois, marcans, et habitans, qui par ci-devant ont accoustumé de gaignier

For England, the more effective enforcement of this ban was not the only reason that made it much more serious than its predecessors, as alarming as the 1447 ban had seemed at the time. It closed out a market that had become, since the 1440s, substantially greater in importance as a result of the Hanseatic League's almost complete exclusion of English merchants from the Baltic cloth trade. As Michael Postan has shown, Antwerp by the 1460s had become vital to the English cloth merchants in providing the only major and feasible access to the large German and Central European markets.[34] Colourfully portraying his fears of the dire consequences, a Commons petitioner in January 1465 maintained that, if the cloth ban continued in force, those engaged in the cloth industry and trade 'shuld be destitute of occupations and become as ydell, which shuld provoke theym to synne and evell livyng, that God defende.'[35] Parliament responded to his (or the Crown's) demand for immediate retaliation, as it had in 1449, by enacting a ban on all imports of Burgundian goods except foodstuffs. The duke of Burgundy was given only two months, until the coming 25 March, to remove his cloth ban before the embargo took effect.[36] In contrast to the last counter-ban, moreover, the Crown this time did enforce it; a patent roll of February 1466, for example, records the seizure of Burgundian goods by the authority of this statute.[37] The bullionist conflict threatened once more to make, in the words of Henry VI, 'alle merchandise ceese.'[38]

leur povre vie à vendre, acheter, et evicer en icelle ville et à l'environ les dits draps d'Angleterre, tant en gros et en detail comme autrement.' They maintained that the merchants lacked enough time to dispose of so many cloths within the month permitted them and further that the confiscations 'seroit la destruction totale des dits bourgois et habitans ... dont les aucuns d'eulx ont mis et employé la pluspart de leur chevanche en l'achat des dits draps.' See also *Ibid.*, II, 1000, no. 1566.

34 Postan, 'Economic and Political Relations,' *Studies in English Trade*, pp. 151-3; Van Houtte, 'La genèse du grand marché international d'Anvers à la fin du moyen âge,' *Revue belge de philologie et d'histoire*, XIX (1940), 87-126; Munro, 'Bruges and the Abortive Staple in English Cloth,' *Ibid.*, XLIV (1966), 1143-7.

35 *Rot. Parl.*, V, 565-6: no. 53. But see also the petition of 1449 in *Ibid.*, V, 150: no. 20, with similar wording.

36 *S.R.*, II, 411-3 (4 Ed. IV, c. 5). The statute demanded that the duke of Burgundy permit the resumption of English cloth sales in all his lands, including the duchy and county of Burgundy, 'si franchement come ceux furent amesnez, cariez, ou convoiez devant les proclamacions de les ditz declaracion et ordenaunce par le dit Duc faitz;' but again it did not mention Flanders. The statutory ban on Burgundian goods was to endure until 'due continuelle reformacion soiet oue et fait par le dit Duc.' The counter-ban, however, was not complete, for it exempted the Hanseatic merchants from its provisions.

37 *Cal. Pat. Rolls 1461-7*, pp. 517-8. The king's officials had seized 389 bales of madder from three Florentine galleys, which these ships had imported from the Low Countries to Sandwich. The confiscation order cited the 1465 statute.

38 Nicolas, *P.P.C.*, VI, 71. See chapter 5, *supra*, pp. 141-2.

Nevertheless, Anglo-Burgundian relations were not so badly impaired that the two rulers refused to enter into negotiations. At that time, Edward IV was particularly anxious not to rupture relations, for he needed Burgundy's support against Louis XI and the French-assisted Lancastrian party. Since Duke Philip's son and heir, Charles Count of Charolais, had become Louis' bitter foe, Edward entertained some hopes of reviving the old Anglo-Burgundian alliance.[39] Edward secured Philip's agreement to hold a conference at Calais on Anglo-Burgundian commercial relations. But the negotiations, conducted during May and June 1465, were fruitless, apparently because neither party was yet ready to offer any concessions.[40] Burgundian involvement in the ensuing *Guerre du Bien Public* and Louis XI's machinations to win over Edward IV effectively delayed the next conference for another nine months.[41] By early 1466, however, both Edward and Count Charles seemed anxious to unite against the increasing menace of the wily King Louis. On 22 March, Edward instructed Warwick ('The Kingmaker') to arrange a marriage alliance between his sister Margaret of York and Count Charles; at the same time, he authorized Warwick to negotiate a repeal of the statutes banning Burgundian goods in return for Philip's removal of the cloth ban.[42]

But this second Anglo-Burgundian conference, conducted at St. Omer and Bruges during April and May 1466, was also a failure and broke down over the bullion dispute. The Burgundian ambassadors demanded the elimination of

---

39 On 28 Mar. 1465 Edward IV issued commissions for negotiating an alliance with Count Charles of Charolais (Rymer, *Foedera*, XI, 540). By this time, Philip's son Charles had become the bitter enemy of Louis XI because of the French king's machinations with the Cröy faction in the ducal council to subvert his powers and to alienate him from Philip. Louis had already demonstrated his intentions to undermine Burgundian power by banning imports of Burgundian salt (1462) and by supporting the rebellious Liégeois. Subsequently, Charles allied himself with the dukes of Berry and Brittany to wage the *Guerre du Bien Public* against Louis XI. See Bonenfant, *Philippe le Bon*, pp. 109-16; Thielemans, *Bourgogne et Angleterre*, pp. 388-420; Vaughan, *Philip the Good*, pp. 379-97. For Louis XI's aid to the Lancastrians and Edward's reactions, see Jacob, *Fifteenth Century*, pp. 534-7.

40 See Rymer, *Foedera*, XI, 541-2 (Edward's commission to negotiate a renewal of the trade treaty, on 8 May 1465.) On 20 June 1465, a Dutch delegation arrived at Calais 'om te spreken van der comanscip van der velle ende wolle;' their complaints were the same as those noted *infra* in note 43. Posthumus, *Bronnen Leidsche Textielnijverheid*, I, 402-3, no. 348:10; other references to the conference in Smit, *Bronnen Handel*, II, 1000, no. 1566.

41 Vaughan, *Philip the Good*, pp. 380-90. Jacob, *Fifteenth Century*, pp. 550-1, and Thielemans, *Bourgogne et Angleterre*, pp. 416-8. Charles defeated Louis XI at the Battle of Montlhéry in July. See note 45 *infra*.

42 Rymer, *Foedera*, XI, 562-4: 'de communicando et tractando cum Duce Burgundiae, super actubus Parliamentorum revocandis.' The commission repeated the provisions of 3 Ed. IV, c. 4, banning certain imports, and 4 Ed. IV, c. 5, embargoing all Burgundian goods.

the 'oppressive' Staple regulations to make the wool trade 'as free as it used to be.'[43] The English ambassadors made no reply to these demands, since they had not been empowered to discuss the Staple issues. They in turn presented their counter-offer of an agreement to terminate both trade bans. But Philip remained intransigent. Despite the pleas from his own Dutch delegates to remove the cloth ban, he refused to do so without a revocation of the Calais bullion law. Warwick then consulted with the Merchants Adventures and their London counterparts, the Mercers, and accepted their demand to continue the embargo against Burgundian goods until Philip relented.[44]

Warwick may well have been satisfied to see the conference fail, for he had fallen victim to Louis XI's wiles and now favoured an Anglo-French alliance directed against Burgundy.[45] Nevertheless, despite the forlorn hope of resolving the monetary conflict and Warwick's opposition to his master's foreign policy, the conference did lay the foundations for a political pact between Edward and Charles. Shortly after, in October 1466, the two signed a treaty of friendship and mutual aid against King Louis.[46] Immediately following Philip's death in June 1467, Charles would cement his alliance with Edward by restoring commercial relations on the English terms which his father had rejected at the 1466 conference.

Philip's intransigence at that conference may have been the product of senility, as though bullionism had become after forty years an *idée fixe* for the aged duke. It may also reflect his perseverance in attempting once more, during those negotiations, to regenerate his long dormant mints, free from English interference. From January 1465 to May 1466, Philip convoked several assemblies of his towns to obtain their agreement on striking a new coinage. His chief

---

43 Posthumus, *Bronnen Leidsche Textilenijverheid*, I, 415, no. 364:8 (21 May 1466): 'den gedeputeerde van Engelant te kennen te geven ende te sprekene van der comanscip van des conincx vellen, die men den coopluyden van desen lande tot Calis upieyde, dairby dat die coopluyden grotelic bezwairt waeren ende noch zijn ... end dat die comanscip vry wair ende hoir loop mochte hebben, als zy van oudts pleget te hebben.'

44 See note 42 *supra* and Thielemans, *Bourgogne et Angleterre*, pp. 420-1, for the letter from William Caxton, Governor of the Merchants Adventurers.

45 Jacob, *Fifteenth Century*, pp. 552-3. According to Jacob, Warwick had become an admirer of Louis XI, who flattered him sedulously during 1464-5; in 1466, Warwick had fought strenuously against the proposed marriage alliance with Count Charles, but his efforts to secure a French alliance failed and only served to increase the enmity between himself and the king. Edward IV, nevertheless, was willing to bargain with Louis, if only to secure better terms from Charles and to discourage Louis' efforts to aid the Lancastrians. In May 1466, Edward prolonged the truce with Louis for two years on condition that neither party assist the enemies of the other.

46 Rymer, *Foedera*, XI, 580-1. On 7 Jan. 1467 Edward IV had again unsuccessfully tried to negotiate a commercial treaty with Duke Philip. *Ibid.*, XI, 576-7.

argument for a debasement was to halt the increasing circulation of various foreign coins, 'feeble in weight and fineness,' many of them struck in close imitation of Burgundian coins. The town assemblies, however, apparently still preferred less drastic solutions: such as a more effectively enforced ban on the influx of debased coins.[47] Philip adopted this measure in November 1465 to retaliate against Edward IV's silver debasement of 1464; his order to confiscate all English silver coins as '*billon*' for his mints was a violation of a long standing tradition to accept English coins.[48] The circulation of foreign debased coins nevertheless continued and apparently become so serious — in supposedly causing a flight of good coins from his lands — that Philip was finally able to issue his coinage ordinance on 23 May.[49] His new coinage, however, represented a relatively timid debasement: only 3.5 per cent for the new gold coinage, and 12.7 per cent for the silver, far less than Edward IV's debasements of 35 per cent and 20 per cent respectively.[50]

Not surprisingly, therefore, Philip's alteration of the coinage was much less successful in stimulating mint production than either his previous ones of

47 The first Burgundian town conferences were held at Brussels in January and March 1465: 'werende die veranderinge vander munte, die mijn vors. genadige heere in meijninge te doen, mitsgaders die provisie vander hagemunte lopende binnen desen landes (January); advis te nemene up de ghebreken van der munte, ende zonderlinghe van den vreemden penninghen die men in 't vorseyden land daghelicx brochte ten grooten quetse ende scade van hem ende van zinen onderzaten' (March). Cuvelier, *Actes*, pp. 102-3, 105-7. Further conferences were held at Brussels in Nov. 1465, and Jan., Feb., Mar., and May 1466. *Ibid.*, pp. 129-31; A.G.R., C. de C., no. 32,518, fo. 26vo. (23 Nov. 1465); fo. 27vo. (20 Jan. 1466); fo. 29r. (9 Mar. 1466); fo. 31vo. (23 May 1466).

48 Varenbergh, *Relations diplomatiques*, pp. 522-3, no. IV:10: 'que puis peu de temps enca, la blance monnoie d'Angleterre est fort multipliees et a prins grant cours ... a plus hault pris beaucoup icelle ne vault.' Précis in Gilliodts-van Severen, *Estaple de Bruges*, II, 135, no. 1072.

49 A.G.R., C. de C., no. 133, fo. 174r.-6r. (version of 14 June 1466; see note 50 *infra*): 'pour ce que en aucunes villes, fortresses, et monnoyes estranges ont este par cy-devant faiz et forgiez deniers dor et dargent ala facon, emprainte, et forme de noz deniers ou assez semblables et iceulx allouez au pris et a valeur de noz deniers, lesquelx toutesfoyes estoyent et sont d'autre et moindre poix et aloy que lesdis notres ... (fo. 175r.);' 'les dis deniers dor et dargent de foible poix et aloy dequoy nosdis pays sont fort remplis tellement que en briefs temps nul bon or ne aussi blance monnoye ne y seront trouve.' (fo. 174r.). The duke decreed that anyone convicted of distributing such foreign coins or of exporting bullion (*billon*) would be banished from his lands forever. See also A.G.R., C. de C., carton 65: bis 1 on the circulation of fraudulent Rhenish coins, chiefly *florins*.

50 Partial text of the 23 May 1466 ordinance in Deschamps de Pas, 'Histoire monétaire des comtes de Flandre,' *Revue numismatique*, 2nd ser., VII (1862), 126-9. Philip ordered the striking of a gold *florin* of 19 carats and a *taille* of 72 to the *marc*; and a silver *double gros* of 6 *den. argent-le-roy* and a *taille* of 82 1/2 to the *marc*. The gold *traite* was £15.10s.9d. *gros*; the silver *traite*, £1.7s.6d. *gros*. See also Spufford, *Monetary Problems*, pp. 120-1. He points out that Philip's florin resembled the Rhenish florin, with the same fineness.

1426-33 or King Edward's. Four mints opened in June and July 1466 but closed a year later,[51] after having received probably little more than old issues for recoinage. As graph VI shows, the gold coinage output (1167 marcs) was especially low. But the Burgundian mints could hardly have expected to receive much gold when, for the first time in forty years, Philip had permitted the English to have the more favourable mint ratio. On the other hand, the duke does not seem to have accepted this disadvantage; for, he convoked three more town assemblies the next year, from February to June 1467, in order specifically to find means of 'combatting the rising prices' for gold coins.[52] But on the opening day of the third conference, 15 June, Philip the Good died, ending his reign as he had begun it with unresolved monetary problems. The new duke of Burgundy, Charles the Rash, continued that conference and achieved some success.[53] On 13 October 1467, he issued a new monetary ordinance for a further debasement of both gold and silver.[54] Two mints re-opened in early 1468 and, as the graph shows, coined significantly increased amounts of gold and silver over the next several years: an average of 29,300 marcs of silver alone during his ten-year reign.[55]

51 The Ghent mint operated from 18 June 1466 to 9 June 1467; the Louvain mint, from 23 June 1466 to 7 July 1467; the Valenciennes mint, from 2 Aug. 1466 to 20 April 1467; and the Dordrecht mint, from 12 June 1466 to 29 June 1467. A.G.R., C. de C., nos. 18,196, 18,069; Acquits de Lille, liasse no. 1512: 4; Van der Chijs, *Munten van Holland*, p. 442; A.R.A. (N.), Rek. no. 4937:X.

52 The monetary conferences were held at Lille from 17-28 February; at Antwerp, from 24-31 May; and at Bruges, from 15-25 June 1467. Cuvelier, *Actes*, pp. 132-45. For the first conference, Philip requested that the delegates be experts on monetary matters and that they bring with them letters from the provincial estates on their deliberations on maintaining his coinage ordinance. For the last conference, the Bailiff of Hainaut reported that Philip had written letters requiring the estates 'ensemble communiquier le fait des monnoyes, qui très excessivement se hauchoient, en especial les florins.' The Hainaut Estates decided that 'le piet de monnoye que l'en vouloit faire sembloit bien prejudiciable à monseigneur meisme et à tous ses pays.' *Ibid.*, pp. 143-5.

53 Charles continued the Bruges conference until 25 June, and then held another between 15 July and 1 August 1467. Cuvelier, *Actes*, pp. 146-50. See also the letter of Arnould Mussche, Master-General of the Mints, dated 28 July 1467: it recommended the debasement which Charles later adopted, on 13 October 1467. A.G.R., C. de C., carton no. 65:2.

54 Complete text in Gilliodts-van Severen, *Archives de la ville de Bruges*, V, 537-54, no. 1101. He raised the gold *traite* to £15.18s.4d. *gros*, and the silver *traite* to 28s.2d. *gros*.

55 The Bruges mint re-opened on 23 January 1468; the Louvain mint on 11 April 1468. (A.G.R., C. de C., nos. 18,706, 18,070.) The large volumes of silver coinage were probably the result of an influx of Central European silver, from the recently opened mines. Hermann van der Wee has also suggested that the Burgundian debasement of 1467, further overvaluing silver in relation to gold — as graph VI clearly shows — provided a profit sufficiently high enough to lure that Central European silver to the Burgundian mints. *Growth of the Antwerp Market*, II, 80-3; see also Nef, 'Mining and Metallurgy,' *C.E.H.*, II, 469-73.

When Charles succeeded his father, however, his primary concern was by no means monetary; indeed, he clearly saw that his father's rigid bullionist policy was a serious hindrance to the realization of his political ambitions: a military alliance with Edward IV to destroy Louis XI once and for all. In June 1467, Charles was again at war with Louis, who had assisted the rebellious Liègeois the previous year in their invasion of Namur and was now inciting them to revolt against the new duke.[56] Thus Charles sought an English army to check Louis on the Burgundian south-west flank, while he later pursued his fatal ambitions along France's eastern frontiers. By this time, Edward had become distrustful of Warwick's pro-French sympathies and was convinced that Louis' aid to the Lancastrian rebels provided a serious threat to his throne.[57] Philip was hardly in his grave, therefore, when the two rulers on 15 July reconfirmed their pact of the previous October 'perpetually and forever.' Each promised to aid the other by any means against all enemies, namely Louis.[58] Charles also agreed, on 20 September, to marry Margaret of York.[59] His final step to complete the alliance was the restoration of commercial relations with England, now even more imperative because of Louis' recently imposed ban on Burgundian goods.[60]

On 24 November 1467, Charles and Edward signed a commercial treaty to guarantee each other's merchants reciprocal rights of free trade for thirty years. The treaty was, in fact, another renewal of the original *intercursus* of 1439, somewhat enlarged to confirm all the privileges which both parties had been granted over the past thirty years.[61] The first and immediate result of the treaty was that the Merchant Adventurers, exiled in Utrecht for three years, returned to Antwerp and Bergen-op-Zoom.[62] As the accompanying Table II suggests,

---

56 Bonenfant, *Philippe le Bon*, pp. 114-6; Pirenne, *Histoire de Belgique*, II, 295-310.

57 Jacob, *Fifteenth Century*, pp. 552-4.

58 Rymer, *Foedera*, XI, 580-1.

59 *Ibid.*, XI, 590. He married Edward's sister on 2 July 1468.

60 Gandilhon, *Louis XI*, pp. 365-71. After Charles' victory over Louis at Péronne in October 1468, Louis agreed *inter alia* to lift this prohibition against Burgundian imports; but he renewed it on October 1470 (pp. 431-3).

61 Rymer, *Foedera*, XI, 591-9, 605-13; précis in Smit, *Bronnen Handel*, II, 1014-5, no. 1578. This treaty, like the one of 1439, was between England, Ireland, and Calais on the one hand, and Flanders, Brabant, and Malines on the other. There is no reason to believe, however, that its provisions excluded Holland and Zealand. Edward IV ratified the treaty on 5 Jan. 1468; Duke Charles, on 20 Feb. 1468.

62 Smit, *Bronnen Handel*, II, 1007-8, no. 1563; see also De Smedt, 'De Engelsche Handel,' p. 592. On 7 Dec. 1469, the Merchants Adventurers received from Bergen-op-Zoom the same charter of privileges that Antwerp had granted them in 1446. Schanz, *Englische Handelspolitik*, II, 170-8, no. 3 (complete text); Smit, *Bronnen Handel*, II, 1031, no. 1609.

the treaty would seem to have encouraged not only a recovery but a boom in London's cloth export trade.

TABLE II

English Cloth Exports, 1466-67 to 1478-79

(Michaelmas) Year	London Denizen Exports (Merchants Adventurers)	Total London Exports	Per cent of the English total	Total Cloth Exports from England
1466-67	8,133	16,241	46	35,388
1467-68	16,594	25,921	63	41,170
1468-69	22,262	25,586	64	39,870
Average				
1465-69	11,859	18,682	53	35,130
1469-70	12,614	18,717	63	29,563
1470-71	13,672	17,680	60	29,530
1471-72*	11,050	17,159	42	40,040
1472-73*	15,524	25,117	72	34,949
1473-74*	16,432	34,290	77	44,538
Average				
1470-74	13,858	22,593	63	35,725
1474-75*	11,959	22,396	71	31,386
1475-76*	19,167	26,102	69	37,789
1476-77*	13,455	30,360	67	45,133
1477-78	19,966	34,796	64	54,177
1478-79	23,080	40,448	71	57,090
Average				
1475-79	17,525	30,820	68	45,115

SOURCE: Calculated from tables in Carus-Wilson, *England's Export Trade*, pp. 102-6.

* The accounts for Bristol are missing for the years 1471-72 to 77; for the computation of total English cloth exports, Bristol's cloth exports have been estimated at 2,347 cloths per annum.

London's particularly rapid expansion in cloth exports also reflects, however, the growing concentration of the cloth trade upon Antwerp.[63] At the same time, the commercial expansion of the South Germans, in exchanging their silver,

63 As previously noted, English cloth merchants had lost access to the Baltic, Scandinavian, and Icelandic markets; and the loss of Gascony by 1453 further reduced their cloth market. See *supra* chapter 5, p. 138 and note 31. Cloth exports from the north-east ports trading to Scandinavia and the Baltic had accounted for about 30-35 per cent of total cloth exports before 1445, but only 10 per cent in 1467-71. Similarly, Bristol's exports had accounted for 20 per cent of total cloth exports before the loss of Gascony, but only 7.5 per cent in 1467-71. Carus-Wilson, *England's Export Trade*, pp. 95-106.

copper, fustians and Rhenish wines for English cloth at Antwerp, contributed significantly to a further expansion of the cloth trade.[64]

Although the 1467 treaty unquestionably provided a brisk tonic for Anglo-Burgundian commerce, it had nevertheless not resolved nor even mentioned the bullionist conflict that had provoked the original rupture in trade relations. To be sure, the Burgundian negotiators at the treaty conference had once more pressed their demands for a reform of the Staple payment regulations.[65] But Charles' decision to accept the treaty without satisfaction on this issue did not signify his willingness to sacrifice Philip's monetary policy entirely as the price for an English alliance. Recognizing the futility and dangers of continued trade embargoes, he merely agreed to leave the Staple dispute for later and calmer consideration. Thus, on 5 January 1468, King Edward announced that another Anglo-Burgundian conference would be held in March to negotiate a separate settlement concerning 'certain exactions, constraints, and ordinances placed on the wool trade at Calais, prejudicial to the subjects of the Duke of Burgundy, and the prohibitions made in his lands against the importation, sale, and distribution of English cloth.'[66] This and subsequent references to Philip's cloth ban are ambiguous, especially in light of the export statistics, but may indicate that the Burgundian resumption of English cloth imports was only a limited or provisional one pending a final agreement with Edward.[67]

---

64 Van Houtte, 'La genèse du grand marché international d'Anvers,' pp. 87-126, and 'Bruges et Anvers: marchés 'nationaux' ou 'internationaux' du XIVe au XVIe siècle?' *Revue du Nord*, XXXIV (1952), 89-104; and Munro, 'Bruges and the Abortive Staple in English Cloth,' pp. 1137-59.

65 See Smit, *Bronnen Handel*, II, 1016, no. 1580; and Thielemans, *Bourgogne et Angleterre*, pp. 469-74, doc. no. 8 (dated only 1467). See also *supra*, pp. 162-3 and note 24.

66 Rymer, *Foedera*, XI, 599-601: 'Non obstant que par lez lettres du dit Entrecours deslors passées et accordéz, soit dit generalement que le dit Entrecours aura Lieu pour tous Denrées et Marchandisez ... pur ce que despeica ont esté meus et suscitéz certains differences, touchans lez dit Entrecours et Communicacion pour raison et à cause de plusours Nouvellettes, Pretenduez d'une partie et d'autre tant à Cause d'ascuns Exactions, Contraintez et Ordonnances, mises sus en le Staple de Calais sur le faitz dez Laines ou prejudice dez Subjettes de nostre dit Cousin le Duc de Bourgoigne ... et dez Defenses faitz en sez dites Paiis de non y Admener, Vendre, ne distribuer les Draps d'Angleterre...' On 20 February Charles issued a similar letter agreeing to hold at Bruges a conference on these issues on 20 March. *Ibid.*, XI, 613-4. While Parliament had not re-enacted the Calais bullion law after its official expiry in Michaelmas 1466, it seems evident that Edward had maintained it.

67 That possibility is suggested by Edward's letter: that, while negotiations continue 'sur les quelz differendez et Nouvelletz,' the commercial treaty 'serroit tenue une fourne en tiel lieu et en dedens tiel jour que par Nous et nostre dit Cousin serront advises et accordéz...' *Ibid.*, XI, 601. Two other possible explanations: that Charles had permitted English cloth imports only for finishing and re-export from the Brabant Fairs; or that the English were now demanding access to the long-forbidden Flemish market. Parliament's ultimatum on Philip's cloth ban,

The promised Anglo-Burgundian trade conference proved difficult to con-
vene, however, as if neither party could agree upon even the agenda. The
negotiations scheduled for March 1468 at Bruges were postponed to May and
then to late June.[68] Since no records are available for such a conference, nor
for another that Edward IV proposed in September, the commercial negotiations may have been delayed for another year.[69] Finally, on 1 June 1469,
an Anglo-Burgundian conference opened at Bruges. To commence the three
months of negotiation, Duke Charles instructed the delegates, including representatives of Middelburg, the Staple Mayor, and his chief officers, to examine
the question of English cloth imports and 'novelties and abuses' in trade relations.[70] At least one issue, the future of the cloth trade, may have been resolved
at this conference; for it is never referred to again during Charles' reign and
copious references over the following year attest to the unhindered sale of
English cloth in Holland, Zealand, and Brabant.[71]

however, had made no such demand to sell cloth in Flanders (*S.R.*, II, 412). In any event
Charles in March 1470 reconfirmed Bruges' staple charter, specifically restating the permanent
Flemish prohibition against English cloth imports. Gilliodts-van Severen, *Archives de la ville
de Bruges*, VI, 12, no. 1107:17. See also note 69 *infra*.

68 Rymer, *Foedera*, XI, 616-7; Smit, *Bronnen Handel*, II, 1016, no. 1580.

69 On 28 Sept. 1468, the Company Court of the Mercers granted two of their members £40
sterl. 'towarde theire Costes and Charges for th'ambassatt of th'enlargying of wollen clothe
in the duke of Burgun landes.' William Caxton, Governor of the Merchants Adventurers (as-
sociated with the London Mercers guild) was also named an ambassador by Edward IV. F.D.
Watney and L. Lyell (eds.), *Acts of the Court of the Mercers' Company, 1453-1527* (Cambridge, 1936), pp. 61-2. A month earlier, in August, the Leyden burgermasters had written to
the Calais Staplers demanding a conference to settle their grievances: 'Itaque ob tales sub-
dolas, dampnosas, injustas astucias et dolositates similes precavendas interdum necesse est
statua et ordinaciones fieri, quibus malorum nociva improbitas et dolosa subtilitas arceantur
et communis vestra ac eciam in negociando utilitas procuretur...' Posthumus, *Bronnen Leidsche Textielnijverheid*, I, 434, no. 383; see also pp. 433-5, nos. 382, 384. In January 1469 a
Leyden delegation visited the Staple 'te spreken van der vryheyt van der Stapele, dat se hiet
een vrye stapel te wesen,' and to complain of the high wool prices and of the poor quality
of the wools sold there. *Ibid.*, I, 460-1, no. 400:7, 8, 9, 10, and 13.

70 Smit, *Bronnen Handel*, II, 1022-3, no. 1594 (to the magistrates of Middelburg, 6 June 1469):
'om te besongierne mitten ambassiators van Ingelant ... upten loep van den Engelschen lakenen ende upte nieuwicheyden ende habusien aen beyden zijden voirtgekeert.' See also Gilliodts-van Severen, *Estaple de Bruges*, II, 183, no. 1125, for safe-conducts issued to John
Prout, the Staple Mayor, and other Staplers, on 11 June.

71 Smit, *Bronnen Handel*, II, 1026-7, no. 1599, and 1047, no. 1631 (Bergen-op-Zoom); 1049,
no. 1636 (Middelburg); 1050, no. 1638 (Antwerp); 1050, no. 1640 (Zealand towns); 1053-4,
no. 1645 (Holland towns); 1061, no. 1661 (Zealand towns); 1076, no. 1680 and 1088, no. 1709
(Bergen-op-Zoom); 1090, no. 1716 (Antwerp); 1091, no. 1718 (Bergen-op-Zoom). From October 1469 to December 1473 only; but thereafter many more references to English cloth sales
until the next cloth ban of 1494.

The Bruges conference also made a valiant attempt to eliminate foreign exchange problems and prevent future monetary conflicts by a coinage convention which it issued on 23 August. In this 'draft' treaty, the English and Burgundian commissioners declared that all coins of both rulers, certain French coins, and Italian *ducats* were to be accepted as legal tender in both countries '*indifferenter*.' Carefully defining the weights and finenesses of all these coins, they agreed upon the exchange rates to fix a common gold to silver ratio of 12:1. The money-of-account systems, therefore, were to be equivalent: one *livre gros* of Flanders to equal one pound *sterling* of England. The monetary theory, however, did not prove susceptible of practical application. When the Burgundian delegates demanded the right to pay for wool at the Calais Staple in either English or Flemish coinage by 'tale' (number), according to this common evaluation, the English commissioners vacillated. Apparently realizing that this demand would nullify the Calais bullion ordinances, they agreed only to refer the issue to King Edward's Council.[72] The Burgundian ducal councillors, on the other hand, appeared unwilling to permit free-trade in bullion.[73] This treaty was never ratified, probably because neither ruler wished to commit himself indefinitely to a stable coinage. Nevertheless, the proposals were significant in offering perhaps the best escape from the evils of mint-competition and the bullionist impasse.

The Burgundians did not achieve a final victory on the Staple and bullion issues for another four years and then only because of Duke Charles' intervention in the Wars of the Roses. In the meantime, English procrastinations following the 1469 Bruges conference had so irritated Charles that he was evidently planning to resume Philip's retaliatory policies. During July 1470, he consulted an assembly of his towns at Bruges on measures that would compel the English to reform the Calais Staple and restore 'free commerce.'[74] But short-

---

72 A.G.R., C. de C., no. 1158, fo. 94-103: 'Ita quod xxᵗⁱ solidi esterlingorum libram faciunt grossorum [Flemish] et contra xxᵗⁱ solidi grossorum libram esterlingorum... Et hunc etiam quanqua in Anglia aut Calesia ubi comiter mercator ex merchas vendentur lane ... talis mercha estimatur valoris xiii s. iv d. [= 1 mark sterling] utriusque monete. In hunc articule, noluerunt consentere domini oratores Anglie...'

73 A.G.R., C. de C., carton 65: bis 1, for the Burgundian report. See comments on this conference in A. De Witte, 'Les relations monétaires entre la Flandre et l'Angleterre jusqu'au XVIIe siècle,' *Revue du droit international*, II (1894), 20. His account is, however, not overly illuminating.

74 Cuvelier, *Actes*, pp. 159-60. From the Leyden account: 'Vander comanship aengaende van der vellen ende wollen die men tot Calis coept ende hailt, dairin dat nuwicheden op gestelt ende hantieringe gedaen ende opgesat worden, dairin by dat die poorteren ende coopluyden van Leyden in der stapule van Calais bezwairt, bedwongen ende benauwert worden boven ouden tractacten ende appunctamenten voirtyts gemaict. Ende dat die comanscip vry mochten

ly after, the mounting policial crisis in England rendered any possible cloth ban quite inopportune. In September, Warwick 'The Kingmaker' invaded England with a French-backed Lancastrian army, forced Edward to flee, and then restored Henry VI. Edward sought refuge with Duke Charles, who had good cause to be gravely alarmed by Warwick's *coup d'état*. Long hostile to Charles, Warwick had promised to supply English forces for Louis XI's invasion of the Burgundian Lowlands; Louis in return had not only financed the Lancastrian expedition but then offered Warwick the counties of Holland and Zealand.[75] Charles was therefore quick to finance Edward's expeditionary force, which successfully invaded England in March 1471 and crushed Warwick's forces at the famous battles of Barnett and Tewkesbury.[76] Once restored to the throne, Edward was called upon to redeem his debt to Charles. After two more Anglo-Burgundian trade conferences, Edward finally agreed in May 1473 to renounce the Calais bullion ordinances.[77]

King Edward then secured from the 1473 Parliament a statute to nullify all previous laws and ordinances that regulated payments at the Calais Staple. More specifically, it permitted the Staplers to accept payments in foreign currencies and to transact bills-of-exchange (in the Lowlands) for transference of these receipts in sterling to London.[78] By this concession, the Staplers were implicitly allowed the unrestricted use of sales credit. Subsequent records show that the wool-buyers of the Lowlands were indeed conducting their trade at the

wesen, ende also vry staen als zy van ouden tyden ende haircommen hadde geweest, dair op dat die Vlamingen, Brabanderen ende die Hollantsche steden hoir beclachten samentliken overgaen, ende begeerden provisie dair op te hebben...'

75 Gandilhon, *Louis XI*, pp. 371-8; Jacob, *Fifteenth Century*, pp. 558-61, 566-9. On 28 Sept. 1470, once Warwick had appeared successful, Louis renewed the ban on Burgundian goods and in December invaded Picardy.

76 Charles supplied Edward with fourteen ships and 50,000 gold *florins*. Gilliodts-van Severen, *Archives de la ville de Bruges*, VI, 61-2.

77 Rymer, *Foedera*, XI, 738-9, 779: Edward IV's instructions for the conferences of March 1472 and May 1473, 'ut ad finalem pacificationem differentiarum et difficultatem.' On 25 July 1474, Edward and Charles renewed the 1467 treaties of commerce, perpetual friendship, and alliance against Louis XI. *Ibid.*, XI, 804-6. At the same time, on 7 July, Antwerp granted the Merchants Adventurers a permanent residence for their trade and concluded a new trade agreement. Verachter, *Archives de la ville d'Anvers*, p. 159, nos. 529-31.

78 *Rot. Parl.*, VI, 60: no. 59. The petitioner argued that the Staplers 'receyved oonly money in gold or silver which hath no cours within this Reame, nor cannot come to the profite of the Kyng, his Roialme, nor of his Merchauntes owners of the said gold and money, withoute eschaunge made in the Landes beyond the See, which eschaunge, if they any make, shuld be unto theym by dyvers other Statutes to excessively grevous and penall.' In reply: 'It is ordeyned and enacted that for any such eschaunge made ... they nor any of them be not hurt, vexed, empleded, empeched, nor empechable.'

Staple according to the traditional 'free commerce' system: *'cum litteris de cambio,'* paying *'pro manibus in prompta pecunia tercius denarius ad numus in sterlingis aut in vestro valore.'*[79]

A final and *pro forma* dismantling of England's century-old bullionist scheme took place at Lille in July 1478, as an adjunct to another renewal of the Anglo-Burgundian commercial treaty. During the negotiations, the Staple officers requested the Burgundians to reaffirm their 1459 prohibition against all wools not purchased at Calais. In return for this guarantee, the Staplers bound themselves to repudiate forever the 1429 Calais Staple Ordinances, article by article.[80] The payment regulations were not then in dispute and, as Eileen Power has noted, the difficult bargaining was conducted over such currently contentious issues as the quality of wools being sold, the proportion of old wools in each sarpler, and the methods of packing the sarplers.[81]

Finally, in negotiating this commercial treaty, the Burgundians made an important concession to the English, who had long protested against Philip the Good's ban on transit-shipments of bullion to Calais.[82] The Burgundian commissioners now agreed by this treaty not to prevent English merchants from shipping bullion through the Burgundian Lowlands, provided that they had acquired the bullion elsewhere.[83] The Burgundians also permitted, as always in the past, the export of legal tender coins, jewelry, and unbroken artifacts of

---

79 Posthumus, *Bronnen Leidsche Textielnijverheid,* I, 613-6, nos. 503, 505 (1478). Posthumus in his *De Geschiedenis van de Leidsche Lakenindustrie,* I, 230, notes that in 1478 the Staplers formally permitted the Leyden merchants to buy woolfells, the most important part of their business, on credit, and by the use of bills-of-exchange; but states that the Staplers were still demanding cash payments for purchases of woolsacks.

80 Rymer, *Foedera,* XII, 77-8; excerpts in Smit, *Bronnen Handel,* II, 1139, no. 1829. The Staplers specifically agreed to enforce no regulation on fixing the prices of wool, to make no 'partition' of receipts, to make no exactions of any part of the payment in bullion, nor to charge buyers higher prices for not supplying bullion. ('Concordatum est quod, si haberi non possit Billona, ad quam tamen habendam mercatores instare poterunt, nichil in recompensam exigetur, et si quid exactum sit restituetur.') The Burgundian 'complaints' voiced *pro forma* are very similar to those presented during the 1467 negotiations. See note 24 *supra*.

81 Rymer, *Foedera,* XI, 78-86; Power, 'The Wool Trade in the Fifteenth Century,' *Studies in English Trade,* pp. 89-90. Flemish references to disputes with the Staple in this and the following periods also concern only such matters as 'pactinghe vander Ingelsche wulle.' Gilliodts-van Severen, *Estaple de Bruges,* II, 225, no. 1183; *Archives de la ville de Bruges,* VI, 80.

82 See *supra* chapter 4, pp. 102-3 and note 27.

83 Rymer, *Foedera,* XII, 74-5: 'poterunt mercatores et subditi Regie Anglie deinceps quascumque massas auri vel argenti, vocatas Billionem, extra Patrias ... Domini Ducis Karoli, noviter defuncti ... proviso quod huius modi Billonam per se aut factores suas emptam...' (Treaty signed by Duchess Marie de Bourgogne). This provision is repeated in the treaty renewal of 3 April 1489. Gilliodts-van Severen, *Archives de la ville de Bruges,* VI, 325, no. 1234.

gold and silver.[84] King Edward, on the other hand, was unwilling to reciprocate with equally liberal measures. That same year, in fact, his Parliament pointedly re-affirmed the long-standing prohibition against the export of all gold and silver: whether in bullion, plate, jewelry, or coin.[85] The king had evidently conceded enough, as the ruler of a commercially less cosmopolitan country, in abrogating the Calais bullion laws.

So far as the records show, the English never again imposed bullionist exactions on wool exports before the demise of the Calais Staple in 1558, nor on the export trade in general. But the old Employment Laws, requiring alien importers to spend their proceeds on English goods, remained on the statute books;[86] and, although Parliament finally permitted the re-export of foreign bullion in 1663, England did not achieve complete free trade in bullion and coin until the passage of Peel's Act in 1819.[87] On the continent, most rulers continued to practice debasement to attract bullion and increase their mint profits. Indeed, both Duke Charles (d. 1477) and his son-in-law Maximilian of Hapsburg exploited their mints extensively to finance their many wars.[88] While English kings kept their coinage stable from 1465 to 1526, Henry VIII found that he could not continue waging his wars with France without resorting to the continental expedient; his 'Great Debasement' (1542-49) was by far the most drastic series of coinage alterations in English history.[89]

Bullionism had thus lost none of its vigour, though later it gradually became primarily a purely monetary rather than fiscal policy and evolved into the more sophisticated economic philosophy known as Mercantilism. In some respects it exists today in both public and governmental concern about trade balances, gold outflows, 'soft currencies,' and foreign exchange crises. It would be foolhardy to question the tenacity and longevity of bullionist-mercantilist concepts, as we come to realize that the late nineteenth- and early twentieth-century era of *laissez-faire* free trade and the international gold standard was but an ephem-

---

84 See *supra* chapter 1, pp. 23-4 and notes 41-2.

85 *S.R.*, II, 454 (17 Ed. IV, c. 1, 1478). The only exemptions permitted were ransoms, payments for English soldiers abroad, and Church ornaments.

86 The same statute (17 Ed. IV, c. 1) also re-affirmed the Employment Act of 5 Hen. IV, c. 9; later Parliament re-enacted it in statutes 1 Ric. III, c. 9 (1483) and 3 Hen. VII, c. 8 (1488).

87 Feavearyear, *Pound Sterling*, p. 4.

88 Spufford, *Monetary Problems*, pp. 141-6; see also H. Van Gelder and M. Hoc, *Les monnaies des Pays-Bas bourguignons et espagnols, 1434-1713* (Amsterdam, 1960), pp. 19-35 for a list of their coinage alterations.

89 Feavearyear, *Pound Sterling*, pp. 46-75, 435-8. Henry VIII's first debasement of 1526, and the only one before the beginning of the 'Great Debasement' in 1542, may be considered as a purely defensive one to adjust the mint prices to the market, and the coinage to the current reduced standard of the circulation.

eral aberration from the historic norm. It would perhaps also be quite impractical and worse, reactionary, to advocate complete *laissez-faire* — which has
never existed as a universally operative and unmodified system — and thus deny
governments the fiscal and monetary tools for regulating the quality, structure,
and growth of their national economies. One should remember, however, that
late-medieval and early-modern rulers also justified their monetary policies in
terms of the 'public welfare:' to protect and foster the commerce of their subjects by remedying the scarcity of money, maintaining the coinage circulation,
preventing the fraudulent use of foreign debased coins and the outflow of good
ones. It was thus necessary to achieve sound money by debasing it. Who can
doubt the sincerity of Philip the Good's monetary ordinance for his last debasement of May 1466 when it announced:

> que ung des principaulx poins de toutes bonnes pollicies sur quoy le
> bien publique, tant de nous comme du peuple, est fondé est de avoir et
> entretenir bonne monnoye, ferme et durable, tant d'or comme d'ar-
> gent.[90]

Quite possibly his argument was this time sincere, for debasements were
often necessary to defend a ruler's coinage, the most evident symbol of his
seigneurial prestige, against foreign mint competition. Nevertheless, the history
of Anglo-Burgundian commercial relations suggests that dogmatic bullionism,
by whatever monetary policy, served only to debilitate and not enhance the
'bien publique.' Competition for bullion was itself a form of war, with commerce as its victim. The subtler continental policy of debasement produced a
chain reaction of coinage alterations and monetary instability in neighbouring
countries; it often caused rampant inflations, undermined confidence in the
money system, and injured relations with foreign merchants. What is strikingly
evident from the monetary history is the trenchant and consistent opposition of
both the English Parliament and the Burgundian 'Estates' to coinage debasement; the Hanseatic Diets' protests against Burgundian debasements were
just as vigorous. England's cruder bullionist policies were no less harmful. If
fully implemented and enforced, they would have destroyed credit, the very
foundation of trade, and then strangled commerce itself with impossible controls. Certainly the clash of opposing policies seriously disrupted Anglo-Burgundian trade in bans, counter-bans, and warfare, and consequently injured
both countries' industries. Although both the English kings and the dukes of
Burgundy may have realized the mutual interdependence of their countries'
economies, each ruler acted as if the other country were the more dependent.
That was the tragic folly of their commercial and monetary policies.

90 A.G.R., C. de C., no. 133, fo. 174vo.

SOME CONCLUSIONS ON ECONOMIC CONSEQUENCES:
a Postscript and a Prelude

In the long run, the most significant consequence of the Anglo-Burgundian bullionist conflicts was to accelerate the transformations of both countries' commercial and industrial economies. The statistics of the following table suggest that the costs of the Calais bullion ordinances very likely had some influence upon three of these closely related transformations: on the one hand, the final, irredeemable decay of both the English wool trade and of the luxury cloth industries of the Low Countries; on the other, the decisive victory of the English cloth trade over all its rivals. At the very least, the statistics indicate that the Burgundians had good cause to be gravely concerned about the imposition of the English bullion regulations:

TABLE III

Average Annual Sales Receipts of the Ypres Drapery Farms, Numbers of Stalls Rented in the Ypres Drapery Halls, English Woolsacks shipped to Calais, and English Broadcloth Exports 1420-4 to 1480-4

Years	Ypres Drapery Farm Sales (1) in £ parisis	Stalls Rented in the Ypres Drapery Halls (2)	English Woolsacks shipped to Calais	English Broadcloth Exports
1420-4	£61.35	423	13,401	36,395
1425-9	58.90	372	13,255	41,510
1430-4	56.32	320	7,508	40,860
1435-9	39.71	216	3,236	42,898
1440-4	40.27	187	9,759	56,944
1445-9	40.55	159	6,592	49,448
1450-4	35.45	109	7,769	37,380
1455-9	34.58	73	7,266	37,542
1460-4	23.72	62	5,315	30,934
1465-9	21.12	71	7,944	35,130
1470-4	19.26	74	7,575	35,725
1475-9	16.76	59	7,950	45,115
1480-4	15.10	27	7,160	55,184

(1) Total of the farms of the excises on wool-purchases, cloth-production, cloth sales, and blue-dyeing (on a weekly basis).

(2) Total of drapers' and *upzetters'* stalls in the *ghemijnghede* and *blaeuwe* Halls.

SOURCES: A.G.R., C. de C., nos. 38,645-708; Carus-Wilson, *England's Export Trade*, pp. 57-69, 91-108.

In brief — and for the moment — it may be argued that the sharply increased costs of English wool, and perhaps most especially the restricted access to credit, steadily drove more and more Flemish and Brabantine drapers out of production. The already expanding English cloth trade quickly filled the vacuum; and when the offending Staple ordinances were finally revoked once and for all in the 1470s, the surviving draperies found themselves unable to regain those markets lost during the long interim. By that time, moreover, their once unexcelled reputation for high quality products could no longer suffice to rescue them, for the English cloth trade had well matched that advantage by gaining secure access to the finishing and dyeing industries of Antwerp and the Dutch towns — in close contact with its chief customers at the Brabant Fairs. To deny the English cloth trade this access would have provided a sound economic rationale for a cloth ban policy; but since retaliation and not protectionism had predominated in Duke Philip's cloth bans, the flood-gates (except in Flanders) remained open. In the 1480s English cloth imports into the Low Countries were indeed likened to an *inundacioni maris immensi*;[1] and only a few hardy remnants of the traditional Flemish and Brabantine draperies had not succumbed. By the early 1550s, when the English cloth trade attained its peak, London's exports alone amounted to some 130,000 cloths a year, of which perhaps 75 per cent was sent to the Low Countries.[2]

This reversal in fortunes of the cross-Channel rivals in turn hastened to fruition two more radical changes in the Low Countries' economy: the shift of commercial hegemony from Bruges to Antwerp; and the expansion of the cheaper *nouvelles draperies* and *draperies légères* (*sayetteries*) to become, successively, the predominant textile industries of the region. First, the rapid waning of Bruges' late-medieval commercial splendour might seem to have been almost inevitable, since that port was so heavily dependent upon the marketing of Flemish woollens. But Bruges might have averted that fate had its *échevins* — and the Flemish in general — been willing to offer the English cloth trade its international commercial and banking facilities: for, as a long-established regional entrepôt, it was the most promising distribution centre when merchants began seeking out the Low Countries' markets and continental access routes for this cloth. Bruges instead let the commercial future slip by default into the hands of its rival on the Scheldt, Antwerp. Having neither a

---

1 D. Schaeffer (ed.), *Hanserecesse 1477-1530*, III, 105 (1487); also cited in Pirenne, 'Une crise industrielle au XVIe siècle,' *Histoire économique de l'occident médiéval*, p. 625.

2 From F.J. Fisher, 'Commercial Trends and Policy in Sixteenth Century England,' in Carus-Wilson, *Essays in Economic History*, I, 153; and W. Brulez, 'Le commerce international des Pays-Bas au XVIe siècle: essai d'appréciation quantitative.' *Revue belge de philologie et d'histoire*, XLVI (1968), 1207 (for Antwerp only).

local cloth industry to protect nor any close ties with the Brabantine drapery towns, Antwerp had eagerly welcomed English cloth imports from at least the 1420s. Antwerp, to be sure, had secured its original commercial foundations in a regional fair for wines, foodstuffs, and raw materials, which continued to be most important during its Golden Age. Yet the trade in English cloths and the finishing industries they required did supply the single most powerful impetus for Antwerp's rapid fifteenth-century development. By the end of the century, its exchange trade of English woollens for Rhenish wines, then South German fustians, silver, and copper, and equally the banking this trade spawned, had attracted merchants from all over Europe. When, finally, Portugal selected this port for its East Indies spice staple, Antwerp had become the leading international entrepôt and financial capital, and as such, the decisive propelling force of the European commercial economy.[3]

Too late did Bruges, seeing itself displaced, realize the folly of Flemish protectionism. In the 1490s, its échevins assiduously sought to lure the English cloth trade away from its rival; but Bruges' proposals to establish a cloth staple were still couched in terms too restrictive, and the English by that time were well content with their investment in Antwerp.[4] Bruges nevertheless did not slip into the same economic decadence that befell the leading drapery town of Ypres. It managed to sustain a decent, if much reduced, level of commercial activity by retaining some regional trade, but especially by gaining the important staple in Spanish wools (1494) and by exporting some products of the Flemish *nouvelles draperies*; it even finally established, in the mid-sixteenth century, its own *nouvelle draperie* and then a *sayetterie*.[5]

The *nouvelles draperies*, while by no means 'new,' first achieved a major importance only from about the mid-fifteenth century, and to some considerable extent they owed their subsequent expansion, directly or indirectly, to the Calais bullion regulations of this period. In the first place, the onerous Staple regulations forced the *nouvelles draperies*, who were largely imitating the cloths of the urban luxury-draperies, to substitute Spanish and Scottish wools more

---

3 See J.A. Van Houtte, 'La genèse du grand marché international d'Anvers à la fin du moyen âge,' *Revue belge de philologie et d'histoire*, XIX (1940), 87-126; Van der Wee, *Antwerp Market*, II, 7-112; Brulez, pp. 1205-21; Renée Doehaerd, *Etudes anversoises: documents sur le commerce international à Anvers, 1488-1514*, I (Paris, 1963), 31-68. (There is, however, no concordance of views on the relative importance of the English cloth and foodstuffs trades).

4 I have discussed this in 'Bruges and the Abortive Staple in English Cloth,' *Revue belge de philologie et d'histoire*, XLIV (1966), 1137-59.

5 M.G. Willemsen (ed.), 'Le règlement sur la draperie brugeoise du 20 septembre 1544,' *Annales de l'Académie Royale d'Archéologie de Belgique*, LXIX (1921), 5-74; L. Gilliodts-van Severen (ed.), *Inventaire diplomatique des archives de l'ancienne école Bogarde à Bruges*, III (Bruges, 1899), 366-87.

and more for the English. Such is the testimony of the Burgundian ambassadors and one of their chief arguments used in attacking the Calais bullion laws.[6] That very reason can be fully documented for one drapery, Wervicq, when ducal intervention was required to rescind its *keure* prohibiting the use of non-English wools;[7] and it seems to be verified by the markedly increased number of *nouvelles draperies* that took up Spanish wools from the 1430s.[8] Since these draperies had already economized by condensing and simplifying the essential process of luxury production — fulling, shearing, and dyeing, they were much better prepared to make this further cost-cutting sacrifice than were the traditional urban industries. Indeed, in so doing, they produced a much cheaper and distinctly different type of cloth which apparently found a more readily available market. Second, one may argue that whatever injuries the Calais ordinances inflicted upon the traditional urban industries assisted the *nouvelles draperies*: by reducing the towns' ability to impose restrictions upon them, and by encouraging a shift of resources into their production. English bullionism played a much less significant role, however, in the revival and expansion of the *sayetteries* and other *draperies légères,* for these industries had never used English wools, but rather the much cheaper, coarser, long-stapled Scottish, German, and local wools.[9] At the most they may have benefited from the shift of resources away from the traditional draperies — enough, perhaps, to help account for the sharp rise in the value of the Hondschoote *sayetterie*'s excise farms from the 1440s.[10] But the era of the *sayetteries'* greatest rate of growth did not really commence until the late fifteenth century, accompanying the European economic recovery and culminating in the boom of the mid-sixteenth century; and its rapid expansion seems to be more closely related to those changes in European commerce, market structure, and income distribution that promoted a larger consumption of cheap, light textiles.

The observation that consumption functions were sometimes more important than production functions in the processes of economic change highlights the dangers of isolating the costs of bullionism in seeking to explain the industrial transformations of England and the Low Countries. The radical alterations in their textile industries and trades were indeed most complex phenomena that had begun long before the period of this study. To be fully understood, they

---

6 F. Morand (ed.), *Chronique de Jean le Fèvre de St. Remy,* II, 378 (in 1435); Smit, *Bronnen Handel,* II, 698, no. 1126 (in 1438); and chapter 6 *supra,* p. 163 (in 1467).

7 Henri De Sagher et al (eds.), *Recueil de documents relatifs à l'histoire de l'industrie drapière en Flandre* (2ᵉ partie), III, 520-1, no. 577 (1458); 527-31, nos. 581-4 (1463).

8 See Introduction *supra,* p. 4 note 16.

9 Coornaert, *Hondschoote,* pp. 189-90.

10 *Ibid.,* tables, pp. 485-7.

must be analyzed in their collective entirety from the thirteenth to the sixteenth centuries, and in the context of the changing European economy as a whole; only then can the significance of the bullionist costs be properly appreciated. Thus, in particular, one must explain why the Flemish and Brabantine luxury draperies were apparently so much more susceptible to irreparable damages from the Calais Ordinances and the English competition than the Dutch cloth industries, which managed to expand in the later fifteenth century, reaching their peak in the early sixteenth century. The answer has to be sought in the differences between their respective industrial and commercial organizations as they evolved by the fifteenth century, the types of cloths produced, and the relative access to their markets. At the same time, the roles of Dutch, Hanseatic, and English trade, the differing effects of coinage depreciation, the restructuring of markets, and the worsening depression of the northern economy are among a number of other subjects that need to be explored. Such is the task that has been set for the sequel to this study.

APPENDIX I

TABLE A

THE COINAGE OF PURE GOLD *MARCS DE TROYES* IN THE MINTS OF ENGLAND AND THE BURGUNDIAN LOW COUNTRIES
1385-1480

All accounts are for Michaelmas years, ending on 29 September of the year stated.

Year	London	Total Flanders	Bruges	Ghent	Malines	Fauquemont
1385	1,091.7	3,230.7			3,230.7	
1386	1,091.7	—				
1387	1,091.7	—				
1388	—	—				
1389	2,608.2	4,619.3		4,619.3		
1390	2,325.7	3,934.8		3,934.8		
1391	2,195.1	1,102.9		167.5	935.4	
1392	2,033.0	935.8	116.0		819.8	
1393	1,632.5	1,591.7	1,566.7		35.0	
1394	1,290.9	2,310.5	2,310.5			
1395	1,290.9	1,342.7	1,342.7			
1396	767.2	783.7	783.7			
1397	1,636.9	2,132.2	1,953.2			179.0
1398	1,636.9	1,443.5	1,264.5			179.0
1399	1,585.5	840.0	819.1			20.9
1400	698.5	666.4	666.4			
1401	698.5	377.0	377.0			
1402	698.5	267.1	267.1			
1403	426.9					
1404	448.6					

Year	London	Calais	Total Burgundian Lowlands	Flanders	Brabant	Namur	Holland
1405	316.4						
1406	515.3						
1407	284.1						
1408	206.8						
1409	—			Ghent			
1410	—		290.6	290.6			
1411	—		153.8	153.8			
1412	9,427.5						
1413	15,336.1		5.3	5.3			
1414	6,722.9		15.7	15.7			
1415	6,722.9		7.4	7.4			
1416	6,722.9						
1417	6,722.9						
1418	2,047.9		47.5	47.5			
1419	2,047.9						
1420	3,715.3						

Year	London	Calais	Total Burgundian Lowlands	Flanders	Brabant	Namur and Hainaut	Holland
				Ghent	Louvain	Namur	Dordrecht
1421	5,631.2		42.1	42.1			
1422	8,461.7	656.9	368.3	368.3			
1423	11,292.2	3,372.6	14.4	14.4			
1424	11,292.2	1,962.5	160.0	160.0			
1425	4,954.6	1,262.3	571.4	517.9		53.5	
1426	2,831.8	702.3	4,585.0	779.4		1,771.4	2,034.2
1427	2,658.9	389.2	5,797.3	2,056.9		1,354.2	2,386.2
1428	2,418.3	191.2	1,489.2	183.7		754.7	550.8
1429	1,457.1	148.1	6,061.4	4,457.5		1,603.9	
1430	1,348.5	164.6	4,715.1*	124.3	3,347.0*	1,061.8	182.0
1431	1,239.8	173.2	8,178.0	4.3	3,569.5	3,390.6	1,213.6
1432	934.1		11,901.4	1.6	1,923.4	7,692.0	2,284.4
1433	700.2		6,065.8			4,969.7	1,096.1
					Brussels	Valenciennes**	
1434	907.1		4,258.6**	3,759.5	205.8	371.0	293.3
1435	575.7		6,804.6	2,708.4	2,470.2		1,626.2
1436	575.7		6,939.5	2,365.7	2,299.8		2,274.0
1437	485.3		3,007.5	837.2	1,989.6		180.7
1438	450.4		1,236.1	820.6	229.4		186.1
1439	640.9		934.7	748.6			186.1
1440	490.1		371.8	232.2			139.6
1441	453.2		—	—			
1442	453.2		148.2	148.2			
1443	453.2		879.1	879.1			
1444	348.0		860.6	860.6			
1445	231.6		423.0	423.0			
1446	229.3		52.7	52.7			
1447	198.9						
1448	154.6						
1449	226.3						
1450	510.4						
1451	389.1						
1452	386.8			Bruges	Malines	Valenciennes	The Hague
1453	275.5						
1454	141.7		6,648.5	3,319.6	1,238.2	1,687.5	403.2
1455	109.9		10,374.4	3,258.7	4,046.1	2,271.5	798.1
1456	116.0		2,784.8	978.7	1,113.9	692.2	
1457	122.1		1,189.4	1,189.4			
1458	120.8		994.6	994.6			
				Ghent			
1459	27.6		206.0	38.5	167.5		
1460	161.7		146.5	92.3	54.2		
1461	—		92.3	92.3			
1462	—		42.3	42.3			

* Louvain, 1429-30: struck for Duke Philip of St. Pol of Brabant.

** The Valenciennes mint output for Nov. 1433-Apr. 1434 is not included in the total output, since the succeeding accounts, to 1444, are missing. With the Valenciennes output included, the total output for 1433-4 would be 4,629.6 marcs.

Year	London	Total Burgundian Lowlands	Flanders	Brabant	Hainaut	Holland
1463	209.6					
1464	209.6					
1465	8,855.9		Ghent	Louvain	Valen-	Dordrecht
1466	8,855.9				ciennes	
1467	—	1,167.4	471.7	502.8	122.9	70.0
			Bruges			
1468	—	1,335.1	1,195.6	139.5		
1469	2,922.6	1,762.9	1,467.2	295.8		
1470	3,272.9	894.3	683.2	211.1		
1471	—	621.9	505.9	116.0		
1472	2,930.8	291.9	198.0	93.9		
1473	2,393.2	98.5	81.8	16.7		
1474	2,191.6	52.7	44.3	8.3		
				Antwerp		
1475	1,875.7	4,234.6	1,998.6	2,236.0		
1476	1,379.0	4,050.9	1,685.7	2,365.3		
1477	1,854.9	1,457.9	960.8	497.1		
1478	1,599.5	1,272.1	680.4	591.7		
1479	1,497.1	842.8	464.3	378.5		
1480	1,976.3	232.8	111.9	120.9		

TABLE B

THE COINAGE OF PURE SILVER *MARCS DE TROYES* IN THE
MINTS OF ENGLAND AND THE BURGUNDIAN LOW COUNTRIES
1385-1480

All accounts are for Michaelmas years, ending 29 September of the year stated.

Year	London	Total Flanders	Bruges	Ghent	Malines	Fauquemont
1385	1,204.0	8,893.3			8,893.8	
1386	1,204.0	—				
1387	1,204.0	—				
1388	—	—				
1389	390.8	8,784.7		8,784.7		
1390	2,476.1	28,007.9		28,007.9		
1391	3,020.4	14,289.0		1,202.3	13,086.7	
1392	379.8	18,989.4	1,472.7		17,516.7	
1393	317.9	10,299.4	9,271.7		1,027.7	
1394	203.1	15,241.4	15,241.4			
1395	203.1	19,275.7	19,275.7			
1396	234.0	22,166.4	22,166.4			
1397	810.8	31,899.1	23,866.7			8,032.4
1398	810.8	31,710.2	23,677.8			8,032.4
1399	1,583.0	21,579.0	19,759.6			1,819.4
1400	316.1	16,304.2	16,304.2			
1401	316.1	8,628.9	8,628.9			
1402	316.1	6,112.2	6,112.2			
1403	177.7					
1404	499.0					

Year	London	Calais	Total Burgundian Lowlands	Flanders	Brabant	Namur	Holland
1405	96.0						
1406	111.5						
1407	88.3						
1408	8.8						
1409	—			Ghent			
1410	—		24,981.8	24,981.8			
1411	—		13,009.7	13,009.7			
1412	1,963.8		26,559.7	26,559.7			
1413	5,739.8		6,338.5	6,338.5			
1414	6,455.5		3,737.4	3,737.4			
1415	6,455.5		1,912.0	1,912.0			
1416	6,455.5		—	—			
1417	6,455.5						
1418	1,452.1		4,757.5	4,757.5			
1419	1,452.1		—	—			
1420	2,042.3		57,905.9	57,905.9			
1421	2,039.8		55,372.3	55,372.3			
1422	2,930.9	1,323.4	67,338.0	65,821.9		1,516.1	
1423	3,822.4	6,513.3	50,434.8	49,164.2		1,270.6	

Year	London	Calais	Total Burgundian Lowlands	Flanders	Brabant	Hainaut and Namur	Holland
				Ghent	Louvain	Namur	Dordrecht
1424	3,821.5	19,314.1	47,764.1	47,281.0		483.1	
1425	2,224.4	25,469.3	21,522.9	20,713.7		809.2	
1426	2,399.2	21,514.6	14,338.3	9,980.1		4,358.2	
1427	2,156.4	19,655.0	1,746.4			1,746.4	
1428	1,605.3	24,074.1	6,323.2	4,598.7		1,724.5	
1429	2,663.0	32,923.5	79,585.8	72,460.7		7,125.1	
1430	2,625.5	36,584.6	68,712.5*	34,992.1	19,467.7*	10,202.0	4,050.7
1431	2,589.6	42,321.2	13,428.1	5,585.4	2,728.3	3,507.4	1,607.0
1432	2,023.9	41,193.3	2,761.7	111.2	360.4	1,446.1	844.0
1433	1,188.6	37,724.0	444.3			125.9	318.4
					Brussels	Valen-ciennes**	
1434	786.6	24,951.7	66,096.2**	57,290.3	511.8	8,519.4	8,294.1
1435	612.7	18,199.5	48,571.7	33,371.0	6,141.7		9,059.0
1436	611.8	8,936.2	40,101.8	26,959.3	8,278.7		4,863.8
1437	754.4	—	24,401.7	13,323.2	9,026.2		2,052.3
1438	2,038.6	—	16,374.3	12,799.9	1,127.3		2,447.1
1439	4,863.8	537.7	12,829.4	10,382.3			2,447.1
1440	1,983.4		4,625.4	2,790.1			1,835.3
1441	1,199.6		—	—			
1442	1,198.7		686.1	686.1			
1443	1,198.7		681.9	681.9			
1444	214.3		671.3	671.3			
1445	285.2		149.0	149.0			
1446	2,081.3		38.0	38.0			
1447	1,509.6		88.0	88.0			
1448	304.5						
1449	749.3						
1450	6,396.4						
1451	9,762.9						
1452	7,876.9						
1453	5,246.6						
				Bruges	Malines	Valenciennes	The Hague
1454	4,341.4			912.5	322.1	557.5	32.9
1455	3,887.0			2,590.5	802.6	1,037.1 586.5	164.3
1456	5,008.3			1,077.8	806.1	238.9 32.8	
1457	6,129.3			20.0	20.0		
1458	5,051.4			66.3	66.3		
1459	4,282.4						
1460	9,717.4						
1461	—						
1462	—						
1463	8,199.9						
1464	8,199.9						

* Louvain, 1429-30: struck for Duke Philip of St. Pol of Brabant.

** The Valenciennes mint output for Nov. 1433-Apr. 1434 is not included in the total output, since the succeeding accounts, to 1444, are missing. With the Valenciennes output included, the total output for 1433-4 would be 74,615.6 marcs.

Year	London	Total Burgundian Lowlands	Flanders	Brabant	Hainaut	Holland
			Ghent	Louvain	Valen-ciennes	Dordrecht
1465	38,178.5					
1466	38,178.5					
1467	—	19,564.4	6,290.1	9,203.8	2,209.7	1,860.8
			Bruges			
1468	—	19,890.1	16,011.1	3,879.0		
1469	11,242.5	30,366.8	22,142.8	8,224.0		
1470	11,129.1	29,202.1	19,125.4	10,076.6		
1471	—	35,732.0	23,601.6	12,130.4		
1472	14,792.7	38,899.9	27,245.1	11,654.8		
1473	9,898.2	35,292.1	25,299.3	9,992.7		
1474	8,271.2	18,700.2	13,703.8	4,996.4		
				Antwerp		
1475	9,909.2	27,303.1	8,571.8	18.731.3		
1476	4,301.4	38,892.2	10,883.7	28,008.5		
1477	4,163.0	18,682.9	10,585.1	8,097.8		
1478	2,887.2	47,689.1	20,465.4	27,223.6		
1479	3,746.8	47,339.2	23,063.4	24,275.8		
1480	2,691.4	46,479.7	21,887.7	24,592.0		

SOURCES FOR THE ENGLISH AND BURGUNDIAN MINT
ACCOUNTS IN TABLES A AND B

ENGLAND

London

Calculated from the tables of the pound-sterling values of the gold and silver mintings, as given in: Sir John Craig, *The Mint: a History of the London Mint from A.D. 287 to 1948* (Cambridge, 1953), Appendix II; and supplemented by G.C. Brooke and E. Stokes, 'Tables of Bullion Coined, 1337-1550,' *The Numismatic Chronicle*, 5th ser., IX (1929), 27-69.

Calais

(a) 20 July 1422 - 31 Mar. 1436: Public Record Office, (L.T.R.) E 364/59, 61-3, 65-6, 69, 72; (K.R.) E 101/192-3; and for some years supplemented by *Calendar of Patent Rolls 1422-1429*, pp. 337-8, 520; *Cal. Pat. Rolls 1429-1436*, pp. 256-7, 259.

(b) Feb. - Mar. 1436, and 1439-40: F.A. Walters, 'Supplementary Notes on the Coinage of Henry VI,' *Numismatic Chronicle*, 4th ser., XI (1911), 172.

The partial accounts given in Rogers Ruding, *The Annals of the Coinage of Great Britain*, I (London, 1840), 84-5, are not reliable.

THE BURGUNDIAN LOW COUNTRIES

FLANDERS

Ghent

(a) 1 Oct. 1388 - 18 Nov. 1389: Archives Générales du Royaume, Chambre de Comptes, comptes en rouleaux, no. 824. An edited version of this account appears in Henri Laurent, *La loi de Gresham au moyen âge* (Brussels, 1933), pp. 163-6, doc. no. 21, but with some errors in the figures.

(b) 18 Nov. 1389 - 7 Jul. 1390: from Laurent, pp. 166-8, doc. no. 22. The compte en rouleau no. 825 for this mint account is missing from the archives.

(c) 7 Jul. - 22 Oct. 1390: A.G.R., C. de C., comptes en rouleaux no. 826. (An edited version of this account is also in Laurent, pp. 171-3, doc. no. 25.)

(d) 17 Jan. 1410 - 17 Feb. 1411: A.G.R., C. de C., comptes en rouleaux no. 827; and Acquits de Lille, liasse no. 936-1.

(e) 23 Oct. 1411 - 1 Jul. 1412: A.G.R., Acquits de Lille, liasse no. 936-2.

(f) 2 Jul. 1412 - 21 Nov. 1419: A.G.R., C. de C., comptes en rouleaux nos. 828-31. (Accounts 2 Jul. 1412 - 3 Jul. 1413 are also in Acquits de Lille, liasse no. 936-3.)

(g) 22 Nov. 1419 - 15 Aug. 1422: A.G.R., Acquits de Lille, liasse nos. 936-4, 6, 8.

(h) 15 Aug. 1422 - 11 Nov. 1424: A.G.R., Acquits de Lille, liasse nos. 937-1, 3, 5.

(i) 11 Nov. 1424 - 10 Apr. 1426: A.G.R., C. de C., reg. no. 580, fo. 47ro.

(j) 22 Nov. 1426 - 23 June 1440: A.G.R., Acquits de Lille, liasse nos. 937: 7-23. (The Ghent accounts of 7 Nov. 1419 - 13 Nov. 1430 were collated with an 18th century precis in A.G.R., C. de C., no. 580, fo. 46ro.-8ro.)

(k) 22 Aug. 1441 - 11 Oct. 1442: Archives Départementales du Nord, Chambre de Comptes, Série B., no. 1606, fo. 32vo.-3ro. (Estimate only, from marginal notations on the number of 'coins in the box' for assay.)

(l) 22 Oct. 1442 - 5 Apr. 1447: A.G.R., Acquites de Lille, liasse nos. 937: 24-6.

(m) 2 May 1459 - 16 Mar. 1462: A.G.R., C. de C., no. 18, 195.

(n) 18 June 1466 - 9 June 1467: A.G.R., C. de C., no. 18, 196.

Bruges

(a) 1 June 1392 - 16 June 1402: A.G.R., C. de C., comptes en rouleaux nos. 776-87.

(b) 2 Mar. 1454 - 25 Mar. 1455: A.D.N., B. 644/15,939. (A partial account, 29 Aug. - 29 Sept. 1454 is in A.G.R., Acquits de Lille, liasse no. 1512-1.

(c) 26 Mar. 1455 - 12 Oct. 1458: A.G.R., C. de C., nos. 18,103-5.

(d) 23 Jan. 1468 - 14 Oct. 1480: A.G.R., C. de C., nos. 18,106-14.

Fauquemont

1 Nov. 1396 - 1 Nov. 1399: A.G.R., C. de C., comptes en rouleaux nos. 2586-7.

MALINES (A separate seignory: mint accounts included under Flanders for the reign of Duke Philip the Bold; under Brabant after 1430).

(a) 9 Sept. 1384 - 4 Dec. 1385: A.G.R., C. de C., comptes en rouleaux nos. 2142-3. (No. 2143 is a copy; an edited version of n. 2142 appears in Laurent, pp. 147-9, doc. no. 9, but it is incomplete.)

(b) 3 Nov. 1390 - 20 Oct. 1392: A.G.R., C. de C., comptes en rouleaux nos. 2145-6, and copies in A.G.R., C. de C., nos. 48,976-7. (Edited versions of the latter also appear in Laurent, pp. 175-7, 184-6, doc. nos. 28, 32; but Laurent incorrectly gives the terminal date of the last account as 24 Oct. 1392.)

(c) 16 June 1454 - 16 June 1456: A.G.R., Acquits de Lille, liasse no. 1512:2-3.

(d) 25 Apr. 1459 - 16 Jan. 1460: A.G.R., Acquits de Lille, liasse no. 1512:5.

NAMUR

23 Oct. 1421 - 10 Oct. 1433: A.G.R., C. de C., nos. 18,203: 1-21; and Acquits de Lille, liasse no. 1933.

BRABANT

Louvain

(a) 15 Sept. 1429 - 20 Mar. 1432: A.G.R., C. de C., no. 18,065-8.

(b) 23 June 1466 - 31 Mar. 1474: A.G.R., C. de C., nos. 18,069-72.

Brussels

4 Sept. 1434 - 31 Dec. 1437: A.G.R., C. de C., nos. 17,986-9.

Antwerp

10 Dec. 1474 - 7 Apr. 1481: A.G.R., C. de C., nos. 17,880: 1-3, 17,881: 1-3. (Texts of these accounts are printed in P.O. Van der Chijs, *De Munten der Voormalige Hertogdommen Braband en Limburg* (Haarlem, 1851), Appendix.)

HAINAUT

Valenciennes

(a) 26 Nov. - 18 April 1434: A.D.N., B. 17,651.

(b) 28 Feb. 1454 - 2 May 1455: A.D.N., B. 31, fo. 149vo.-50ro.

(c) 9 May 1455 - Mar. 1456: marcs struck calculated from the coinage issues given in P. Spufford, *Monetary Problems and Policies in the Burgundian Netherlands, 1433-96* (Leyden, 1970), p. 184. His source citation was A.G.R., Acquits de Lille, no. 937bis (from his researches of 1956-60). But this account is now apparently missing: I did not find it in using this same bundle in 1963, nor in rechecking it in 1970. I must also express my indebtedness to Mr. Spufford's admirable study for the references to the Valenciennes accounts of 1433-4 and 1454-5 in the Lille Archives (A.D.N.).

(d) 2 Aug. 1466 - 20 Apr. 1467: A.G.R., Acquits de Lille, liasse no. 1512:4.

The mint accounts for Feb. 1437 - Mar. 1439, and Jul. 1441 - Oct. 1444 are missing (Spufford, p. 177).

HOLLAND

Dordrecht, Zevenbergen, and The Hague

(a) 23 Nov. 1425 - 24 Dec. 1427 (Dordrecht): Algemeen Rijksarchief (Nederland), Rekeningen van de Grafelijkheidsrekenkamer te 's-Gravenhage, no. 4937:I.

(b) 12 Dec. 1429 - 20 Feb. 1433 (Zevenbergen and perhaps also Dordrecht): A.R.A. (N.), Rek. no. 4937:II (with an account of subsidiary revenues and disbursements, 12 Dec. 1429 - 16 Mar. 1433, in no. 4937:III).

(c) 23 Jan. 1434 - 27 June 1440 (Dordrecht): A.R.A. (N.), Rek. no. 4937:IV-VII.

(d) 1 May 1454 - 4 Aug. 1455 (The Hague): A.R.A. (N.), Rek. no. 4937:VIII-IX.

(e) 12 July 1466 - 29 June 1467 (Dordrecht): A.R.A. (N.), Rek. no. 4937:X.

All of these accounts, except, curiously enough, that of 12 Dec. 1429 - 20 Feb. 1433 (Zevenbergen), have been printed, in extracts or in precis, in P.O. Van der Chijs, *De Munten der Voormalige Graafschappen Holland en Zeeland* (Haarlem, 1858), pp. 373-7, 399, 402, 404, 413, 426, 429, and 442. The Dordrecht accounts for 1 Jan. 1442 - 7 Feb. 1446, and 1463-5 are missing. *Note*: Both the location of the mint and the period of minting for account (b), A.R.A. (N.), rek. no. 4937:II, are difficult to determine. The mint-masters have noted that the minting took place at Dordrecht between 12 Dec. 1429 and 7 Apr. 1432 (n.s.); but they record the striking of gold *clinquaerts* (only from 8 Aug. 1430) to 20 Feb. 1433 (n.s.), and then of demi-*clinquaerts* to 20 Feb. 1434 (n.s.). A subsequent marginal notation states that the minting in fact took place at Zevenbergen, until 20 Feb. 1434 (n.s.). This latter date, however, is probably erroneous, since the next account, no. 1437:III, records subsidiary receipts and disbursements from 12 Dec. 1429 to 16 Mar. 1433 (n.s.); and no. 1437:IV records that the striking of the new, reformed coinage at Dordrecht commenced on 23 Jan. 1434 (n.s.). Account no. 1437:III, fo. 2ro., records a messenger's journey to the Zevenbergen mint on 29 Dec. 1429; but the mint may subsequently have been returned to Dordrecht (Ch. 3, p. 76). In A.D.N., B. 639/15,567 may be found a partial mint account for Zevenbergen that records the minting of 412.78 gold *marcs* in April 1430 (from an English subsidy supplied in *nobles*); since it may have been included in the above account, I have not added this gold output to the Dordrecht-Zevenbergen column in Table A.

I have used only those mint-accounts for the mints of the Low Countries that were directly controlled by the dukes of Burgundy; and also only those mints within the Flemish monetary orbit. Thus the mints of the duchy and county of Burgundy, and the mints of Picardy (Amiens and St. Quentin), which struck coins of the French royal type, have not been included. In the Archives Générales du Royaume may also be found other mint accounts for several towns of the pre-Burgundian era: Vilvorde (1409 and 1417), Louvain (1410-11), Maastricht (1418-9), and Brussels (1420-1). They have all been printed in Frederick Verachter (ed.), *Documents pour servir à l'histoire monétaire des Pays-Bas* (Antwerp, 1849), pp. 107-8, 110-4, 119-20, 125, 140-3.

Method of Computing the Mint Outputs

All the mint-account statistics in these tables are given in the mint-weight unit of the Burgundian Low Countries (and of France), the *marc de Troyes*. As described in chapter one, it contained 8 Paris ounces and weighed 244.753 grams. The English mint weight was the Tower Pound of

12 Tower or 11.25 Troy ounces, weighing 349.912 grams. (See chapter 1 *supra,* note 10, for the sources.) To make the mint accounts comparable, I converted the English Tower Pound weights into the equivalent *marcs de Troyes* by the ratio of 1.429 *marcs* to the Tower Pound. That this ratio is indeed valid for the period of this study is confirmed by several Flemish monetary ordinances: they consistently describe the English noble struck between 1412 and 1464 at a *taille* of 50 to the Tower Pound as being equal in weight to a *taille* of 35 to the *marc.* Thus:

$$\frac{1.x}{50} = \frac{1 \text{ marc}}{35} = \frac{50 \text{ marc}}{35} = 1.429 \text{ } marcs.$$

(A.G.R., C. de C., no. 580, fo. 85r.; no. 18,069, fo. 3r.; no. 1158, fo. 94vo.)

The gold *marcs* in the tables are in terms of 'fine gold,' 99.48 per cent pure. The silver marcs are those of the commercially pure *argent-le-roy,* 95.83 per cent pure silver. The English standard, however, was only 92.50 per cent pure, thus containing 96.52 per cent as much silver as *argent-le-roy.* This percentage was used to convert the English silver mint-outputs into *argent-le-roy marcs de Troyes.*

The Burgundian Mint Accounts

Practically all of the Burgundian mint accounts ran for irregular periods, though averaging about one year. For convenience the English fiscal year of Michaelmas (29 Sept.) to Michaelmas was employed for these accounts. To make them run for such annual periods, I first calculated the *monthly* average for each account and then multiplied this average by the number of months in the account preceding Michaelmas and by those following Michaelmas. For each mint and mint-year, the apportionments so calculated, often over several accounts, were then summed to arrive at the annual Michaelmas figures given in the tables. (Those accounts running for less than a year were, of course, left intact and added on to the apportionments of the preceding or succeeding account for that year.) One should note, however, that the results are in effect only averages; moreover, they represent only the estimated mint output within the given Michaelmas year and not necessarily a total of 12 months of mint activity. The accounts themselves generally indicated only the first and last days of minting.

The English Mint Accounts

London

In general, the figures presented by Craig did run for Michaelmas years. In the few instances of accounts for irregular periods, the same apportionment of the figures was made, by using monthly averages, as with the Burgundian accounts. More often, only the combined minting value for two or more years was given; for these, the annual averages computed can be seen in the repetition of the figures in the tables. The major problem was to convert Craig's figures of the pound sterling values of the coinages struck into coinage weights: first, it was necessary to divide these figures by the current *traite* per Tower Pound for gold and silver, and then to convert the Tower Pound weights into *marcs de Troyes.*

Calais

There are no complete, extant mint accounts for Calais and the statistics given in the tables can only be estimates, derived from considerable computation. The Public Record Office accounts cited, (L.T.R.) E 364 and (K.R.) E 101, do provide complete annual accounts, usually for Michaelmas years, from 1422 to 1436; but these accounts provide only the combined total of the seignorages on gold and silver, lumped together. The accounts cited in the *Calendar of Patent Rolls,* however, do provide separately the weights of pure gold and silver struck; but for each metal, only the combined totals for several years of minting are given, for four periods: 20 July 1422 - 30 Jan. 1424,, 25 Feb. 1424 - 31 Jan. 1428, 20 Feb. 1428 - 3 Aug. 1431, and 31 Oct. 1431 - 30 Sept. 1432. These accounts, moreover, do not seem complete though it seems fairly certain that no more gold was struck at Calais after 3 Aug. 1431.

To obtain annual estimates of the gold and silver mint-outputs at Calais, between 1422 and 1436, the following procedure was used:

(a) The seignorage revenues on the gold and silver mintings listed in the *Cal. Pat. Rolls* were calculated for each of the given periods, according to the seignorage rates listed in Craig, Appendix I.

(b) These gold and silver seignorage receipts were then added together, and the relative proportion of receipts accounted for by each metal, in each of the periods, was calculated. These percentages provided an estimate of the average annual ratio of gold to silver mintings for each period.

(c) By means of these percentages, the separate amounts of gold and silver seignorage receipts were calculated for each year from the complete mint-receipt accounts in the P.R.O.

(d) These separate and annual seignorages on gold and silver were then converted back into pure metal, in terms of *marcs de Troyes*.

The defect of this procedure, of course, is that it must necessarily assume that the ratio of gold to silver mintings for any given period — e.g. 25 Feb. 1424 to 31 Jan. 1428 — was constant throughout that period.

TABLE C

BURGUNDIAN MINT PRICES AND RATIOS

THE *TRAITES* AND BULLION PRICES OF GOLD AND SILVER,
PER *MARC DE TROYES*, AND THE GOLD, SILVER, AND *TRAITE* RATIOS
AT THE MINTS OF THE BURGUNDIAN LOW COUNTRIES, 1384-1477

The mint prices for gold and silver bullion are expressed in a decimal *livre gros*, per *marc de Troyes*. In this table, the mint prices for gold, taken from the ordinances or the mint-accounts, have been adjusted to a gold *marc* of 23 7/8 carats fineness, so that they may correspond to the English mint standard and ratios. The mint prices for silver are in terms of *argent-le-roy* of 12 *deniers* fineness (23/24ths pure), as they are expressed in the mint accounts.

The ratios are as follows:

$$\text{Gold ratio:} \qquad \frac{\text{Gold mint price}}{\text{Traite for silver}} = \frac{x}{1}$$

$$\text{Ratio of the Traites:} \qquad \frac{\text{Traite for gold}}{\text{Traite for silver}} = \frac{x}{1} \ (\text{or}, \ \frac{1}{x})$$

$$\text{Silver Ratio:} \qquad \frac{\text{Silver mint price}}{\text{Traite for gold}} = \frac{1}{x}$$

Year	GOLD		SILVER		RATIOS		
	Traite	Mint Price	Traite	Mint Price	Gold	Traites	Silver
July 1384	£ 8.551	£ 8.229	£ .833	£ .716	9.88	10.27	11.94
April 1386	£10.160	£ 9.906	£ .933	£ .867	10.62	10.89	11.72
Oct. 1386	£10.160	£ 9.906	£ .950	£ .890	10.43	10.69	11.41
April 1387	£12.128	£11.734	£1.152	£1.038	10.19	10.53	11.69
Oct. 1388	£13.529 (Noble)	£12.603	£1.256	£1.100	10.03	10.77	12.30
Feb. 1389	£13.529	£12.710	£1.256	£1.100	10.12	10.77	12.30
July 1389	£13.529	£13.031	£1.256	£1.100	10.38	10.77	12.30
Dec. 1389	£ 9.550	£ 9.198	£ .950	£ .850	9.68	10.05	11.24
Dec. 1389	£ 9.550	£ 9.248	£ .950	£ .850	9.73	10.05	11.24
Jan. 1391	£ 9.550	£ 9.248	£ .958	£ .858	9.65	9.97	11.13

Year	GOLD		SILVER		RATIOS		
	Traite	Mint Price	Traite	Mint Price	Gold	Traites	Silver
Jan. 1393	£ 9.550	£ 9.349	£ .950	£ .875	9.84	10.05	10.91
April 1407	£ 8.356 (Noble - proposed)	£ 8.180	£ .883	£ .788	9.26	9.46	10.61
	£ 8.444 (Ecu - proposed)	£ 8.193	£ .883	£ .788	9.27	9.56	10.72
? 1407	£ 8.444 (Ecu - proposed)	£ 8.193	£ .866	£ .800	9.46	9.75	10.56
July 1407	£ 9.651	£ 9.383	£ .950	£ .875	9.88	10.16	11.03
Aug. 1409	£ 8.143	£ 7.891	£ .816	£ .758	9.67	9.98	10.74
Jan. 1414	£ 8.143	£ 7.984	£ .816	£ .758	9.78	9.98	10.74
Dec. 1416	£ 9.144	£ 8.636	£1.000	£ .863	8.64	9.14	10.60
June 1418	£11.514	£11.260	£1.133	£1.058	9.94	10.16	10.88
Sept. 1427	£12.338	£12.171	£1.133	£1.058	10.74	10.87	11.66
Nov. 1428	£14.325	£14.027	£1.284	£1.200	10.92	11.16	11.94
Oct. 1433	£13.500	£13.300	£1.200	£1.138	11.08	11.25	11.87
Jan. 1454	£14.922	£14.623	£1.200	£1.138	12.19	12.44	13.12
July 1456	£14.922	£14.723	£1.200	£1.138	12.27	12.44	13.12
May 1466	£15.457	£14.997	£1.375	£1.317	10.91	11.24	11.74
Oct. 1467	£15.834	£15.363	£1.408	£1.350	10.91	11.25	11.73
Mar. 1474	£15.834	£15.363	£1.408	£1.366	10.91	11.25	11.59
Oct. 1477	£18.095	?	£1.600	£1.516	?	11.31	11.93

SOURCES: See the sources for the mint accounts in Tables A and B.

See also the ordinances cited in Louis Deschamps de Pas, 'Essai sur l'histoire monétaire des comtes de Flandre de la maison de Bourgogne,' *Revue numismatique*, 2nd ser., VI (1861), 106-39, 211-37, 458-78; VII (1862), 117-43, 351-65, 460-80; XI (1866), 172-219.

Alphonse De Witte, *Histoire monétaire des comtes de Louvain, ducs de Brabant, et marquis de Saint-Empire Romain,* II (Antwerp, 1896), *passim*; Archives Générales du Royaume, Chambre de Comptes, reg. no. 132, fo. 59r.-60r.; no. 133, fo. 174r.-9vo.; no. 580, fo. 85r.-9r., 92r.-4r.; cartons 65: bis 1, 65:2.

TABLE D

ENGLISH MINT PRICES AND RATIOS

THE *TRAITES* AND BULLION PRICES OF GOLD AND SILVER,
PER TOWER POUND, AND THE GOLD, SILVER, AND *TRAITE* RATIOS
AT THE ENGLISH MINTS (LONDON AND CALAIS), 1361-1471

The mint prices for gold and silver bullion and the *traites* are expressed in a decimal pound sterling, per Tower Pound. In this table the mint prices for silver, as taken from the ordinances, have been adjusted from the English silver standard of 11 oz. 2 dwt. silver to one of 12 *deniers argent-le-roy* (23/24), so that the ratios may be comparable to those of the Burgundian Lowlands. The mint prices and *traites* for gold are in terms of the English fineness standard of 23 7/8 carats.

| Year | GOLD | | SILVER | | RATIOS | | |
	Traite	Mint Price	Traite	Mint Price	Gold	Traites	Silver
June 1361	£15.000	£14.750	£1.295	£1.252	11.39	11.58	11.98
Nov. 1411	£16.667	£16.416	£1.554	£1.505	10.56	10.73	11.07
Apr. 1413	£16.667	£16.375	£1.554	£1.502	10.54	10.73	11.10
Jul. 1421	£16.667	£16.416	£1.554	£1.502	10.56	10.73	11.10
Aug. 1464	£20.833	£18.333	£1.943	£1.709	9.44	10.73	12.19
Mar. 1465	£22.500	£21.458	£1.943	£1.709	11.04	11.58	13.17
Sept. 1466	£22.500	£21.458	£1.943	£1.779	11.04	11.58	12.64
Sept. 1467	£22.500	£21.775	£1.943	£1.805	11.21	11.58	12.47
Apr. 1471	£22.500	£22.125	£1.943	£1.865	11.39	11.58	12.06

SOURCES:

Sir John Craig, *The Mint: A History of the London Mint from A.D. 287 to 1948* (Cambridge, 1953), pp. 423-4.

G.C. Brooke and E. Stokes, 'Tables of Bullion Coined, 1337-1550,' *The Numismatic Chronicle*, 5th ser., IX (1929), 27-69.

C.E. Blunt and C.A. Whitton, 'The Coinages of Edward IV and Henry VI (Restored),' *British Numismatic Journal*, XXV (1948), 53-7.

Calendar of Close Rolls 1360-64, pp. 292-3.

Cal. Close Rolls 1413-19, pp. 64-6.

Cal. Close Rolls 1419-22, pp. 204-5, 230-5.

Calendar of Patent Rolls 1461-67, pp. 370-1.

Cal. Pat. Rolls 1467-77, pp. 138-9, 313-5.

TABLE E

TRAITES OF THE GOLD AND SILVER MARCS, RATIOS OF THE GOLD
AND SILVER TRAITES, AND THE SEIGNORAGE RATES ON GOLD
AND SILVER MINTING AT THE NAMUR MINT, 1426-1433

Date	Traite of the Gold *Marc**	Traite of the Silver *Marc*	Ratio of the Traites	Seignorage as a percentage of the Traites	
				on gold	on silver
July 1426	£15.68	£1.07	14.65	5.30 %	2.33 %
Dec. 1426	£15.68	£1.08	14.52	5.30 %	2.32 %
Sept. 1427	£14.11	£1.08	13.07	5.30 %	2.32 %
June 1428	£15.11	£1.20	12.59	3.95 %	2.08 %
Jan. 1429	£15.61	£1.30	12.01	3.83 %	1.92 %
June 1429	£16.03	£1.35	11.87	1.74 %	2.47 %
Dec. 1430	£16.07	£1.35	11.90	1.47 %	1.85 %
Mar. 1431	£16.07	£1.35	11.90	.98 %	1.23 %
Apr. 1431	£16.20	£1.35	12.00	.97 %	1.23 %
Sept. 1431	£16.33	£1.35	12.09	.97 %	1.23 %
Dec. 1431	£17.14	£1.44	11.90	3.68 %	1.74 %
Dec. 1432	£17.80	£1.44	12.36	5.31 %	1.74 %
May 1433	£18.80	£1.56	12.08	5.43 % —3.44 %	5.09 %

* Gold marcs converted to the English standard of 23 7/8 carats.

SOURCE: A.G.R., C. de C., reg. no. 18,203:1-21 and Acquits de Lille, liasse no. 1933.

TABLE F

THE TRAITE, BRASSAGE, AND SEIGNORAGE CHARGES ON THE MINTING OF GOLD MARCS DE TROYES IN FLANDERS, FROM 1384 TO 1433, AND IN THE BURGUNDIAN LOWLANDS, FROM 1433 TO 1477, IN *LIVRES GROS*

(a) marc of 23 1/2 carats

(b) marc of 23 3/4 carats

(c) marc of 24 carats

Date and Coin	Traite of the gold *marc*	Brassage per *marc*	Per Cent of the traite	Seign- orage per *marc*	Per Cent of the traite	Total Mint Charges as per cent of the traite
July 1384 Heaume (a)	£ 8. 8s. 4d.	2s. 4d.	1.39 %	4s. 0d.	2.37 %	3.76 %
April 1386 Heaume (a)	£10. 0s. 0d.	1s. 7d.	.79 %	3s. 5d.	1.71 %	2.50 %
April 1387 Angel (a)	£11.18s. 9d.	2s. 0d.	.84 %	5s. 9d.	2.41 %	3.25 %
Oct. 1388 Angel (a)	£11.18s. 9d.	2s. 0d.	.84 %	2s. 9d.	1.15 %	1.99 %
Oct. 1388 Noble (b)	£13. 9s. 2d.	4s. 3d.	1.58 %	14s. 2d.	5.26 %	6.84 %
Feb. 1389 Noble (b)	£13. 9s. 2d.	4s. 3d.	1.58 %	12s.1/2d.	4.47 %	6.05 %
July 1389 Noble (b)	£13. 9s. 2d.	4s. 3d.	1.58 %	5s. 8d.	2.10 %	3.68 %
Dec. 1389 Noble (b)	£ 9.10s. 0d.	3s. 0d.	1.58 %	4s. 0d.	2.10 %	3.68 %
Dec. 1389 Noble (b)	£ 9.10s. 0d.	3s. 0d.	1.58 %	3s. 0d.	1.58 %	3.16 %
Jan. 1393 Noble (b)	£ 9.10s. 0d.	3s. 0d.	1.58 %	1s. 0d.	.53 %	2.11 %
Apr. 1407* Noble (b)	£ 8. 6s. 3d.	2s. 4d.	1.41 %	1s. 2d.	.70 %	2.11 %
Apr. 1407* Ecu (b)	£ 8. 8s. 0d.	2s. 4d.	1.39 %	2s. 8d.	1.59 %	2.98 %
July 1407* Ecu (b)	£ 9.12s. 0d.	2s.10d.	1.48 %	2s. 6d.	1.30 %	2.78 %
Aug. 1409 Ecu (b)	£ 8. 2s. 0d.	2s. 2d.	1.34 %	2s.10d.	1.75 %	3.09 %
Jan. 1414 Ecu (b)	£ 8. 2s. 0d.	2s. 2d.	1.34 %	1s. 0d.	.63 %	1.95 %
Dec. 1416 Noble (a)	£ 9. 0s. 0d.	3s. 0d.	1.68 %	7s. 0d.	3.88 %	5.56 %

* Proposed only.

Date and Coin	Traite of the gold *marc*	Brassage per *marc*	Per Cent of the traite	Seign-orage per *marc*	Per Cent of the traite	Total Mint Charges as per cent of the traite
June 1418 Heaume (a)	£11. 6s. 8d.	2s. 8d.	1.18 %	2s. 4d.	1.03 %	2.21 %
Nov. 1422 Heaume (a)	£11. 6s. 8d.	2s. 2d.	.96 %	2s.10d.	1.25 %	2.21 %
June 1425 Noble (c)	£14. 0s.11d.	?	?	4s. 2d.	1.48 %	?
June 1426 Clinquaert (c)	£15.15s.3 1/2d.	?	?	16s. 8d.	5.30 %	?
Sept. 1427 Noble (c)	£12. 6s. 9d.	2s. 4d.	1.34 %	1s. 0d.	.41 %	1.75 %
Nov. 1428 Noble (c)	£14. 8s. 0d.	2s. 6d.	.88 %	3s. 6d.	1.22 %	2.10 %
Oct. 1433 Philippus (c)	£13.10s. 0d.	2s. 6d.	.94 %	1s. 6d.	.56 %	1.50 %
Jan. 1454 Lion (c)	£15. 0s. 0d.	2s. 0d.	.67 %	4s. 0d.	1.33 %	2.00 %
July 1456 Lion (c)	£15. 0s. 0d.	2s. 0d.	.67 %	2s. 0d.	.67 %	1.34 %
May 1466 Florin (c)	£15.10s. 9d.	8s. 1d.	2.59 %	1s. 2d.	.38 %	2.97 %
Oct. 1467 Florin (c)	£15.18s. 4d.	8s. 3d.	2.59 %	1s. 2d.	.37 %	2.96 %
Oct. 1474 Florin (c)	£18. 3s.9 1/2d.	?	?	1s. 6d.	.41 %	?
Dec. 1474 Florin (c)	£18. 3s.9 1/2d.	?	?	1s. 5d.	.41 %	?

SOURCES: See the sources of the Burgundian mint accounts for Tables A-B, and of the monetary ordinances, for Table C. In no instance did the mint accounts for the period immediately following an ordinance (when coins were actually struck) contradict the particulars of that ordinance; but in some years, the mint accounts note changes in the mintage fees that are not authorized by any *extant* monetary ordinance.

Note that up until June 1425 the *traite* of the *marc* was calculated on the basis of the alloy of the gold coin being struck; thereafter, on the basis of a hypothetical *marc* of 24 carats.

TABLE G

THE TRAITE, BRASSAGE, AND SEIGNORAGE CHARGES ON THE MINTING
OF SILVER MARCS DE TROYES IN FLANDERS, FROM 1384 TO 1433,
AND IN THE BURGUNDIAN LOWLANDS, FROM 1433 TO 1477,
IN LIVRES *GROS*

Date	Traite of the marc *argent-le-roy*	Brassage per marc	Per Cent of the traite	Seign-orage per marc	Per Cent of the traite	Total Mint Charges as Per Cent of the traite
July 1384	16s.8d.	1s. 4d.	8.00 %	1s.0d.	6.00 %	14.00 %
Apr. 1386	18s.8d.	1s.1 1/2d.	6.68 %	2 1/2d.	1.12 %	7.80 %
Oct. 1386	19s.0d.	1s.1 1/2d.	5.20 %	2 1/2d.	1.10 %	6.30 %
Apr. 1387	23s.0d.10m.	1s. 7d.	6.87 %	8d.10m.	3.03 %	9.90 %
Oct. 1388	25s.1d.14m.	2s. 5d.14m.	9.79 %	8d.	2.65 %	12.44 %
Dec. 1389	19s.0d.	1s. 8d.	8.75 %	4d.	1.75 %	10.50 %
Jan. 1391	19s.2d.	1s. 8d.	8.70 %	4d.	1.74 %	10.44 %
June 1393	19s.0d.	1s. 2d.	6.14 %	4d.	1.75 %	7.89 %
Apr. 1407*	17s.8d.	1s. 2d.	6.60 %	9d.	4.25 %	10.85 %
1407*	17s.4d.	10d.	4.72 %	6d.	2.88 %	7.60 %
Jul. 1407	19s.0d.	1s. 2d.	6.14 %	4d.	1.75 %	7.89 %
Aug. 1409	16s.4d.	1s. 0d.	6.12 %	2d.	1.02 %	7.14 %
Dec. 1416	20s.0d.	1s. 5d.	7.08 %	1s.4d.	6.67 %	13.75 %
June 1418	22s.8d.	1s. 2d.	5.13 %	4d.	1.47 %	6.60 %
Nov. 1428	25s.8d.4m.	1s.2 1/4d.	4.55 %	6d.	1.95 %	6.50 %
Oct. 1433	24s.0d.	1s. 1d.	4.51 %	2d.	.69 %	5.20 %
May 1466	27s.6d.	1s.1/2d.	3.79 %	1 1/2d.	.45 %	4.24 %
Oct. 1467	28s.2d.	1s.1/2d.	3.70 %	1 1/2d.	.44 %	4.14 %
Mar. 1474	28s.2d.	8 1/2d.	2.52 %	1 1/2d.	.44 %	2.96 %
Oct. 1474	32s.0d.	1s. 2d.	4.36 %	6d.	1.56 %	5.92 %

* Proposed only.

SOURCES: See Table I.

TABLE H

SEIGNORAGE ON THE MINTING OF GOLD COINS IN THE BURGUNDIAN LOWLANDS FOR DUKES PHILIP THE GOOD AND CHARLES THE RASH, 1419-20 TO 1476 7
IN *LIVRES GROS*

Michaelmas Years	Total Seignorage Receipts	Flanders	Namur and Hainaut	Brabant	Holland
		Ghent	Namur	Louvain*	Dordrecht
1419-20	Nil				
1420-1	5	5			
1421-2	43	43			
1422-3	2	2			
1423-4	23	23			
1424-5	103	103			
1425-6	2,156	162	1,146		848
1426-7	3,761	1,725	1,042		994
1427-8	692	9	453		230
1428-9	1,547	778	770		
1429-30	351	22	286		43
1430-1	1,656	1	554	813	288
1431-2	5,088		4,268	331	489
1432-3	5,459		5,242		217
			Valenciennes**	Brussels	
1433-4	326	282	28	22	22
1434-5	588	203		263	122
1435-6	559	177		211	171
1436-7	259	63		182	14
1437-8	97	62		21	14
1438-9	70	56			14
1439-40	28	17			11
1440-1	—	—			
1441-2	11	11			
1442-3	66	66			
1443-4	65	65			
1444-5	32	32			
1445-6	4	4			
1446-7	Nil				
1447-8	Nil				
1448-9	Nil				
1449-50	Nil				
1450-1	Nil				
1451-2	Nil				
1452-3	Nil				

* The seignorage produced at the Louvain mint in 1429-30 for Duke Philip of St. Pol of Brabant has not been included.

** The Valenciennes mint's seignorage for Nov. 1433 - Apr. 1434 is not included in the total receipts, since the succeeding accounts are missing. If included, the total would be £354 gros.

Michaelmas Years	Total Seignorage Receipts	Flanders	Hainaut	Brabant	Holland
		Bruges	Valenciennes	Malines	The Hague
1453-4	1,329	663	337	248	81
1454-5	2,075	652	454	809	160
1455-6	535	174	138	223	
1456-7	129	129			
1457-8	99	99			
		Ghent			
1458-9	38	4		34	
1459-60	20	9		11	
1460-1	9	9			
1461-2	4	4			
1462-3	Nil				
1463-4	Nil				
1464-5	Nil				
1465-6	Nil				
		Ghent	Valenciennes	Louvain	Dordrecht
1466-7	84	28	7	29	20
1467-8	78	70		8	
1468-9	103	86		17	
1469-70	52	40		12	
1470-1	36	29		7	
1471-2	17	12		5	
1472-3	6	5		1	
1473-4	3	3			
				Antwerp	
1474-5	310	152		158	
1475-6	295	128		167	
1476-7	103	68		35	

SOURCES: See the sources of the mint-accounts for Tables A and B.

Notes on the seignorage tables and their method of computation are appended to the following Table I.

TABLE I

SEIGNORAGE ON THE MINTING OF SILVER COINS IN THE BURGUNDIAN LOWLANDS FOR DUKES PHILIP THE GOOD AND CHARLES THE RASH, 1419-20 TO 1476-7
IN *LIVRES GROS*

Michaelmas Years	Total Seignorage Receipts	Flanders Ghent	Namur and Hainaut Namur	Brabant Louvain*	Holland Dordrecht
1419-20	965	965			
1420-1	923	923			
1421-2	1,130	1,098	32		
1422-3	848	819	29		
1423-4	808	788	20		
1424-5	353	345	8		
1425-6	226	166	60		
1426-7	48		48		
1427-8	123	77	46		
1428-9	2,035	1,812	223		
1429-30	1,316	875	340		101
1430-1	283	140	70	42	31
1431-2	55	3	36	3	13
1432-3	14		10		4
			Valen-ciennes**	Brussels	
1433-4	553	477	71	6	69
1434-5	430	278		77	75
1435-6	369	225		104	41
1436-7	243	111		115	17
1437-8	141	107		14	20
1438-9	107	87			20
1439-40	39	23			16
1440-1	—	—			
1441-2	6	6			
1442-3	6	6			
1443-4	6	6			
1444-5	1	1			
1445-6	Nil	Nil			
1446-7	1	1			
1447-8	Nil				
1448-9	Nil				
1449-50	Nil				
1450-1	Nil				
1451-2	Nil				
1452-3	Nil				

* The seignorage produced at the Louvain mint in 1429-30 for Duke Philip of St. Pol of Brabant has not been included.

** The Valenciennes mint's seignorage for Nov. 1433 - Apr. 1434 is not included in the total receipts, since the succeeding accounts are missing. If included, the total would be £624 gros.

Michaelmas Years	Total Seignorage Receipts	Flanders	Hainaut	Brabant	Holland
		Bruges	Valenciennes	Malines	The Hague
1453-4	8	3	5		
1454-5	23	7	5	9	2
1455-6	12	7	3	2	
1456-7	1	1			
1457-8	3	3			
1458-9	Nil				
1459-60	Nil				
1460-1	Nil				
1461-2	Nil				
1462-3	Nil				
1463-4	Nil				
1464-5	Nil				
1465-6	Nil				
		Ghent		Louvain	Dordrecht
1466-7	122	39	14	58	12
1467-8	124	100		24	
1468-9	189	138		51	
1469-70	183	120		63	
1470-1	279	203		76	
1471-2	243	170		73	
1472-3	221	158		63	
1473-4	117	86		31	
				Antwerp	
1474-5	601	152		449	
1475-6	974	235		739	
1476-7	491	265		226	

SOURCES: See the sources of the mint-accounts for Tables A and B.

SPECIAL NOTES: for Tables H and I.

(1)   Annual estimates of the seignorage revenues were calculated by apportioning the receipts, when available in the accounts, over a Michaelmas year. When no seignorage receipts were provided in the accounts, the seignorages were estimated by multiplying the number of marcs struck for the given year (as listed in Tables A and B) by the current seignorage rates (as listed in Tables F and G).

(2)   These two tables provide estimates of only the gross seignorage revenues (not including the *remèdes* and bullion confiscations). They do not attempt to indicate the *net* seignorage profits on minting: first, because a large number of the mint accounts are incomplete, without any indication of expenditures; and second, because the medieval accounting procedures are so different from the modern that to estimate accurately the true current costs (including amortizations), to be deducted from mint revenues, is extremely difficult, if not impossible. (See chapter I, p. 21 n. 32b).

(3)   The Namur mint: when Duke Philip the Good purchased the county of Namur with its mint in 1421, the agreement provided Philip with only two-thirds of the seignorage profits and Count John of Namur with the other third; but when Count John died in 1429, Duke Philip then acquired the total seignorage. In these tables, the total Namur seignorage receipts have been given, and not just the two-thirds accruing to Duke Philip (up to 1429).

TABLE J

FINENESS, TAILLE, VALUE, AND TRAITE PER MARC DE TROYES
OF THE GOLD COINS STRUCK IN THE BURGUNDIAN LOWLANDS,
1384-1477

fineness — out of 24 carats
taille — number of coins struck to the marc
of the fineness given
value — officially prescribed value in the
gros money-of-account system

Date	Name of Coin	Fineness in Carats	Taille to the marc	Official Value	Traite Value of the gold marc (pure)*
July 1384	Heaume	23 1/2	50 1/2	3s.4d.	£ 8. 8s. 4d.*
Oct. 1386	Heaume	23 1/2	60	3s.4d.	10. 0s. 0d.*
Apr. 1387	Heaume (Angel)	23 1/2	47 3/4	5s.0d.	11.18s. 9d.*
Oct. 1388	Noble	23 3/4	31 2/3	8s.6d.	13. 9s. 2d.*
Dec. 1389	Noble	23 3/4	31 2/3	6s.0d.	9.10s. 0d.*
Apr. 1407	Noble (proposed)	23 3/4	31 2/3	5s.3d.	8. 6s. 3d.*
Apr. 1407	Ecu (proposed)	23 3/4	42	4s.0d.	8. 8s. 0d.*
Jul. 1407	Ecu (proposed)	23 3/4	48	4s.0d.	9.12s. 0d.*
Aug. 1409	Ecu	23 3/4	54	3s.0d.	8. 0s. 2d.*
Aug. 1409	Noble	23 3/4	31 2/3	5s.0d.	7.18s. 4d.*
Dec. 1416	Noble	23 1/2	36	5s.0d.	9. 0s. 0d.*
June 1418	Heaume	23 1/2	68	3s.4d.	11. 6s. 8d.*
June 1425	Noble (also Namur)	23 1/2	35 1/2	7s.8d.	14. 0s.11d.*
Nov. 1425	Clinquaert (Dordrecht)	17	67	3s.4d.	15.15s. 3d.
Jul. 1426	Clinquaert (also Namur)	17	67	3s.4d.	15.15s. 3d.
Sept. 1427	Noble	23 7/8	35 1/4	7s.0d.	12. 6s. 9d.
June 1428	Clinquaert (Namur only)	16	67 1/2	3s.0d.	15.3s.9 1/2d.
Nov. 1428	Noble	23 1/2	35 1/4	8s.0d.	14. 8s. 0d.
Feb. 1429	Clinquaert (Namur only)	15 1/2	67 1/2	3s.0d.	15.13s. 7d.
June 1429	Clinquaert (Namur only)	15 1/2	67 1/2	3s.1d.	16.2s.2 1/4d.

* Traite calculated in terms of the fineness of the coin struck; thereafter, in terms of a hypothetical marc of 24 carats.

Date	Name of Coin	Fineness in Carats	Taille to the marc	Official Value	Traite Value of the gold marc (pure)
Dec. 1430	Clinquaert (Namur only)	16	68	3s.2d.	16. 3s. 0d.
Apr. 1431	Clinquaert (Namur only)	15 7/8	68	3s.2d.	16. 5s. 7d.
Sept. 1431	Clinquaert (Namur only)	15 3/4	68	3s.2d.	16.8s.2 1/4d.
Dec. 1431	Clinquaert (Namur only)	15	68	3s.2d.	17. 4s. 7d.
Dec. 1432	Pieter (Namur and Louvain)	19	68	4s.2d.	17.17s.9 1/2d.
May 1433	Pieter (Namur only)	18	68	4s.2d.	18.17s.9 1/2d.
Aug. 1433	Pieter (Namur only)	18	68	3s.1 1/2d.	14. 3s. 5d.
Oct. 1433	Philippus	23 13/16	67 1/2	4s.0d.	13.10s. 0d.
Jan. 1454	Lion	23	57 1/2	5s.0d.	15. 0s. 0d.
May 1466	Florin	19	72	3s.5d.	15.10s. 9d.
Oct. 1467	Florin	19	72	3s.6d.	15.18s. 4d.
Oct. 1474	Florin	19	72	4s.0d.	18.3s.9 1/2d.

SOURCES: See Tables A-C and E.

TABLE K

FINENESS, TAILLE, AND TRAITE PER MARC DE TROYES, *ARGENT-LE-ROY*,
OF THE SILVER DOUBLE GROS STRUCK IN THE BURGUNDIAN LOWLANDS,
1384-1477

fineness	—	out of 12 deniers *argent-le-roy*, with 24 grains to one denier
taille	—	number of double gros (2d.) coins struck to the marc of the fineness given
traite	—	in shillings and pence of the *gros* money-of-account system (with 24 mites to 1d.)

Date	Fineness in deniers and grains	Taille to the marc	Traite Value of the marc *argent-le-roy*
July 1384	6 deniers	50	16s.8d. gros
Apr. 1386	6 den.	52	18s.8d.
Oct. 1386	6 den.	57	19s.0d.
Apr. 1387	5 den. 4 gr.	59 1/2	23s.0d.10m.
Oct. 1388	4 den. 20 gr.	60 1/2	25s.1d.14m.
Dec. 1389	6 den.	57	19s.0d.
Jan. 1391	6 den.	57 1/2	19s.2d.
June 1393	6 den.	57	19s.0d.
Apr. 1407*	6 den.	53	17s.8d.
1407 ?*	6 den.	52	17s.4d.
July 1407	6 den.	57	19s.0d.
Aug. 1409	6 den.	49	16s.4d.
Dec. 1416	5 den.	50	20s.0d.
June 1418	6 den.	68	22s.8d.
1422**	5 den.	50	20s.0d.: Namur only
July 1425	5 den.	53	21s.2d.12m.: Namur
July 1426	4 den. 22 1/2 gr.	53	21s.5d. 4m.: Namur
Dec. 1426	4 den. 23 gr.	54	21s.7d. 4m.: Namur
June 1428	4 den. 12 gr.	54	24s.0d.: Namur
Nov. 1428	5 den. 8 gr.	68 1/2	25s.8d. 4m.: Flanders
Jan. 1429	4 den. 4 gr.	54	26s.0d.: Namur
June 1429	4 den.	54	27s.0d.: Namur
Dec. 1431	3 den. 18 gr.	54	28s.9d.14m.: Namur
May 1433***	6 den.	70	31s.1d. 7m.: Namur
Aug. 1433	6 den.	70	23s.4d.: Namur
Oct. 1433	6 den.	72	24s.0d.
May 1466	6 den.	82 1/2	27s.6d.
Oct. 1467	6 den.	84 1/2	28s.2d.
Oct. 1474	5 den.	80	32s.0d.

* Proposed only.
** From Oct. 1421, Duke Philip the Good struck double gros at Namur of 6 den. fineness and a taille of 68; the exact date of this stronger coinage (the same as the Flemish double gros of Dec. 1416) is unknown, except that it is noted for that year in the Namur mint account.
*** Namur *plaque* of 8 esterlins, or 2 2/3d. gros. (3 esterlins = 1d.) Value reduced to 2d. gros in August 1433.
SOURCES: See sources for Tables A-C and E.

APPENDIX II

ASSAY OF FOREIGN DEBASED AND COUNTERFEIT COINS CIRCULATING IN BRABANT: CONDUCTED AT THE LOUVAIN MINT, 21 DECEMBER 1430

The mint master's report compares the precious metal contents of the Burgundian coins with those of their imitations. The 'surplus' noted in each case indicates the profit to be made per *marc de Troyes* of precious metal in circulating the debased foreign coins in Brabant. All figures, except those in square-brackets, are those of the Louvain mint-master.

A. SILVER COINS: struck in imitation of the Burgundian *cromstaert*

[fineness:	5 deniers 8 grains *argent-le-roy*
taille to the marc:	68 1/2 to the *marc de Troyes*
official value:	8 esterlins of Brabant = 2 2/3d. gros
	of Brabant = 2d. gros of Flanders
traite of the marc:	34s.2d. gros Brabant =
	25s.8d.4 mites gros Flemish]

1. *Cromstaert of Rumène* [Rummen]: by the Demoiselle de *Wesemal* [Wezemaal]

fineness:	4 deniers 18 grains
taille:	72 to the marc
current rate:	8 esterlins = 2 2/3d. gros Brab.
traite:	40s.6d. gros Brabant
surplus per marc:	76 *placques* [= 6s.4d. gros Brab. = 18.54 %]

2. *Cromstaert of Reyckem* [Reckheim]: by Guillaume de Sombrecht [sic: Sombreffe]

fineness:	4 deniers 3 grains
taille:	72 to the marc
current rate:	8 esterlins [= 2 2/3d. gros Brab.]
traite:	46s.11d. gros Brab.
surplus per marc:	155 *placques* [sic: should be 153 pl.]
	= 12s.9d. gros Brab. [= 37.32 %]

3. *Cromstaert* [or *Placque*] of Tournay [of King Charles VII of France]

fineness:	5 deniers
taille:	69 to the marc
current rate:	1 cromstaert [= 8 est. Brab. = 2d. gros Flemish]
traite:	27s.7d.18 mites gros Flemish
	[= 36s.9d.9 mites gros Brabant]
surplus per marc:	23 1/2d. gros Flemish [= 1s.11d.12 mites gros Flemish =
	2s.7d.9 mites gros Brabant = 7.65 %]

4. *Gryffon of Liège**

fineness:	4 deniers
taille:	72 to the marc
current rate:	2 *placques* [= 2d. gros Brabant]
traite:	36s.0d. gros Brabant
surplus per marc:	22 *placques* Brab. [= 1s.10d. gros Brabant = 5.37 %]

5. *Staende Mannekens of Guillaume de Sombrecht** [sic: Sombreffe-Reckheim]

fineness:	4 deniers
taille:	109 to the marc
current rate:	2 *placques* [= 2d. gros of Brabant]
traite:	54s.6d. gros Brabant
surplus per marc:	244 *placques* [= 20s.4d. gros Brab. = 59.51 %]

B. GOLD COINS: *Counterfeits* *Coin Imitated*

1. *Gryffon or Florin of Liège,*
   and *Ecu of Liège*

fineness:	14 1/2 carats	
taille:	69 1/2 to the marc	
current rate:	37 1/2d. gros Flem.	
	[= 4s.2d. gros Brab.]	
traite:	£17.11s.6d. gros Flem.	
surplus:	32s.9d. gros Flem.	
	[= 43s.8d. gros Brab. = 13.70 %]	

Schild [*Ecu* or *Klinkaert*]
of Louvain

[16 carats
68 to the marc]
37 1/2d. gros Flem.
[= 4s.2d. gros Brab.]
£15.18s.9d. gros Flem.

2. *Ecu of Rumène* [Rummen]: struck
   by the Lady of Wezemaal

fineness:	13 1/2 carats
taille:	69 1/2 to the marc
current rate:	37 1/2d. gros Flem.
traite:	£18.18s.1d. gros Flem.
surplus:	£2.19s.4d. gros Flem.
	[= £3.19s.4d.13m. gros Brab. = 18.61 %]

Schild [*Klinkaert*]
of Louvain

[16 carats
68 to the marc]
37 1/2d. gros Flem.
£15.18s.9d. gros Flem.

3. *Couronne of Tournay* of Charles VII

fineness:	20 1/2 carats
taille:	68 1/2 to the marc
current rate:	49d. gros Flem.
traite:	£16.5s.1d. gros Flem.
surplus:	14s.3d. gros Flem.
	[= 18s.11d.12m. gros Brab. = 4.58 %]

Pieter of *Louvain***

[21 carats
68 to the marc]
49d. gros Flem.
£15.10s.10d. gros Flem.

4. *Maille of the Rhine*
   [Rummen-Wezemaal]

fineness:	14 1/2 carats
taille:	74 to the marc
current rate:	43d. gros Flem.
traite:	£21.9s.8d. gros Flem.
surplus:	£5.10s.11d. gros Flem.
	[= £7.7s.6d.10m. gros Brab. = 34.80 %]

Imperial *Florin****

[19 carats
72 to the marc
42d. or 43d. gros Flem.]
£15.18s.9d. gros Flem.

5. *Mailles of Arnhem* or *Arnoldus*
   of the Duke of Guelders ****

fineness:	12 1/2 carats	
taille:	77 to the marc	
current rate:	28d. gros Flem.	
traite:	144 *mailles* and 20d. gros Flem. [sic]	£15.18s.9d. gros Flem.
	= £16.17s.0d. gros Flem.	
	[sic: should be £17.5s.0d. gros]	
surplus:	18s.3d. gros Flem.	
	[sic: should be 26s.3d. gros Flem. = 35s.0d. gros Brabant = 8.24 %]	

* These two silver coins of Liège and Sombreffe were not in fact true counterfeits of the *crom-staerts*, though their issuers may have hoped that they might be accepted as such. They circulated at a rate of 2 esterlins less than that of the various *cromstaerts*, but even so were considerably overvalued.

** The Louvain *pieter* was in fact, however, itself originally a counterfeit of the Tournay *cou-ronne*; for the latter was first struck by Charles VII in May 1427 (at Tournay), while the former was first struck, by Duke Philip of St. Pol, only in May 1430. See Marcel Hoc, *Histoire moné-taire de Tournai*, pp. 95 et seq.; A.G.R., C. de C., no. 18,065.

*** The report unfortunately provided no particulars about the florin so imitated, saying only 'contrefaictes apres celles de l'empereur que fait forgier ledit Wesemal audit lieu de Rumène.' But the fineness and taille of the Imperial florin of that period were found in another report in A.G.R., C. de C., carton 65: bis 1; and the *traite* per marc of the Imperial florin was deduced from the 'surplus' accorded the *maille* of the Rhine. If the Imperial florin's current rate was 43d. gros Flem., the same as that of the Rhenish *maille*, the traite of the florin's gold *marc* would thus have been £16.3s.0d. gros Flem.; if it was instead 42d. gros, then £15.18s.4d. gros, which is very close to the *traite* of the florin's gold *marc* as given above. Nevertheless, it is very possible that the florin's current rate was 43d. gros, and thus that the florin was overvalued by 1d. gros Flemish.

**** The mint-assayors, or the scribe, evidently made an error in calculating the *traite* of the gold *marc* for the Arnhem *Maille* or *Arnoldus*, because a gold marc should have yielded 147.84 *mailles* (77 × 24/12.5), or 147 *mailles* and 23 1/2d. gros. Flem., not 144 *mailles* 20d. gros. Flem. The *traite*, at 28d. gros. Flem. per *maille*, would then have been £17.5s.0d. gros (per marc of 24 carats). An 18th-century Flemish copy of this report does in fact give a *traite* value of £17.4s.10 1/2d. gros Flem.; and thus a surplus of £1.6s.1 1/2d. gros. Flem. This *maille, Arnoldus,* or *florin* of Guelders apparently did not achieve its harmful effects as a counterfeit imitation of better foreign coins, as did the other coins listed. From the mint-master's report, it would seem that its fineness had been reduced, while the *maille* continued to circulate at its former rate, or at least above its true intrinsic worth. According to another manuscript in carton 65: bis 1, the Guelder *Arnoldus* or *maille* had deteriorated in fineness from 14 carats — once 18 carats — to just 11 1/2 carats by the mid-1430s. For that matter, the same manuscript states that the *florin* of neighbouring Jülich had been debased from 19 to 18 5/12 carats; the *postulaat* of Utrecht, from 17 to 15 carats; and the Rhenish *Fredericus*, from 16 to 14 carats in the same period.

SOURCES: A.G.R., Chambre de Comptes, carton 65: 2 (uncatalogued) for the original French text, collated with an 18th-century Flemish copy in A.G.R., C. de C., reg. no. 580, fo. 92r. The fineness and taille for each of the gold and silver coins struck at the Louvain mint were taken from the corresponding Louvain mint-accounts (4 Oct. 1430 to 18 March 1431) in A.G.R., C. de C., reg. no. 18,067.

APPENDIX III

ESTIMATED ANNUAL EXPORTS OF ENGLISH WOOLSACKS BY DENIZENS
AND OF BROADCLOTHS FROM LONDON BY DENIZENS
AND BY ALL MERCHANTS, 1415-1485

Year Ending Michaelmas	Denizen Exports of Wool-sacks	Denizen Cloth Exports from London	Total Cloth Exports from London
1415	12,180	2,974	20,519
1416	12,453	3,457	13,422
1417	13,485	3,193	11,291
1418	14,623	4,040	10,790
1419	14,832	3,875	13,884
1420	11,384	4,780	14,102
1421	11,832	2,716	8,607
1422	13,402	4,420	15,601
1423	14,476	6,748	23,168
1424	15,913	8,224	14,394
1425	11,195	8,274	22,291
1426	12,247	4,223	19,330
1427	16,083	3,849	15,101
1428	15,351	3,635	17,059
1429	11,398	6,195	17,334
1430	7,066	6,973	18,664
1431	10,433	10,530	17,735
1432	10,540	13,334	16,317
1433	8,663	12,719	16,358
1434	838	9,890	17,681
1435	12,923	8,699	17,255
1436	2,531	2,084	8,544
1437	66	3,449	14,569
1438	156	8,879	19,630
1439	505	8,848	23,840
1440	17,731	9,165	24,037
1441	6,395	8,412	22,987
1442	965	9,881	27,154
1443	13,563	10,794	24,816
1444	10,141	8,129	21,837
1445	1,447	13,140	22,895
1446	16,153	6,847	16,086
1447	2,154	8,673	20,947
1448	9,542	4,555	12,215
1449	3,665	5,157	10,301
1450	14,370	6,548	11,598
1451	5,456	8,048	17,487
1452	9,054	8,128	14,231
1453	7,372	11,523	19,241
1454	2,593	4,113	11,761
1455	13,798	10,606	19,373
1456	4,597	7,937	16,634
1457	3,306	5,446	12,575
1458	8,249	10,636	21,041
1459	6,379	9,989	18,822
1460	3,703	5,136	11,740
1461	9,098	6,825	14,805

Year Ending Michaelmas	Denizen Exports of Wool-sacks	Denizen Cloth Exports from London	Total Cloth Exports from London
1462	2,224	12,940	22,361
1463	4,214	9,893	15,050
1464	7,334	12,207	19,803
1465	6,642	2,962	8,185
1466	6,325	9,342	17,475
1467	9,159	8,133	16,241
1468	8,189	16,594	25,921
1469	9,407	22,262	25,586
1470	9,464	12,614	18,717
1471	2,204	13,672	17,680
1472	10,255	11,050	17,159
1473	6,904	15,524	25,117
1474	9,048	16,432	34,290
1475	8,495	11,959	22,396
1476	11,886	19,167	26,102
1477	977	13,455	30,360
1478	10,016	19,966	34,796
1479	8,375	23,080	40,448
1480	7,860	20,748	40,513
1481	10,001	23,105	44,743
1482	7,230	20,557	41,195
1483	5,150	9,373	26,581
1484	5,561	12,567	31,384
1485	5,406	15,197	37,564

SOURCES: Carus-Wilson, *England's Export Trade*, calculated from tables in pp. 56-69, 91-109. In her tables, Prof. Carus-Wilson presented only the raw or actual customs accounts figures for each of England's thirteen official export ports. It was not possible simply to sum these export figures for each year, because rarely did all or even most of the accounts run for precisely one Michaelmas year: sometimes for only 5 months, sometimes for more than 2 years. Thus estimates of annual exports (for each port) had to be computed by the same method employed in calculating the mint accounts: the monthly average of the longer of two consecutive accounts was taken and that average was multiplied by the number of months preceding Michaelmas in the account and by the number following Michaelmas .The apportionments so derived were then summed to arrive at an estimate for each Michaelmas year for each port. The estimates for the thirteen ports were then summed to arrive at the figures for estimated annual total exports. Fewer such calculations were required for the London cloth export accounts, which more often ran for complete Michaelmas years. (This method of calculation was the one which Prof. Carus-Wilson used to construct her graphs at the end of the volume.)

BIBLIOGRAPHY

MANUSCRIPT SOURCES

BELGIUM

Archives Générales du Royaume (A.G.R.)

Chambre de Comptes (C. de C.): Registres

Général

no. 17:	Chambre de Comptes du Brabant
nos. 131-3:	registres des chartes du duché de Brabant-Limburg (monetary ordinances)
no. 579:	évaluation des monnaies, mesures (15th century)
no. 580:	registre aux affaires des monnaies (1250-1689)
no. 1,158:	registre touchant les affaires des monnaies de Flandres (1418-1546)
nos. 13,925-7:	comptes des baillis de l'Ecluse
nos. 23,250-1:	Den Gouden Burgoins Guldenen
nos. 49,850-5:	comptes des droits d'importation (draps d'Angleterre)

Comptes des Monnaies (mint accounts)

nos. 17,880-2:	Antwerp (1474-1507)
no. 17,985:	Brussels (1420-1)
nos. 17,986-9:	Brussels (1434-7)
nos. 18,064-72:	Louvain (1410-1, 1429-32, 1467-74)
nos. 18,073-4:	Maastricht (1418-9)
no. 18,094:	Vilvoorde (1417)
nos. 18,103-30:	Bruges (1455-8, 1468-1507)
nos. 18,195-200:	Ghent (1459-62, 1466-7, 1482-5, 1489)
no. 18,203 (1-21):	Namur (1421-33)
no. 18,242 (1-3):	Malines (1485-9)
nos. 48,976-7:	Malines (1390-2)

Comptes généraux des communes de Flandres

nos. 32,461-564:	Bruges (1406-1502)
nos. 38,635-722:	Ypres (1406-1500)
nos. 42,521-625:	Franc de Bruges (1395-1512)

Chambre des Comptes: Cartons

cartons 65, 65:bis 1, 65:2	monetary ordinances, reports of mint-masters, letters of officials on monetary affairs, from ca. 1380-ca. 1700 (uncatalogued and unsorted)

Comptes en rouleaux: Monnaies (mint accounts)

nos. 776-87	Bruges (1392-1402)
nos. 824-6:	Ghent (1388-90)
nos. 827-31:	Ghent (1410-9)
nos. 2142-6:	Malines (1390-2)
nos. 2586-7:	Fauquemont (1396-9)
nos. 2588-9:	Louvain (1394-5, 1384-6, respectively)
no. 2592:	Louvain and Vilvoorde (1392-3)

Acquits de Lille: liasses des monnaies (mint accounts)

no. 931	various monetary ordinances and mint reports
no. 936 (1-8):	Ghent (1411, 1419-20)
no. 937-bis:	Ghent (1422-40, 1442-7)
no. 1512:1	Bruges (1454)
nos. 1512:2-3, 5	Malines (1454-6, 1459-60)
no. 1512:4	Valenciennes (1466-7)
no. 1933:	Namur (1421-3)

Trésor de Flandre, Série I

nos. 2365-73: monetary ordinances and reports of monetary conferences

GHENT: Municipal Archives (Stadsarchief van Gent - S.V.G.)

no. 591/431 (draps d'Angleterre)

BRUSSELS: Municipal Archives (Archives de la ville de Bruxelles - A.V.B.)

no. XVI:	Het Wit Correctieboek
nos. 1435-7:	ordinances and *keuren* of the Brussels drapery, 15th and 16th centuries

THE NETHERLANDS

Algemeen Rijksarchief te 's-Gravenhage

Rekeningen van de Grafelijkheidsrekenkamer te 's-Gravenhage, no. 4937: I-X
Mint accounts of Dordrecht, Zevenbergen, and The Hague, 1425-1467.

FRANCE

Archives départementales du Nord, Lille (A.D.N.)

Série B (Chambre de Comptes)

Cartons B., nos. 615-44: monetary ordinances, reports of mint-masters and monetary officials

Mint accounts and reports (Ghent, Bruges, Valenciennes)

B. 31
644/15,939
1606
17,651
19,960/19,312
19,975/19,402

GREAT BRITAIN

H.M. Public Record Office

Patent Rolls
C 47/15-9
C 67/25

Treaty Rolls (Calais and France)
C 76/84-141 (1399-1470)

Exchequer: King's Remembrancer (largely Calais accounts)
(K.R.) E 101/190-8 (1421-1470)

Exchequer: Lord Treasurer's Remembrancer - Foreign Accounts (Calais)
(L.T.R.) E 364/59-104 (1421-1470)

PRINTED SOURCES

PRIMARY SOURCES (Documentary and Statistical)

BARTIER, John, and VAN NIEUWENHUYSEN, Andrée, eds., *Les ordonnances de Philippe le Hardi, de Marguerite de Mâle, et de Jean Sans Peur, 1381-1419*, Vol. I: *Les ordonnances de Philippe le Hardi et de Marguerite de Mâle, du 16 octobre 1381 au 31 décembre 1393*, Recueil des ordonnances des Pays-Bas (1ʳᵉ série: 1381-1506), Brussels, 1965.

BERNARD, Jacques, ed., *Recueil des traités de paix, de trêve, de neutralité, et d'autres actes publics*, Vol. I, Amsterdam, 1700.

BONENFANT, Paul, ed., 'Actes concernant les rapports entre les Pays-Bas et la Grande-Bretagne de 1293 à 1468 conservés au château de Mariement,' *Bulletin de la Commission Royale d'Histoire de Belgique*, CIX (1944), 53-125.

BORMANS, J.H., ed., *Les gestes des ducs de Brabant (De Brabantsche Yeesten)*, Vol. III, Brussels, Hayez, 1869.

BRIE, F.W.D., ed., *The Brut*, Early English Text Society, Vol. II, London, 1908.

BROOKE, C.G., and STOKES, E., 'Tables of Bullion Coined, 1337-1550,' *The Numismatic Chronicle*, 5th series, IX (1929), 27-69.

CARUS-WILSON, E.M., and COLEMAN, Olive, eds., *England's Export Trade 1275-1547*, Oxford, Clarendon Press, 1963.

CHAPLAIS, Pierre, ed., 'Documents concernant l'Angleterre et l'Ecosse anciennement conservés à la Chambre des Comptes de Lille (XIIᵉ-XVᵉ siècles),' *Revue du Nord*, XXXVIII (1956), 185-210.

CRUMP, C.G., and JOHNSON, C., 'Tables of Bullion Coined Under Edward I, II, III,' *The Numismatic Chronicle*, 4th series, XIII (1913), 200-45.

CUVELIER, Joseph, ed., *Actes des Etats Généraux des anciens Pays-Bas (1427-1477)*, Commission Royale d'Histoire, Brussels, Palais des Académies, 1948.

DEHAISNES, M. l'Abbé, and FINOT, M. Jules, eds., *Inventaire sommaire des archives départementales du Nord antérieures à 1790: Archives Civiles, Série B*, Vol. I:1, Lille, 1899.

DELEPIERRE, Octave, and WILLEMS, M.F., eds., *Collection des keuren ou statuts de tous les métiers de Bruges*, Ghent, Annoot-Braeckman, 1842.

DE PAUW, Napoleon, ed., *Ypre Jeghen Poperinghe*, Ghent, Siffer, 1899.

DE SAGHER, Henri, DE SAGHER, Johan, VAN WERVEKE, Hans, WYFFELS, Carlos, eds., *Recueil de documents relatifs à l'histoire de l'industrie drapière en Flandre: deuxième partie - le sud-ouest de la Flandre depuis l'époque bourguignonne*, 3 vols, Commission Royale d'Histoire, Brussels, Palais des Académies, 1951-66.

DE SMET, J.J., ed., 'Kronyk van Jan van Dixmude,' *Corpus Chronicorum Flandriae*, III (Brussels, 1856), 35-109.

DEVILLERS, Leopold, ed., *Cartulaire des comtes de Hainaut*, 6 vols., Académie Royale de Belgique, Brussels, Hayez, 1892.

DEVON, Frederick, ed., *Issues of the Exchequer, Henry III - Henry VI*, London, 1837.

DIEGERICK, I.L.A., ed., *Inventaire analytique et chronologique des chartes et documents appartenant aux archives de la ville d'Ypres*, 5 vols., Bruges, Vandecasteele-Werbrouck, 1853-60.

DOEHAERD, Renée, ed., *Les relations commerciales entre Gênes, la Belgique, et l'Outremont d'après les archives notariales génoises aux XIIIᵉ et XIVᵉ siècles*, Vols. II and III: *Textes*, Institut Historique Belge de Rome: Etudes d'histoire économique et sociale, Brussels, Palais des Académies, 1941.

DOEHAERD, Renée, and KERREMANS, Charles, eds., *Les relations commerciales entre Gênes, la Belgique, et l'Outremont d'après les archives notariales génoises, 1400-1440*, Institut Historique Belge de Rome, Brussels, Montagne de la Cour, 1952.

DOEHAERD, Renée, ed., *Etude anversoises: documents sur le commerce international à Anvers, 1488-1514*, 3 vols., Paris, S.E.V.P.E.N., 1963.

DOUET-D'ARCQ, L., ed., *La chronique d'Enguerran de Monstrelet*, 5 vols., Paris, Renouard, 1860-1.

ESPINAS, Georges, and PIRENNE, Henri, eds., *Recueil de documents relatifs à l'histoire de l'industrie drapière en Flandre: première partie - des origines à l'époque bourguignonne,* 4 vols., Commission Royale d'Histoire, Brussels, 1906-20.

GACHARD, L.P., ed., *Inventaire des archives des Chambres de Comptes des Archives Générales du Royaume de Belgique,* Vol. I, Commission Royale d'Histoire, Brussels, 1858.

GACHARD, L.P., ed., *La Bibliothèque Nationale à Paris: notices et extraits des manuscrits qui concernent l'histoire de Belgique,* 2 vols., Commission Royale d'Histoire, Brussels, 1875-7.

GACHARD, L.P., ed., *Collection de documents inédits concernant l'histoire de la Belgique,* 3 vols., Brussels, Haumann, 1833-5.

GAILLARD, Edward, ed., *Glossaire flamande de l'inventaire des archives de Bruges,* 2 vols., Bruges, Gaillard, 1879-82.

GAIRDNER, James, ed., *The Paston Letters, 1422-1509,* 6 vols., London, Chatto and Windus, 1896-1904.

GILLIODTS-VAN SEVEREN, Louis, ed., *Cartulaire de l'ancien consulat d'Espagne à Bruges, 1re partie: 1280 à 1550,* Bruges, De Plancke, 1901.

GILLIODTS-VAN SEVEREN, Louis, ed., *Cartulaire de l'ancienne estaple de Bruges,* 2 vols., Bruges, Société d'Emulation, 1904-8.

GILLIODTS-VAN SEVEREN, Louis, ed., *Cartulaire de l'ancien grand tonlieu de Bruges,* 2 vols., Bruges, Société d'Emulation, 1906-8.

GILLIODTS-VAN SEVEREN, Louis, ed., *Coûtume de la ville de Bruges,* 2 vols., Coûtumes des pays et comté de Flandre, Brussels, 1875.

GILLIODTS-VAN SEVEREN, Louis, ed., *Inventaire des archives de la ville de Bruges,* 6 vols., Bruges, E. Gaillard, 1871-8.

GILLIODTS-VAN SEVEREN, Louis, ed., *Inventaire diplomatique des archives de l'ancienne école Bogarde à Bruges,* 3 vols., Bruges, De Plancke, 1899.

GILLIODTS-VAN SEVEREN, Louis, ed., 'Les relations de la Hanse teutonique avec la ville de Bruges au commencement du XVIe siècle,' *Compte rendu des séances de la Commission Royale d'Histoire,* 4e série, VII (1879-80), 175-282.

GRAY, H.L., ed., 'Tables of Enrolled Customs and Subsidy Accounts, 1399-1482,' in E. Power and M. Postan, eds., *Studies in English Trade in the Fifteenth Century,* London, Routledge and Kegan Paul, 1951 (1933).

GREAT BRITAIN, H.M. Public Record Office, *Calendars of the Close Rolls: Edward III - Edward IV,* 35 vols., London, 1896-1953.

GREAT BRITAIN, H.M.P.R.O., 'Calendar of the French Rolls, 1 - 10 Henry V,' *The Forty-Fourth Annual Report of the Deputy Keeper of the Public Records,* London, 1883, pp. 543-639.

GREAT BRITAIN, H.M.P.R.O., 'Calendar of the French Rolls, Henry VI,' *The Forty-Eighth Annual Report of the Deputy Keeper of the Public Records,* London, 1887, pp. 217-450.

GREAT BRITAIN, H.M.P.R.O., *Calendars of the Patent Rolls: Edward III - Edward IV,* 36 vols., London, 1891-1900.

GREAT BRITAIN, 'Historical Manuscrupts Commission,' *Various Collections,* Vol. IV, London, 1907.

GREAT BRITAIN, Parliament, *Rotuli Parliamentorum ut et Petitiones et Placita in Parliamento,* 6 vols., London, 1767-77.

GREAT BRITAIN, Record Commission (Tomlins, T.E., Raithby, J., et al, eds.), *The Statutes of the Realm,* 6 vols., London, 1810-22.

GRUNZWEIG, A., ed., *Correspondance de la filiale de Bruges des Medici,* Commission Royale d'Histoire, Brussels, 1931.

HÖHLBAUM, K., KUNZE, K., and STEIN, W., eds., *Hansisches Urkundenbuch,* 10 vols., Verein für Hansische Geschichte, Halle and Leipzig, 1876-1939.

KERVYN DE LETTENHOVE (Baron), ed., 'Programme d'un gouvernement constitutionnel en Belgique au quinzième siècle,' *Bulletin de l'Académie Royale des sciences, des lettres, et des beaux-arts de Belgique,* 2e série, XIV (1862), 218-50.

KOPPMAN, K., ed., *Die Recesse und andere Akten der Hansetäge von 1236 bis 1430,* 8 vols., Die Historische Kommission bei der Königl. Akademie der Wissenschaften, Leipzig, 1870-97.

JOHNSON, Charles, ed., *The 'De Moneta' of Nicholas Oresme and English Mint Documents*, London, Thomas Nelson, 1956.

KUSKE, Bruno, ed., *Quellen zur Geschichte des Kölner Handels und Verkehrs im Mittelalter*, 2 vols., Gesellschaft für Rheinische Geschichtskunde, no. 23, Bonn, 1917-23.

LAMEERE, M.J., SIMONT, H., eds., *Recueil des ordonnances des Pays-Bas: deuxième série, 1506-1700*, Vol. V, Commission Royale d'Histoire, Brussels, 1910.

MALDEN, H.E., ed., *The Cely Papers*, Vol. I, Royal Historical Society, Camden Third Series, London, 1900.

MORAND, François, ed., *Chronique de Jean le Fèvre de St. Remy*, 2 vols., Paris, Renouard, 1876.

NICOLAS, N.H., ed., *Proceedings and Ordinances of the Privy Council of England*, 6 vols., London, 1834-7.

NYS, Charles, ed., *Inventaire des chartes et documents appartenant aux archives de la ville d'Anvers*, Antwerp, Manceaux, 1858.

PALGRAVE, Sir Francis, ed., *Kalendars and Inventories of the Treasury of His Majesty's Exchequer*, Vol. II, London, Public Record Office, 1836.

PEGOLOTTI, Francesco Balducci, *La Practica della Mercatura* (ed. Allan Evans), Cambridge, Mass., Medieval Academy, 1936.

PIOT, Charles, ed., *Inventaire des chartes, cartulaires, et comptes en rouleaux de la ville de Léau*, Commission Royale d'Histoire, Brussels, 1879.

POSTHUMUS, Nicolaas W., ed., *Bronnen tot de Geschiedenis van de Leidsche Textielnijverheid, 1333-1795*, Vol. I: *De Middeleeuwen*, Rijks Geschiedenkundige Publicatiën no. 8, The Hague, 1910.

PREVENIER, W., ed., *Handelingen van de Leden en van de Staten van Vlaanderen, 1384-1405: Excerpten uit de Rekeningen der Steden, Kasselrijen en Vorstelijke Ambtenaren*, Commission Royale d'Histoire, Brussels, 1959.

PRIEM, F., ed., *Précis analytique des documents des archives de la Flandre-Occidentale à Bruges: comptes du Franc*, 2 vols., Bruges, Vandercasteele-Werbrouck, 1844.

ROPP, G. von der, ed., *Hanserecesse, 1431-1476*, Zweite Abteilung, 7 vols., Verein für Hansische Geschichte, Leipzig, 1876-92.

RUDING, Rogers, ed., *Annals of the Coinage of Great Britain and Its Dependencies*, Vol. I (3rd ed.), London, John Hearne, 1840.

RYMER, Thomas, ed., *Foedera, Conventiones, Literae, et Acta Publica*, 12 vols., London, 1709-12.

SCHÄFER, Dietrich, and TECHEN, Friedrich, eds., *Hanserecesse, 1477-1530*, Dritte Abteilung, 2 vols., Verein für Hansische Geschichte, Leipzig, 1910-3.

SCHANZ, Georg, ed., *Englische Handelspolitik gegen Ende des Mittelalters*, Vol. II: *Zoll- und Handelsstatistik, Urkunden und Beilagen*, Leipzig, Duncker and Humboldt, 1881.

SCOTT, M.E., and GILLIODTS-VAN SEVEREN, Louis, eds., *Le Cotton Manuscrit Galba: documents pour servir à l'histoire des relations entre l'Angleterre et la Flandre de 1341-1473*, Commission Royale d'Histoire, Brussels, 1896.

SMIT, H.J., ed., *Bronnen tot de Geschiedenis van den Handel met Engeland, Schotland, en Ierland, 1150-1485*, 2 vols., Rijks Geschiedenkundige Publicatiën nos. 65-6, The Hague, 1928.

STEVENSON, Joseph, ed., *Letters and Papers Illustrative of the Wars of the English in France During the Reign of Henry VI of England*, 2 vols., Rerum Britannicarum Medii Aevi Scriptores, London, Longman and Green, 1861-4.

TAWNEY, R.H., and POWER, Eileen, eds., *Tudor Economic Documents*, 3 vols., London, Longman and Green, 1924.

UNGER, W.S., ed., *Bronnen tot de Geschiedenis van Middelburg in den Landsheerlijken Tijd*, 3 vols., Rijks Geschiedenkundige Publicatiën nos. 54, 61, 75, The Hague, 1923-31.

UNGER, W.S., ed., *De Tol van Iersekeroord: Documenten en Rekeningen, 1321-1572*, Rijks Geschiedenkundige Publicatiën, Kleine Serie no. 29, The Hague, 1939.

VANDEN BUSSCHE, Emile, ed., *Inventaire des archives de l'état à Bruges: section première - Franc de Bruges (chartes)*, Vol. I, Bruges, 1881.

VANDER LINDEN, Hermann, ed., *Itinéraires de Philippe le Bon, duc de Bourgogne, et Charles, comte de Charolais*, Commission Royale d'Histoire, Brussels, 1940.

VAN DOREN, R.J., ed., *Inventaire des archives de la ville de Malines*, Vol. I, Malines, 1859.

VAN DUYSE, Prudent, and DE BUSSCHER, Edmond, eds., *Inventaire analytique des chartes et documents appartenant aux archives de la ville de Gand*, Ghent, Annoot-Braeckman, 1867.

VAN EVEN, E., ed., *Inventaire chronologique et analytique des chartes et autres documents appartenant aux archives de la ville de Louvain, 1125-1793*, Louvain, J. Savonne, 1873.

VAN LIMBURG-BROUWER, P.A.S., ed., *Boergoensche Charters, 1428-1482*, Uitgegeven van wege de Nederlandsche Koninklijke Academie van Wetenschappen, The Hague, Martinus Nijhoff, 1869.

VAN MARLE, Raimond, ed., *Le comté de Hollande sous Philippe le Bon*, The Hague, Martinus Nijhoff, 1908.

VAN MIERIS, Frans, ed., *Groot Charterboek der Graaven van Holland, van Zeeland, en Heeren van Vriesland*, 4 vols., Leyden, 1754-6.

VERACHTER, Frederick, ed., *Documents pour servir à l'histoire monétaire des Pays-Bas*, Antwerp, De Braey, 1840.

VERACHTER, Frederick, ed., *Inventaire des anciens chartes et privilèges et autres documents conservés aux archives de la ville d'Anvers, 1193-1856*, Antwerp, Van Merlen, 1860.

WARNER, G., ed., *The Libelle of Englysche Polycye*, Oxford, 1926.

WATNEY, F.D., and LYELL, L., eds., *Acts of the Court of the Mercers Company, 1453-1527*, Cambridge, 1936.

WILLEMS, J.F., ed., *Les gestes des ducs de Brabant (De Brabantsche Yeesten)*, Vol. II, Brussels, Hayez, 1843.

WILLEMSEN, M.G., ed., 'Le règlement sur la draperie brugeoise du 20 septembre 1544,' *Annales de l'Académie royale d'archéologie de Belgique*, LXIX (1921), 5-74.

WILLEMSEN, M.G., ed., 'Le règlement général de la draperie malinoise de 1544,' *Bulletin du cercle archéologique de Malines*, XX (1910), 1-115.

WRIGHT, Thomas, ed., *Political Poems and Songs Relating to English History, 1327-1485*, Vol. II, London, Longman and Green, 1861.

SECONDARY SOURCES

ALLMAND, C.T., 'The Anglo-French Negotiations, 1439,' *Bulletin of the Institute of Historical Research*, XL (1967), 1-33.

ARMSTRONG, C.A.J., 'La double-monarchie France-Angleterre et la maison de Bourgogne, 1420-1435: le déclin d'une alliance,' *Annales de Bourgogne*, XXXVII (1965), 81-112.

BARNES, F.R., 'The Taxation of Wool, 1327-1348,' in George Unwin, ed., *Finance and Trade Under Edward III*, London, Cass and Co., 1962 (1918).

BARTHELEMY, Anatole, *Essai sur les monnaies des ducs de Bourgogne*, Dijon, Lamarche, 1850.

BARTIER, John, *Légistes et gens de finances au XVᵉ siècle: les conseillers des ducs de Bourgogne, Philippe le Bon et Charles le Téméraire*, Mémoires de l'Académie Royale de Belgique, Classe des Lettres, Vol. L, Brussels, 1957.

BIGWOOD, Georges, *Le régime juridique et économique du commerce de l'argent dans la Belgique du moyen âge*, Mémoires de l'Académie Royale de Belgique, Vol. XIV, Brussels, 1921.

BLOCH, Marc, 'Le problème de l'or au moyen âge,' *Annales d'histoire économique et sociale*, I (1933), 1-34.

BLOCH, Marc, *Esquisse d'une histoire monétaire de l'Europe*, Cahiers des Annales, no. 9, Paris, Armand Colin, 1954.

BLUNT, C.E., and WHITTON, C.A., 'The Coinage of Edward IV and of Henry VI (Restored),' *British Numismatic Journal*, 3rd ser., XXV (1945-8), 4-59, 130-82.

BONENFANT, Paul, *Philippe le Bon*, Brussels, Renaissance du Livre, 1955.

BOVILL, E.W., *The Golden Trade of the Moors* (2nd ed., rev. R. Hallett), London, Oxford University Press, 1968.

BOWDEN, Peter, 'The Wool Supply and the Woollen Industry,' *Economic History Review,* 2nd ser., IX (1956), 44-51.

BOWDEN, Peter, *The Wool Trade in Tudor and Stuart England,* London, MacMillan and Co., 1962.

BRULEZ, W., 'Le commerce international des Pays-Bas au XVIᵉ siècle: essai d'appréciation quantitative,' *Revue belge de philologie et d'histoire,* XLVI (1968), 1205-21.

CALMETTE, Joseph, *Les grands ducs de Bourgogne,* Paris, Albin Michel, 1949.

CARTELLIERI, Ode, 'Philippe le Bon et le roi de France en 1430-1431,' *Annales de Bourgogne,* I (1929), 78-83.

CARUS-WILSON, Eleanora M., *Medieval Merchant Venturers,* London, Methuen, 1954.

CARUS-WILSON, E.M., 'The Iceland Trade,' in E. Power and M. Postan, eds., *Studies in English Trade in the Fifteenth Century,* London, Routledge and Kegan Paul, 1933, pp. 155-84 (reprinted as 'The Iceland Venture,' in *Medieval Merchant Venturers,* pp. 98-142).

CARUS-WILSON, E.M., 'The Origins and Early Development of the Merchant Adventurers Organization in London,' in *Medieval Merchant Venturers,* pp. 143-80.

CARUS-WILSON, E.M., 'The Overseas Trade of Bristol in the Fifteenth Century,' in Power and Postan, eds., *Studies in English Trade in the Fifteenth Century,* pp. 183-246 (and in *Medieval Merchant Venturers,* pp. 1-97).

CARUS-WILSON, E.M., 'Trends in the Export of English Woollens in the Fourteenth Century,' in *Medieval Merchant Venturers,* pp. 239-64.

CARUS-WILSON, E.M., 'The Woollen Industry,' in M. Postan and E. Rich, eds., *The Cambridge Economic History,* II *(Trade and Industry in the Middle Ages),* Cambridge, 1952, pp. 355-429.

CASTELLANE, Comte de, 'Les monnaies d'argent du système flamand frappées à Tournai au nom de Charles VII,' *Revue numismatique,* 2nd ser., IV (1898), 103-15.

CHALON, Renier, *Recherches sur les monnaies des comtes de Hainaut,* Brussels, 1848 (and *Supplement:* Brussels, 1852).

CHALON, Renier, *Recherches sur les monnaies des comtes de Namur,* Brussels, 1858.

CIPOLLA, Carlo M., 'Currency Depreciation in Medieval Europe,' *Economic History Review,* 2nd ser., XV (1963), 413-22.

CIPOLLA, C.M., *Money, Prices, and Civilization in the Mediterranean World,* Princeton, N.J., 1956.

COCKSHAW, Pierre, 'Le fonctionnement des ateliers monétaires sous Philippe le Hardi,' *Bulletin du cercle d'études numismatiques,* VII (1970), 24-36.

COLEMAN, D.C., 'An Innovation and its Diffusion: the 'New Draperies',' *Economic History Review,* 2nd ser., XXII (1969), 417-29.

COORNAERT, Emile, *Un centre industriel d'autrefois: la draperie-sayetterie d'Hondschoote (XIVᵉ-XVIIIᵉ siècles),* Paris, Presses Universitaires de France, 1930.

COORNAERT, Emile, 'Draperies rurales, draperies urbaines: l'évolution de l'industrie flamande au moyen âge et au XVIᵉ siècle,' *Revue belge de philologie et d'histoire,* XXVIII (1950), 59-96.

COORNAERT, Emile, *Une industrie urbaine du XIVᵉ au XVIIᵉ siècles: l'industrie de la laine à Bergues-Saint-Winoc,* Paris, Presses Universitaires de France, 1930.

CRAIG, Sir John, *The Mint: a History of the London Mint from A.D. 287 to 1948,* Cambridge, University Press, 1953.

DAENELL, E.R., *Die Blütezeit der deutschen Hanse: Hansische Geschichte von der zweiten Hälfte des XIV. bis zum letzten Viertel des XV. Jahrhunderts,* 2 vols., Berlin, 1905.

DAUMET, Georges, *Calais sous la domination anglaise,* Arras, 1902.

DECOURDEMANCHE, J.A., *Traité pratique des poids du moyen âge,* Paris, Leroux, 1915.

DE ROOVER, Raymond, 'Anvers comme marché monétaire au XVIᵉ siècle,' *Revue belge de philologie et d'histoire,* XXXI (1953).

DE ROOVER, Raymond, 'La balance commerciale entre les Pays-Bas et l'Italie au XVᵉ siècle,' *Revue belge de philologie et d'histoire,* XXXVII (1959), 374-86.

DE ROOVER, Raymond, *The Bruges Money Market Around 1400 (with Statistical Supplement by Hyman Sardy)*, Verhandelingen van de Koninklijke Vlaamse Academie voor Wetenschappen, Letteren, en Schone Kunsten van België, Klasse der Letteren, Vol. XXX, no. 63, Brussels, 1968.

DE ROOVER, Raymond, *L'évolution de la lettre de change. XIVᵉ-XVIIIᵉ siècles*, Paris, 1953.

DE ROOVER, Raymond, *Gresham on Foreign Exchange*, Cambridge, Mass., Harvard University Press, 1949.

DE ROOVER, Raymond, *Money, Banking, and Credit in Medieval Bruges: Italian Merchant Bankers, Lombards, and Money-Changers*, Cambridge, Mass., Harvard University Press, 1948.

DE ROOVER, Raymond, 'New Interpretations of the History of Banking,' *Journal of World History*, II (1954), 38-76.

DE ROOVER, Raymond, 'The Organization of Trade,' in M. Postan and E. Rich, eds., *Cambridge Economic History*, III *(Economic Organization and Policies in the Middle Ages)*, Cambridge, 1963, pp. 42-156.

DE ROOVER, Raymond, *The Rise and Decline of the Medici Bank*, Cambridge, Mass., Harvard University Press, 1963.

DESCHAMPS DE PAS, Louis, 'Essai sur l'histoire monétaire des comtes de Flandre de la maison de Bourgogne, et description de leurs monnaies d'or et d'argent,' *Revue numismatique*, 2nd ser., VI (1861), 106-39, 211-37, 458-78; VII (1862), 117-43, 351-65, 460-80; XI (1866), 172-219. (Reprinted, with appendices, as *Essai sur l'histoire monétaire des comtes de Flandre de la maison de Bourgogne*, Paris. 1863.)

DESCHAMPS DE PAS, Louis, 'Etude sur les monnaies de Calais,' *Revue de la numismatique belge*, XXXIX (1883), 175-224.

DE SMEDT, Oscar, 'De Engelsche Handel te Antwerpen in de Jaren 1305-1515,' *Bijdragen tot de Geschiedenis*, XV (1924), 585-97.

DE SMEDT, Oscar, *De Engelse Natie te Antwerpen in de XVIde Eeuw, 1496-1582*, 2 vols., Antwerp, De Sikkel, 1950-4.

DE STURLER, J., *Les relations politiques et les échanges commerciaux entre le duché de Brabant et l'Angleterre au moyen âge: l'étape des laines anglaises en Brabant et les origines du développement du port d'Anvers*, Paris, E. Droz, 1936.

DE WITTE, Alphonse, *Histoire monétaire des comtes de Louvain, ducs de Brabant, et marquis du Saint-Empire Romain*, 2 vols., Antwerp, De Backer, 1894-6.

DE WITTE, A., 'Les relations monétaires entre la Flandre et l'Angleterre jusqu'au XVIIᵉ siècle: notes numismatiques,' *Revue du droit international*, II (1894), 1-22.

DICKINSON, Joycelyne G., *The Congress of Arras, 1435: a Study in Medieval Diplomacy*, Oxford, Clarendon Press, 1955.

DIEUDONNÉ, A., *Manuel des poids monétaires*, Paris, 1925.

DOEHAERD, Renée, *L'expansion économique belge au moyen âge*, Brussels, Renaissance du Livre, 1946.

DOLLINGER, Philippe, *La Hanse, XIIᵉ-XVIIᵉ siècles*, Paris, Aubier, 1964.

ENGEL, A. and SERRURE, R., *Traité de numismatique du moyen âge*, 3 vols., Paris, Ernest Leroux, 1891-1905.

ESPINAS, Georges, *La draperie dans la Flandre française au moyen âge*, 2 vols., Paris, Picard, 1923.

FAVRESSE, Felicien, *Etudes sur les métiers bruxellois au moyen âge*, Brussels, Université Libre de Bruxelles, 1961.

FEAVEARYEAR, Sir Albert, *The Pound Sterling: a History of English Money* (2nd ed., revised by E.V. Morgan), Oxford, Clarendon Press, 1963.

FISHER, F.J., 'Commercial Trends and Policy in Sixteenth Century England,' in E.M. Carus-Wilson, ed., *Essays in Economic History*, I (London, 1954), 152-72.

FRYDE, E.B., and M.M., 'Public Credit, with Special Reference to North-West Europe,' in Postan and Rich, eds., *Cambridge Economic History*, III, 451-71.

FRYDE, E.B., 'Financial Resources of Edward III in the Netherlands, 1337-1340,' *Revue belge de philologie et d'histoire*, XL (1962), 1168-87; XIV (1967), 1142-1216.

GAILLIARD, J., *De Ambachten en Neringen van Brugge*, 2 vols., Bruges, Baillard, 1854.

GANDILHON, Renée, *La politique économique de Louis XI*, Paris, 1914.

GENICOT, Leopold, 'Crisis: From the Middle Ages to Modern Times,' in M. Postan, ed., *Cambridge Economic History*, I (*Agrarian Life of the Middle Ages*), 2nd ed., revised, Cambridge, 1966, pp. 660-742.

GIRARD, A., 'Un phénomène économique: la guerre monétaire, XIVᵉ-XVᵉ siècles,' *Annales*, II (1940).

GRAS, N.S.B., *The Early English Customs System*, Harvard University Press, 1918.

GRAUS, F., 'La crise monétaire du XIVᵉ siècle,' *Revue belge de philologie et d'histoire*, XXIX (1951), 445-54.

GRAY, H.L., 'English Foreign Trade from 1446 to 1482,' in E. Power and M. Postan, eds., *Studies in English Trade in the Fifteenth Century*, London, 1933, pp. 1-38.

GRAY, H.L., 'Production and Exportation of English Woollens in the Fourteenth Century,' *English Historical Review*, XXXIX (1929), 13-35.

GREAVES, Dorothy, 'Calais Under Edward III,' in G. Unwin, ed., *Finance and Trade Under Edward III*, London, Cass., 1962 (1918).

HANEFFE, J. De Chestret de, *Numismatique de la principauté de Liège et de ses dépendances*, Brussels, Hayez, 1890.

HARRISS, G.L., 'The Struggle for Calais: an Aspect of the Rivalry between Lancaster and York,' *English Historical Review*, LXXV (1960), 30-53.

HAWARD, W.I., 'Financial Transactions between the Lancastrian Government and the Merchants of the Staple from 1449 to 1461,' in E. Power and M. Postan, eds., *Studies in English Trade in the Fifteenth Century*, London, 1933, pp. 293-320.

HECKSCHER, Eli F., *Mercantilism*, 2 vols. (trans, Shapiro, revised ed. E.F. Soderlund), London, Allen and Unwin, 1955.

HEERS, Jacques, *Gênes au XVᵉ siècle: activité économique et problèmes sociaux*, Paris, S.E.V.P.E.N., 1961.

HELLEINER, Karl F., 'The Population of Europe from the Black Death to the Eve of the Vital Revolution,' in E. Rich and C. Wilson, eds., *The Cambridge Economic History*, IV (*The Economy of Expanding Europe in the Sixteenth and Seventeenth Centuries*), Cambridge, 1967, pp. 1-95.

HERLIHY, David, *Medieval and Renaissance Pistoia: the Social History of an Italian Town, 1200-1430*, New Haven, Yale University Press, 1967.

HOC, Marcel, *Histoire monétaire de Tournai*, Brussels, Société Royale de Numismatique de Belgique, 1970.

HOLMES, G.A. 'The 'Libel of English Policy',' *English Historical Review*, LXXVI (1961), 193-216.

HUIZINGA, Johan, *The Waning of the Middle Ages (De Oogst van de Middeleeuwen)*, London, Penguin Books, 1955 (1924).

JACOB, E.F., *The Fifteenth Century (1399-1485)*, Oxford History of England, Vol. VI, Oxford, Clarendon Press, 1961.

JANSMA, T.S., 'Philippe le Bon et la guerre hollando-wende (1438-1441),' *Revue du Nord*, XLII (1960), 5-18.

KERLING, Nelly J.M., *Commercial Relations of Holland and Zealand with England from the late 13th Century to the Close of the Middle Ages*, Leyden, E.J. Brill, 1954.

KETNER, F., *Handel en Scheepvaart van Amsterdam in de Vijftiende Eeuw*, Leyden, E.J. Brill, 1946.

KIRBY, J.L., 'Issues of the Lancastrian Exchequer and Lord Cromwell's Estimates of 1433,' *Bulletin of the Institute of Historical Research*, XXIV (1951), 121-51.

KIRBY, J.L., 'Financing of Calais Under Henry V,' *Bulletin of the Institute of Historical Research*, XXIII (1950).

LAFAURIE, Jean, *Les monnaies des rois de France: Hughes Capet à Louis XII*, Paris, Emile Bourgey, 1951.

LANDRY, Adolphe, *Essai économique sur les mutations des monnaies dans l'ancienne France de Philippe le Bel à Charles VII*, Paris, Honoré Champion, 1910.

LAURENT, Henri, 'Crise monétaire et difficultés économiques en Flandre aux XIVᵉ et XVᵉ siècles,' *Annales d'histoire économique et sociale*, V (1933), 156-60.

LAURENT, Henri, *Un grand commerce d'exportation au moyen âge: la draperie des Pays-Bas en France et dans les pays méditerranéens (XIIᵉ-XVᵉ siècles)*, Paris, E. Droz, 1935.

LAURENT, Henri, *La loi de Gresham au moyen âge: essai sur la circulation monétaire entre la Flandre et le Brabant à la fin du XIVᵉ siècle*, Brussels, Université Libre de Bruxelles, 1933.

LE PATOUREL, John, 'L'occupation anglaise de Calais au XIVᵉ siècle,' *Revue du Nord*, XXXIII (1951), 228-41.

LIÈVRE, Louis, *La monnaie et le change en Bourgogne sous les ducs Valois*, Dijon, Berthier, 1929.

LIPSON, Ephraim, *The Economic History of England*, Vol. I: *The Middle Ages* (7th ed.), London, Black, 1937; Vols. II and III: *The Age of Mercantilism* (3rd ed.), London, Black, 1951.

LIPSON, Ephraim, *A Short History of Wool and Its Manufacture*, London, Heinemann, 1953.

LIPSON, Ephraim, *The History of the English Woollen and Worsted Industries*, London, 1921.

LOPEZ, Robert S., 'Back to Gold, 1252,' *Economic History Review*, 2nd ser., IX (1956), 219-40.

LOPEZ, R.S., 'Hard Times and Investment in Culture,' in *The Renaissance: a Symposium*, New York, 1953, reprinted in K. Dannenfeldt, ed., *The Renaissance*, Boston, Heath and Co., 1959, pp. 50-63.

LOPEZ, R.S., 'The Origin of the Merino Sheep,' *The Joshua Starr Memorial Volume: Studies in History and Philology*, Jewish Social Studies, no. 5, New York, 1953, pp. 161-8.

LOPEZ, R.S., 'The Trade of Medieval Europe: the South,' *Cambridge Economic History*, II (Cambridge, 1952), 257-354.

LOPEZ, R.S., and MISKIMIN, H.A., 'The Economic Depression of the Renaissance,' *Economic History Review*, 2nd ser., XIV (1962), 408-26.

LOPEZ, R.S., MISKIMIN, H.A., and CIPOLLA, C.M., 'The Economic Depression of the Renaissance: Rejoinder and Reply,' *Economic History Review*, 2nd ser., XVI (1964), 519-29.

MCKISACK, May, *The Fourteenth Century (1307-1399)*, Oxford History of England, Vol. V, Oxford, Clarendon Press, 1959.

MACPHERSON, David, *Annals of Commerce*, Vol. I, London, 1805.

MILLER, Edward, 'Economic Policies of Governments: France and England,' in M. Postan and E. Rich, eds., *Cambridge Economic History of Europe*, III (Cambridge, 1963), 290-339.

MILLER, F., 'The Middelburgh Staple, 1383-1388,' *Cambridge Historical Journal*, II (1926), 74-7.

MISKIMIN, Harry A., *The Economy of Early Renaissance Europe, 1300-1460*, Englewood Cliffs, N.J., Prentice-Hall, 1969.

MISKIMIN, H.A., 'Monetary Movements and Market Structure: Forces for Contraction in Fourteenth- and Fifteenth Century England,' *Journal of Economic History*, XXIV (1964), 470-90.

MISKIMIN, H.A., *Money, Prices, and Foreign Exchange in Fourteenth Century France*, New Haven, Yale University Press, 1963.

MOLLAT, Michel, 'Recherches sur les finances des ducs Valais de Bourgogne,' *Revue historique*, CCXIX (1958), 285-321.

MOLLAT, M., JOHANSEN, P., POSTAN, M., SAPORI, A., VERLINDEN, C., 'L'économie européenne à la fin du moyen âge,' in *Rendiconti del Xᵉ Congresso di Scienze Storiche (Supplement)*, Rome, 1955.

MUNRO, John H., 'Bruges and the Abortive Staple in English Cloth: an incident in the shift of commerce from Bruges to Antwerp in the late fifteenth century,' *Revue belge de philologie et d'histoire*, XLIV (1966), 1137-59.

MUNRO, J.H., 'The Costs of Anglo-Burgundian Interdependence,' *Revue belge de philologie et d'histoire*, XLVI (1968), 1228-38.

MUNRO, J.H., 'An Economic Aspect of the Collapse of the Anglo-Burgundian Alliance, 1428-1442,' *The English Historical Review*, LXXXV (1970), 225-44.

NEF, John U., 'Mining and Metallurgy in Medieval Civilization,' in Postan and Rich, eds., *Cambridge Economic History*, II (Cambridge, 1952), 430-93.

NEF, J.U., 'Silver Production in Central Europe, 1450-1618,' *Journal of Political Economy*, XLIX (1941).

OMAN, Charles, *The Coinage of England*, Oxford, Clarendon Press, 1931.

OUTHWAITE, R.B., *Inflation in Tudor and Early Stuart England*, Studies in Economic History: the Economic History Society, London and Toronto, MacMillan, 1969.

OWEN, Leonard, *The Connection between England and Burgundy during the First Half of the Fifteenth Century*, London, Simpkins Marshall, 1909.

PERROY, Edouard, 'L'administration de Calais en 1371-1372,' *Revue du Nord*, XXXIII (1951), 218-27.

PERROY, Edouard, *The Hundred Years' War* (trans. David Douglas), London, Eyre and Spottiswoode, 1959.

PERROY, Edouard, 'A l'origine d'une économie contractée: les crises du XIVᵉ siècle,' *Annales*, IV (1949), 167-82.

PIRENNE, Henri, 'Une crise industrielle au XVIᵉ siècle: la draperie urbaine et la 'nouvelle draperie' en Flandre,' in *Histoire économique de l'occident médiéval* (ed. E. Coornaert), Paris, De Brouwer, 1951, pp. 621-43.

PIRENNE, Henri, *Histoire de Belgique*, Vols. I-III, Brussels, 1907-8 (reissued by Renaissance du Livre, Brussels, 1956, as Vols. I-II).

PIRENNE, Henri, 'Le mouvement économique et social au moyen âge,' in *Histoire économique de l'occident médiéval* (ed. E. Coornaert, Paris, 1951), pp. 157-498.

PIRENNE, Henri, 'Nicolas Rolin,' *Biographie nationale de Belgique*, XIX (1907), 828-39.

PLANTET, L., and JEANNEZ, L., *Essai sur les monnaies du comté de Bourgogne*, Lons-le-Saunier, 1855.

POERCK, Guy de, *La draperie médiévale en Flandre et en Artois: technique et terminologie*, 3 vols., Bruges, De Tempel, 1951.

POSTAN, Michael, 'Credit in Medieval Trade,' *Economic History Review*, 1st ser., I (1928), 236-62; reprinted in Carus-Wilson, ed., *Essays in Economic History*, I (London, 1954), 61-87.

POSTAN, Michael, 'Economic and Political Relations of England and the Hanse, 1400-1475,' in Power and Postan, eds., *Studies in English Trade in the Fifteenth Century*, London, 1933, pp. 91-154.

POSTAN, Michael, 'Revision in Economic History: the Fifteenth Century,' *Economic History Review*, 1st ser., IX (1938), 160-7.

POSTAN, Michael, 'Some Economic Evidence of Declining Population in the Later Middle Ages,' *Economic History Review*, 2nd ser., II (1950), 221-46.

POSTAN, Michael, 'The Trade of Medieval Europe: the North,' in Postan and Rich, eds., *The Cambridge Economic History*, II (Cambridge, 1952), 119-256.

POSTHUMUS, Nicolaas W., *De Geschiedenis van de Leidsche Lakenindustrie*, Vol.I: *De Middeleeuwen, Veertiende tot Zestiende Eeuw*, The Hague, Martinus Nijhoff, 1908.

POWER, Eileen, 'The Wool Trade in the Reign of Edward IV,' *Cambridge Historical Journal*, II (1926), 17-35.

POWER, Eileen, *The Wool Trade in English Medieval History*, London, Oxford University Press, 1941.

POWER, Eileen, 'The Wool Trade in the Fifteenth Century,' in Power and Postan, eds., *Studies in English Trade in the Fifteenth Century*, London, 1933, pp. 39-90.

PRESTWICK, Michael, 'Edward I's Monetary Policies and their Consequences,' *Economic History Review*, 2nd ser., XXII (1969), 406-16.

PREVENIER, W., 'Réalité et histoire: le quatrième membre de Flandre,' *Revue du Nord*, XLIII (1961), 5-14.

QUICKE, F., *Les Pays-Bas à la veille de la période bourguignonne, 1356-1384*, Brussels, 1947.

RAMSAY, Sir J.H., *Lancaster and York: a Century of English History*, 2 vols., Oxford, University Press, 1892.

RAMSAY, Peter, 'Overseas Trade in the Reign of Henry VII: the Evidence of the Customs Accounts,' *Economic History Review*, 2nd ser., VI (1953), 173-82.

REDDAWAY, T.F., 'The King's Mint and Exchange in London, 1343-1543,' *English Historical Review*, LXXXII (1967), 1-23.

RENOUARD, Yves, 'Le commerce de l'argent au moyen âge,' *Revue historique*, CCIII (1950), 41-52.

RITCHIE, Nora, 'Labour Conditions in Essex in the Reign of Richard II,' in Carus-Wilson, ed., *Essays in Economic History*, II (London, 1962), 91-111.

ROBINSON, W.C., 'Money, Population, and Economic Change in Late Medieval Europe,' *Economic History Review*, 2nd ser., XII (1959), 63-76 (with rejoinder by Michael Postan, 77-83).

RUSSELL, J.C., *British Medieval Population*, Albuquerque, University of New Mexico Press, 1948.

SABBE, Etienne, *Anvers: métropole de l'occident, 1492-1566*, Brussels, Renaissance du Livre, 1952.

SANDEMAN, G.A.C., *Calais Under English Rule*, Oxford, 1908.

SCHANZ, Georg, *Englische Handelspolitik gegen Ende des Mittelalters mit besonderer Berücksichtigung des Zeitalters der beiden ersten Tudors Heinrichs VII und Heinrichs VIII*, Vol. I, Leipzig, Duncker and Humbolt, 1881.

SCHRÖTTER, Friedrich, *Wörterbuch der Münzkunde*, Berlin, Walter de Gruyter, 1930.

SHAW, W.A., *The History of Currency, 1252-1894*, London, Wilson and Milne, 1895.

SMIT, H.J., *De Opkomst van den Handel van Amsterdam*, Amsterdam, 1914.

SMITH, Adam, *An Inquiry into the Nature and Causes of the Wealth of Nations* (1776, ed. Edwin Cannan), New York, Modern Library, 1937.

SPUFFORD, Peter, 'Coinage, Taxation, and the Estates General of the Burgundian Netherlands,' *Anciens pays et assemblées d'états (Standen en Landen)*, XL (1966), 63-88.

SPUFFORD, Peter, 'Continental Coins in Late Medieval England,' *British Numismatic Journal*, 3rd ser., XXXII (1963), 127-39.

SPUFFORD, Peter, *Monetary Problems and Policies in the Burgundian Netherlands, 1433-1496*, Leyden, E.J. Brill, 1970.

STEEL, Anthony, *The Receipt of the Exchequer, 1377-1485*, Cambridge, University Press, 1954.

STEIN, Walter, 'Die Merchant Adventurers in Utrecht von 1464-1467,' *Hansische Geschichtsblätter*, XXVII (1899), 179-89.

THIELEMANS, Marie-Rose, *Bourgogne et Angleterre: relations politiques et économiques entre les Pays-Bas bourguignons et l'Angleterre, 1435-1467*, Brussels, Presses Universitaires, 1966.

THOMPSON, J.D.A., *Inventory of British Coin Hoards, A.D. 600-1500*, Royal Numismatic Society Publications, Oxford, 1956.

THOMPSON, J.D.A., 'Continental Imitations of the Rose Noble of Edward IV,' *British Numismatic Journal*, 3rd ser., XXV (1949), 183-208.

UNWIN, George, 'The Estate of Merchants, 1336-1365,' in G. Unwin, ed., *Finance and Trade Under Edward III*, London, Cass and Co., 1962 (1918), pp. 179-255.

VAN DER CHIJS, P.O., *De Munten der Voormalige Hertogdommen Braband en Limburg van de Vroegste Tijden tot aan de Pacificatie van Gend*, 2 vols., Haarlem, Bohn, 1851.

VAN DER CHIJS, P.O., *De Munten der Voormalige Graafschappen Holland en Zeeland van de Vroegste Tijden tot aan de Pacificatie van Gend*, Haarlem, Bohn, 1858.

VAN DER WEE, Hermann, 'L'échec de la réforme monétaire de 1407 en Flandre vu par les marchands italiens de Bruges,' in *Studii in Onore di Amintore Fanfani*, Vol. III, Milan, 1962, pp. 579-89.

VAN DER WEE, Hermann, *The Growth of the Antwerp Market and the European Economy, Fourteenth to Sixteenth Centuries*, 3 vols., The Hague, Martinus Nijhoff, 1963.

VAN GELDER, H. Enno, 'Aantekeningen bij de Vlaamse Muntslag, 1384-1434,' *Revue belge de numismatique*, CVII (1961), 137-53.

VAN GELDER, H. Enno, and HOC, Marcel, *Les monnaies des Pays-Bas bourguignons et espagnols, 1434-1713: répertoire général*, Amsterdam, J. Schulman, 1960.

VAN HOUTTE, J.A., 'Anvers aux XVe et XVIe siècles,' *Annales*, XVI (1961), 248-78.

VAN HOUTTE, J.A., *Bruges: essai d'histoire urbaine*, Brussels, Renaissance du Livre, 1967.

VAN HOUTTE, J.A., 'Bruges et Anvers, marchés 'nationaux' ou 'internationaux' du XIVe au XVIe siècle,' *Revue du Nord,* XXXIV (1952), 89-108.

VAN HOUTTE, J.A., 'La genèse du grand marché international d'Anvers à la fin du moyen âge,' *Revue belge de philologie et d'histoire,* XIX (1940), 87-126.

VAN HOUTTE, J.A., 'The Rise and Decline of the Market of Bruges,' *Economic History Review,* 2nd ser., XIX (1966), 29-47.

VAN HOUTTE, J.A., NIERMEYER, J.F., ROMEIN, J., VAN WERVEKE, Hans, eds., *Algemene Geschiedenis der Nederlanden,* Vol. III: *De Late Middeleeuwen, 1305-1477,* Utrecht, N.V. Standaard Boekhandel, 1961.

VAN NIEUWENHUYSEN, Andrée, 'Le transport et le change des espèces dans la recette générale de toutes les finances de Philippe le Hardi,' *Revue belge de philologie et d'histoire,* XXXV (1957), 55-65.

VAN UYTVEN, Raymond, 'La Flandre et le Brabant, 'terres de promission' sous les ducs de Bourgogne?' *Revue du Nord,* XLIII (1961), 281-318.

VAN UYTVEN, Raymond, *Stadsfinanciën en Stadsekonomie te Leuven van de XIIde tot het einde der XVIde Eeuw,* Verhandelingen van de Koninklijke Vlaamse Academie, Klasse der Letteren no. 44, Brussels, 1961.

VAN WERVEKE, Hans, *Bruges et Anvers: huit siècles du commerce flamand,* Brussels, Editions de la Librairie Encyclopédique, 1944.

VAN WERVEKE, Hans, 'Currency Manipulation in the Middle Ages: the Case of Louis de Mäle, Count of Flanders,' *Transactions of the Royal Historical Society,* 4th ser., XXXI (1949), 115-27.

VAN WERVEKE, Hans, 'Economic Policies of Governments: the Low Countries,' in Postan and Rich, eds., *Cambridge Economic History,* III (Cambridge, 1963), 340-60.

VAN WERVEKE, Hans, 'De Ekonomische en Sociale Gevolgen van de Muntpolitik der Graven van Vlaanderen, 1337-1433,' *Annales de la Société d'Emulation de Bruges,* LXXIV (1931), 1-15; reprinted in *Miscellanea Mediaevalia,* Ghent, E. Story-Scientia, 1968, pp. 243-54.

VAN WERVEKE, Hans, 'Essor et déclin de la Flandre,' in *Studii in Onore de Gino Luzzatto,* Milan, 1949, pp. 152-60; reprinted in *Miscellanea Mediaevalia,* Ghent, 1968, pp. 3-11.

VAN WERVEKE, Hans, *De Omvang van de Ieperse Lakenproductie in de Veertiende Eeuw,* in *Mededelingen van de Koninklijke Vlaamse Academie voor Wetenschappen, Letteren, en Schone Kunsten van België, Klasse der Letteren,* Vol. IX:2, Antwerp, 1947.

VAN WERVEKE, Hans, 'Industrial Growth in the Middle Ages: the Cloth Industry of Flanders,' *Economic History Review,* 2nd ser., VI (1954), 237-45.

VAN WERVEKE, Hans, 'Monnaie de compte et monnaie réelle,' *Revue belge de philologie et d'histoire,* XIII (1934), 123-52; reprinted in *Miscellanea Mediaevalia,* Ghent, 1968, pp. 133-57.

VAN WERVEKE, Hans, *De Muntslag in Vlaanderen Onder Lodewijk van Male,* in *Mededelingen van de Koninklijke Vlaamse Academie voor Wetenschappen, Letteren, en Schone Kunsten van België, Klasse der Letteren,* Vol. XI:5, Brussels, 1949.

VAN WERVEKE, Hans, 'De Vlaamse Munthervorming van 1389-1390,' *Nederlandsche Historiebladen,* I (1938), 336-47; reprinted in *Miscellanea Mediaevalia,* Ghent, 1968, pp. 268-80.

VARENBERGH, Emile, *Histoire des relations diplomatiques entre le comté de Flandre et l'Angleterre au moyen âge,* Brussels, 1874.

VAUGHAN, Richard, *Philip the Bold: the Formation of the Burgundian State,* London, Longmans Green, 1962.

VAUGHAN, Richard, *John the Fearless: the Growth of Burgundian Power,* London, Longmans Green, 1966.

VAUGHAN, Richard, *Philip the Good: the Apogee of Burgundy,* London, Longmans Green, 1970.

VICENS VIVES, Jaime, *An Economic History of Spain* (3rd ed., trans. F.M. Lopez-Morillas), Princeton, Princeton University Press, 1969.

VINER, Jacob, *Studies in the Theory of International Trade,* New York, Harper, 1937.

WALKER, A. Stanley, 'The Calais Mint, 1347-1470,' *British Numismatic Journal,* 2nd ser., VI (1921-2), 77-112.

WALTERS, Frederick A., 'The Silver Coinage of the Reign of Henry VI,' *Numismatic Chronicle*, 4th ser., II (1902), 224-66.

WALTERS, F.A., 'The Gold Coinage of the Reign of Henry VI,' *Numismatic Chronicle*, 4th ser., III (1903), 236-310.

WALTERS, F.A., 'The Coinage of Richard II,' *Numismatic Chronicle*, 4th ser., IV (1904), 326-52.

WALTERS, F.A., 'The Coinage of Henry IV,' *Numismatic Chronicle*, 4th ser., V (1905), 247-306.

WALTERS, F.A., 'The Coinage of Henry V,' *Numismatic Chronicle*, 4th ser., VI (1906), 172-218.

WALTERS, F.A., 'The Coinage of the Reign of Edward IV,' *Numismatic Chronicle*, 4th ser., IX (1909), 132-219.

WALTERS, F.A., 'The Stamford Find and Supplementary Notes on the Coinage of Henry VI,' *Numismatic Chronicle*, 4th ser., XI (1911), 153-73.

WARD, Grace, 'The Early History of the Merchants Staplers,' *English Historical Review*, XXXIII (1918), 297-319.

WATSON, Andrew M., 'Back to Gold - and Silver,' *Economic History Review*, 2nd ser., XX (1967), 1-34.

WHITTON, C.A., 'The Heavy Coinage of Henry VI,' *British Numismatic Journal*, 2nd ser., XXIII (1938-41), 59-90, 206-68, and 399-438.

INDEX